Hugo Gernsback and
the Century of Science Fiction

Hugo Gernsback and the Century of Science Fiction

GARY WESTFAHL

CRITICAL EXPLORATIONS IN
SCIENCE FICTION AND FANTASY, 5
Donald E. Palumbo *and* C.W. Sullivan III, *series editors*

McFarland & Company, Inc., Publishers
Jefferson, North Carolina, and London

CRITICAL EXPLORATIONS IN SCIENCE FICTION AND FANTASY
(a series edited by Donald E. Palumbo and C.W. Sullivan III)

1. *Worlds Apart? Dualism and Transgression in Contemporary Female Dystopias* (Dunja M. Mohr, 2005)
2. *Tolkien and Shakespeare: Essays on Shared Themes and Language* (edited by Janet Brennan Croft, 2007)
3. *Culture, Identities and Technology in the* Star Wars *Films: Essays on the Two Trilogies* (edited by Carl Silvio and Tony M. Vinci, 2007)
4. *The Influence of* Star Trek *on Television, Film and Culture* (edited by Lincoln Geraghty, 2007)
5. *Hugo Gernsback and the Century of Science Fiction* (Gary Westfahl, 2007)

LIBRARY OF CONGRESS CATALOGUING-IN-PUBLICATION DATA

Westfahl, Gary.
Hugo Gernsback and the century of science fiction / Gary Westfahl.
    p. cm. — (Critical explorations in science fiction and
    fantasy ; 5)
    Includes bibliographical references and index.

    ISBN-13: 978-0-7864-3079-6
    softcover : 50# alkaline paper ∞

    1. Gernsback, Hugo, 1884–1967 — Criticism and interpretation.
2. Science fiction, American — History and criticism.   3. Science
fiction — History and criticism. I. Title.
PS3513.E8668Z93   2007
813'54 — dc22   2007010957

British Library cataloguing data are available

Cover illustration ©2007 Wood River Gallery

Manufactured in the United States of America

McFarland & Company, Inc., Publishers
  Box 611, Jefferson, North Carolina 28640
  www.mcfarlandpub.com

To my wife

LYNNE LUNDQUIST WESTFAHL

who, during twenty-five years
of watching me work on projects like this,
has endured her own century of science fiction

Acknowledgments

First, and most prosaically, I should thank all of the editors who received, reviewed, and published earlier versions of some of the materials that appear in this book, sometimes offering their input and influencing textual revisions: they are R. D. Mullen, Arthur B. Evans, Istvan Csicsery-Ronay, Jr., Veronica Hollinger, Rob Latham, and Carol McGuirk, editors of *Science Fiction Studies,* where appeared earlier versions of "The Popular Tradition of Science Fiction Criticism, 1926–1980" (26.2 [July 1999]:187–212), "Wanted: A Symbol for Science Fiction" (22.1 [March 1995]: 1–21), and "Evolution of Modern Science Fiction: The Textual History of *Ralph 124C 41+*" (23.1 [March 1996]: 37–92); David Pringle, editor of *Interzone,* where an earlier version of "Cremators of Science Fiction: Brian Stableford and John Clute on Hugo Gernsback and His Legacy" appeared (#130, April 1998); Cambridge University Press and James Redmond, editor of *Themes in Drama: Vol. 14, Melodrama* (Cambridge: Cambridge University Press, 1993), where an earlier version of "'Man against Man, Brain against Brain': The Transformation of Melodrama in Science Fiction" appeared; AMS Press and George Slusser, Roger Galliard, Paul Alkon, and Daniéle Chatèlain, editors of *Transformations of Utopia: Changing View of the Perfect Society* (New York: AMS Press, Inc., 1999), where an earlier version of "Gadgetry, Government, Genetics, and God: The Forms of Science Fiction Utopia" appeared; and the University of Georgia Press and George Slusser and Tom Shippey, editors of *Fiction Two Thousand: Cyberpunk and the Future of Narrative* (©1992 by the University of Georgia Press, Athens, Georgia 30602; all rights reserved), where an earlier version of "'The Gernsback Continuum': Cyberpunk in the Tradition of Science Fiction" appeared. Of these people, Arthur B. Evans additionally warrants special thanks because of the important roles he played in first inspiring me to create this book and in assisting me while first shaping its contents.

The research for this book required a number of hard-to-find documents, but I was fortunately able to find most of them within the enormous resources of the J. Lloyd Eaton Collection of Science Fiction and Fantasy Literature, housed in the Tomàs Rivera Library of the University of California, Riverside, and I thank everyone who works there, including Melissa Conway, Darien Davies, Sheryl Lewis, and especially Sara Stilley, for their assistance. I should also thank the Interlibrary Loan Department of Rivera Library for providing me with copies of the issues of *Modern Electrics* containing the first publication of Gernsback's *Ralph 124C 41+*, the issues of *The Electrical Experimenter* containing the first publication of his *Baron Münchhausen's New Scientific Adventures*, and the two issues of *Technocracy Review*. Hal Hall of Texas A&M University libraries provided me with copies of some important secondary sources. Several years ago, the late R. D. Mullen was kind enough to send me a copy of the version of *Ralph 124C 41+* which appeared in *Amazing Stories Quarterly*, while with similar kindness Edward James sent me a copy of the 1952 British edition of that novel. Richard Bleiler provided some key assistance in finding information about Hugo Gernsback's family.

Many other colleagues should be thanked for offering assistance and support in these and related research projects, and the short list of names would include Mike Ashley, Amy Chan Kit Sze, John Clute, James Gunn, John Grant, Donald M. Hassler, Fiona Kelleghan, David Langford, Farah Mendlesohn, Andy Sawyer, Darrell Schweitzer, Fred Shapiro, and Wong Kin Yuen.

For assistance in planning and preparing this manuscript, I owe a great deal of thanks to Donald E. Palumbo.

Finally, and as always, I thank Michael Paul Wong and my colleagues at the University of California, Riverside's Learning Center, as well as David Werner and other colleagues in the University of LaVerne's Educational Programs in Corrections, for providing a supportive work environment, and I thank my wife, Lynne, and my children, Allison and Jeremy, for enduring my absences during yet another project. Sacrificing her own best interests, Lynne merits special recognition for buying me the laptop computer on which I prepared this manuscript, believing that it would allow me to become even more productive, and hence would allow me to spend even more time working on projects such as this book.

Table of Contents

Introduction

Mike Ashley begins the Preface to his and Robert A. W. Lowndes's *The Gernsback Days: A Study of the Evolution of Modern Science Fiction from 1911 to 1936* by noting, correctly, that "In recent years there has been a resurgence of interest in Hugo Gernsback, and the start of a serious study of the contributions he made to the development of science fiction" (9). Ashley himself, of course, played a major role in that resurgence by means of several publications like *The Gernsback Days*, his article "Mr. G. and Mr. H. G.," and *The Time Machines: The Story of the Science-Fiction Pulp Magazines from the Beginning to 1950*. To a modest extent, my own work was also a factor, especially a series of articles later assembled as *The Mechanics of Wonder: The Creation of the Idea of Science Fiction* and other research now presented here.

One could further point to numerous studies by other researchers during the last two decades that testify to a renewed attentiveness to Gernsback and his achievements: the Eric Leif Davin interviews with some of Gernsback's editors and writers which appear in his *Pioneers of Wonder: Conversations with the Founders of Science Fiction*; Deborah Elkin's "Hugo Gernsback's Ideas of Science and Fiction, 1915–26"; Fred Erisman's "Stratemeyer Boys' Books and the Gernsback Milieu"; Ron Miller's "Hugo Gernsback, Skeptical Crusader"; several articles by Sam Moskowitz, including "Amazing Encounter: MacFadden's Takeover of Gernsback's Company," "Henrik Dahl Juve and the Second Gernsback Dynasty," "Hugo Gernsback and Edgar Rice Burroughs," "The Return of Hugo Gernsback," and "The Rise and Fall of the First Gernsback Empire"; Maria Orlando's "Hugo Gernsback: The Inventor, The Prophet, and the Father of Science Fiction"; Andrew Ross's "Getting Out of the Gernsback Continuum"; Mark Siegel's *Hugo Gernsback: Father of Modern Science Fiction, with Essays on Frank Herbert and Bram Stoker*; Brian Stableford's "Creators of Science Fiction 10: Hugo Gernsback"; and Daniel Stashower's "A Dreamer Who Made Us Fall in Love with the Future." It is also worth noting that some recent studies of twentieth-century science fiction, such as Edward James's *Science Fiction in the 20th Century*, Brooks Landon's *Science Fiction after 1900: From the Steam Man to the Stars*, and Brian Attebery's "The Magazine Era: 1926–1960" in Edward James and Farah Mendlesohn's *The Cambridge Companion to Science Fiction*, tend to include more references to Gernsback, and to speak of him more sympathetically, than earlier studies of the genre. In the context of all these publications, one might reasonably question the need for another book devoted to the topic of Hugo Gernsback.

And yet, I believe, the most important argument regarding Hugo Gernsback has still not been presented in its fullest form, and this book, if not its ideal embodiment, nevertheless represents a more comprehensive presentation of that argument than any previous efforts.

As a way of introducing this argument, it is useful to contrast the different reasons why Mike Ashley and I were separately drawn to study Gernsback's career. Ashley was a dedicated scholar of the science fiction magazines — and he remains the most knowledgeable expert in that field — and during the course of his research, he grew dissatisfied with the then-standard portrayals of Hugo Gernsback's role in the history of science fiction magazines. To many in the 1970s and 1980s, Gernsback was only the man who had instructed and encouraged authors to write bad science fiction, who had published and praised the bad science fiction that resulted from his efforts, and who consequently had functioned only as a brief and baleful influence on the genre, so that later editors needed to struggle to overcome the damage that he had done. Ashley did not believe this story, and he has managed, by means of the research presented in his books, to persuasively refute it. Ashley has shown that Gernsback in fact wanted to encourage the writing of superior science fiction; that he worked individually with some authors to achieve those ends; and that, especially during the time in the early 1930s when his associate David Lasser, Managing Editor of *Wonder Stories*, was dedicated to these goals, he managed to achieve some tangible results in the form of improved stories published in his magazines. Ashley has thus corrected the historical record, and he has established that Gernsback actually had a salutary effect on the early development of science fiction.

Still, Ashley's argument is a limited argument, as suggested by the subtitle of *The Gernsback Days*, which explicitly focuses only on the years from 1911 to 1936, the time when Gernsback was most active as a magazine editor publishing science fiction stories. Ashley admirably succeeded in demonstrating that Gernsback was a good editor, and a good influence, during that era. But my concerns have always been much broader than that. My ambition in the 1980s was to study science fiction in all forms, at all times, and I wanted to begin my work by finding, or constructing, an explanatory matrix to guide such wide-ranging studies. My first, misguided attempt was a proposed dissertation which would have examined the (purported) history of science fiction from the Renaissance to the early nineteenth century. When I (understandably) began to doubt that the origins of science fiction could in fact be located in the era of Francis Bacon and *The New Atlantis*, I decided that I needed an introductory chapter that would consider the origin of, and patterns of usage in, the term "science fiction"; this led me to Gernsback's magazines, and that is where I discovered the true origins of science fiction.

From my perspective, therefore, the questions of whether Gernsback published bad stories, or encouraged writers to publish bad stories, were basically irrelevant. I came to recognize that Gernsback had effectively created the genre of science fiction and had imprinted his image upon all of its texts; that he had had an impact on all works of science fiction published since 1926, regardless of whether he played any direct role in their publication; that he had influenced perceptions of the works published before 1926 now acknowledged as science fiction; and that the overall effects of his work were overwhelmingly positive, as demonstrated by the vibrant, fascinating genre that he had fashioned. The proof of his importance, then, would come not from a reconsideration of the stories published in his *Amazing Stories* or *Wonder Stories*, but rather from a reconsideration of the entire genre of science fiction — a recognition of its unique power and durability, and a further acknowledgment that that power and durability could be largely attributed to Gernsback's contributions.

Thus, while I continued to study Gernsback's commentaries and fiction, my attention was constantly being diverted into other areas — such as later novels and stories, films, and television programs — that could all be illuminated and better appreciated by relating their contents back to Gernsback's ideas as he had expressed them in his editorials and his fiction. These explorations, as published in various forums, served both to buttress my developing argument and to bring some variety into a lengthy research project that was otherwise focused on diligently explaining the theories of Gernsback and his most prominent successor, John W. Campbell, Jr.

It was my original design to present all of these materials in the form of a comprehensive study to be entitled *The Mechanics of Wonder: The History of the Idea of Science Fiction*. But the tale grew in the telling, to say the least, and the original manuscript had time to deal with science fiction and its criticism after 1950 in only the most cursory of fashions. Then, after two scholarly publishers otherwise persuaded of its merits rejected the book solely because it was still very lengthy, I heeded suggestions to shorten the text by eliminating virtually all of the materials involving more recent developments.

This new book on Gernsback is hardly inattentive to the era when he was most active as a science fiction editor and writer; indeed, in certain areas—such as the convoluted history of his novel *Ralph 124C 41+*, his efforts to promote science fiction by means of symbols, and the role played by early amateur magazines, or fanzines, in the growth of science fiction—this book is more comprehensive than its predecessor. But the major novelty of this project, as indicated in its title, is to restore the full dimensions of my original argument—to examine Hugo Gernsback's impact on the entire century of science fiction since he first began his writing and publishing career. Earlier versions of seven chapters in this book have previously appeared in various anthologies and journals, as detailed in the Acknowledgments and the Bibliography; yet all of those materials have now been expanded and updated, and I also include a significant amount of new material that has never been published. In particular, having previously focused on those aspects of Gernsback's career that were most obviously influential—his major magazines, *Amazing Stories* and *Wonder Stories*, and his novel *Ralph 124C 41+: A Romance of the Year 2660*—this book seeks, by means of its entirely new fourth and ninth chapters, to place these works in the context of his entire career and to closely examine those Gernsback publications that were less influential, such as his short-lived magazines *Technocracy Review* and *Science-Fiction Plus* and his novel *Baron Münchhausen's New Scientific Adventures*, garnering new insights into science fiction along the way. All these materials work together to convey the major argument I have alluded to: science fiction as it is observed today is the house that Hugo Gernsback built, and no matter which of its many rooms one ventures into, there are always lingering signs of his powerful presence.

In recent years, I also have touched upon Gernsback and his work in a number of other articles, including "The Dance with Darkness," "Superladies in Waiting," and "Where No Market Has Gone Before," which could not be aptly incorporated into this volume (though all are cited in the bibliography). However, in observing the overall course of my career, some might detect a movement away from Hugo Gernsback, since most of my publications in recent years have said little or nothing about him. Still, I would argue that Gernsback has not been marginalized in my work, but rather has been internalized, subtly guiding and shaping my research and my thoughts. In this respect, having first served as an outspoken and idiosyncratic champion of Gernsback, I have now become, like innumerable other science fiction writers and commentators, someone who constantly reflects Gernsback's influence without explicitly acknowledging that influence. The difference is that, unlike some of those people, I am very much aware of the wellspring of my ideas, and I can still periodically return to, and gain new strength from, that invaluable resource. That is why I have benefited from preparing this book, and that is why I hope that others will benefit from reading it.

PART I

HUGO GERNSBACK THE EDITOR

1

Cremators of Science Fiction

Brian Stableford and John Clute
on Hugo Gernsback and His Legacy

Hugo Gernsback has always been a man who provokes extreme reactions; he has been both effusively praised, and scornfully criticized, for his contributions to the development of science fiction. The December, 1997 issue of the British science fiction magazine *Interzone* included two particularly strong attacks — one a vicious character assassination of the man, the other an implicit assault upon the power of his legacy; and although I had previously resolved to conclude my work on Gernsback's career with the completion of the manuscript of *The Mechanics of Wonder: The Creation of the Idea of Science Fiction,* the pieces were so appalling as to inspire me to plunge back into additional research in order to thoroughly refute them, the eventual result being this second book.

Surprisingly, the authors of these attacks were both distinguished figures, properly regarded as two of our most erudite and insightful commentators on science fiction: Brian Stableford and John Clute. For years, Stableford has produced books, articles, and reviews that have been widely appreciated as valuable sources of information and ideas about science fiction, while Clute, long renowned for his excellent science fiction reviews, earned new prominence as a co-editor or author of definitive reference works. Both men have earned the Science Fiction Research Association's Pilgrim Award for their lifetime contributions to science fiction scholarship. And yet, as I will demonstrate, when they turned to the subjects of Hugo Gernsback and his effects on science fiction, they proved to be dead wrong.

The knowledgeable Mike Ashley anticipated me in criticizing Stableford's piece, "Creators of Science Fiction, 10: Hugo Gernsback" in a letter published in the February, 1998 issue of *Interzone*, politely commenting that "I find myself wondering about the depth of Brian's research" (5). He evidently found himself unable to say bluntly that the article, as is highly uncharacteristic of Stableford, included several factual errors. Gernsback's Menograph in *Ralph 124C 41+* was a thought-recording device, not a "thought-reading device" (47). Clement Fezandié was not "The only writer featured in *Science and Invention* who did new work for *Amazing Stories*" (48); G. Peyton Wertenbaker also contributed new stories to both magazines. It is not true that in launching *Amazing Stories,* Gernsback's "first intention was to use the magazine as a vehicle for reprinting the popular works of Jules Verne and H. G. Wells, using other reprints (including some from Gernsback's other magazines) as fillers" (48); in fact, he never intended to make *Amazing Stories* an all-reprint magazine, since he announced plans to publish new stories in the first issue and stated the same more emphatically in a special announcement in the second issue (which also featured a new story). Stableford asserts that E. E. "Doc" Smith, Stanton A. Coblentz, and John Taine were writers who emerged in the 1930s, since they "had previously found no market for their extravagant imaginative fiction" (49); in truth, they had all begun publishing in the 1920s, not the 1930s, and the first two began their careers in Gernsback-edited magazines. The 1923 issue of *Science and Invention* was not "given over" to science fiction (48), since it included only six science fiction stories in the midst of numerous scientific articles that represented the magazine's typical fare. It is not true that Gernsback "got [Edgar Rice] Burroughs to write *The Master Mind of Mars* for the 1927 *Amazing Stories Annual*" (48); as explained in Irwin Porges's *Edgar Rice Burroughs: The Man Who Created Tarzan,* Burroughs had earlier written the novel for *Argosy* and offered it to Gernsback only after the magazine had rejected it. Gernsback first met Sam Moskowitz in 1950, not 1953 (49). One might protest that these are generally minor and not particularly grievous errors, but in a piece by a person universally acclaimed as one of the world's greatest experts in science fiction, it is shocking to find any errors at all. All one can conclude is that Stableford did not know very much about Gernsback before writing his article, and he did not bother to learn more than a minimal amount before rushing to his judgments.

However, any distress about incidental mistakes fades in the face of the egregious inaccuracy of the overall argument. Here is what Stableford would have you believe: it was not until the 1950s that Moskowitz "offered Gernsback heroic status as 'the Father of Science Fiction.' There is, however, no conspicuous evidence that Gernsback had any interest in science fiction per se until that fateful meeting with Moskowitz, whose extravagant flattery seems to have been very gratefully received" (48). While acknowledging as he must that Gernsback did write and publish some science fiction, Stableford identifies

1933, the year when Gernsback launched his magazine *Sexology*, as the moment when Gernsback completely cut all ties with science fiction, and "For the next 20 years Gernsback showed not the slightest interest in science fiction — until he met the worshipful Sam Moskowitz, and was told that he was the father of a precious orphan" (49).

There is regrettably no polite way to characterize this account, because it is simply not true. One could write a book presenting mountains of evidence to disprove it; indeed, both Ashley and I have essentially done exactly that (Ashley and Robert A. W. Lowndes's *The Gernsback Days*; my *The Mechanics of Wonder*). Here are some salient facts: during every decade of his life in America, Gernsback wrote science fiction, wrote about science fiction, and published science fiction — usually extensively. Between 1926 and 1936, he launched six science fiction magazines and wrote two dozen editorials and one article focused on the topic of science fiction. And what about the two decades when Stableford says he "showed not the slightest interest in science fiction"? In truth, he repeatedly demonstrated a strong and enduring interest in science fiction. In 1939, he contributed a guest editorial, "Science Fiction," to a new science fiction magazine also called *Science Fiction*; in 1940, he published three issues of a science fiction comic book, *Superworld Comics*; in 1942, he wrote a short science fiction story, "The Infinite Brain" for the magazine *Future Combined with Science Fiction;* in 1943 (not the late 1950s, as Stableford implies), he began to privately publish annual magazine parodies featuring his "fiction and futurology" (50), which he mailed out as Christmas cards; and while at first each one had a different farcical title (such as Tame [parodying *Time*], Digest of Digests [parodying *Reader's Digest*], and Jollier's [parodying *Collier's*]), in the 1950s each one was entitled Forecast, so that Gernsback had effectively started to publish his own annual science fiction fanzine. Also in 1950, he arranged for the republication of his science fiction novel *Ralph 124C 41+,* did some revisions (as will be discussed), and wrote a new "Preface" for this Second Edition.

Particularly objectionable is the hypothesis, stated as fact, that Moskowitz first identified Gernsback as "the father of science fiction" in the 1950s and gave Gernsback the idea that he merited that appellation. In the first place, throughout his active career as a science fiction editor from 1926 to 1936, Gernsback repeatedly and proudly praised himself as a pioneer in the field: for example, in 1929, he wrote, "I started the movement of science fiction in America in 1908 through my first magazine, 'MODERN ELECTRICS'" ("Science Wonder Stories" 5). In 1934, he chose a later starting date but still labeled himself the instigator of the "movement": "Not until 1926, when I launched my first Science Fiction magazine, was any concerted movement possible.... The movement since 1926, has grown by leaps and bounds until today

there are literally hundreds of thousands of adherents of Science Fiction...."
("The Science Fiction League" 1061).

In the second place, during the decade following his departure from the
field when he sold *Wonder Stories* in 1936, there is additional textual evidence
in science fiction magazines that Gernsback and those around him were keenly
aware of his significant role in launching the modern genre of science fiction.
In his 1939 guest editorial for *Science Fiction,* he identified himself as the person who had started the tradition of science fiction: "When I coined the term
'science fiction' way back in 1926, in the first science-fiction magazine (Amazing Stories) which was published by me at that time, I perhaps did not fully
realize what I had let loose on an unsuspecting and unprepared world" ("Science Fiction" 3); in addition, the Table of Contents of that issue identified
Gernsback at "the founder of 'Science Fiction'" (4).

In the third place, by the time of the June, 1942 issue of *Future Combined with Science Fiction,* which published Gernsback's "The Infinite Brain,"
somebody — either Gernsback himself or his former editor, Charles D. Hornig,
who was also the editor of *Future*—had developed the specific belief that the
proper term for Gernsback's role was "father." The contents page of that issue
identified him as the "father of magazine science-fiction" (4); the introduction on the first page of the story similarly called him "the Father of Science
Fiction Magazines" (40). An unsigned feature in that issue, "Station X," presumably written by Hornig, begins with an extended tribute to his contributions which concludes with another announcement that Gernsback had been
a "father" to science fiction:

> This issue of Future will be on all stands in April. Now April is a very distinc-
> tive month, as oldtimers will tell you, in the world of science fiction, for the
> very first issue of the very first all-science fiction magazine bore that date. April,
> 1926.
>   Science fiction, as a modern pulp-magazine proposition, designed to satisfy
> the desires of tens of thousands of enthusiasts all over the world [for, up to the
> recent conflict you *could* obtain your favorite magazine in any part of the
> world], is now sweet sixteen.

After a paragraph describing the appearance and contents of the first issue of
Amazing Stories, the column continues:

> And the man who edited this pioneer magazine, sixteen years ago, was one
> already well known to thousands of readers of such magazines as "Science and
> Invention," "Radio News" and the old "Electrical Experimenter"—Hugo Gersn-
> back.
>   Hugo Gernsback remained at the post of that first magazine for some years,
> then later brought out the second title, *Science Wonder Stories.* In 1930, the third
> title appeared, under the old Clayton banner. By that time, science fiction mag-
> azines were off to a solid start. There have been ups and downs ever since, but

the number of titles have increased nonetheless. And today they are still going strong.

We think this is a particularly fine occasion upon which to present a short-short science fiction tale by the "father of science fiction magazines," and hope you'll enjoy *The Infinite Brain* ["Station X" 100].

Finally, a couple of years later, one even finds Gernsback's significant role in creating the genre of science fiction being recognized in publications outside of the field of science fiction. In December, 1943, when reporters from *Time* and *Newsweek* magazine were interviewing Gernsback about his first magazine parody "Christmas card," he unquestionably identified himself to those who interviewed him as the father of science fiction, using that precise term, since both magazines, in their January 3, 1944 issues, printed versions of the claim: Gernsback "is also generally credited with being the father of the modern science-fiction pulps" ("Greetings, Electronitwits!" 54) and is "The father of pseudo-scientific fiction" ("Gernsback, the Amazing" 40). Now, I have been accused in the past of presenting excessive amounts of data in support of certain contentions; but when one is in the position of essentially being forced to describe one of science fiction's most distinguished scholars as an outright liar, one necessarily wishes to accumulate and present all available information in order to support such a surprising and unfortunate conclusion.

To be sure, one cannot disagree with Stableford's point that Gernsback was an unscrupulous businessman who was hardly averse to profiting from his predilection for science fiction; but data confirming some underlying sincerity in his interest is overwhelming, and the many readers of *Amazing Stories* and its successors perceived that interest as sincere and responded accordingly. It is hard to believe that Gernsback could have had such an undeniable and profound impact on people like Moskowitz, Donald A. Wollheim, and John W. Campbell, Jr. if he had been doing it only for the money, if he had really, in Stableford's words, "always regarded his offspring — and treated it — as a contemptible bastard" (50).

So, why would the normally reliable and judicious Stableford produce such a sloppy and slanderous diatribe? Demonstrably, Stableford has an agenda, one with no place in it for Gernsback. As a champion of the "scientific romance," a tradition he observes in Britain from 1888 to 1950, he must discern a lamentable error of judgment in most histories of science fiction: after discussing H. G. Wells at length, they unaccountably abandon the Mother Country, nodding briefly only in the direction of Olaf Stapledon and C. S. Lewis, and rather than discussing major writers like John Gloag and S. Fowler Wright, they lavish attention on a grubby American and his loathsome magazines. Perhaps, then, by casting him only as an avaricious charlatan falsely elevated in importance by the myth-making Moskowitz, Stableford can persuade historians to de-emphasize this rude upstart and the literature he engendered. But it is a hard road to travel, with too many facts in the way.

However, while erasing a person from the history books by rewriting the past is problematic, another method is available: rewriting the future. That is, examining someone of conspicuous accomplishments, one can confidently predict that everything the person achieved will soon wither and fade away, so that future historians will most likely ignore the person. Do you dislike Bill Gates? Well, you might concoct a scandalous "unauthorized biography" charging that Gates is merely an opportunistic crook who swindled his way to the top by stealing other people's ideas. However, you could also gather any available evidence of nascent weaknesses in the Microsoft empire to contend that the company will soon collapse, with all of its products forgotten. Either way, you are striving to reduce Gates to insignificance; and it is by following the latter sort of strategy that my friend John Clute has been waging his own, more subtle campaign against Gernsback and his legacy.

Throughout the 1990s, whenever someone of importance in the field of science fiction died, Clute seemed driven to interpret that death as another portentous sign of the impending death of science fiction itself. After Moskowitz died, Clute (in "Mantra, Tantra, and Specklebang," *Ansible* No. 118) called science fiction "a genre intimately tied to the lives of those who created it as a literature and as a subculture, and who are dying now or dead," and went on to say, "I personally find myself thinking — as I thought when Isaac Asimov died — that the genre is, inevitably, losing its default voices. That ... sf had become far too amorphous to know long before Sam Moskowitz ceased his acts of knowing.... That he carried the template of his era down with him when he died." In his column "Been Bondage" for the December, 1997 *Interzone,* he again sounded this elegiac note, describing the deaths of Judith Merril and George Hay as "a warning shot at the heart of genre" and asserting that the literature they championed is now "mostly history," "a bondage of the been" (52).

Fresh Clute is delightful; stale Clute, much less so. Many other giants of science fiction have perished, or will soon perish, and one hopes that Clute will never again feel impelled to employ these occasions to offer a funeral oration for the premature burial of science fiction. So, a few words of gentle protest seem to be in order.

The last time I saw Clute was at the 1996 World Science Fiction Convention in Los Angeles, in a large auditorium crowded with people, many of them far from elderly. That evening, Clute was handed a Hugo Award, in the form of a costly and beautiful statuette, for the Best Related Book of 1995, his popular *SF: The Illustrated Encyclopedia.* And at that time, taking part in a lavish videotaped presentation amidst throngs of enthusiasts, he said nothing about participating in the death throes of a doomed and inexorably declining movement; in that setting at least, it would have been a difficult argument to make.

The problem with Clute's position is that he espouses a Great Man (or Great Person) theory of science fiction history: for decades, the genre was held together by its Great People; now, one by one, those Great People are dying; and when they are gone, the genre itself will lose its shape and quickly disintegrate. However, science fiction is better regarded as a successful institution, and one characteristic of such institutions is that they continue to survive even after the deaths of prominent constituents. The United States endured after the deaths of George Washington, John Adams, and Thomas Jefferson; science fiction endured after the deaths of Gernsback, Campbell, and Wollheim, and it has continued to endure after the deaths of Moskowitz, Merril, and Hay. It is incongruous to hear Clute lamenting the loss of science fiction's "default voices" because he himself (like Stableford, to a lesser extent) has now *become* one of those voices, with a prose style — highly literate, bordering on the pretentious, but always motivated by an urgent desire to *communicate*, not merely play with words — that ideally reflects some current attitudes towards science fiction.

That is how institutions work: one figure dies, but another takes her place, doing the same job in a different but equally suitable way. The Book Review Department, first headed by Damon Knight, is now run by John Clute. Judith Merril capably led the Annual Anthologies Division, but Gardner Dozois, David Hartwell, and others are currently in charge. Special Research Projects were long supervised by Sam Moskowitz, but Mike Ashley has now taken control. Some members of the Default Voices Committee departed, so new members have been recruited.

Science fiction is a successful institution, in large part, because Hugo Gernsback ably supervised its initial construction. He provided the genre with a name, a critical theory justifying its importance and value, and a literary history. He exemplified the potential of science fiction in his own novel *Ralph 124C 41+*. He effectively promoted the genre by means of words and images, gradually establishing science fiction as a recognized facet of popular culture. He established the first international organization of fans, the Science Fiction League, in 1934 (which Stableford somehow neglected to mention); and though he may have done so, as Frederik Pohl maintained in *The Way the Future Was*, primarily to make money, he still beat the drum for that organization with remarkable vigor, featuring lengthy reports on League activities in every remaining issue of *Wonder Stories* that he edited. Even as the League itself faded away, the organizational impulse remained, expressed in various successor associations, and science fiction soon became a genre bolstered by a well-organized and energetic support group. Several decades later, science fiction is still functioning pretty well, with more than enough talented writers producing original and memorable work, and with a small army of dedicated science fiction fans carrying on all its traditional enterprises.

Because no institution lasts forever, one can legitimately worry about the long-term viability of both the literature and the community of science fiction, and I have myself speculated about possible scenarios for its eventual demise. But today, the beast most definitely remains alive and kicking, and it seems indefensible, and even a bit rude, to seize upon every one of its personal tragedies as ineluctable evidence of its imminent death. Science fiction will perish only in response to a body blow, not a glancing wound. It will not die because a few beloved old people pass away, and it will not die because John Clute announces that it must.

When the perspicacious Clute repeatedly proclaims that science fiction is about to die, based on at best insufficient evidence, the unavoidable speculation is that Clute actually *wishes* science fiction as we know it to die; but why? The problem for the Canadian Clute, like the British Stableford, may be that the institution of science fiction was originally an *American* institution, and both fandom and the literature it espoused have retained a strong American flavor even as Gernsback's "movement" expanded to other nations and continents. (George Hay, for example, was undeniably British, but he was also a devotee of Campbell and a one-time follower of L. Ron Hubbard.) So, if the institution, the genre, even the *idea* of science fiction fades away, there may ensue a regrettable absence of large and vibrant organizations dispensing attractive awards, but authors and readers would otherwise be free to create and enjoy imaginative literature without the oppressive atmosphere of American-ness associated with the term "science fiction." And this is, perhaps, the utopia that Stableford and Clute dream of, explaining why Stableford endeavors to remove America from the past of science fiction, while Clute endeavors to remove America from its future.

Now, I fully realize that there are sensitive issues of national pride involved here. The panoply of American culture, much of it lacking in artistry or appeal, has spread — some might say like a disease — throughout the world. People in many countries may justifiably believe that their distinctive native cultures are being overwhelmed by an ugly tsunami of jeans, Coca Cola, and MTV. In the case of science fiction, commentators may resent, and seek to resist, the excessive influence of American authors and approaches, and rewriting history or redacting the future so as to minimize the American presence may seem an appropriate procedure to liberate their worlds from suffocating cultural oppression. And it was undoubtedly emotions like these that inspired

Stableford to dismiss my first defense of Gernsback and his centrality (in *Foundation* No. 47) with the comment, "Mr. Westfahl has all the charm and sensitivity of the typical American tourist, and thus knows exactly how to put the British and Europeans firmly in their place" (Aldiss, James, and Stableford, "On 'On the True History of Science Fiction'" 29).

Still, one must note, resentment about cultural oppression can go both ways. Reflecting habits that centuries of independence have not erased, numerous Americans continue to display a deferential attitude towards the Mother Country and all of its works. For decades, Sunday nights on American public television have featured a procession of dull, mediocre BBC dramas, under the infuriating umbrella title of *Masterpiece Theatre*, which find a large and loyal audience of American viewers who evidently believe that celluloid was invented primarily for the purpose of recording actors with British accents dressed in impeccable period costumes delivering speeches to each other; and every year, an insufferably tedious movie of similar ilk invariably garners widespread critical acclaim and several Oscar nominations. American commercials selling pricey or supposedly upscale products habitually employ British performers and British settings to communicate the high status of persons using the product; an extremely expensive but otherwise unremarkable car called the Rolls-Royce remains an American icon of automotive superiority. Devotion to the Royal Family is as strong in America as it is in Britain, amply evidenced by the unrelenting American media coverage of Princess Diana's death and the endless stream of tacky Diana "souvenirs" still being advertised and purchased by American consumers.

Do I sound rabidly anti–British? Nothing could be farther from the truth; why, some of my best friends are British ... really. But there is a point to be made: back at the time when Americans were generally content to mind their own business, it was the British who were brutally and peremptorily imposing their own culture on countries throughout the world, implanting a residual belief in British superiority that is still held by some residents of its former colonies and correspondingly resented by other residents of those nations. Thus, when critics born in or residing in Britain begin to belittle major figures in American science fiction, implicitly promoting the superiority of their British counterparts, or when they visibly long for the end to an American-dominated science fiction tradition, presumably in order to engender a literature that might be ... well, a bit more British in its tone and timbre, then many Americans may start to feel that the British have once again come to put the Americans firmly in their place.

Yet all of these essentially irrelevant emotions about national cultures need to be removed from the picture, so we can dispassionately confront the narrow questions of the origins and status of modern science fiction. Making absolutely no general claims about the superiority or inferiority of things American or British, I do not find it culturally chauvinistic to assert that Americans, led by Hugo Gernsback, were the first people to truly recognize what science fiction was and how important it was, and they were the first people to forge the field into a genre with recognized attributes and an effective support system, so that the triumph of the American model of science fiction was not merely a side effect of American postcolonial hegemony, but was rather a triumph richly earned, due to the tireless efforts of Gernsback, his colleagues, and his successors. And this book, among other things, will be providing a detailed defense of that claim, demonstrating how Gernsback's critical writings and fiction helped to make American science fiction into a body of literature which has succeeded beyond anyone's dreams.

In light of Gernsback's contributions, then, I do not find it unreasonable to ask commentators to discuss the founder of the American tradition of science fiction in a reasonably thorough and accurate manner, or to ask them to display some respect for the power and durability of his works and the works of the others who followed in his footsteps. It is, one might say, what the default voices of science fiction should be doing.

2

The Popular Tradition of Science Fiction Criticism, 1926–1980

It has been, by any measure, one of history's most extensive discussions about one particular branch of literature. The conversation was started in the 1920s by the editors and writers of American pulp magazines, who offered their thoughts in editorials, blurbs, articles, reviews, and ancillary materials; next, readers joined in with letters, followed by editorial replies and additional responses from other readers. The dialogue then moved outside of the magazines into private correspondence, personal interactions at meetings and conventions, newsletters and fanzines, and critical studies and bibliographies published by small presses. At first a conversation primarily involving Americans, it soon spread to England and Europe and, eventually, to countries all over the world. And before the last few decades, it has been a discussion with relatively little participation or input from people formally trained and officially qualified to discuss literature. For want of a better term, call it the popular tradition of science fiction criticism.

As no one can credibly deny, Hugo Gernsback was the man who launched this tradition and established its initial agenda, and some of his contributions are almost universally acknowledged: that he began publishing the first true science fiction magazine, *Amazing Stories*, in 1926; that by means of skillful marketing and proselytizing, he persuaded readers, other publishers, and eventually the entire world to believe in the existence of "science fiction" as a distinct category of literature; that he brought previously separated people with an interest in science fiction together, both informally through his magazines' letter columns and formally by founding the first fan organization, the Science Fiction League; and that he thus set in motion the process that culminated in the vast science fiction community that we observe today. My own argument that Gernsback represented the first major critic, and remains the most important critic, of science fiction is acknowledged less universally,

17

though historians of the genre will invariably quote from a Gernsback editorial or two to convey, at least, that he did present some ideas regarding the nature and purpose of science fiction.

Still, in light of the many commentaries on science fiction written before Gernsback's era, as systematically documented in Arthur B. Evans's "The Origins of Science Fiction Criticism: From Kepler to Wells," one might challenge the importance and originality of Gernsback's work; just as Sam J. Lundwall once charged that "in a sense ... Americans had stolen" a "heritage" of European science fiction *literature*, "transforming it and vulgarizing it and changing it beyond recognition" (*Science Fiction: An Illustrated History* 201), one might charge that Gernsback's only contribution was to steal and vulgarize an earlier tradition of science fiction *criticism*.

There are two points to make in response. First, like everyone else of his era, Gernsback had only a limited awareness of previous commentaries and no sense that there even existed a previous "tradition" of science fiction criticism to build upon or borrow from. Second, despite some resonances with the ideas of earlier commentators, Gernsback's theories of science fiction significantly differed from preceding efforts in several significant respects.

What Gernsback knew about previous commentaries on science fiction can be quickly summarized. As I note elsewhere, Gernsback published — and almost certainly wrote — a 1911 review of Mark Wicks's *To Mars Via the Moon* which echoed that book's "Preface," and Wicks undoubtedly influenced both Gernsback's fiction and his ideas about science fiction. As publisher of George Allan England's 1923 story "The Thing from — Outside," Gernsback may have read his "Facts about Fantasy" or engaged in conversations or correspondence with him about science fiction. Gernsback's strong affinity for the works of Jules Verne probably brought him into contact with some comments on those works, by Verne himself and others, and perhaps even discussions of other writers like Edgar Allan Poe and H. G. Wells that Gernsback was less enamored of. However, Gernsback almost certainly never read any contemporary book reviews, literary magazines, prefaces to literary works, or critical studies, and he did not research such materials from previous eras; names like Felix Bodin, William Wilson, and Edgar Fawcett were unknown to him. So, like others before him, Gernsback developed most of his ideas about science fiction entirely on his own, unaware that earlier commentators had made similar observations.

Moreover, Gernsback did more than unknowingly echo what others had already said about science fiction. To explain how his commentaries differed from previous commentaries, I can offer this alliterative list:

Completeness. Gernsback defined the basic characteristics of science fiction, described several different purposes in and different audiences for science fiction, argued for the unique importance of science fiction, and sketched out a history of the genre. Even aspects of science fiction seemingly neglected in his editorial pronouncements, like the use of science fiction as a vehicle for satire and social commentary, surfaced at least occasionally in comments on individual works published in *Amazing Stories*, like the introduction to Wells's *The Island of Dr. Moreau* which stated that "it is our opinion that Mr. Wells has tried to sketch a travesty upon human beings" (637).

Conviction. Gernsback sincerely believed that science fiction was an important genre and took it very seriously. While his innovative suggestion that science fiction stories might describe future inventions so carefully as to justify patents is regularly ridiculed, that idea played a key role in validating science fiction as a uniquely significant form of literature which could play a role in not only *predicting*, but actually *creating*, the future, making the genre "a world-force of unparalleled magnitude" ("The Science Fiction League" 1062). In contrast, one observes England lightheartedly discussing the genre as a little more than a profitable shell game, while Brian Stableford notes that "It is surely a sad discovery to find H. G. Wells, in the preface to his collected scientific romances, offering embarrassed and sarcastic excuses for ever having written them, and promising (after the fashion of a flasher begging mercy from a magistrate) not to do it again now that he has seen the error of his ways" (*Scientific Romance in Britain, 1890–1950* 331–332).

Context. Other previous commentators sometimes discussed science fiction as a form of literature to come only in the future (like Felix Bodin) or one represented only by a single example (like William Wilson). Gernsback not only regularly connected his ideas to authors now esteemed as science fiction pioneers, like Poe, Verne, Wells, and Edward Bellamy (all listed in his first *Amazing Stories* editorial, "A New Sort of Magazine") but he published monthly magazines featuring several old and new examples of the form that were discussed in lengthy introductions that habitually strived to relate the stories, however tendentiously, to Gernsback's theories. Composition teachers who regularly urge student writers to support their ideas with specific evidence and examples will understand why Gernsback's commentaries, buttressed with a wealth of such support, had more impact than other analyses that lacked such a range of older and contemporary illustrative examples.

Communication. Unlike earlier commentators who expressed their ideas in a review here or preface there that usually was little read and quickly forgotten, Gernsback repeated his arguments about science fiction every month, for three years in a magazine with a circulation over 100,000, and for several years thereafter in other widely read magazines. Other publishers noticed his success and produced magazines that paid lip service to his ideas even if they did not exactly follow them; readers absorbed his arguments and wrote letters in response to them; Gernsback's word "science fiction" crept into the dictionaries and into public discourse; and sporadic outbursts of commentary on science fiction were supplanted by a true, continuing conversation. It is Gernsback's ability to forcefully communicate his ideas, and to elicit a strong response to those ideas, that most clearly separates him from all his predecessors; and, if no other documentation is provided, the sheer bulk of science fiction criticism after Gernsback, in contrast to the sporadic commentaries before Gernsback, conclusively demonstrates his enormous impact.

The first clear statement of Gernsback's theories came in the first issue of *Amazing Stories*, where Gernsback announced that "By 'scientifiction' I mean the Jules Verne, H. G. Wells, and Edgar Allan Poe type of story—a charming romance intermingled with scientific fact and prophetic vision" ("A New Sort of Magazine" 3).[1] He thus began to establish a distinguished literary history for his proclaimed genre, and he clearly defined its three basic elements: "charming romance," a narrative framework, later described in less elevated terms as "thrilling adventure" ("Science Fiction Week" 1061); "scientific fact," lengthy explanations of present-day scientific principles incorporated into the story; and "prophetic vision," detailed descriptions of possible new scientific discoveries or inventions.

Science fiction correspondingly had three functions: the narrative could provide "entertainment," the scientific information could furnish a scientific "education," and the accounts of new inventions could offer "inspiration" to inventors, who might proceed to actually build the proposed invention or something similar to it. Correspondingly, there were three natural audiences for science fiction: the general public, seeking to be entertained; younger readers, yearning to be educated about science; and working scientists and inventors, anxious to find some stimulating new ideas.

By means of editorial comments and republication of older works, Gernsback also presented an early picture of the history of science fiction: an era of little conspicuous activity before 1800; a century of isolated pioneers inspired by the Industrial Revolution and other scientific advances, beginning with Poe and prominently including Verne and Wells; and the modern era, marked by vast increases in the number of science fiction works and by the growing prominence of Gernsback's own vision.

Without a doubt, Gernsback's simplistic but persuasive set of ideas had a powerful effect on the early readers and writers of science fiction, since his arguments are regularly recapitulated in readers' letters and in their more extended commentaries of the 1920s and 1930s. Furthermore, while one might attempt to explain away the letters and "Guest Editorials" found in Gernsback's magazines—suggesting that they resulted from Gernsback's ideologically selective publication, readers eager to win contests attempting to curry favor with Gernsback, or even Gernsback making up supportive letters — the fact that editorials and letters echoing those ideas also appeared in the magazines of Gernsback's early competitors would seem inarguable evidence of his substantive influence.

But Gernsback himself did not remain a major force in the field for very long, for reasons that remain controversial. It is a matter of public record that in early 1929, his company went bankrupt and he lost control of his publications, including *Amazing Stories*, which forced him to start over with two new science fiction magazines, *Science Wonder Stories* and *Air Wonder Stories,* soon combined as *Wonder Stories*; but this and other later magazines never matched the success of *Amazing Stories.* However, the reasons behind his ruinous bankruptcy are disputed: according to Sam Moskowitz's account, "Hugo Gernsback: 'Father of Science Fiction,'" in *Explorers of the Infinite,* based on Gernsback's own testimony, Gernsback had been forced into bankruptcy by a devious rival, Bernarr McFadden; but others, such as Steve Perry and Brian Stableford, believe that Gernsback was the devious one, and that the bankruptcy represented his botched scheme to avoid his debts while retaining assets like *Amazing Stories.* What has never to my knowledge been noted is that this was also a time when Gernsback experienced a terrible personal tragedy: on November 19, 1928, his three-year-old daughter Bernett was killed in a car accident when she darted away from a nursemaid to retrieve some pennies she had dropped ("Taxi Kills a Child Retrieving Pennies"). Perhaps, then, a distraught Gernsback began to pay less attention to his business affairs during the time, resulting in the bankruptcy; it is even possible that the horribly ironic reason she died — chasing after pennies — caused him to temporarily reconsider the merits of his notorious desire to make money, further contributing to his financial collapse.[2]

In any event, in the second phase of Gernsback's career as a science fiction editor, he maintained a certain amount of visibility and influence, but by the mid–1930s, his one remaining science fiction magazine, *Wonder Stories,* was failing to garner a sufficient number of readers, and he sold the magazine to another company in 1936. Despite various later efforts as a writer and editor, he would never regain the prominence in the field that he had enjoyed in the 1920s and 1930s. Still, Gernsback was never entirely forgotten, and when he died in 1967, the man editing *Amazing Stories* at the time, Harry Harrison, paid tribute to his pioneering work and pervasive influence in noting that "There are very few men who have singlehandedly shaped and created an entire form of literature, and who have lived to see it grow to a vital fruition" ("Continuity" 2).

Following Gernsback's departure from science fiction in 1936, other editors in the 1930s took on leading roles in contributing to and supervising the continuing discussion of science fiction, though none offered any noteworthy innovations or departures from Gernsback's original theories. In fact, most sought only to truncate, or weaken, his ideas.

Gernsback's former assistant T. O'Conor Sloane, who edited *Amazing Stories* from 1929 to 1938, began presenting a slightly different picture of science fiction in his very first editorial: "The basic idea of the magazine was the publication of fiction, founded on, or embodying always some touch of natural science.... To [our authors] it is a pleasure we are sure, to enter the realm of fiction, and use their knowledge there, for the instruction, as well as amusement of their readers" ("Amazing Stories" 103). Sloane's definition of science fiction — "fiction, founded on, or embodying always some touch of natural science" — included only fiction and science, with no mention of prophecy or prediction, and his announced purposes for the genre included only "instruction" and "amusement," with no mention of providing stimulating ideas for scientists or, indeed, of engaging in any serious effort to offer predictions of the future. Refusing to acknowledge those aspects of science fiction which made the genre most interesting and potentially most important, Sloane's magazines, perhaps inevitably, seemed languid in contrast to the exuberance of Gernsback's magazines.

Three other major editors — Harry Bates, the first editor of *Astounding Stories of Super-Science* (later *Astounding Stories*); Mort Weisinger, first editor of *Wonder Stories* under new owners who renamed it *Thrilling Wonder Stories*; and Ray Palmer, who succeeded Sloane as editor of *Amazing Stories* — reduced Gernsback's agenda in another way, neglecting the elements of science and education while continuing to profess a continuing commitment to them. Thus, even though Bates's first editorial announcement sounded congruent with Gernsback's ideas — "ASTOUNDING STORIES ... is a magazine whose stories will anticipate the scientific achievements of To-morrow — whose stories will not only be strictly accurate in their science but will be vividly, dramatically, and thrillingly told" (cited in Clarke, *Astounding Days* 8–9) — he noticeably places more emphasis on the stories' narrative qualities than on their scientific qualities — reflecting his private opinions that Gernsback's *Amazing Stories* was "awful stuff.... Cluttered with trivia! Packed with puerility. Written by unimaginables!" and that his magazine should emphasize "story elements of action and adventure," not science ("Editorial Number One" x, xiii). A similar concern for exciting narrative can be detected in opening remarks from editors Weisinger — "Our objective will always be to provide the most thrilling and entertaining fiction possible — while never ignoring basic scientific truths" ("The New Thrilling Wonder Stories" 10) — and Palmer — "Insofar as the basic subject matter is founded upon scientific research, it will be essentially a true story magazine although thrilling tenseness of adventure will still form a part of the many features yet to come" ("The Observatory by the Editor" 8).

Yet the major science fiction magazine editor of the 1930s, F. Orlon Tremaine of *Astounding Stories*, embraced Gernsback's complete picture of the genre as fiction, science, and prophecy — speaking of one "story that ... those of you who like carefully projected scientific thought will like" ("Ad Astra" 7) — and agreed that its works could provide entertainment, education, and stimulating ideas — stating "There is no more interesting or educational reading anywhere" ("Star Dust" 65), and "Astounding Stories holds a unique and important place in scientific achievement.... Perhaps we dream — but we do so logically, and science follows in the footsteps of our dreams" ("Blazing New Trails" 153). Still, in addition to both announcing and demonstrating his increased attention to the literary quality of science fiction, Tremaine significantly departed from Gernsback's agenda in one respect: his picture of the characteristic audience of science fiction. Whereas Gernsback had aspired to a mass audience, Tremaine argued that science fiction readers were by nature a small, elite group, "members of that inner circle who see and understand a vision that is beyond the ken of the vast multitude" ("Looking Ahead" 155).

In discussing science fiction commentaries of the 1930s, scholars have naturally focused on magazine editors, since the pulp magazines of that era were undoubtedly the genre's most widely read, influential, and accessible publications. But other publications were taking note of science fiction, most notably writer's magazines, which began publishing articles explaining how to write science fiction. The first of these came from Gernsback himself— "How to Write 'Science' Stories," in the February, 1930 issue of *Writer's Digest*— but other such articles would soon follow from popular writers like S. P. Meek, Ross Rocklynne, and Henry Kuttner.

Also during the 1930s, growing numbers of fan organizations and individual fans started to produce their own publications, the fanzines, which collectively represent a vast and largely unexplored territory for science fiction scholars. While the fanzines of the 1930s varied in quality and included large amounts of inconsequential material, some of their contents have had a lasting impact; Harry Warner, Jr., for instance, notes that the enduring terms "B.E.M." (for Bug-Eyed Monster) and "space opera" originated in early fanzines (*All Our Yesterdays* 234, 41). Since both represent pejorative references to the illustrations and stories then appearing in the science fiction magazines, they illustrate the important role that fanzines could play: as forums for commentary beyond the control of magazine editors, they could provide vigorous, even acidic criticisms of the contents of those magazines. Further, by displaying occasional discontent with the routine space adventures of the era, they anticipated later critical voices and helped to inspire the reforms and improvements of the 1940s often attributed (incorrectly, I have argued) solely to Campbell's editorial genius.

As one example of what the fanzines were doing, four essays by Clyde F. Beck that appeared in one fanzine, *The Science Fiction Critic*, along with a newly written "Author's Preface," were gathered together in 1937 and published as *Hammer and Tongs*. While both tiny (only 28 pages of text, plus a one-page bibliography) and obscure (only a small number of copies were published by the same amateur press that produced *The Science Fiction Critic*), *Hammer and Tongs* qualifies as the first book devoted entirely to science fiction criticism. And while Beck apologized in his preface for his failure "to formulate a sketch of a system of criticism of this new type of romance" (ix), he nonetheless makes an interesting effort to blend the principles of Wells (which he is familiar with and refers to) and the concerns of Gernsback and contemporary fans.

Like some later commentators, Beck dislikes the term "science fiction," "which not only is self-contradictory, but does not properly define the type of story to which it is applied" (viii); accepting Wells's principle that the science is there simply to provide an air of verisimilitude, Beck suggests the term "pseudo-scientific fantasy" would be more appropriate (ix). In his nearest approach to a complete definition of the genre, he lists "the three things fundamental to good science fiction": the author "has founded the plot upon a plausible development of scientific theory, he has maintained an atmosphere of reality in unfamiliar circumstances, and he has shown to a certain extent a consciousness of purpose in writing" (5). Noting that "This last is perhaps the most often lacking in contemporary science fiction," Beck demonstrates a strong interest in purposes beyond Gernsback's, declaring that "its possibilities for allegorical satire and imaginative projection of present social trends are unparalleled" (5). Anticipating the concerns of later critics for stronger characterization in science fiction, he states that "The author is free of space and time, of the imposed restraint of our present discontents; but all too often he forgets that he is not free of men and women, that he must write of real people after all if he is to interest real people" (xiv). And comments about individual authors and stories can be much more scathing than anything a magazine would have printed: "writers such as Van Lorne, Skidmore, Jones, and the like are continually fouling the pages of the magazines with illiterate, maudlin, or merely foolish drivel" (16).

However, when Beck complains about the "loose thinking of authors, who with or without degrees, abandon in writing science fiction the vigorous habit of mind which is the prime requisite of science," and goes on to point out their frequent "misuse of scientific terms" (2), he conveys the strong concern for scientific accuracy that was characteristic of Gernsback-era commentators. Thus, in emphasizing both literary values and scientific accuracy, Beck reminds modern readers of the later criticism of Damon Knight and James Blish, though Beck's *Hammer and Tongs* was far too brief and fleeting a discourse to have the impact of Knight's and Blish's works.

The next major figure in the popular tradition of science fiction criticism was Campbell, who assumed editorial control of *Astounding Stories* in 1937 and came to dominate the field in the 1940s by publishing superior new writers like Isaac Asimov, Robert A. Heinlein, and A. E. van Vogt and by offering his own vigorous, and increasingly pugnacious, editorial commentaries.

While Campbell accepted Gernsback's three defining principles — fiction, science, and prophecy — he broadened all three to identify and celebrate expanded possibilities in the genre. Not merely "charming romance" or "thrilling adventure," science fiction, according to Campbell, could adopt a wide variety of generic models; he also announced on several occasions that good writing skills and strong characterization were key elements in science fiction stories (though many would argue that the stories he published increasingly failed to reflect such priorities). The presentation of scientific data was still important, but it could be accomplished, in the manner of Heinlein, with brief comments and indirect references; Campbell also broadened the concept of "science" to include fields like the social sciences and parapsychology as potential material for stories. And the prophecies of science fiction had to involve not only plausible new inventions, but consideration of how those inventions might affect human society, so that writers would have to develop a detailed picture of an imagined future world that incorporates those inventions.

Campbell's discussions of science fiction also explained, far more than Gernsback's, how science fiction should be written: the author begins with an innovative idea, then employs a process of scientific thinking, or extrapolation, to develop a complete background from that idea, and finally allows a narrative to evolve out of that background; ideally, the story will naturally emerge almost by itself from the background material, without conscious craftsmanship.

In describing the purposes of science fiction, Campbell accepted Gernsback's goals of entertainment, education, and stimulating ideas, but he also focused on several new purposes: by presenting challenging scientific puzzles to solve, science fiction stories might train young people to think more scientifically; more broadly, science fiction stories could provide analyses of possible new scientific innovations — to anticipate problems before they occur — and imaginative reconsiderations of past and present situations. In these ways, science fiction could be "a way of considering the past, present, and future from a different viewpoint, and taking a look at how else we *might* do things ... a convenient analog system for thinking about new scientific, social, and economic ideas — and for re-examining old ideas" ("Introduction," *Prologue to Analog* 10, 13). Oddly, even as he expanded the purposes of science fiction, he followed Tremaine in limiting the genre's envisioned audience, regarding it as too demanding for the general public or young people without a strong interest in science.

Finally, while his discussions of science fiction history were less frequent and less prominent than Gernsback's, Campbell during his career did articulate two interestingly divergent visions of science fiction history. First, he claimed that it primarily represented a modern literature whose first major practitioner was H. G. Wells: "Science-fiction finds no counterpart in the entertainment of history" ("Future Tense" 6). Later, he argued that science fiction represented a long literary tradition that included many distinguished authors of the past: "While most people tend to think of [science fiction] as being Jules Verne and H. G. Wells up-to-date, perhaps we might better remember that the tradition goes back earlier to Gulliver's Travels and even to Aesop's Fables" ("Introduction," *Cloak of Aesir* 13–14).

Overall, in articulating a more broad and sophisticated vision of what science fiction was, how it should be written, why it should be written, and where it came from, Campbell both harkened back to some of the ideas of commentators before Gernsback and laid the groundwork for modern critical approaches to science fiction.

Before 1950, the history of the popular tradition of science fiction criticism can properly focus on the major figures of Gernsback and Campbell. After 1950, such a narrow focus is no longer possible, for from 1950 to 1980, there were many influential commentators talking about science fiction, and all of them played a role in the tradition and deserve some attention. A few figures are more important than others, but even these others are important to consider in part as representatives of larger movements.

In every sense of the word, what happened to science fiction in the 1950s was indeed an explosion. There was a tremendous increase in the amount of science fiction written and published as science fiction, in a plethora of new magazines and in hardcover and paperback books; many writers went beyond traditional markets to present science fiction in a variety of new forums; and science fiction became prominent in the media of films and television. Accompanying this explosion, several new commentators of note emerged, and these can be roughly grouped into four categories: new magazine editors; book reviewers; anthologists; and editors and authors of books about science fiction.

There were, of course, other science fiction editors besides Campbell in the 1940s, but other than Palmer — who faded from prominence by the end of the decade — they generally had little influence. In the 1950s, however, two major new magazines emerged. One of these — *The Magazine of Fantasy and Science Fiction*, first edited by J. Francis McComas and Anthony Boucher, then by Boucher alone — chose to be somewhat reticent in proclaiming attitudes and theories about science fiction. They published no editorials or readers' letters, offering commentaries only in the form of book reviews by Boucher and others. Still, the magazine's intent (evident in its title) to blur distinctions between science fiction and fantasy, and its manifest commitment to literary quality, were undoubtedly influential even if its policies were not explicitly proclaimed. Judith Merril has argued for Boucher as the major figure of science fiction in the 1950s:

> He brought literary standards and literary status, both, into the specialty field.... He approached his editorship with a revolutionary concept: the idea that science-fantasy [as he preferred to call the whole field of rational-imaginative-speculative fiction] *could be well-written.*
>
> Boucher carried this to an unheard-of extreme. He would not buy a story just for the idea; he had to like the writing.... Boucher's function as book reviewer was no less important than as editor. He had, at least part of the time, brilliant competition.... But for the writers, it was Boucher's accolades that counted, and for thousands of new readers of s-f books, it was Boucher's guidance they trusted.
>
> I said earlier that science fiction today is catching up with science; Anthony Boucher was the dominant force in the fifties when science fiction began to catch up with fiction ["What Do You Mean: Science? Fiction?" 79–80].

The other editor, H. L. Gold of *Galaxy*, was more loquacious. His editorials and introductions to anthologies generally offered little more than restatements of Campbell's principles: he said that the "job [of science fiction] is simply to speculate, skillfully and intelligently and dramatically and above all entertainingly, on any and every possibility we can fashion out of observable fact, theory, hypothesis, and outright guesses" ("Introduction" ix) and said the science fiction writer must "*extrapolate*, which is the process of taking a known fact or theory of today and carrying it just as far as imaginative logic can take it" ("In This Corner" ix). Thus, Gold accepted Campbell's ideas that science fiction is a literature based on scientific "fact or theory" imaginatively extended through "extrapolation." And in one comment on science fiction history, he seemed inclined to accept the expansive view of the later Campbell, listing only ancient writers as the possible originators of the form: "There is no way of setting the birth date of science fiction. Some authorities claim that Plato was the father. Other authorities trace paternity back to Homer, the Bible" ("Program Notes" ix).

However, Gold did offer some changes. First, though an early contest involving flying saucers was said to have "a scientific intent" ("For Adults Only" 3), Gold wrote little about scientific content and scientific accuracy in science fiction, and he largely abandoned efforts to defend science fiction as a way of inspiring future inventions or considering future possibilities, since "science fiction is not in the prediction business" ("Program Notes" xi). When a reference to science appears in Gold's writing, it was given little prominence; he said once that "What science fiction must present entertainingly is speculation. Not prophecy, but fictional surmises based on present factors, scientific, social, political, cultural, or whatever" ("Step Outside" 2).

Instead of discussing the scientific value of science fiction, Gold placed greater emphasis on its literary value. An early editorial claimed that "We are inducing fine writers in other branches of literature to try their hand in science fiction" ("It's All Yours" 3) and said that his policy "merely applies the standards of *any* legitimate branch of literature to science fiction" ("Yardstick for Science Fiction" 3). He particularly called for more mature and thought-provoking science fiction: his first editorial proclaimed that

> Science fiction, everybody agrees, or seems to, has finally come of age....
> GALAXY *Science Fiction* proposes to carry the maturity of this type of literature into the science fiction magazine field, where it is now, unfortunately, somewhat hard to find. It establishes a compound break with both the lurid and the stodgy traditions of s-f magazine publishing. From cover design to advertising selections, GALAXY *Science Fiction* intends to be a mature magazine for mature readers ["For Adults Only" 2].

He said in his second editorial that "We have challenged writers to present themes that could not be sold elsewhere ... themes that are too adult, too profound or revolutionary in concept for other magazines to risk publishing" ("It's All Yours" 3). In these ways, Gold claimed that "GALAXY and its writers are opening new paths in science fiction" ("Ask a Foolish Question" 159).

Despite these early assertions of the seriousness and maturity of science fiction, Gold also placed stress on the role of science fiction as pure entertainment; "The first goal" of science fiction, he said, "is entertainment ... [which] ranges all the vast distance from staring through keyholes to staring through telescopes, from racetracks to treatises, scatology to seismography" ("Step Outside" 2). Thus, while his magazine became famous — or notorious — for heavy-handed satire, Gold did not announce such goals for science fiction; it was according to his statements simply a medium for providing well-crafted and entertaining stories. (Ironically, it was the later Campbell who would place more emphasis on science fiction as social commentary.) Thus, as Sloane to some extent reduced and trivialized Gernsback's arguments for science fiction, Gold to some extent reduced and trivialized Campbell's arguments for science fiction — though he must be commended as an editor for the quality of fiction he published in the 1950s, which was far superior to that of Campbell's *Astounding Science-Fiction* during that decade.

While *Astounding Science-Fiction, The Magazine of Fantasy and Science Fiction* and *Galaxy* are generally seen as the major magazines of the 1950s, Damon Knight has also praised *Thrilling Wonder Stories* and *Startling Stories*, edited by Samuel Merwin, Jr. from 1944 to 1951 and afterwards by Samuel Mines, as "successful and influential.... [Merwin] upgraded the magazines to a point about equidistant among the three leaders" ("Beauty, Stupidity, Injustice, and Science Fiction" 79). Ashley has lauded Samuel Mines as "a key figure in furthering the frontiers of science fiction ... [who] challenged writers to experiment with daring themes" and celebrates his decision to publish Philip Jose Farmer's controversial *The Lovers* ("Introduction: From Bomb to Boom" 89–90).[3] If Mervin and Mines remain obscure, unlike the reviewing Boucher and the editorializing Gold, it is undoubtedly because they offered no striking pronouncements or extended analyses of science fiction, primarily influencing the development of science fiction by their editorial decisions.

In the 1950s, science fiction criticism first became a regular and respected activity, most prominently taking the form of regular book reviews in magazines and amateur publications. Four figures deserve special mention.

The first two are Damon Knight and James Blish. Knight was the first person, despite his achievements as a writer and editor, to gain a reputation primarily as a science fiction critic, and the first person to win a Hugo Award for his criticism, collected in his 1956 book *In Search of Wonder* (revised and expanded in 1967). He burst onto the scene in 1945 with a blistering fanzine attack on the logic and style of A. E. van Vogt's *The World of Null-A*; and in his 1952 introduction to a series of reviews in *Science Fiction Adventures*, reprinted in *In Search of Wonder*, Knight offered this critical manifesto:

> As a critic, I operate under certain basic assumptions, all eccentric, to wit:
> 1. That the term "science fiction" is a misnomer, that trying to get two enthusiasts to agree on a definition of it leads only to bloody knuckles; that better labels have been devised [Heinlein's suggestion, "speculative fiction," is the best, I think], but that we're stuck with this one; and that it will do us no particular harm if we remember that, like "The Saturday Evening Post," it means what we point to when we say it.
> 2. That a publisher's jacket blurb and a book review are two different things, and should be composed accordingly.
> 3. That science fiction is a field of literature worth taking seriously, and that ordinary critical standards can be meaningfully applied to it: e.g., originality, sincerity, style, construction, logic, coherence, sanity, garden-variety grammar.
> 4. That a bad book hurts science fiction more than ten bad notices [1].

A few years later, Blish, writing as "William Atheling, Jr.," began writing reviews of science fiction magazines for various amateur and semiprofessional magazines; his columns were collected in *The Issue at Hand* (1964) and *More Issues at Hand* (1970). Like Knight, Blish began with a statement of critical principles:

> The function of a critic in this field, as it is in others, is two-fold: First of all, he must ask that editors and writers be conscious of the minimum standards of competence which apply in the writing of all fiction; secondly, he must make reasonably clear to his non-professional readers what those standards of competence are.... Technical competence in story-telling is of course not the sole factor which turns a piece of fiction into a work of art. Freshness of idea, acuity of observation, depth of emotional penetration are all crucial; and there are other such factors. But technical competence is the one completely indispensable ingredient.... For the few antibiotic-resistant cases who insist that science fiction is too aberrant a medium to be judged by the standards of other kinds of fiction, we can reply flatly and without much desire to be polite that we are not interested in any form of fiction which cuts itself off from human life and human values [*The Issue at Hand* 13–14].

There are three interesting features in the approaches of Knight and Blish.

First, for the first time in the history of the popular tradition, we encounter science fiction commentators who explicit identify themselves as critics. Interestingly, Boucher's introduction to the first edition of *In Search of Wonder* also argued that "All the rest of us ... are primarily reviewers; damon knight [sic], in most of his published assessments of science fiction and particularly in those gathered here, is a critic" (vi).

Second, like Gold, Knight and Blish insisted that science fiction be judged by "ordinary critical standards" and "the minimum standards of competence which apply in the writing of all fiction." In a sense, this was nothing new, since both Gernsback and Campbell outwardly agreed that science fiction should pay heed to literary values. But those men also devised special apologies for the genre's literary lapses: when a reader complained about "tripe" in a recent issue of *Wonder Stories*, an editor replied, "The art of writing these stories is young" ("The Reader Speaks," *Wonder Stories*, June, 1931 132). And, discussing the difficulty of creating a thoroughly worked-out background for a science fiction story, Campbell maintained that "science-fiction is an extremely difficult medium in which to produce good work — really good work" ("Introduction," *The Man Who Sold the Moon* 12). So Gernsback implied that science fiction should be judged by special and lenient standards because it is such a new genre, and Campbell suggested that science fiction should be judged by special and lenient standards because it was such a unusually hard genre. But Knight — implicitly — and Blish — explicitly — brushed these claims of special privilege aside.

In essence, both men advocated practicing what Campbell had preached — stories that broke away from conventional boundaries, stories with involving characters, stories which addressed science and its issues in imaginative and provocative ways — and, in critiques of particular novels and stories, they repeatedly insisted on certain standards: logical plotting, realistic characterization, and competent prose style.

Employing the standards of all fiction, Knight promised to regularly give "bad notices" to works that deserve them, and Blish announced that "criticism, if it is to be of any use at all, must among other things be merciless" (*The Issue at Hand* 22). And they therefore announced the end of science fiction's era of boosterism. When the genre was just beginning, and its writers were few and untalented, enthusiasts nevertheless tried to give them the benefit of the doubt, to promote all works of science fiction as worthwhile regardless of their quality, and harsh critiques like Beck's — at least in widely distributed publications — were rare. Now, with the genre well established and many talented writers in the field, it was time to work to improve the genre by, among other things, criticizing inferior works. Knight said it is valuable to "rip a bad work of art to shreds" so one can "find out how it is made" (*In Search of Wonder* 22) — and thus to learn how to make one better — while Blish similarly argued that "the whole point of telling a man he is doing something the wrong way is the hope that next time he will do it right" (*More Issues at Hand* 1–2).

Third, Knight and Blish moved away from the obsessive concern for scientific explanation and prediction that preoccupied Gernsback and Campbell. Knight suggested that the term used to describe the genre should not even include the word "science" (and in the 1960s, some commentators would actually attempt to replace Gernsback's term with Knight's preferred "speculative fiction"). And responding to editor Kendell Foster Crossen's call to "throw the science out of science fiction," Blish said, "To be sure, the story's the thing" (*The Issue at Hand* 45, 46). Still, both men paid attention to the quality of the science in science fiction. Arguing against Alfred Bester's position that "the science in [a science fiction story] is unimportant," Knight responded, "When Bester suggests that people don't turn to science fiction for information, of course he's right; but people don't turn to s.f. for misinformation, either" (6). And while criticizing Charles Eric Maine's *High Vacuum*, Knight defined these standards:

> For the record, again, I don't expect any science fiction writer to do graduate work in physics before he writes a space opera. If a writer makes a blunder in higher mathematics or theoretical physics, he is safe from me — I am no expert, and will never notice it. The gross errors in this novel are in the area of common knowledge [as if a Western hero should saddle up a pueblo and ride off down the cojone]; any one of them could have been corrected by ten minutes with a dictionary or an encyclopedia [*In Search of Wonder* 100].

Blish agreed that "respect for facts ... is fundamental to fiction, not just science fiction alone, but all fiction" (*The Issue at Hand* 46).

In a way, then, Knight and Blish seemed to return to the lax standards of Bates, Weisinger, and Palmer — that a tremendous amount of freedom in dealing with science in science fiction is permissible as long as one does not "ignor[e] basic scientific truths." The difference is that Knight's and Blish's commitment to scientific accuracy is muted but sincere; when they notice obvious errors, they chastise them rather severely. Thus, unlike the earlier magazines that attempted to minimize the factor of science, Knight and Blish do take science seriously, even while agreeing that it is not the only important issue.

While their reviews thus balanced an insistence on "ordinary critical standards" with some attentiveness to scientific accuracy, they did not always place emphasis on the latter factor, primarily because, perhaps, they saw no need to; Knight has privately commented that "I don't think either of us ever said that science (broadly defined) was not central to the genre. If we didn't spend much time on that, it was because the importance of 'science' (meaning speculation about other worlds, the future, imaginary inventions, etc.) was universally taken for granted" (Letter to Gary Westfahl, March 6, 1992). However, persons reading their reviews, and noting the stress on literary values, might get the impression that "ordinary critical standards" were in fact the central issue; and one feature of the subsequent New Wave movement was an effort to further minimize the genre's emphasis on scientific matters.

This parallel discussion is not meant to imply that Knight and Blish were identical in their approach and their impact. Knight primarily reviewed science fiction books, while Blish concentrated on the magazines; Knight maintained a breezy and accessible style, while Blish — perhaps trapped by the pseudonym of Atheling — sometimes affected an irritatingly pompous manner; and Knight published in mainstream magazines while Blish wrote for amateur magazines, so that Knight undoubtedly had more visibility and influence.

A third reviewer, P. Schuyler Miller, generally receives little attention or respect — Malcolm J. Edwards notes that he "was not a particularly demanding critic" ("P. Schuyler Miller" 808); but he did write a monthly column of reviews for *Astounding Science-Fiction* and its successor *Analog Science Fiction/Science Fact* for twenty-four years — from 1951 to his death in 1974 — making him by far the most prolific science fiction reviewer. And while he was not as highly esteemed as Knight or Blish for his critical acumen, Miller also had some influence on the field. For example, he was the first prominent commentator to use the term "hard science fiction," and his scattered comments on the form during the early 1960s helped to establish the nature and boundaries of that subgenre; he was also the first to use the expression "new wave" in reference to British writers of the 1960s.[4] Other columns devote a considerable amount of serious attention to juvenile science fiction, along with occasional discussion of older science fiction "classics" and fantasy. His contribution, then, may have been to make readers more aware of the various subcategories of science fiction that were then emerging, arguing in effect that these deserved special consideration instead of lumping all works together simply as "science fiction."

In the 1960s and 1970s, a fourth major reviewer emerged, science fiction writer Algis Budrys, whose sharp and idiosyncratic reviews for *Galaxy* were eventually republished in book form as *Benchmarks: Galaxy Bookshelf* in 1985.

The first hardcover anthology of science fiction to appear was Groff Conklin's 1946 *The Best of Science Fiction* (though *Adventures through Space and Time*, edited by Raymond J. Healy and J. Francis McComas, was actually the first to be prepared and accepted for publication). In his introduction, attempting to present science fiction to a wider audience, Conklin in one way followed the approach of Gernsback, dignifying the genre by placing it in the context of an extended literary history; he first accepted the early nineteenth century as the time the genre originated, stating that "the modern concept of science fiction, though it remained without the name, began at about the time when science itself began to have a broad, popular interest" (xxi), and went on to discuss *The Moon Hoax*, Poe, Fitz-James O'Brien, Verne, Conan Doyle, Ambrose Bierce, Jack London, H. Rider Haggard, and Mark Twain's *A Connecticut Yankee in King Arthur's Court* before listing "the elder statesmen of modern science fiction" as Wells, George Allan England, Garrett P. Serviss and others" (xxi–xxii). And he praised Gernsback, who "will always be remembered by both writers and addicts with the respect due to a pioneer," and Campbell, who "has created a magazine which ... maintains an inordinately high level of well-written and effective stories" (xxiii).

However, Conklin departed from the vision of Gernsback and Campbell in one crucial respect:

> science fiction, despite its treading on the toes of nuclear physics, has no business claiming the robes of the prophet ... fun, after all, is the primary import of science fiction, which, like the detective story and the fairy tale as well, has one purpose, clear and simple: the purpose of entertaining you. It is first as entertainment that *The Best of Science Fiction* is offered, with only a slight and faintly uneasy salaam to the writers who have put their imaginations to the practical problem of what nuclear fission might involve in the way of social and political change [xvi, xviii].

Thus, Conklin, like Gold, attempted to play down the important functions of science fiction proclaimed by Campbell — though he still acknowledged such functions as a secondary aspect of the genre.

Conklin went on to edit numerous anthologies that were each generally devoted to a different science fiction topic — robots, space travel, other dimensions, mutants, and the like. Science fiction was a growing field, which generated a need for some kinds of subdivisions; and Conklin's collections were influential in setting up canons of stories of certain types and in establishing the convention of categorizing science fiction works by subject matter — unlike Miller's tendency to categorize by different types of audiences.

The first regular series of science fiction anthologies began with *The Best Science Fiction Stories: 1949*, edited by Everett F. Bleiler and T. E. Dikty, followed by five successor volumes; and while these volumes did not have a major impact, their work had some interesting features. In their "Preface" to the first volume, Bleiler and Dikty began by claiming that "Many of the greatest figures in world literature have written what might be called science-fiction.... A short list would include Daniel DeFoe [sic], W. H. Hudson, Aldous Huxley, Edgar Allan Poe, Jean Jacques Rousseau, Jonathan Swift, and H. G. Wells" (19), thus following the strategy of Gernsback and Conklin in striving to establish the respectability of the form. And two of their "cogent reasons to demonstrate that science-fiction has value"—"its scientific truth, its educational value"— recall Gernsback: in saying, "there has been a large middle-ground where science-fiction and history have conveniently met, and many apt predictions have resulted. Nor has science-fiction been without repercussions on the life of the individual" (20), they restated Gernsback's argument for the power of science fiction prophecy, although their examples of its impact — the founding of the Royal Academy in response to Francis Bacon's *The New Atlantis* and the attempted establishments of actual utopian societies in response to Bellamy — extended beyond the realm of inventions. And, while acknowledging this claim can be "overestimate[d]" or "overrate[d]," they agreed that "Science-fiction, it is true, can offer a palatable mass of facts for easy consumption" (20–21). But their third argument for the genre was more expansive and original: that it can offer "an insight and investigation into a specific aspect of life which no other means can offer: the relation of man to science" (21).

After emphasizing this broad and powerful role, however, they oddly retreated, in the "Preface" to their second volume, to argue for a strong connection between science fiction and detective fiction:

> In addition to their parallel evolution science-fiction and the whodunit share a closely related innermost essence. The detective story ... is intellectually oriented. It proposes an intellectual problem which the reader is intended [or not intended] to solve. It is ultimately an exercise for the imagination. Science-fiction is similarly intellectually aimed; often it is just as much a riddle or puzzle tale as the whodunit. And both stress Mystery ... in modern science-fiction, as

the reader of this book will notice, the science is almost always imaginative, and surprise endings are common. In science-fiction, stories which are the exegesis of a scientific idea are obviously closer to the whodunit than stories which stress an adventure element ... the science-fiction story — at present and increasingly in the future — is supplanting the detective story [19–20].

In a way, this attitude was a natural outgrowth of Campbell's emphasis on science fiction as a way to train people to think in a scientific manner; but Bleiler and Dikty were proposing a major truncation of the genre. The "adventure element" — the basis of science fiction's broad appeal since Gernsback — was now viewed as a vestigial and unimportant element; and there are here no arguments for science fiction as a way to anticipate and influence future developments or to comment on present-day society. Instead, science fiction becomes little more than a stimulating brain-teaser.

Judith Merril, who edited twelve "Year's Best" anthologies from 1955 to 1967, became the preeminent anthologist of her era, in part because she definitely presented and argued a consistent and provocative position. In rambling commentaries surrounding her eccentric choices of stories from all sorts of writers and publications — not just those associated with science fiction — Merril effectively maintained that there were not after all large differences between science fiction and other forms of literature, thus making another appeal, in a way, for judging science fiction by "ordinary critical standards." And this, of course, is another effect of a growing genre — the effort to break down barriers so that it can grow some more. To further broaden the field, Merril started a campaign to replace "science fiction" with the more general — and ameliorative — "SF"; as she explained in 1967,

> *Science fiction* as a descriptive label has long since lost whatever validity it might once have had. By now it means so many things to so many people that ... I prefer not to use it at all, when I am talking about stories. *SF* [or generically, s-f] allows you to think *science fiction* if you like, while I think *science fable* or *scientific fantasy* or *speculative fiction*, or [once in a rare while, because there's little enough of it being written, by any rigorous definition] *science fiction* ["Introduction," *SF: The Best of the Best* ix].

Later in her career as an editor, Merril became an enthusiastic advocate of the New Wave, celebrated in her 1960s book reviews for *The Magazine of Fantasy and Science Fiction* and in her 1968 anthology *England Swings SF*— and the next critical movement in the history of the idea of science fiction, to be discussed shortly. When Merril left the scene in the late 1960s, two other series of "year's best" anthologies carried on her tradition — one edited by Donald A. Wollheim and Terry Carr, the other by Harry Harrison and Brian W. Aldiss, each offering exemplary stories as well as introductory commentaries. After these series ended in the 1970s, other editors have carried on the tradition of annual anthologies, including Wollheim and Carr (in separate series), Frederik Pohl, Gardner Dozois, and David G. Hartwell and Kathryn Cramer.

Amidst growing number of hardcover science fiction anthologies and novels, the 1940s and 1950s also witnessed the first appearances of books about science fiction written by well-known authors and editors in the field. There were critical anthologies featuring essays on science fiction by well-known writers and editors, including *Of Worlds Beyond: The Science of Science Fiction Writing* (1947), edited by Lloyd Arthur Eshbach; *Modern Science Fiction: Its Meaning and Its Future*, edited by Reginald Bretnor (1953); and *The Science Fiction Novel: Imagination and Social Criticism*, edited by Basil Davenport (1959), who also wrote the brief critical study *Inquiry into Science Fiction* (1955). Much later, Bretnor produced two additional anthologies, *Science Fiction, Today and Tomorrow* (1974) *and The Craft of Science Fiction* (1976).

While Hal Clement had explained the process of writing hard science fiction in an pioneering essay, "Whirligig World," that appeared in *Astounding Science-Fiction* in June, 1953, L. Sprague de Camp in the same year offered more general guidance in *The Science Fiction Handbook* (1953), the first book about how to write science fiction, which was revised and republished in 1975. Other books of this sort followed, including the Science Fiction Writers of America's *Writing and Selling Science Fiction* in 1976.

Sam Moskowitz, the most diligent researcher in the science fiction community, produced numerous biographical essays on science fiction writers of the past and present, later gathered into two volumes — *Explorers of the Infinite: Shapers of Science Fiction* (1963) and *Seekers of Tomorrow: Masters of Modern Science Fiction* (1966) — while a third collection of his essays, *Strange Horizons* (1976), explored issues like feminism and anti–Semitism in early science fiction. One company, Advent Publishers of Chicago, was particularly energetic in publishing such critical books, including the aforementioned collections of Knight's and Blish's reviews and studies like Alva Rogers's *A Requiem for Astounding* (1964). There were also published histories of fandom itself, most notably Moskowitz's *The Immortal Storm* (1954), focusing on the 1930s, and Harry Warner, Jr.'s *All Our Yesterdays* (1969) and *A Wealth of Fable* (1976), focusing on the 1940s and 1950s. In his *The Universe Makers* (1971), veteran author and editor Donald A. Wollheim persuasively epitomized the science fiction monomyth, the predicted future common to most science fiction: a near future of great troubles, followed by successful human expansion throughout the Galaxy, contact with alien life, and ultimately an approach to God. And, as the science fiction movement grew more international in character, Swedish fan Sam J. Lundwall brought a distinctly European, and often irascible, tone to science fiction commentaries with his books *Science Fiction: What It's All About* (1971) and *Science Fiction: An Illustrated History* (1977).

There is no time for detailed discussions of all of these books, and it is difficult to generalize about them. They reflected first of all some desire to explain, and even codify, the process of writing science fiction, something attempted in some of the essays in Eshbach's anthology and in de Camp's book. There was an ongoing concern for the literary history of science fiction which on the one hand led to massive bibliographical compilations and on the other hand inspired some, anticipating the expansiveness of later academics, to incorporate much of the history of Western literature into the field. For example, in *The Science Fiction Handbook*, de Camp, under the rubric of "imaginative literature," created an absurdly grand context for the genre by dragging in scores of ancient and medieval works: Homer's *Odyssey* and other "early epics are full of details that modern readers recognize as elements of science fiction or fantasy"; in *The Clouds*, Aristophanes "invented the mad scientist," and in *The Birds*, he "conceived the earth satellite vehicle"; "Dickens introduced the theme of time travel in *A Christmas Carol*" (7–8, 13). However, while Moskowitz's books did include some older figures, his focus was on the life and works of twentieth-century writers, and some of his chapters remain the definitive biographies of their subjects. Essays wrestled with the aforementioned questions of boundaries — how to divide up the burgeoning genre, and how, or whether, to divide science fiction from other genres and mainstream literature. There were efforts to explain the purpose of science fiction — often echoing the portentousness of Campbell — tentative explorations of science fiction in other media (film, radio, television), and complaints about the dismissive attitudes of outside critics. Overall, these various contributions are best viewed as continuations of the tradition of fanzine commentaries, now striving for a sense of dignity appropriate to the format of hardcover publication, and their ultimate value may have been to extend discussion of the issues raised by science fiction to readers who were not familiar with fandom.

In addition to critical studies, one cannot forget the bibliographies: after scattered efforts to create a complete and comprehensive bibliography of science fiction literature in the 1930s, regularly discussed in the "Science Fiction League" column of *Wonder Stories*, the first major bibliography in book form appeared in 1948, Everett F. Bleiler's *The Checklist of Fantastic Literature*, revised and expanded as *The Checklist of Science Fiction and Supernatural Fiction* in 1978. Bleiler's lifelong research later engendered two massive compilations, *Science-Fiction: The Early Years* (1990) and *Science-Fiction: The Gernsback Years* (1998). Another significant contribution came from Donald

Henry Tuck, whose comprehensive bibliography, *The Encyclopedia of Science Fiction and Fantasy through 1968*, appeared in 1974 and 1982. And there were many others, most notably Robert Reginald and William Contento, who would continue this work in the 1980s and afterwards.

Of course, even as books and bibliographies found a wider audience, fandom continued to produce fanzines, and as fandom itself grew larger and more diverse, the fanzines became more numerous and variegated. I happen to be especially familiar with one fanzine from this era, the California-based *Rhodomagnetic Digest*, because one of its contributors was J. Lloyd Eaton, whose science fiction collection became the basis of the J. Lloyd Eaton Collection of Science Fiction and Fantasy Literature, now housed at the University of California, Riverside. To indicate what sorts of virtually unknown, but potentially valuable, materials may be found in these fanzines, consider the August, 1950 issue of the *Rhodomagnetic Digest*. In additions to letters from Isaac Asimov, Ray Bradbury, and August Derleth, the issue features an essay, "Literature and Science Fiction" by Norman Siringer, which displays an unexpected awareness of developments in contemporary literature (interestingly linked to the scientific method) and reads at times like a manifesto for the New Wave of the 1960s. Here are some edited excerpts from this striking piece:

> Since the influence of James Joyce upon modern literature has greatly changed concepts of style, it has become increasingly more difficult to set a formula or plan for the successful use of various ingredients within the framework of a writing of given length to give the guarantee of literary merit. Yet experimentation with stylistic or organizational devices — stream of consciousness, expressionism, impressionism, etc.— have made modern literature, like modern art and modern music, more flexible and better adapted to the specific needs or purposes of the writer....
>
> The renaissance of science shattered the remaining icons. The twentieth century man has a scientific mind, which is essentially an imaginative and a doubting mind. He will not accept the attitudes and codes of his father without first subjecting them to analysis. He realizes that society is constantly changing and that it must change if it is to progress. Antiquated laws, theories of conduct, political systems must be discarded once they are no longer useful.
>
> Our literature today is probing, recklessly truthful, freed from restraining taboos....
>
> Modern literature is internationalist ... the modern writer is interested in people of other countries and races and writes of them with a scientific approach. Why are these people downtrodden? How can their economic and cultural standards be improved? Literature of the past would not have permitted a *Grapes of Wrath* because the reading public was composed of the wealthy who were not concerned with the plight of the masses. Race relations was not a popular subject because everyone was convinced that the Negro was inferior to the White and that the Christians were justified in any economic or political crimes committed against the heathens.
>
> This is the moral quality of modern literature, the heritage open to the writer

of science fiction. Science fiction can best flourish in a democracy; under a dictatorship, as under a Victorian society with certain rigid obligations to the status quo, an imaginative medium for speculation about future man is an impossibility without a guarantee of respect for existing moral, religious or economic standards. And this is not the method of a scientist.

Science fiction suffers primarily from its confinement to the pulp magazines. Even the better American pulps are subject today to the same codes and taboos that restricted the writer for the *Golden Argosy, Hoffman's Adventure, All Story,* and *Blue Book....*

Science fiction is becoming increasingly significant as a method of literary expression, and will attract abler writers than it holds today... [20–22].

Other articles in the *Rhodomagnetic Digest,* while lighter in tone, also had insights to convey. In the July–August, 1951 issue, Barbara Scott's "The Girls in Their Cosmic Dresses" offered a bemused survey of the women featured in magazine science fiction illustrations:

The conventional, semi-dressed young miss of science fiction illustration has some good points, a couple of which are only too obvious, and some which require elucidation. She shows, for instance, that artists of today have an unbounded confidence in a brighter world tomorrow. Obviously the weather of the future is going to be more temperate, possibly sub-tropical, because that's the only kind of weather the gals are ever dressed for[.]

Another thing the artists have confidence in is that medical science will get around to discovering the secret of eternal youth. For no science fiction heroine ever manages to get past a smoothly feminine thirty, and most of them are in a state of suspended teen-age animation. One reason is obvious — how would the customary plump middle aged creature look in one of those panty-bra combinations?

Wonderful, everlasting warm weather, eternal youth — what else does the woman of the future face? Obviously she is beautiful — in fact, nothing else ever seems to exist except a standard level of feminine pulchritude, a pulchritude so all-pervading that even monsters of another world and another species are attracted to her and keep running away with her, being chased withal by tall, tanned young men with blasters and disintegrators. Surely the best of all possible lives — and one that has almost nothing to do with the story — or the future — or facts — or science [16–18].

Overall, the stereotypical view that science fiction fans functioned solely as a conservative, constraining force on the genre does not seem justified, and further investigation of the fanzines may provide future scholars with other surprises.

In the 1960s, Michael Moorcock in England, and Harlan Ellison in America, became the major spokesmen for the New Wave movement. Of the two, Moorcock was perhaps more radical and energetic in his views, although the magazine he inherited, *New Worlds SF,* was a consistent failure, sustained for most of his tenure by a government grant. Still, Moorcock's openness to controversial and unusual stories, and his impassioned editorials in favor of new directions in what he preferred to call "speculative fiction" or "sf," undoubtedly influenced science fiction writers, if not the larger science fiction community. A passage from one editorial entitled "Why So Conservative?" can serve to represent Moorcock's views:

> At the time of *The Space Merchants* and *The Stars My Destination*, sf was the best popular reading available, almost without question. But the literary climate and the social climate have changed. Things are better. Sf is not alone.... Sf is still an ideal medium for social satire, philosophical argument, prophetic warning, and so on — but is now not the only medium. What we choose to call the "mainstream" is doing almost everything that sf was doing ten or twenty years ago — and it is doing it better than sf was doing it then! ... [Sf] must develop its own standards, its own conventions and it must take its subject matter from every possible source. Otherwise it will remain what it was until fairly recently — the fat, intelligent, often sardonic, colorfully-dressed eunuch of liter-ature.... [These stories] are trying to cope with the job of analyzing and inter-preting various aspects of human existence, and they hope that in the process they succeed in entertaining you [3, 156].

In a way, deemphasizing science (here represented only tangentially in the phrase "prophetic warning") and emphasizing literary values was an old story by the time Moorcock appeared; still, in its fondness for modern writers of "mainstream" fiction, and its call for "subject matter from every possible source," Moorcock's manifesto suggests a new and stronger commitment to literary quality and experimentation.

While less esteemed by some critics — Aldiss spoke of his efforts as a "fake revolution" (*Trillion Year Spree* 304) — Harlan Ellison ultimately proved the most important figure in the New Wave because with his enormously suc-cessful and influential anthologies, *Dangerous Visions* (1967) and *Again, Dan-gerous Visions* (1972), as well as other writings, he made the New Wave into a popular movement. One of his advantages over Moorcock was that Ellison had grown up with, and had been influenced by, the theories of Gernsback and Campbell — even if he himself was not aware of it — and he thus could articulate the principles of the New Wave in a manner that readers with a tra-ditional commitment to the genre and its ideas could appreciate, if not endorse.

Despite his familiarity with earlier traditions, Ellison did declare that he was leading a "revolution" ("Introduction: Thirty-Two Soothsayers" 19) and in fact attempted to demolish several aspects of the Gernsback and Camp-bell paradigms. Like others of his time, he regularly used the term "specula-tive fiction," and his nearest approach to a definition of the form included only tangential references to scientific thought:

> In any definition of speculative fiction, there is an unspoken corollary: the most effective fiction in the genre is that which touches on reality in as many places

as possible while maintaining the mood of speculation.... The reader must be able to draw the lines of extrapolation from his own experience or environment — the world in which he lives today — through the intervening linkages of logic, emerging at the new place to which the writer has taken him ["A Voice from the Styx" 121].

Ellison's only concern for science, in fact, was that writers should avoid scientific errors by the use of a "dodgem explanation" or "writer's tricks" (*The Other Glass Teat* 40) — standards that were much lower than Knight's or Blish's.

In addition to an effort to further diminish science as an issue in the genre, Ellison, like Moorcock, wanted science fiction to become more of an experimental and "avant-garde" literature — in "The Waves in Rio," he listed several writers as "the 'avant-garde' in speculative fiction" (11); he sought to eliminate young readers as a characteristic audience of the genre — "I do not write specifically for fourteen-year-old boys *or* their mommies" ("The Waves in Rio" 13); and like others before him, he specifically denied that science fiction was in any way prophetic — "In the mistaken belief that just because I occasionally write fantasy stories extrapolating some bizarre future America I am privy to Delphic insights, the editors of the [*Los Angeles*] *Times* have asked me to unleash some wry conceits about what we can expect. Little do they understand that writers are merely paid liars and we know no more than the rest of you" ("Cheap Thrills on the Road to Hell" 159). Also, in keeping with his expansive views of the genre, he was willing to expand the history of science fiction to the point where it became a joke:

> My own personal seminal influence for the fantasy that is the basis for all great speculative fiction is the Bible.... Speculative fiction in modern times *really* got born with Walt Disney in his classic animated film *Steamboat Willie*, in 1928. Sure it did. I mean, a mouse that can operate a paddle-wheeler?
>
> It's as sensible a starting place as Lucian, after all, because when we get right down to the old nitty-gritty, the beginning of speculative fiction was the first Cro-Magnon who imagined what it was like out there snuffling around in the darkness just beyond the fire ["Introduction: Thirty-Two Soothsayers" 20–21].

However, Ellison's efforts to refashion the genre so radically provoked a violent counter-reaction, and he was later driven to a more conciliatory attitude towards traditional science fiction: "no one is suggesting that the roots of science fiction be ignored or forgotten or cast aside. Solid plotting, extrapolation, trends and culture, technology — all of these things are staples that are necessary to keep the genre electric and alive" ("A Time for Daring" 112). Finally, in the 1970s, as if worn out by the battle, Ellison abandoned his crusade to reform science fiction and retreated from the field altogether, angrily resigning from the Science Fiction Writers of America and insisting that his works not be published as "science fiction."

At the same time that the New Wave was having a strong effect on the popular tradition of science fiction criticism, an entirely new tradition moving according to its own rhythm was emerging: academic science fiction criticism. While I have criticized the theories and attitudes that permeate some of these studies, these represented progress in one crucial respect: because these authors were trained literary scholars and researchers, they could avoid the naive assumptions, poor reasoning, haphazard documentation, and incohesiveness that sometimes marred the work of the amateur scholars. And when these critics happened to address works considered central by the science fiction community, the results were often demonstrably superior.

As one telling example, one might compare Alexei Panshin's *Heinlein in Dimension* (1968) to H. Bruce Franklin's *Robert A. Heinlein: America As Science Fiction* (1980). Both books have an identical format: an introductory biographical sketch, followed by brief discussions of Heinlein's novels and stories in chronological order, and ending with a bibliography of his works. However, Franklin was first of all more thorough than Panshin, listing several Heinlein items that Panshin had missed, and his analyses of individual works were consistently more insightful and rewarding. Consider their discussions of "By His Bootstraps." Panshin said the story

> is convincing evidence that Heinlein had mastered the art of planning his stories. It is an intricate bit of foolery involving a man meeting himself half a dozen times along the path from Time A to Time B. It is an amusing set piece, logical and beautifully worked out.... "By His Bootstraps" is tightly constructed, as intricate as a bit of musical comedy choreography, and arrives at a destination, while "Elsewhere" slops every which way and simply ends. Neither has anything to get your teeth into.... "By His Bootstraps" is a neatly composed, though completely empty, example of the [intensely recomplicated story] [28, 93].

Panshin's dismissive account surely derives from his reading of a Heinlein letter to John W. Campbell, Jr., later reprinted in *Grumbles from the Grave* (1989), in which Heinlein says that the story "is still hack — a neat trick, sure, but no more than a neat trick. Cotton candy" (22). Panshin thus falls victim to one of the most common mistakes made by untrained critics: believing everything that authors say about their own works.

However, there were several good reasons why Heinlein might have wanted to avoid discussing the serious implications of the story with the outspokenly political Campbell; and Franklin, willing to hypothesize that there might be more to the story than Heinlein reported, studied it more carefully and offered this assessment:

> one of his masterpieces. Rigorous in its logic, this tale penetrates deeply into the implications of the myth of the free individual.... On one level, the story is an ingenious exploration of the problem of identity in time, and the associated

questions of the relations between determinism and free will. Diktor has created himself out of Bob Wilson, but without conscious choice until after it has already happened.

"By His Bootstraps" is also a dramatic display of the trapped ego, creating a world out of images of itself. It is thus the first fully developed manifestation of the solipsism which will become one of Heinlein's main themes. This solipsism is the ultimate expression of the bourgeois myth of the free individual, who supposedly is able to lift himself from rags to riches by his own bootstraps.... Diktor is a grandiose enlargement of Robinson Crusoe, with the entire planet his island. In fact, the first man Wilson meets in the future throws himself on his knees and arises as "his Man Friday." All the people of this world ... are now "docile, friendly children," "slaves by nature." What they lack is "the competitive spirit," "the will-to-power": "Wilson had a monopoly on that."

But this "monopoly" is also a state of supreme loneliness, as well as boredom.... Wilson's sexuality in both worlds is barren. He can only reproduce himself, as he, a self-created being, suggests in his final words, promising himself, his only kind of son, a great future.... On still another level, "By His Bootstraps" displays this world-embracing egoism as the center of political imperialism. When Diktor asks the first Bob Wilson to return briefly to his own time, his purpose is to acquire some tools to be used in colonizing this undeveloped land.... The prime thing he needs is certain books: Machiavelli's *The Prince*, *Behind the Ballots* by political machine boss James Farley, *How to Win Friends and Influence People* by Dale Carnegie, and Adolf Hitler's *Mein Kampf* [55–57].

Franklin finds the story far from "completely empty" and filled with much "to get your teeth into"—not "cotton candy" at all. Manifestly, if asked to recommend one critical study of Heinlein to a busy scholar, most would name Franklin's book instead of Panshin's.

Still, if representatives of the popular tradition did not always do well in head-to-head competition with the academics, there remained an important place for them in the 1960s and 1970s. For one thing, the academics tended to play favorites, devoting the bulk of their attention to certain selected writers like Mary Shelley, Wells, Olaf Stapledon, Philip K. Dick, Stanislaw Lem, and Ursula K. Le Guin, while leaving vast amounts of the territory of science fiction essentially unclaimed. Thus, those who wished to study science fiction comprehensively, or to examine authors who had not been admitted to the academic canons, still needed to rely on the surveys and bibliographies prepared by representatives of the popular tradition. In addition, as some of the academics followed the tendency of their tribe and increasingly emphasized critical theory and arcane jargon, there arose some hostility towards academic criticism in the science fiction community, as their analyses appeared increasingly distant from the central issues and seminal authors of their tradition as they perceived it.

However, the 1970s also brought new prominence to figures who straddled the boundaries of fandom and academia, maintaining membership in both groups and thus achieving, in themselves at least, a merging of the two traditions. Of course, there had always been people connected to both communities, since both J. O. Bailey, author of the first academic study of science fiction, and R. D. Mullen, co-founded of *Science Fiction Studies*, had ties to fandom. But the two major histories of science fiction produced in the 1970s garnered more attention: Brian W. Aldiss's *Billion Year Spree: The True History of Science Fiction* (1973) and James Gunn's *Alternate Worlds: The Illustrated History of Science Fiction* (1975). Both authors were professional writers with strong ties to the science fiction community; Gunn had a Ph.D. in English and was a tenured professor at the University of Kansas; and Aldiss, while lacking formal literary training, had educated himself to the point where he was comfortable as a speaker at academic conferences and a book reviewer for the *Oxford Mail*. Although Aldiss's book, emphasizing major authors and often denigrating the American tradition, seemed more academic in spirit, while Gunn's book, endeavoring to put in a good word for all authors and emphasizing the American tradition, seemed more popular in spirit, neither history of science fiction seemed either purely popular or purely academic, and both were perhaps stronger for that reason, suggesting that both traditions had much to gain from cooperation and interaction. They further indicated that, as the 1980s approached, it was going to become more and more difficult to keep the popular and academic traditions separate, since other emerging commentators, like John Clute, Gary K. Wolfe, and Susan Wood, had feet firmly planted in both camps.

While I will leave it to others to discuss and praise the contributions of academic science fiction criticism, the virtues of the popular tradition are clear: an unwavering belief in the unique power and importance of science fiction; a catholic enthusiasm for its various manifestations; and a commitment to examine and discuss virtually every work that emerged under its aegis. In contrast, academic critics may regard science fiction as no more or less valuable than other forms of literature; may like some science fiction and intensely dislike the rest of it; and may be highly selective in examinations of works in the genre. To many, such attitudes will seem only commonsensical in contrast to the naive belief, bumptious enthusiasm, and obsessive commitment of the popular tradition. Yet love and devotion, for people or for forms of literature, can yield uniquely valuable results, and I believe that the commentaries produced by the loving and devoted members of the science fiction community, considered collectively, are every bit as interesting and stimulating as, if not more so than, those produced by members of the academic community. And those who ignore the popular tradition will be forever hampered in their efforts to understand the genre of science fiction.

3

Wanted

A Symbol for Science Fiction

Hugo Gernsback first announced his quest in a 1928 editorial entitled "$300.00 Prize Contest — Wanted: A Symbol for Scientifiction." As a justification for this contest, Gernsback explained:

> The thought occurred to me ... that what scientifiction needs at present is some sort of a label — an emblem, or a trade-mark, so to speak. Scientifiction is too good a thing just to be used as a word in mere letters. It should have some dignity, and the idea itself of scientifiction should have its own crest, henceforth.... A design — a coat-of-arms — a flag — an emblem or, whatever you may call it, is wanted for "scientifiction." Whatever it is, there must be no question as to its meaning. It must be self-explanatory — it must be descriptive of "scientifiction" [5].

As is often the case, Gernsback's action can be interpreted primarily as an expression of his desire for profit: in the short run, he wanted a contest that might temporarily increase sales of and interest in *Amazing Stories*, and in the long run, he wanted a distinctive symbol he could use to encourage browsers to notice and purchase his science fiction magazines. However, as is also often the case, Gernsback's initiative has a broader significance that far transcends any concern for his possibly tainted motives.

For when critics compile lists of "definitions of science fiction," they invariably consider only *verbal* definitions; and of course these represent the most natural and productive ways to define any literary genre. However, when people set out to design symbols to epitomize the genre of science fiction, they are effectively creating *visual* definitions of science fiction. And while pictorial representations can never match the clarity and subtlety of verbal definitions, they still can be regarded as a potentially valid alternative approach to the problem of definition and might be usefully examined both for information about the attitudes towards science fiction of the people who created and used them and as possible influences on the attitudes of those people who regularly saw them.

I will define a *symbol for science fiction* as a simple design or drawing explicitly or implicitly intended to represent the entirety of science fiction, or at least the entirety of the science fiction offered by a particular magazine or company. I do not include words or letters, however stylized, that serve that purpose (usually the letters "SF"), unless shaped so as to suggest a definite visual image (like the Berkley Books symbol described below). When symbols become larger and more elaborate, as on some magazines' Table of Contents pages or on book covers, they are better described not as symbols but as *illustrations of science fiction*; while not my focus here, I sometimes discuss these as related relevant data. I have found symbols for science fiction in five places: the results of Gernsback's contest, to my knowledge the only public and collective effort to achieve such a symbol; the Table of Contents pages of some science fiction magazines; spines or title pages of books published as part of a company's science fiction series; the cover illustrations of books about science fiction; and symbols placed on the spines of science fiction books in public libraries.[1]

At the time he launched his contest, Gernsback had in a way already created and used one symbol for science fiction: the drawing on every Table of Contents page in *Amazing Stories* of "Jules Verne's Tombstone at Amiens Portraying His Immortality," where a Verne clad only in a white robe is seen coming out — almost flying out — of an opened coffin. As the first of several ironies that permeate this study, one notes how strange it is that the first symbol Gernsback presented for his "new" genre of scientifiction was the tombstone of a dead author — albeit one projecting an optimistic message about transcending death.[2]

To stimulate contestants, Gernsback designed one possible symbol which Frank R. Paul painted for the cover of the April, 1928 issue. Within a gigantic eye, the bottom of the white of the eye presents a sort of pageant of Earth history — from left to right, dinosaurs, mammoths, cavemen, a host of figures from history, and a mob of undifferentiated, unclothed people undoubtedly representing future humanity. Within the pupil of the eye — depicted as two large gears with a small gear between them — are scenes of technological progress: a train and a car, doctors performing an operation, modern weapons, an airplane, even what looks like a flying saucer. As Gernsback described it, "The big eye represents the mind's eye. Within that eye, you have, in a pictorial presentation, everything that is represented by scientifiction."

Gernsback was evidently dissatisfied with this creation — he added that "I admit that many of our readers could give the world a much better representation of the word 'scientifiction,' which is what this contest is all about" ("$300.00 Prize Contest" 5) — and evidently dissatisfied with the symbols his readers sent in: though he first said that "Prize-winning announcements will be made in our July issue," he delayed revealing the results until the September, 1928 issue. And, while he claimed the prize-winning symbol was a combination of three entries, the symbol introduced in that issue was actually his own invention, although one influenced by those suggestions; the disparities between the entries and Gernsback's final symbol are evident.

As Gernsback explained the process of creating the symbol, he began with the First Prize design, by A. A. Kaufman, where Science is represented by the gear wheel, while the pen

> represents the fiction part. Here, then, we have Fact and Theory. After we had been satisfied that Mr. Kaufman's idea was the best one, we started to amplify the original idea. In doing so, we borrowed the shape and design of the second prize winner, Mr. Clarence Beck; and from the third prize winner, Mr. A. J. Jacobson, we borrowed those two extra wheels, these to mesh with Mr. Kaufman's single wheel.... It was our aim to incorporate as much science as possible in the design, so the frame of the design, representing structural steel, suggests more machinery. The flashes in the central wheel represent Electricity. The top of the fountain pen is a test tube, which stands for Chemistry; while the background with the moon and stars and planet, give us the science of Astronomy. ("Results of $300.00 Scientifiction Prize Contest").[3]

As someone who enjoyed tinkering with machinery, Gernsback liked the mechanical style of Kaufman's design (recall that he told Paul to make the eye's pupil resemble two gears); but Gernsback had defined scientifiction as "a charming romance intermingled with scientific fact and prophetic vision" ("A New Sort of Magazine" 3), which stipulated three elements in the genre: narrative, science, and prophecy. To simply have one gear producing "scientifiction" would not properly display the double role of science and prediction in creating the story, so he had to borrow the double gears of Jacobson's design — with labels changed from "Science" and "Fiction" to "Fact" and "Theory" — to accord with his theories. Other embellishments — lightning flashes, steel beams, test tube, and planet Saturn — perhaps reflect some fear that the symbol was too abstract, creating a need for more literal futuristic images.

These two symbols Gernsback created are both, in their way, quite interesting. In the first, having various scenes from the past, present, and future depicted within a gigantic eye — "the mind's eye," as Gernsback put it — suggests that science fiction might be primarily regarded as a special *type of seeing or perception.* Arguably, the symbol represents the first crude anticipation of the idea that science fiction is best regarded as a special form of *cognition* — most famously and meticulously developed in Darko Suvin's familiar definition of science fiction as "the literature of cognitive estrangement." And the motif of the *eye* has sometimes been employed in later symbols for science fiction: the illustration on the cover of L. David Allen's *Cliff's Notes: Science Fiction, an Introduction* (1973) was a large eye with Earth as its center; the Leo and Diane Dillon cover illustrations for the three-volume Berkley paperback editions of Harlan Ellison's anthology *Dangerous Visions* prominently featured eyes; the logo for Phantasia Press was two stylized P's shaped to resemble either one face or two faces in profile with prominent eyes; and a large eye, with a number of different scenes depicted within, regularly adorned covers of the magazine *Science Fiction Eye*.

In the second symbol, the moving gears that guide the pen suggest that science fiction might be primarily regarded as a special *process or method of writing*. And this became the recurring theme of John W. Campbell, Jr., who attempted to cast science fiction as a thought-experiment carried out in the manner of a scientific experiment. Despite the prominence of this theme, however, only a few symbols for science fiction have — arguably — attempted to describe the genre in this fashion. One could count the mathematical symbol often displayed on the cover or spine of Campbell's *Analog: Science Fiction/Science Fiction* — an arrow with an superimposed arc — as an effort to depict the process of creating an "analog" for present-day reality, explained in Campbell's "Introduction" to *Prologue to Analog* as a central science fiction approach. Also, the cover of the journal *Extrapolation* throughout the 1980s and 1990s might be viewed as a two-dimensional picture of the process of extrapolation often said to exemplify the process of writing science fiction; that is, instead of extending a line showing known data into the unknown future, one begins with a known pattern — an upside-down and invested "e" — and endlessly duplicates that pattern across an unknown plane.[4] At this time, as noted, Gernsback was defining science fiction in his editorials as a form of narrative that included descriptions of scientific fact and possible scientific developments. Therefore, both of his symbols for science fiction — ironically — intimate definitions of the genre that were far more sophisticated than the verbal formula he was then promulgating.

Generally speaking, the other entries Gernsback reprinted in the September, 1928 issue lack interesting features. In keeping with styles of illustration then popular, several offered figures designed as personifications of science, wisdom, or the scientist (as seen, for instance, in Beck's mythological characters). One of them, E. J. Byrne's Ninth Place winner, apparently satisfied Gernsback's need for a three-part representation of science fiction as narrative, science, and prophecy — a book and quill pen flanked by a chemical beaker and a magic lamp — but no sense of dynamic interaction is conveyed, and the association with genies and fantasy could not have pleased Gernsback, who then regularly denounced stories which lacked a scientific basis as "fairy tales." Purcell O. Schube's Honorable Mention winner depicted a hovering brain with eyes projecting rays onto a book with a left page reading "Progress of Man Today" and a right page reading "Progress of Man Tomorrow," which might be interpreted as a writer's imagination connecting present-day facts with futuristic predictions — but could also be interpreted as the first alien employed to represent science fiction (a symbol discussed below). Overall, if the fourteen displayed designs were the best ones Gernsback received, one understands why Gernsback took so long to select — or create — a winning symbol. Apparently, he had given his readers a difficult assignment.

While Gernsback established the policy of printing the winning symbol on every cover of *Amazing Stories*, and retained the drawing of Verne's tombstone on its Table of Contents page, he commissioned artwork of a significantly different sort for the Table of Contents pages of his later magazines. These collages of various fantastic scenes merit brief mention because they visibly retreat from the innovative implications of his symbols and foreshadow future, more prosaic symbols for science fiction. Two of these offer a mildly interesting contrast: *Science Wonder Stories* (later *Wonder Stories*) offered an embracing couple and two earnest men holding copies of the magazine while, over their heads, a gigantic and beautiful woman — Science?— holds a few little persons taken from a large stream of people moving through an array of strange planets — presumably representing what those readers are reading about;[5] while *Science Wonder Quarterly* offered a different sort of collage — a woman facing a man in a television screen, an immense ray, strange machinery, and, at the bottom, a man holding a pen — looking like a young Gernsback — presumably representing the author creating these visions. One can extract from these two illustrations an argument: that science fiction is primarily intended either as a stimulus for readers' imagination or as an expression of the authors' imagination. So, in a way, each resolves in different ways an ambiguity in Gernsback's first symbol — is the "mind's eye" the reader's eye or the writer's eye? (Whether Gernsback or his artists were aware of this issue, of course, is questionable.)

Other illustrations in this position lack any interesting features. *Amazing Stories Quarterly* presents a straightforward collage of various fantastic scenes — strange birdlike creatures, rocketships flying in the air, a futuristic city with skyscrapers and elevated highways, several planets, and a person looking at a woman in a circular television screen; the picture in *Air Wonder Stories* is painfully dull — two airplanes representing slight improvements on then-modern technology flying toward each other; and the collage in *Wonder Stories Quarterly* recalls the historical imagery of Gernsback's first symbol — at the bottom, one sees dinosaurs and a cavemen, on the sides, a scientist in a laboratory and a futuristic city, at the top an array of planets and spacecraft — but without the framing device of the gigantic eye. All these illustrations anticipate the common message in most of the later symbols for science fiction — that science fiction represents only *stories about certain topics*, such as space travel, other planets, alien creatures, amazing inventions, and future cities. Not a form of perception or a process of writing, then, science fiction is simplistically reduced to a group of stories united only by their attention to some unusual subjects.

This shift in ways of symbolizing science fiction became apparent in 1934, when Gernsback again confronted this problem. While the prize-winning symbol appeared on some later issues of *Amazing Stories*, either on the cover or the Table of Contents page, it was eventually removed, and neither Gernsback nor his successor T. O'Conor Sloane gave evidence of any further interest in the issue. However, in 1934, when Gernsback launched the Science Fiction League in an issue of *Wonder Stories*, he reasoned that such an organization required some sort of identifying symbol. In "The Science Fiction League: An Announcement," Gernsback first presented "The emblem of the LEAGUE, which has been finally decided upon" (933): a circular design featuring a rather rotund spaceship flying through space with the Earth in the background, surrounded by the words "Science Fiction League." His next editorial, "The Science Fiction League," further explained that this symbol would be an "Insignia (also called lapel buttons) to make it possible for LEAGUE members to recognize each other" and could be used to claim "courtesy discounts" from certain bookstores. In neither editorial did Gernsback offer any detailed explanation of this symbol's significance — perhaps because he did not approve of its implications — save to say in the latter that it was "a distinctive as well as a striking design," (1063, 1065); however, the definitions conveyed by such a symbol are clear enough: science fiction means *stories about space travel*, or *stories about spaceships*.

In choosing this "emblem" for his Science Fiction League, Gernsback acknowledged a visible change in the genre since the first appearance of *Amazing Stories*. In the stories he published and his editorials, Gernsback had never privileged stories about space travel; that was merely one of many subjects available to science fiction writers. Indeed, his theories in one respect marginalized such stories, since the purported goal of giving working scientists useful ideas for inventions might be better accomplished by stories about earthbound scientists in their laboratories than stories about space explorers trekking across an unknown planet. And early issues of *Amazing Stories* did not predominantly feature space stories, so it is not surprising that none of Gernsback's contestants thought of a spaceship as a symbol for science fiction. However, his readers made it clear that they wanted more stories about space travel; for example, a 1927 Gernsback editorial reported that his "Youngest

Reader" "unhesitatingly stated that he preferred stories of space and of interplanetarian travel" ("Amazing Youth" 625), and Sloane's first editorial for *Amazing Stories* in 1929 noted that "We have published many stories on interplanetary travel. This subject remains a great favorite with our readers" ("Amazing Stories" 103). Responding to this increasing demand for space travel stories — also fueled by the popularity of E. E. "Doc" Smith's novels — Gernsback's *Wonder Stories Quarterly* launched in 1932 an "Interplanetary Plots" contest, in which readers could send in plot outlines that could be given to experienced writers. As more and more stories of this type appeared, science fiction in the 1930s seemed to be evolving into a literature about space travel; and, in becoming, I believe, the first person to choose a spaceship to represent science fiction, Gernsback was simply responding to this new reality — one which, ironically, he neither desired nor directly inspired.

Whether influenced by the League's emblem or not, *the spaceship* soon became the most common symbol for science fiction: during World War II, when *Astounding Science-Fiction* switched to digest size, for example, its Table of Contents page featured a spaceship on the left margin. And in the late 1940s and 1950s, when science fiction small presses appeared and other publishers launched science fiction lines, the need for an identifying emblem often yielded pictures of spaceships. The Frederick Fell Company developed a symbol for "Fell's Science Fiction Library" that recalled the League emblem — a spaceship in a circle — though now the ship is pointed straight up, taking off from Earth with a city in the background, not flying in space; the Winston juvenile science fiction novels and Avalon Books both employed an almost identical, though simplified symbol; and the early symbol for Doubleday Science Fiction was a spaceship flying out of a book. When foreign publishers launched science fiction lines, their identifying symbols were often similar: In Great Britain, publisher Hennel Locke used a picture of a spaceship for its "space fiction"; in France, books in the Fleuve Noir science fiction series had spaceships of various designs on their spines; and in Germany, publisher AWA Verlag imitated the Winston symbol. Finally, when public libraries started to include science fiction books, they often marked their spines with the symbol of a spaceship; in *The Lost Garden*, Laurence Yep recalls that in the late 1950s "every science-fiction book was marked by a rocket ship on the spine; and I would go through the children's room at the Chinatown and North Beach branches as well as the Main Library, looking for anything with a blue rocket on its spine" (78). And I found a blue rocketship — perhaps the same symbol Yep looked for — on the spine of one book from the San Bernardino County Free Library. Admittedly, many of these symbols emerged forty or fifty years ago, but the power of the spaceship as a symbol for science fiction has hardly diminished; in 1993, for example, when Baen Books decided to use a new symbol for its science fiction books, they adopted a picture of a stylized flying spaceship.

Gernsback may have also played a part in promoting another common symbol for science fiction: *the planet Saturn*, long popular in astronomical illustrations because of its striking appearance. As early as 1923, the cover of Gernsback's special "Scientific Fiction" issue of *Science and Invention* prominently featured Saturn, though the planet did not figure in the story; and as noted, Gernsback added a picture of Saturn to his prize-winning symbol. One symbol for science fiction books in the Claremont Public Library was an outline of Saturn overlaying another moon or planet; for its science fiction books, Berkley Books devised a stylized "B" with the bottom turned into a circle with a large encompassing ring, obviously to resemble Saturn; German publisher Wilhelm Goldman Verlag marked science fiction books by a picture of Saturn with a large "G" on the planet; and today, Saturn is the official symbol of the Science Fiction Channel, projected in the lower right-hand screen during all its programs.

Images of other astronomical phenomena are also employed: for years, *Galaxy* magazine unsurprisingly adorned its Table of Contents page with a picture of a galaxy; for his magazine *Science-Fiction Plus*, Gernsback developed a special symbol — a star on top of a sphere — to designate stories that were scientifically accurate; and Starlog Books employed as an emblem five stylized "SF's" arranged as a five-pointed star.

After the atomic bomb explosion in 1945 and the new prominence that event brought science fiction, the then-standard picture of *the atom*— a small round nucleus surrounded by four elliptical electron orbits — became another symbol for science fiction. Prime Press published Lester del Rey's ... *And Some Were Human* with a large atom symbol on the cover; an atom surrounding the letters "SF" was the symbol of the science fiction published by the British company Weidenfeld & Nicolson; and when Leisure Books launched a line of low-priced "Inflation Fighter" science fiction novels in the 1970s, the only illustration on the covers was a typical atom. Before atomic energy, of course, the most wondrous form of energy known was electricity; and the most prominent image of electricity, *the lightning bolt*, has been occasionally used to represent science fiction: Gernsback added lightning bolts to his design, and the 1993 covers of *The Science Fiction Research Association Review* featured a design that connected the letters "S" and "F" with a stylized lightning bolt.

Two other types of symbols for science fiction do not appear to be as common as they might be: an *astronaut*, seen holding a smiling crescent moon on the title pages of science fiction books from Greenberg: Publisher, an imprint of Gnome Press, and seen flying on a book past the planet Saturn on other Gnome Press science fiction books; and a *robot*, pictured sitting at a desk looking through some type of periscope on the title pages of Fantasy Press books.

In addition to finding all these types of symbols in isolation — the eye, spaceship, Saturn, atom, lightning bolt, astronaut, and robot — one sometimes observes various sorts of combinations of these symbols. The trademark of Advent Publishers, for instance, combined pictures of Saturn and an eye. The two most popular symbols — the spaceship and Saturn — were frequently combined: science fiction books from British publisher Boardman and Company sported a picture of a spaceship flying past Saturn and another planet; the most recent symbol used in the Ontario City Library is a spaceship in front of Saturn; and one symbol found in the Los Angeles Country Library system was a picture of a spaceship flying towards Saturn. Another combination found is a spaceship and the moon: French publisher Fernard Nathan adopted the symbol of a spaceship flying in the front of the moon, and a symbol on New England Science Fiction Association books is a crescent moon accompanied by a spaceship. Combining spaceships with energy symbols, an older identifying mark used in the Ontario City Library is a spaceship in front of an atom, and the symbol for Carey Rockwell's *Tom Corbett, Space Cadet* books was a spaceship in front of a lightning bolt.

For examples of more complex combined symbols, one can turn to Hugo Gernsback himself, who conspicuously returned to his original quest for a symbol of science fiction in his 1953 magazine *Science-Fiction Plus*. Since the magazine included no advertisements, there was a need for some sort of illustration in each issue's back cover, and on four occasions during the magazine's seven-issue run the back cover featured Frank R. Paul illustrations of science fiction. The painting on the back of the first issue of *Science-Fiction Plus* (March, 1953), entitled "The Spirit of Science Fiction," was not described in a blurb within the magazine, but its meaning was evident enough: it featured a depiction of the Solar System, including the Sun and the planet Saturn, with an immense spectral hand emerging from one small planet (presumably the Earth) and reaching up toward an array of galaxies above the Solar System. The back cover of the second issue (April, 1953), "Science Fiction Views the Cosmos," was described in this way in a blurb:

> The eye-shaped nebula on the lower left symbolizes the eye of science-fiction. It watches the creation of new worlds as the forces of nature shape them. At the lowest point we see the simplest atom — with one circling electron, hydrogen. Next, the helium atom, then lithium — on and on, through more and more complex atoms. Vast electrical forces are let loose during the act of creation — symbolized by the flashes and the sinuous electromagnetic waves.
>
> Finally, the new spiral-shaped world grows rapidly in ever-widening circles — the expanding universe now recedes into the infinite void ["The Back Cover" 47].

The back cover of the fourth issue (June, 1953), "Science Fiction Explores the Cosmos," was again unexplained by a blurb; it showed a naked man, accompanied by strange objects, flying upward toward a bright cluster of machinery. Despite their differences, all three images primarily rely upon astronomical imagery, with some use of pictures of the atom and of machinery, and depict science fiction as an effort to somehow look upward, or to move upward, into the cosmos.

Somewhat more imaginative was the fourth and final effort to symbolize science fiction, which appeared on the back cover of the sixth issue (October, 1953). Entitled "The Elements of Science Fiction," it is described in great detail in a blurb within the magazine:

> The symbolization of science fiction as suggested by many of its components is graphically expressed in a unique illustration on our back cover. The form is that of a functioning robot, motivated by an electronic brain. Its head is Mount Palomar Observatory, and its nose the 200-inch telescope, which gathers light rays billions of light years away and helps piece together the mystery of the universe. Its ears are search radar units, which collect the electronic waves of the stars. The trunk of the body is a complex atomic generator that represents the foundation of our future progress. The right arm is a rocket ship reaching for the stars, and its fingers exploratory off-shoot ships. The left arm is the Hayden Planetarium projector, which brings the stars and planets close to us and shows us the mechanics of our universe. At the waist, searchlight beams foretell the progress of scientific research. The legs are radio and television masts comprising the structure of modern communication, while the feet are caterpillar tractors capable of surmounting many natural obstacles. The huge crystalline growth symbolize the exploration and conquest of distant and alien worlds. The blazing sun, at left, shows how it appears on an airless planet!
>
> Famed veteran artist Frank R. Paul, in his inimitable style, portrayed the idea which was conceived by the editor ["The Back Cover" 19].

This image not only again brings together astronomical and mechanical imagery, but it also incorporates the most common symbol of science fiction, the rocketship. The blurb also has two revelatory aspects: its introductory phrase "the symbolization of science fiction" explicitly announces a resumption of Gernsback's 1928 quest, and this particular image, unlike the other, is specifically described as an idea "conceived by the editor" — and this must be a reference to Gernsback himself, as reported by the magazine's other editor, Sam Moskowitz, who states that the images in "The Elements of Science Fiction" "were doubtless the ideas of Gernsback, who had long been fond of such intricate representations" ("The Return of Hugo Gernsback" Part IV 224). Clearly, then, his 1928 contest for a symbol for science fiction was not merely a momentary act of expediency, but a reflection of a persistent concern that also manifested itself in his 1934 symbol for the Science Fiction League and in these 1953 paintings for *Science-Fiction Plus*.

Still, all of these variations on the common patterns of astronomical, mechanical, and electrical imagery did not exhaust all the possibilities, including one type of symbol for science fiction that Gernsback never employed: a picture of *an unusual alien or strange creature.* For example, the symbol of the science fiction publisher Shasta Press was a picture of a reptilian alien reading a book; the singular symbol for British publisher Dennis Dobson's "Science Adventure Fiction" was three strange horselike creatures; a comical alien using his nose as a pencil is on the 1977 McGraw-Hill cover of L. Sprague and Catherine Crook de Camp's *Science Fiction Handbook — Revised*; and the insect-like "Eaton Alien" has at times represented the Eaton Conferences on Science Fiction and Fantasy — although without the wholehearted support of the conference coordinators.[6]

Although stuffy academics — and magazine and book publishers who wish to maintain an aura of dignity — may resist aliens as symbols of science fiction, they are more popular in the less dignified world of science fiction fandom: images of aliens are ubiquitous on the covers of fanzines, and one fan organization, the Lunarians, employs as its emblem a little alien in a spacesuit sitting on the Moon and reading a book.

All definitions of science fiction conveyed by such symbols are crude and inadequate: as noted, a picture of a spaceship or spaceman implies that science fiction means *stories about space travel or spaceships,* or stories about astronomy and engineering; a picture of Saturn or another planet or star implies that science fiction means *stories about space,* or stories about astronomy; a picture of a robot implies that science fiction means *stories about amazing machines,* or stories about engineering; a picture of an atom or lightning bolt implies that science fiction means *stories about amazing energy,* or stories about physics; and a picture of an alien implies that science fiction means *stories about space creatures*— one cannot add "or stories about exobiology" since such aliens, usually crude combinations of human and animal features, are manifestly not products of a biologically informed imagination.

There are two patterns in these common symbols for science fiction. First, with the possible exception of the alien, all symbols suggest that science fiction is primarily focused on "hard sciences" like astronomy, physics, and engineering; and all symbols involve elements that are associated with juvenile science fiction, or science fiction in film and television. The popularity and ubiquity of these symbols, then, is not without significance. Commentators often complain that science fiction is wrongly and exclusively linked to stories about spaceships, monsters, and machines, while stories about, say, new medical treatments or new political systems are marginalized. Discussing science fiction films, for example, Harlan Ellison complains,

The public image of what *is*, and what *ain't*, science fiction film — an image as twisted as one of Tod Browning's freaks — is the result of decades of paralogia, arrogant stupidity, conscious flummery, and amateurism that have comprised the universal curriculum of *milieu* that passes for filmic education for a gullible audience. If it goes bangity-bang in space; if it throbs and screams and breaks out of its shell with slimy malevolence; if it seeks to enslave your body, your mind, your gonads or your planet; if it looks cuddly and beeps a lot, it's "sci-fi.... Thus, when one is asked by the Director of an upcoming Film Festival what movies should be scheduled as peachykeen for the "Sci-Fi Section," and you suggest *Charly, Seconds, Wild in the Streets* [1968], and *Yellow Submarine* [1968], expect the querulous stare and the reply, "But that ain't sci-fi." Not a cranking spaceship or giant arachnid as far as the eye can glom ["Introduction — Lurching Down Memory Lane" 10; my ellipsis].

Note that the kinds of films that Ellison belittles are exactly those that would be well represented by symbols of science fiction like a spaceship, Saturn, atom, lightning bolt, robot, or alien; while the films he celebrates do not fit any of those symbols. Therein may lie another explanation for the improper attitudes he describes. Those who believe that science fiction should focus on hard science, one might argue, have been able to develop or seize upon powerful and evocative symbols, like the spaceship, Saturn, or the atom, to convey that linkage; while those who believe that science fiction should emphasize the soft sciences or more general "speculation" have been unable or disinclined to develop symbols to better reflect their own ideas about the genre. And this is a problem, perhaps, that these people must confront; before Ursula K. Le Guin wonders again why science fiction is so often stigmatized as juvenile space fiction, she might first consider the fact that today, in thousands of libraries across the country, some worker has diligently pasted a picture of a spaceship on the spines of all her books. Surely, there is a possible connection here.

    If these symbols for science fiction are unduly influencing readers' perceptions of science fiction, there is the more insidious danger that they will influence writers' and editors' perceptions as well. Consider the Winston juveniles. The employee who first drew that spaceship probably thought it was only an appropriate description of the sorts of science fiction the company would be publishing; but once such a symbol is in place, it can affect the attitudes of everyone associated with it. Consciously or not, Winston editors may have started to look for or solicit stories about spaceships; and consciously or not, prospective authors for the company may have started to produce more stories about spaceships. It may not be coincidental, then, that the Winston juveniles were almost exclusively novels about outer space and space travel; what would be more natural, when one knows that a picture of a spaceship is going to be on the cover and title page? And today, the spaceship symbol of Baen Books visually reinforces its opinions (though already known) about the types of science fiction books it wishes to receive from writers. Thus, like verbal definitions of science fiction, visual definitions may function as restrictive prescriptions.

To rise above the simplicity of such symbols, one might look at the cover illustrations on books about science fiction; though these may not reflect the opinions or preferences of their authors,[7] they do represent valid data regarding common perceptions of science fiction. An approach anticipated by the Table of Contents pages of Gernsback's magazines is the *fantastic collage*: the 1978 Octopus Books cover of Robert Holdstock's *Encyclopedia of Science Fiction* juxtaposes a number of striking images, including Robby the Robot from the film *Forbidden Planet*, two spaceships, the moon, and a space station; and the 1980 Seaview Books cover of Ed Naha's *The Science Fictionary* includes photographs of the moon from George Méliès' *Le Voyage dans La Lune*, the alien from *This Island Earth*, Frederic March as *Dr. Jekyll and Mr. Hyde*, and the space travelers from *Destination Moon*. Another frequent choice is the *alien landscape*: the 1960 Ballantine cover of Kingsley Amis's *New Maps of Hell* sports a Richard M. Powers cover painting depicting three bizarre aliens on a barren landscape with a spaceman, rocketship, and futuristic city in the background and with a pink sky prominently featuring the planet Uranus; the 1978 Chicago Review Press cover of George S. Elrick's *Science Fiction Handbook for Readers and Writers* shows strange cities on rocky platforms resembling mushrooms with stars and glowing globules in the sky; and the 1975 A&W Visual Library cover of James Gunn's *Alternate Worlds: The Illustrated History of Science Fiction* shows a landscape of ice mountains, with a spaceship on the ground in front of an immense red sun taking up most of the sky. These collages or landscapes may prominently include common symbols for science fiction — spaceships, planets, and aliens — thus reinforcing associations between science fiction and spaceships, monsters, and machines; but by featuring a number of different images, they also suggest a more variegated genre.

Another strategy has been to symbolize science fiction with *adaptations of famous artworks or artistic styles*. The Hyperion Press editions of older science fiction works featured on their cover a sketch of a naked man, in the style of ancient Greek pottery illustration, with a space helmet on — a juxtaposition that visually conveys the theme of "Classics of Science Fiction." The 1976 Bowker Books cover of Neil Barron's *Anatomy of Wonder* simply reproduced a portion of a painting by Hieronymus Bosch showing a number of grotesque witches and demons. And the only illustration in the 1993 St. Martin's Press edition of John Clute and Peter Nicholls's *The Encyclopedia of Science Fiction* is adapted from Leonardo da Vinci's sketch of a man's body pointing in five directions — though the man's head is now reptilian and there are stars in the background. Clearly such choices reflect some desire to dignify the genre by association with past masters; they might be said to illustrate — humorously in the Hyperion symbol, seriously in the *Encyclopedia* symbol — the contradiction that science fiction is on the one hand seen as a continuation of ancient mythology and on the other hand seen as bold projections of new and unknown futures. Canada's Tesseract Books uniquely employs a depiction of a tesseract, or four-dimensional cube, to suggest the otherworldly nature of its books.[8]

Finally, as artistic statements in themselves, some modern journals about science fiction — like *Monad: Essays on Science Fiction* and *Science Fiction Studies* — have eschewed all illustrations, which could reflect displeasure with the common symbols used for science fiction, a belief that symbols of science fiction are undignified or inappropriate, even a sense that science fiction is impossible to depict or summarize in visual terms. But as already suggested, this may mean that some important players are abandoning the playing field to their opponents.

For, as I have attempted to demonstrate, symbols for science fiction, like definitions of science fiction, do not emerge spontaneously from the literature they represent; rather, they are created by people with specific opinions about the nature and priorities of that literature. If most common symbols can be traced back to Gernsback or to people who thought like Gernsback, then it is not surprising that the symbols reflect what many would argue are inaccurate or juvenile impressions or science fiction, and it is not surprising that such attitudes persist so strongly even today. And as one way to overturn or modify these views of the genre, critics might legitimately attempt to create new symbols for science fiction that would match the evocative power of the spaceship or Saturn while at the same time conveying a quite different opinion about its true nature and priorities.

With this thought in mind, one might consider the covers of two science fiction anthologies which sought to vigorously challenge traditional attitudes: Larry McCaffery's *Storming the Reality Studio*, which privileges those science fiction works which can be seen as precursors or examples of postmodern fiction; and Ursula K. Le Guin and Brian Attebery's *The Norton Book of Science Fiction*, which privileges recent stories of high literary value and, usually, little scientific content. McCaffery's cover is a collage, but one radically different from pictures of spaceships and robots: a dog (?) flying with a table and some apparatus on its back, and the skull of a steer attached to various bits of machinery. Le Guin and Attebery's cover is an alien landscape, but one radically different from scenes of aliens and strange planets in the sky: a woman stands on a shore facing four immense blue spheres hovering over the water. The nature of those spheres is completely undefined: are they force fields? Magic bubbles? Products of the woman's imagination? Like the collections they represent, these covers tear science fiction away from conventional associations with science and machinery to make an entirely different statement about the nature of the genre — perhaps only that science fiction means *stories about something out of the ordinary*. While such images, considered as visual definitions of science fiction, are really no more profound than pictures of spaceships, they do suggest unexplored possibilities in creating other new and different symbols for science fiction.

Perhaps, then, someone today might launch a new contest that would borrow Gernsback's title — "Wanted: A Symbol for Science Fiction" — without necessarily reflecting his opinions; because, I would argue, neither Gernsback's original contest nor seven decades of subsequent efforts have yielded a truly satisfactory symbol for science fiction.

4

Peaks and Valleys

Hugo Gernsback's Career as a Science Fiction Editor

Hugo Gernsback's first science fiction magazine, *Amazing Stories*, was an unqualified success, selling a respectable number of copies, enduring in various incarnations for over seventy years after Gernsback lost control of the magazine in 1929, and spawning a companion magazine, *Amazing Stories Quarterly*, which lasted for several years. His second major magazine — originally two magazines, *Science Wonder Stories* and *Air Wonder Stories*, merged after one year into *Wonder Stories*—was almost as successful, enduring for almost two decades after Gernsback sold the magazine in 1936 (though renamed *Thrilling Wonder Stories)* and also spawning an accompanying quarterly. For that reason, discussions of Gernsback's influence on science fiction, including my own *The Mechanics of Wonder*, have quite naturally emphasized these two titles, drawing the bulk of their materials and evidence from their pages.

It is equally natural for commentators to neglect Gernsback's other magazines which featured science fiction or which were related to science fiction. Several of his early science magazines — *Modern Electrics*, *The Electrical Experimenter*, *Science and Invention*, *Practical Electrics*, *Radio News*, and *The Experimenter*—may have published science fiction stories in some issues, but they otherwise had little to do with science fiction, and they apparently did not appeal to the people who would later form the science fiction community. Another magazine of marginal significance launched around the time of *Wonder Stories*, *Scientific Detective Monthly* (later *Amazing Detective Tales*), attracted few readers and vanished after one year. Gernsback's other failures in this area include his *Technocracy Review* (two issues in 1933), a nonfiction magazine addressing an issue of obvious interest to science fiction readers; a science fiction comic book, *Superworld Comics* (three issues in 1940), and another science fiction magazine, *Science-Fiction Plus* (seven issues in 1953). Manifestly, none of these ventures had much of an impact on science fiction; however, examining their contents and considering *why* they were unsuccessful can serve to illuminate some interesting characteristics of twentieth-century science fiction, the genre that Gernsback created but was never able to entirely control.

Science fiction scholars who thumb through the pages of Gernsback's first two magazines, *Modern Electrics* and *The Electrical Experimenter*, will find themselves in a new and different world, and one which generally has little relationship to their own interests. With the exception of Gernsback's own fiction, the science fiction stories published in these magazines were uniformly inconsequential and have been appropriately forgotten. The vast majority of the pages of these magazines were devoted to now-outdated articles about developments in the fields of radio and electronics, accompanied by shorter contributions by technically-minded readers describing their own minor achievements or asking questions about their technical problems or possibly patentable ideas.

The April, 1911 issue of *Modern Electrics* in which Gernsback's novel *Ralph 124C 41+* first appeared is typical. The issue began with news reports and articles, some signed, some unsigned: "The Practical Electrician, Chapter 1" by "Professor W. Weiler," translated by Gernsback (pages 3–6), which continued to run in all later 1911 and 1912 issues; "Fontana Mast" (7–8); "The 'Singing Spark' System of Wireless Telegraphy" (9–11); "Photographic Phonograph" (12–13); "Paris Letter" (14–16), news of inventions from Europe; "Condenser for High-Power Transmitters" (16–17); Gernsback's editorial (18); and the first installment of *Ralph* (19–20). Next was the "Experimental Department," (21–34), descriptions of their new inventions from various readers (including, that month, Lewis Mumford), and a few more articles and features: "A Portable Wireless Telegraph Outfit" (34–35); "Flying Sparks," a page of cartoons (36); "Wireless Telegraph Contest," (37–39), where readers were invited to send photographs and descriptions of their radio equipment; and a page listing "Electrical Patents for the Month" (40). Then came the "Oracle" (41–54), answering technical questions from readers, and finally, advertisements (52–64) chiefly aimed at inventors, offering help with patents, various types of electrical equipment, a program to "Learn Electricity," the products of Gernsback's Modern Electrics Publications, and Gernsback's book *The Wireless Telephone*. Later issues introduced two new but similar features: an "Aeronautic Department" and another question-and-answer section, "Advice on Patents." Two 1912 issues included suitable-for-framing portraits of Thomas Alva Edison and Nicolas Tesla. Other than the cartoons and jokes that were used as fillers, the only other non-scientific feature of the magazine was Gernsback's occasional humor column, "The Wireless Screech," which parodied various features in *Modern Electrics*—an "Idiotorial" followed by farcical articles, news reports, and reader questions.

None of this seems like it would be particularly interesting to science fiction readers, despite occasional reports from writers like Robert A. Heinlein that they had once been avid readers of magazines like *The Electrical Experimenter*. But a comprehensive (if not necessarily exhaustive) survey of the readers' departments in the issues of *Modern Electrics* which serialized Gernsback's *Ralph 124C 41+*, and the issues of *The Electrical Experimenter* which serialized Gernsback's *Baron Münchhausen's New Scientific Adventures*, revealed no names of people who went on to become science fiction writers or prominent science fiction fans; thus, there is little tangible evidence of any significant overlap between the readers of Gernsback's scientific magazines and the later readers of his science fiction magazines. Undoubtedly, most science fiction readers were keenly interested in scientific facts and new scientific discoveries, but it seems, despite certain statements from Gernsback to the contrary, that few of them spent a lot of time tinkering in their basement laboratories or endeavoring to create significant new inventions.[1]

Still, if these magazines are generally not important to science fiction scholars, they may be worth examining by other sorts of scholars. For example, the relationship between *Modern Electrics* and the prominent thinker Lewis Mumford is one interesting area for exploration. He records in his autobiographical *My Works and Days: A Personal Chronicle* that "in my youth, as a zealous reader of Hugo Gernsback's Modern Electrics, I shared my generation's pious belief in our future" (14); and Donald L. Miller notes in *Lewis Mumford: A Life* that Mumford's first publication, at the age of fifteen, was an eight-line article on "new breakthroughs in radio receivers" published in *Modern Electrics* (34). Yet it has apparently not been noted that Mumford published repeatedly in the magazine. In looking at all issues from 1911 and 1912, for example, I found no piece that matched Miller's description—presumably, if Mumford was fifteen at the time, it appeared in 1910—but Mumford did make five contributions to the "Experimental Department" of the magazine in those years. (The department invited people to describe their inventions and awarded prizes to the best ones.) The first, "Unique Variable Condenser," as by "L. C. Mumford," appeared in the January, 1911 issue (577); "A Portable Receiving Outfit," as by "Lewis C. Mumford," appeared in the April, 1911 issue (29–30); "The Ultimate," as by "L. O. Mumford," appeared in the June, 1911 issue (179); "A Reply," as by "Lewis C. Mumford," appeared in the September, 1911 issue (269) (not a description of an invention, but a caustic response to another correspondent's report that he had "improved" upon an invention previously described by Mumford); and "Improved Electrolytic Detector," as by "Lewis C. Mumford," appeared in the April, 1912 issue (40). The first won the First Prize of two dollars; the others, all Honorable Mentions, presumably earned Mumford 25 cents each. These pieces offer only the sort of shop-talk that characterized the magazine and provide no insights into the developing thoughts of young Mumford; but they at least prove that the man who would later write the influential *The Story of Utopia* read, as a young man, the magazines that first published Gernsback's singular contribution to that tradition.

As for Gernsback's *The Electrical Experimenter*, the "Question Box" section in the April, 1916 contains one query from a noteworthy source:

> Morris K. Jessup, Rockville, Ind., desires us to tell him: 1. How to make a selenium cell. 2. Where he can find a book on the "fourth dimension" [720].

This is undoubtedly the same Morris K. Jessup who later wrote a controversial book about UFOs, entitled *The Case for the UFO* (1955), which was followed by two additional books on the same topic before Jessup's death by apparent suicide in 1959; and while one cannot guess why he would seek to construct a selenium cell, his other request does intriguingly suggest that, even at the age of fifteen, the young Jessup was already interested in otherworldly matters. And in the June, 1916 issue, a featurette entitled "Portable Wireless Set of Lilbert Young" includes a photograph of the note's author showing him proudly standing behind his "portable radio station" and revealing, unquestionably and surprisingly, that he was an African-American (112). Thus, even if Gernsback was not reaching and influencing future science fiction readers with these scientific magazines, he may have been reaching and influencing some other, unexpected sorts of readers.

Gernsback's science magazines of the 1920s — particularly *Science and Invention* — merit more attention from science fiction scholars, for several reasons. Science fiction stories appeared more frequently: instead of precisely one story per issue — the pattern of *Modern Electrics* and *The Electrical Experimenter* — there were often two stories per issue. Gernsback began to feature some better, and better-known, authors, such as Ray Cummings, George Allan England, and A. Merritt; even H. G. Wells was represented by a reprint of "The Star" in the March, 1923 issue of *Science and Invention*. And stories now tended to begin with substantive introductions, in which one can observe Gernsback or his associate T. O'Conor Sloane developing and rehearsing some of the ideas about science fiction that would were soon to be promulgated in the pages of *Amazing Stories*. For example, in the August, 1923 issue, this is how G. Peyton Wertenbaker's "The Man from the Atom" was introduced:

If you are interested in Einstein's Theory of Relativity, you cannot afford to miss this story. It is one of the big scientific stories of the year and is worth reading and rereading many times. If the Theory of Relativity has been a puzzle to you, this story, written in plain English, cannot fail to hold your interest from start to finish. The thoughts expressed in this story are tremendous. It will give you a great insight, not only into the infinitely large, but also the infinitely small. Better yet, relativity is brought home to you in a most ingenious and easily understandable manner — EDITOR [Introduction to "The Man from the Atom" 329].

This is precisely the sort of introduction, emphasizing the scientific content and value of the story to come, which would become a regular feature of Gernsback's *Amazing Stories* and *Wonder Stories*.[2]

As it happens, the August, 1923 issue is also of unusual interest because it is described on the cover as the "Scientific Fiction Number" of the magazine, because Wertenbaker's story inspired the cover painting, and because the issue included an unprecedented six stories (although one of them, a Gernsback vignette entitled "The Electric Duel," is often misidentified as an article). Clearly, Gernsback was attempting to test the potential appeal of a science fiction magazine, and it is occasionally argued that it therefore represents the world's first science fiction magazine. But that argument is refuted if one examines the Table of Contents page for that issue, which shows that the issue, like other issues of *Science and Invention*, was mostly devoted to scientific articles and scientific features; there were certainly more science fiction stories than usual, but they did not constitute the entirety — or even a majority — of the issue's contents. Further, while one might expect a science fiction magazine to feature an editorial about science fiction, the actual editorial in that issue, entitled "Predicting Future Inventions," did as the title indicated discuss a topic of obvious relevance to science fiction. However, except for four sentences about Verne's predicted submarine and six sentences about Gernsback's predicted electromagnetic weapon in "The Magnetic Storm," the editorial did not focus on, or even explicitly mention, science fiction itself.

Thus, it still seems correct to begin the story of the science fiction genre with the first issue of *Amazing Stories* in 1926, despite Gernsback's later desire to emphasize the period from 1911 to 1926 as the genre's most significant formative period. However, it is easy to understand why Gernsback would always look back on this period with particular fondness. This was the time when Gernsback was only publishing magazines that dealt with practical science — his true specialty — and he was doing so with the feeling that he was both a genuine expert in the field and an active contributor to its progress with his numerous suggestions for useful inventions. Later, some of his magazines would involve other fields, such as science fiction literature, where he had less knowledge and participated mainly as a spectator, not a contributor. In addition, the 1910s and 1920s were the time when Gernsback was most involved in the day-to-day business of editing magazines as their principal editor; he chose and arranged the contents, and if there was a space to be filled a day before the issue had to be sent to the printers, it was Gernsback who needed to write something to fill the gap. Later, as he grew more attentive to other business ventures, Gernsback would leave most of the day-to-day editing work to subordinates; so it was that T. O'Conor Sloane undoubtedly did most of the work on *Amazing Stories,* David Lasser and Charles D. Hornig did most of the work on *Wonder Stories,* and Sam Moskowitz did most of the work on *Science-Fiction Plus.* Gernsback may have still been around to write editorials, overrule certain decisions, and make other contributions, but he was not the principal architect of these magazines as he had been in the case of *Modern Electrics* and *The Electrical Experimenter.* They, in a sense, were his babies, and hence they were the magazines he was naturally most nostalgic about, and most willing to talk about in later years.

Gernsback's magazines in the 1920s were generally successful, but after the Great Depression, he like many others was finding it harder to make a profit. One response was to try launching other magazines in search of new success; and one of these, *Technocracy Review,* became one of his most interesting failures.

The 1933 magazine *Technocracy Review,* of course, was not really a science fiction magazine, since it featured no stories, only articles about technocracy. Still, this was a subject of obvious relevance to science fiction, and Gernsback did attempt to attract its readers to his new magazine by means of a large advertisement in *Wonder Stories,* so it would appear to merit some discussion. This is particularly important because, as will be noted, what little has been said about this rarely-seen magazine may be inaccurate.

To readers unfamiliar with *Technocracy Review,* its most surprising aspect might be the declaration of policy that appears alongside the editorial on page 53 of its second issue: "*Technocracy Review* voices no opinion of its own. It aims to publish all opinions whether for or against Technocracy." Surely, one might reason, since technocracy involves placing scientists in positions of political power, and since Hugo Gernsback was well known to be enthusiastic about all matters scientific, he should have been a strong supporter of technocracy, and he should have been publishing a magazine which reflected that supportive attitude. Instead, not only did his magazine indeed publish both articles that praised technocracy and articles that criticized technocracy, but Gernsback himself, in his own writings on the subject, sounded frankly skeptical about the whole idea.

For people to understand why this was the case, it is necessary to explain that, in the 1930s, the term "technocracy" evidently had a somewhat different meaning than it does today; in particular, it was regarded more as an economic theory than as a political theory.

Explaining what technocracy meant to people in the 1930s is difficult, because its chief proponent, Howard Scott, was a rather mysterious figure — so much so that an article about him in the second issue of *Technocracy Review* was entitled "Howard Scott — Technocracy's Mystery Man" — and he did little to convey his beliefs in a clear and cohesive way to the general public. It is also true that, at the time, different people seemed to have somewhat different ideas about the full meaning of the term. However, relying most heavily on an unusually lucid article by the magazine's Managing Editor, David Lasser — "How Technocracy Works" — and making some inferences of my own, I might offer this general overview.

The key assumption of technocracy was that the only rational way to assess the value of an object was by measuring how much energy was needed in order to produce it. Now, when human beings first began to use currency, one must assume, there was generally a strong correlation between the energy needed to produce a product and its price: if securing materials to build a product and/or actually building the product involved little expenditure of energy, the artisan would charge a low price; if securing the materials and/or building the product required a great deal of energy, the artisan would charge a high price. Under these conditions, with prices for products that corresponded reasonably well to the energy needed to make those products, economic systems could remain stable.

Unfortunately, with the rise of industrialization in the nineteenth century, this desirable situation began to break down. Some industries modernized rapidly so that it required less and less energy to produce a product, while other industries did not; yet prices for particular products tended to remain the same as they had been in the past, despite these unevenly distributed changes in their requirements for energy. There also seems to be, among supporters of technocracy, an implicit mistrust of any system that relies on the unpredictable fluctuations of supply and demand, instead of the fixed quantity of energy, to determine prices. Furthermore, as the barons of industry reinvested the not always justifiable profits that they were making from selling their products, Scott believed that one result was an inevitable and constant increase in the amount of debt accumulated by each individual, an additional factor undermining economic stability. As a result of all these problems, Scott opined in the 1920s, modern industrial society was headed for a complete economic collapse. When he first said this, no one paid much attention to him; but when a major economic collapse actually occurred in the early 1930s, Scott suddenly seemed like a prophet, and his ideas suddenly seemed to be worth taking seriously.

So, how was society supposed to solve the problem of its collapsed economy? As a first step, Scott had initiated in the 1920s what he described as an "energy survey" of the United States, attempting to scientifically determine precisely how much energy was being used to produce every product. Presumably, this data would prove essential to any effort to revive and restructure the economy, although Scott himself declined to spell out what sorts of reforms would be needed, enigmatically declaring that "*Technocracy proposes no solution*" to the problems facing the world in the 1930s ("Technocracy Speaks" 43). Other proponents of technocracy, however, offered more specific ideas about what needed to be done.

First, employing data from the energy survey, the irrational and unstable price system would be abolished, and the value of all products sold and bought would be determined by the amount of energy needed to create the products, as measured by new units to be called "energy credits." In addition, the total amount of energy produced by a country would be calculated, and that amount would be divided by the number of citizens in that country; then, each citizen would be annually issued an equal amount of "energy credits," and they would use their "energy credits" to sell and buy products.

At this point, one might reasonably wonder how all of this relates to technocracy as the term is understood today. However, it was clear that the complex process of establishing energy values and issuing energy credits could not credibly be entrusted to conventional politicians without a scientific background; instead, as a necessary element in the system, technically trained people would have to be in charge of society. Thus, what is now regarded as the central tenet of technocracy — a government controlled by scientists — initially emerged only as a minor corollary to a proposed economic system, and with the interesting exception of Gernsback himself, few people at the time seemed interested in discussing the benefits or drawbacks of a government controlled by scientists. In fact, the overriding concern of commentators on technocracy was an entirely different question: were radical reforms like these actually the best, or the only, way to quickly end America's Great Depression?

With some knowledge about what the term "technocracy" meant to people in the 1930s, one readily realizes why Gernsback was extremely skeptical about the merits of technocracy. In the first place, as everyone acknowledges, Gernsback was very fond of money, constantly sought to obtain as much money as possible, and would obviously resist any proposal that threatened his stockpile of money. "Energy credits" would strike such a man as an untested, dubious replacement for the money he was so fond of, and he would be particularly resistant to any plan to redistribute national income on an equitable basis, which of course would significantly reduce his annual income.

However, for obvious reasons, Gernsback could not publicly state, "I am opposed to implementing technocracy because it means that I would no longer be a wealthy man." He had to find another reason to justify his opposition to the idea.

What Gernsback noticed was this: the people behind technocracy, like Scott, were generally not first-rate scientists, and he could detect a number of minor scientific errors in the arguments they presented, which he seized upon and discussed in his article "Technocracy vs. Science." These errors not only discredited them as reliable experts, in Gernsback's view, but they also conveyed a crucial flaw in technocracy: its supporters were not true *scientists*, but were merely *technicians,* and the term they had created, "technocracy," manifestly involved a proposed government headed by technicians, not scientists — which is to say, a government headed by second-raters. As Gernsback explained the problem:

> There is, as will be seen, a huge difference between the two. The Technician, as a rule, takes the output of the Scientist. The Scientist comes first, the Technician second. Science does all the difficult work, such as research, invention, etc., and technology takes this raw product and puts it out as a finished article.
>
> As a rule, the scientist is more careful and knows his subject from the ground up, whereas the technologist is not so well versed in the theory ["Technocracy vs. Science" 83].

Therefore, to create a truly superior government, it would be necessary to place true scientists at the top, a proposed system that Gernsback describes with one of his typically unappealing neologisms:

> Indeed, it would not be a bad idea to start immediately a new cult which I would term SCIENTOCRACY, and the men who head this particular cult would, of course, be SCIENTOCRATS — offering Scientocracy, in opposition to Technocracy, as the direction of the country and its resources by Scientists and not by Technicians ["Technocracy vs. Science" 83].

Still, Gernsback did not elaborate on this proposal, and one suspects that, deep in his heart, he remained strongly in favor of maintaining the status quo and thus of insuring his own continuing prosperity. To solve the problem of the Great Depression, he had proposed, in his previous article "The Machine and the Depression," a much more modest reform: *"the taking out of industry and of all business all minors below the ages of 21 and, if necessary, all married women"* ("The Machine and the Depression" 23). According to Gernsback, this would create a sufficient number of jobs for adult males (the presumed heads of their households) and thus relieve widespread economic misery. One also notes that this is a proposal which served Gernsback's own interests, since it would have absolutely no effect on Gernsback's personal wealth.

In its first two issues, *Technocracy Review* published a number of articles on the subject, most of them reprinted from other sources along with original articles by Gernsback and Lasser; the second issue, for example, offered Gernsback's editorial "Whither Technocracy?" (53); Norman Thomas's "Who Shall Control Society?" (54–59); Wayne M. Weishaar's "Howard Scott — Technocracy's Mystery Man" (60–65); Frederick Soddy's "Men, Machines and Money" (66–67); Lasser's "How Technocracy Works" (68–73, 88–89); Charles N. Edge's "In Defence of the Price System" (74–77, 91); C. C. Furnas's "The Two-Hour Working Day" (78–81, 90); Gernsback's "Technocracy vs. Science" (82–85, 92); Roger Magadoux's "The Commodity Dollar" (86–88); and three features: a letter column, "Comments from Our Readers" (93–94); "Book Reviews," covering four books about technocracy (95); and "Opinions from Public Men," brief excerpts from publications about technocracy (96). In his editorial in the second issue, Gernsback confidently proclaimed that

> My own opinion in the matter, is, that while the public furor no doubt will die down somewhat, Technocracy will be with us always. It is already today inextricably entwined with economics and politics, and the chances are that in the future it will remain in the same position, or it may become even a greater force ["Whither Technocracy?" 53].

And Lasser at least had every intention of continuing the magazine indefinitely, since the introduction to Lasser's article in the second issue described it as "the first of a series of articles on the meaning of Technocracy, and the kind of society it proposes to supersede our present form" (Introduction to "How Technocracy Works" 68). In fact, of course, both Gernsback and Lasser were wrong: technocracy quickly faded into obscurity, and *Technocracy Review* never published a third issue. Clearly, the magazine had proven to be a complete failure in attracting readers; however, given its relevance to current concerns and obvious relationship to the futuristic concerns of science fiction, one must inquire: why was it a complete failure?

In answering this question, one first notes that, amidst all of the economic discussions, there were sporadic attempts in the pages of *Technocracy Review* to connect its contents to science fiction. In "The Machine and the Depression," as part of his effort to explain America's economic difficulties, Gernsback introduced the device of a "visitor from Mars" who, "after looking around him, would sadly shake his head and wonder if all humanity had not gone stark mad"; Gernsback then provides an extended speech by the Martian that details the reasons for his dismay ("The Machine and the Depression" 21–22). Manifestly, Gernsback believed that it was both natural and persuasive to introduce an element of science fiction to convey an argument about current economic conditions. Further, brief biographies of Gernsback and Lasser in *Technocracy Review* unambiguously attempt to relate their work in the field of science fiction to their articles on technocracy: in the second issue, Gernsback is described as "an inventor of numerous radio and mechanical devices, and the author of a book projecting future civilization, 'Ralph 124C41+' published early in the twentieth century" (83), while in the first issue, Lasser is identified as "managing editor of Wonder Stories, which deals fictionally with the scientific possibilities of the future, and the recreation of society through science" (5). Such comments suggest that publishing science fiction stories, and publishing articles about technocracy, are both complementary aspects of a concerted effort to predict and to shape future society.

In truth, though, the contents of *Technocracy Review* were almost completely unrelated to the stories then appearing in the science fiction magazines. In *Science-Fiction: The Gernsback Years,* Everett F. Bleiler and Richard Bleiler do discuss one story, Nat Schachner's "The Robot Technocrat" (in *Wonder Stories,* March, 1933), which was "According to rumor ... commissioned by editor David Lasser, who regarded Technocracy favorably," and was undoubtedly published as part of an effort to promote *Technocracy Review,* because "through no coincidence ... a full-page advertisement for Gernsback's new magazine, *Technocracy Review*" appeared facing the editorial page in the same issue (359). However, in the Bleilers' topical index to the 1835 stories published in science fiction magazines from 1926 to 1936, this is only one of nine stories listed under "Technocracy," and only this story, Schachner's "The Revolt of the Scientists" and its two sequels (*Wonder Stories,* April, May, and June, 1933), and Abner J. Gelula's "Hibernation" (*Amazing Stories,* July, 1933) appear, based on the Bleilers' summaries, to include any detailed considerations of economic issues. The other four stories listed under "Technocracy"— Eando Binder's *Enslaved Brains* (*Wonder Stories,* July, August, and September 1934), Miles J. Breuer's "A Problem in Communication" (*Astounding Stories,* September, 1930), Victor Endersby's "When the Top Wobbled" (*Amazing Stories,* February, 1936), and Joslyn Maxwell's *The Outpost on the Moon* (*Wonder Stories,* December, 1930, January, 1931, and February, 1931)— merely depict repressive societies headed by scientists. Doing the math reveals, then, that almost precisely one-half of one percent of the science fiction stories published during this decade had anything to do with technocracy.

In making these observations about Gernsback's dislike of technocracy, and about science fiction's general lack of interest in technocracy, by the way, I stand in rare disagreement with Mike Ashley, who makes these comments in *The Time Machines:*

> Technocracy was a movement to involve science more in the socio-economic decision-making process. Gernsback gave it his whole-hearted support, even to the extent of launching a new [though short-lived] magazine called *Technocracy*

Review. Technocracy also featured strongly in *Wonder Stories*, mostly in the works of Nat Schachner where science was ultimately shown to triumph [78].

However, as already indicated, Ashley is not offering an accurate description of what technocracy meant to people in the 1930s; Gernsback's own words manifestly demonstrate that he was not a supporter of technocracy; and as shown by the Bleilers' exhaustive survey, one cannot say that technocracy was "featured strongly" in any science fiction magazine of the era. It was not even a major aspect of Schachner's works, since the Bleilers identify only four of his forty-two stories from 1930 to 1936 as works involving technocracy.

Early science fiction's evident paucity of interest in economic matters, and the evident failure of *Technocracy Review* to attract science fiction readers, therefore suggest a characteristic of science fiction, then and now, that I observed in my article "In Search of Dismal Science Fiction": namely, throughout its history, science fiction has rarely dealt with speculative economics, making virtually no efforts to employ futuristic settings to comment on current economic conditions or to suggest alternative economic systems. Why this has always been the case would be an issue for extended discussion, but there may be a simple explanation for why this was true during the 1930s: by and large, readers of that era were turning to science fiction in order to *escape* worries about the Great Depression; reading something like *Technocracy Review,* however, would only serve to keep *reminding* them to worry about the Great Depression.

As a sidelight, it is also possible that the short-lived *Technocracy Review* had a major impact on the duration and visibility of Gernsback's own career as a science fiction editor. Before Gernsback fired him in August, 1933, David Lasser, as Managing Editor of *Wonder Stories*, was making a determined effort to improve the quality of the science fiction being published in the magazine (as Mike Ashley has exhaustively demonstrated), and if he had remained in control of the magazine (instead of being replaced by the less capable Charles D. Hornig), *Wonder Stories* might have been more successful in the following years, and Gernsback might not have found it necessary to sell the magazine in 1936. Thus, he might have remained a major figure in science fiction publishing throughout the 1930s and 1940s. But what inspired Gernsback to make the unwise decision to fire Lasser? As suggested by Lasser himself in an interview that appeared in Eric Leif Davin's *Pioneers of Wonder,* it may have simply been a way of saving some money: "Gernsback had to cut costs where he could. So, after he fired me, he hired a young kid [Hornig] to replace me at half my salary. That was a big savings for him" (57). Lasser also suggests that Gernsback may have been disturbed because he was spending so much time on political activities instead of working exclusively on *Wonder Stories.* Still, as one factor in Gernsback's decision, one cannot discount the possibility that he simply disliked Lasser's political views. Gernsback was manifestly a supporter of capitalism, while Lasser was an avowed socialist. And their short-lived experience in jointly editing *Technocracy Review* in early 1933 might have brought their previously-ignored political differences to the forefront.

Just as it is easy to see why Gernsback was unenthusiastic about tech-nocracy, it is also easy to see why the idea appealed to Lasser. In the first place, it clearly represented a form of socialism, involving redistribution of income and a strong government controlling all aspects of society. In addi-tion, because technocracy was a theory seemingly supported by scientific evi-dence and reasoning, it would harmonize with Lasser's other interests in advanced technology and space travel. One suspects that publishing *Technoc-racy Review* was mainly Lasser's idea, so that Gernsback had some reason to resent Lasser when the magazine so spectacularly failed. But the magazine also served to reveal, and even emphasize, their large political differences, as Gerns-back surely read Lasser's articles supporting technocracy, while Lasser surely read Gernsback's articles criticizing technocracy. Granted, there is no explicit textual evidence in anything said by or about Lasser that identifies *Technoc-racy Review* as a factor in his departure from *Wonder Stories*; still, one has to suspect that the seeds of the discord between Gernsback and Lasser that cul-minated in his firing were first sown during the time when they were both working on that obscure magazine.

While one might write an alternate history in which Lasser remained with Gernsback and Gernsback remained in the science fiction field after 1936, the fact remains that Gernsback did sell *Wonder Stories* to another pub-lisher in 1936 and thus abandoned science fiction entirely for a while. Obvi-ously, however, he was still paying some attention to the field, and he surely noticed two significant developments in 1939. First, some new science fiction magazines were appearing, suggesting a new interest in the genre; indeed, as a favor to a friend, publisher Louis Silberkleit, Gernsback contributed a guest editorial to the first issue of one of those magazines, *Science Fiction*, which was also being edited by the man he had chosen to replace Lasser as editor of *Wonder Stories,* Charles D. Hornig. In many ways, this editorial introduced what would be standard features of Gernsback's later writings on science fiction: some boasting of the role he had played in introducing and promot-ing the genre, comments about its natural appeal to "the younger generation," complaints that truly scientific stories were being supplanted by "the 'fairy-tale' type of fiction" (3), and expressions of optimism that science fiction as he had conceived it would nevertheless endure and continue to expand. There was only one surprising omission: while noting that science fiction was "a great stimulus to the imagination" (3), Gernsback failed to make arguments about the educational value of science fiction or its specific role in providing scientists with ideas for new inventions — perhaps at the request of a publisher and an editor who had no desire to emphasize such points in garnering an audience for their new magazine. Placed in a forum where he was no longer in control, it seems, Gernsback was willing to compromise a bit, and to tactfully refrain from characterizations of science fiction that some people in 1939 might deem unpalatable or unprofitable.

The second significant development in 1939 was the huge popularity of a relatively new sort of periodical: the comic book, a form which had received a tremendous boost from the remarkable success of two new superheroes, Superman and Batman. In light of these developments, then, it would have been perfectly logical for Gernsback to seek to exploit both the renewed popularity of science fiction and the new popularity of comic books by launching a science fiction comic book — and in 1940, that is precisely what Gernsback did. For scholars who are unable to purchase the rare and expensive copies of *Superworld Comics,* and scholars who cannot travel to the few libraries in the world which include this publication, examining the three issues which appeared in 1940 can prove extremely difficult. Thus, I consider myself fortunate to have finally obtained a blurry, and sometimes illegible, copy of the first issue of *Superworld Comics,* so that I can provide a partial report on the contents of this unusual Gernsback "magazine" (which is, by the way, the dignified term that Gernsback always used in describing his comic book).

Since the early days of *Amazing Stories,* Gernsback had expressed a strong desire to attract young readers to science fiction, publishing a 1927 editorial, "Amazing Youth," which discussed "the percentage of youthful readers who find food for thought and a great stimulus through the pages of the magazine" (625). A comic book, then, would seem like an ideal way to particularly address children and provide imaginative stories and features which would awaken their interest in scientific matters. In large part, that is what *Superworld Comics* strived to do, although Gernsback strangely chose to open his magazine with an article addressed "To Parents and School Teachers."

In this piece published in the comic book's inside front cover (attributed only to "The Publishers," though Gernsback almost certainly wrote it), one observes Gernsback modifying his approach to science fiction to downplay the features suitable only for adults — stimulating prophecies to inspire inventors — and to emphasize those elements more suitable for children — exciting entertainment and useful scientific information. In "To Parents and School Teachers," there was no reason to stress the comic's virtues as involving fiction, especially since that was always conveyed by the slogan on the bottom of the front cover: "Super Action Wonders — Adventures!" Rather, Gernsback reassured parents and teachers about the comic's "educational value" by calling attention to the quiz "How Smart Are You?," printed on the inside back cover, with questions that can be answered by consulting the stories and features in the comic book: "By this means the young reader can test his knowledge after reading the magazine, and then entertain himself and his friends with knowledge thus acquired." And, if the child neglects to perform this important task, Gernsback goes on to advise the parents to make sure that he does: "It is suggested that you test the young reader's knowledge after he has perused the magazine by asking him the questions enumerated on the inside back cover. We would be very much pleased to hear from those interested in the educational value of this magazine, in this respect."

Even if some aspects of the comic did not provide this sort of specific information, Gernsback at least noted that its predictions were all scientifically plausible; in bold type, he declared that "All features are based on present-day science" and "all are within the realm of possibility." Just as Gernsback once presented the contents of *Amazing Stories* as a wholesome alternative to "the so-called 'sex-appeal' type of story that seems so much in vogue" ("Thank You!" 99), he now presents the sober-minded contents of *Superworld Comics* as a wholesome alternative to the more extravagant adventures in other comic books: in "this magazine," he boasts, "No superhuman feats impossible of accomplishment are ever printed," which seems a direct slap at Gernsback's most popular competitor in this arena, DC Comics' Superman.

In reading this introductory article, one can tentatively identify one of the reasons why *Superworld Comics* failed. Reflecting the sort of old-fashioned attitude that one might expect in a man who was fifty-six years old, Gernsback evidently imagined that most comic books were purchased by parents to give to their children, or at least that most parents closely supervised their children's reading material in order to remove any item that was not worthwhile. In such a situation, designing a comic book that appealed to parents would be essential. In reality, most children in 1940 undoubtedly purchased their own comic books, and their parents probably did not bother to do more than glance at the comic books they were reading. Thus, viable comic books had to appeal primarily to children; yet, in emphasizing how much parents would love to have their children reading *Superworld Comics,* Gernsback was effectively doing everything in his power to drive children away.

However, the broader reason *Superworld Comics* did not achieve success, I would argue, is it was such a surprisingly conventional comic book, and hence could not stand out from the crowd of new comic books then appearing and find its own loyal audience. With their years of experience in editing science fiction magazines, Gernsback and his colleague Charles D. Hornig were seemingly in a position to blaze new trails by producing a true science fiction comic book, featuring the sorts of extravagant space adventures found in the science fiction magazines of the day. Instead, either because Gernsback was already losing touch with current developments in science fiction or simply because he was being overly cautious in entering a new arena, the contents of *Superworld Comics* were depressingly similar to the contents of all the other comic books then on the market.

One problem may have been that comic books in those days had sixty-four pages, and generally ran few if any advertisements (the first issue of *Superworld Comics* had only one, an advertisement for a machine to "Make Your Own Records at Home" on the back cover), leaving Gernsback and Hornig with lots of pages that needed to be filled with something, even if it had little or nothing to do with the announced priorities of *Superworld Comics*. This is the only way to explain why the 64 pages of the first issue included 20 pages of oddities — humorous pieces that have no relationship to science or science fiction. These were: a three-page reprint of Winsor McKay's famous comic strip "Little Nemo in Dreamland" (under that title, not the more familiar "Slumberland") (57–59)[3]; a three-page reprint of a similar strip attributed to "Silas," "Dream of the Mince Pie Fiend" (60–62); four pages of "Fables in Rhyme" (28–31), and two pages of "Educatin' Edgar" (52–53), both by Art Helfant; a three-page adventure of "Alibi Alice" by Ruth Leslie (34–36); a page, "Fun with Heads" (44), showing a number of heads that also look like different heads when viewed upside-down; and one page of "Cookoo Nuts" (27), visual puns submitted by readers, a feature Gernsback had first employed in his 1920s humor magazine *Tidbits*. Another humorous vignette, "Smarty Artie" (54–56), might be regarded as genuine science fiction, since it involves the amusing consequences of using static electricity from cats to generate power — which also the theme of an early science fiction story Gernsback published in *Modern Electrics,* Jacque Morgan's "The Scientific Adventures of Mr. Fosdick: The Feline Light and Power Company Is Organized" (1912); however, its style and tone place the piece firmly in the category of funny comics for children, not science fiction.

In addition, the first issue featured 11 pages of features which presented scientific information or described proposed activities with some arguable educational value; and it was these, more than the science fiction adventures, which Gernsback deployed as the primary conduit for the valuable scientific information he had promised to provide. One of these is credited to Gernsback: a two-page illustrated article entitled "Humans and Martians" (32–33), wherein he presented the theories of Martian physiology which, as will be discussed in Chapter 9, he had first introduced in *Baron Münchhausen's New Scientific Adventures* and would also figure in the Mitey Powers story of this issue of *Superworld Comics* and in his 1953 story "The Exploration of Mars." There were also two pages presenting surprising facts under the title of "Unbelievable, but True!" (50–52); two pages of information about "Wonders of Other Worlds" and "Super Distance Marvels" (63, 64); and four pages describing do-it-yourself activities under the titles "Fun with Magic," "Fun with Coins," "Fun with Toothpicks," and "Fun with Paper Stunts" (46–49).

A final item of purported educational value, "The Junior Inventor" (37), warrants special discussion. While Gernsback could not characterize any of the stories in *Superworld Comics* as potential inspirations for youthful inventors, he could at least encourage a spirit of youthful inventiveness by means of this feature, in which he invited children to send in their ideas for simple but useful inventions created out of household objects. The first item presented was attributed to Gernsback's own daughter, Bertina Gernsback, who was indeed as the caption stated eleven years old and a resident of New York City at the time; she had purportedly come up with the idea of bending a wire coat hanger in order to create a shoe tree. One might suspect that it was not really her idea, but at least it was possible; it seems much less likely, in the first issue of a new comic book, that the other submissions to this new feature actually came from real children living in such distant places as St. Louis, Missouri, San Francisco, California, and even Manila, the Phillipines!

Finally, the first issue of *Superworld Comics* featured four extended stories that unquestionably fell into the category of science fiction, although three of them were very much standard comic book fare, involving heroes in the present day battling against ordinary criminals. While only one of these stories — "Buzz Allen The Invisible Avenger!" — is specifically attributed to a known pseudonym of Hornig, Derwin Lesser (the others being either unattributed or attributed to unfamiliar names), it is generally assumed that Hornig, with some assistance from Gernsback, had a hand in writing all four of them. But the three conventional stories in no way reflect Gernsback's priorities for science fiction, since they include absolutely nothing in the way of educational scientific explanations for their posited wonders.

One of these stories, "Detective Crane: The Case of Super-Speed" (38–43, 45), involves a hero who, at least in this adventure, displays no unusual abilities; he is simply an ordinary detective investigating some baffling robberies who infiltrates "Spider" Morgan's gang and discovers that the criminal is using "weird science" to make him and his henchmen "live a thousand times faster than normal" (40) so they can invisibly rob trains in a matter of seconds. The criminals learn of Crane's true identity, but at that moment policemen burst into their hideout to rescue Crane and apprehend the criminals. Another hero, "Buzz Allen The Invisible Avenger!" (12–19), seemed the sort of character close to Gernsback's heart — a "radio ham" who, while trying out a new type of tube in his radio set, accidentally discovers the secret of invisibility, which he uses to oppose the criminal who murdered his father because he refused to pay protection money; in the final panel, Buzz vows to continue using his invention to oppose organized crime. "Introducing Hip Knox Super Hypnotist" (20–26) offered the comic's only costumed hero: a frail, effeminate young man wearing a turban and a one-piece suit featuring a large eye on his chest. Rescued as a baby by an inventor named Knox who endowed him with amazing hypnotic powers, Hip Knox can in an unexplained fashion instantly place any person he encounters under hypnotic control, as illustrated by zigzag lines emanating from his bulging eyes; he is the opposed by the "mortal enemy of the Knox family" (25), Eric MacFadden, who develops a helmet that prevents its wearer from being hypnotized. Thanks to his "sixth sense" (25), Hip can foil his first plan, but fears that MacFadden might be successful the next time.

This third, otherwise unremarkable story commands some attention because of its apparent relationship to Gernsback's own career; for "Eric Macfadden" is surely a reference to Bernarr MacFadden, the famed bodybuilder turned health entrepreneur who was notoriously involved in the effort to drive Gernsback into bankruptcy in 1929. As he is illustrated, Eric MacFadden bears a resemblance to Bernarr MacFadden, including a moustache such as the one that Bernarr MacFadden grew in his later years, and the first time we see Eric MacFadden, he is posing with his right arm extended straight out from his shoulder to his elbow, then straight up from his elbow to his hand — the classic stance of a bodybuilder showing off the muscles in his arms! Eleven years after his run-in with Bernarr MacFadden, it appears, Gernsback still bore a grudge. The story's conclusion is also strange: the first adventure of a comic book superhero usually concludes with the hero vowing to devote his life to fighting crime or other worthwhile goals; "Introducing Hip Knox Super Hypnotist" concludes with the hero fretting about his own survival, wondering if he will be able to survive MacFadden's next attack. In creating a superhero seemingly worried more about himself than about other people, critical observers might speculate, was Gernsback conveying an aspect of his own personality? Was the name "Hip Knox," while obviously a reference to hypnotism, also intended as a faint echo of Gernsback's old pseudonym, "Fips"?

Finally, there was one story which did feature the elements of aliens and space travel more commonly found in science fiction — "Mitey Powers Battles the Martians on the Moon" (1–11) — although the story was visibly influenced more by the Flash Gordon comic strip and serials than by any stories then appearing in the science fiction magazines. This story, illustrated by Frank R. Paul, was also the only story that incorporated true scientific facts (as occasional footnotes). Astronomer Professor Wingate is ridiculed when he announces that supposed meteors striking the Earth are actually missiles being fired by hostile Martians on the Moon; his daughter's boyfriend, Mitey

Powers, decides to build a spaceship and travels to the Moon in order to prove the Professor is correct, discovering during the journey that the daughter, Nina Wingate, has come along as a stowaway. They then are captured by Martians who are similar in appearance to those found in *Baron Münchhausen's New Scientific Adventures* and "The Exploration of Mars"; but unlike those placid residents of a utopian Martian civilization, these Martians more closely resemble those of H. G. Wells's *The War of the Worlds* (recently prominent because of Orson Welles's October, 1938 radio adaptation), intent upon conquering Earth "to make room for our own. Mars is growing colder, airless and less and less fertile!" (5) Rescued by Earth soldiers sent to the Moon when it is realized that Professor Wingate was correct, Mitey Powers proposes a suicide mission to blow up the Martians' projectile weapon, but a companion takes his place and dies while bringing an end to the Martians' scheme. Also, while being held captive by the Martians, Mitey undergoes a process which "doubled Mitey's mental and physical abilities" (6), perhaps establishing a rationale for later spectacular feats, although none occur in this first adventure. Clearly, Mitey Powers was regarded as the magazine's star, since he appeared on the covers of all three issues, always battling some menace in outer space, and his adventures do seem more exciting and innovative than the others; but this single feature was obviously not enough to make the entire comic book a success.

Overall, in considering *Superworld Comics,* one observes a Hugo Gernsback who is now growing older and becoming less able to adjust to changing circumstances. A person in Gernsback's situation, surveying the comic book market in 1940, might have made one of two decisions. First, resolving to emulate the success of others, he could have carefully studied the competition and come up with attractive heroes resembling Superman and Batman, and these heroes might have been successful though not really innovative. However, it seems that Gernsback did not really understand why those other heroes were popular and hence could not come up with viable alternatives to them. While virtually all successful comic books of its era featured costumed superheroes performing "superhuman feats impossible of accomplishment," Gernsback's comic provided only one costumed superhero, and Hip Knox was visually unappealing and reliant upon a power that led to little visual excitement (zigzag lines come out of his eyes, and opponents are rendered motionless). One also notes that most successful superheroes of the era performed their feats in disguise, using evocatively descriptive names (Superman, Batman, Captain Marvel, Wonder Woman, Green Lantern, etc.), while they lived ordinary lives using their real names; this pattern of secret identities added variety to the stories and could generate suspenseful subplots involving the possible revelation of the hero's secret. Gernsback's heroes had no qualms about using their real names, making no efforts to conceal their identities.

Gernsback's second course of action would have been to move in new directions and to produce the first true science fiction comic book, a policy that would later be successfully followed by comic books like *Planet Comics* in the 1940s and *Mystery in Space* and *Strange Adventures* in the 1950s. But Gernsback seemingly lacked the nerve to launch such a bold departure from current comic books. Instead, he eqeuivocated, essentially coming up with a conventional comic book with an overlay of scientific gimmicks and features, resulting in a publication that was insufficiently exciting to attract comic book readers, and insufficiently science-fictional to attract science fiction readers.

Thus, *Superworld Comics* represented Gernsback's missed opportunity to bring genuine science fiction into the realm of comic books — an opportunity that others with a background in science fiction would later exploit.[4] However, recognizing that the comic book was not succeeding, Gernsback followed his typical pattern in quickly abandoning an unprofitable enterprise.

Still, even after the swift failure of *Superworld Comics*, Gernsback continued to demonstrate his ongoing attachment to the field by beginning to produce, in 1943, a series of annual, self-published parodies of popular magazines which were sent as Christmas cards to his friends. In each of these were humorous vignettes and futuristic stories written by Gernsback; it will be recalled that the first of these parodies was the subject of articles in *Time* and *Newsweek* magazine, briefly making them prominent. By 1951, these annual compilations were entitled Forecast, so that Gernsback, in effect, was now publishing his own annual fanzine, though one doubts that he would have described these efforts with that term, and it seems that few if any of these publications found their way into the fanzine collections of science fiction fans.[5] For the most part, then, some of the contents of Gernsback's Christmas gifts became known to the science fiction community only in 1953, when Gernsback, heartened by the invitation to serve as the Guest of Honor at the 1952 World Science Fiction Convention and well aware that the field of science fiction magazines was booming once again, decided to launch what would prove to be his final science fiction magazine, *Science-Fiction Plus*, which among other new stories would republish a number of those privately-published Gernsback pieces.

In the seven issues of *Science-Fiction Plus*, Gernsback wrote six editorials about science fiction, often including some interesting observations about the genre. Yet in some respects, his most revelatory writings about his relationship to science fiction in the 1950s were two nonfiction pieces that ostensibly had nothing to do with the genre.

The first was an item he contributed to the first issue as an example of a feature he planned to include in every issue, "Stranger Than Science Fiction" — a brief discussion of some unusual but true scientific fact which could earn their authors a $10 prize. Gernsback's piece, entitled "We All Live in the Past," makes this point:

> Man resents the future instinctively because *nature has condemned us everlastingly to live in the past.* We never perform an act in the "present."
> Our fastest reflexes are already old when we perceive them. Every gesture, even the blinking of an eyelid, is in the past [...].
> Look at your watch — *you see only what time it was,* not what time it *is!* Even with light moving at 186,000 miles an hour, it takes a small fraction of a second for the watch image to reach the retina in your eye [...].
> And that is probably the chief reason why Science-Fiction enthusiasts like to roam in the future ... it is exhilarating to get away from the dead and gone past....
> ["We All Live in the Past" 38; all italics and unbracketed ellipses are the author's].

The second was the editorial he contributed to the magazine's sixth issue, "The Mighty Mite: *Homo Sapiens*: A Study in Futility," in which he contrasted the vast age and size of the universe with the short lifespan of human beings:

> If we think in terms of geological time, man's span of life on this planet is so microscopically short that it becomes useless to express it in figures [...].
> Yet man wants to roam the stars — not in spirit but in person. Vain and futile thought! The *nearest* star, *Alpha Centauri,* is less than 4 light years away — 23 ½ billion miles. At the fantastic, sustained speed of 1,000 miles a second — which man may not reach in hundreds of years — it would take 1,492 years for a round-trip! What about a comparatively near star 100 light years away, or a medium distant one, 10,000 light years away? The figures are a travesty on our puny life span.
> Hence man's bitter realization that most of our mighty striving is in vain — *our time scale is totally out of gear with our physical surroundings.* The time factor of the Universe is suited for the gods who live forever, not for the human mite who lives and dies during the span of a clock tick ["The Mighty Mite" 2].

Since Gernsback in the 1920s and 1930s was so focused on the future, and so optimistic about human space travel, what could have inspired this sudden attentiveness to the past, and this new pessimism about human progress in conquering space? One answer would be that these thoughts reflected Gernsback's perceptions of his own changed status. Launching a science fiction magazine in the 1920s, Gernsback saw himself as an avatar of the future; launching another science fiction almost 30 years later, Gernsback suspected that he was now a representative of the past. And in the 1920s, Gernsback recognized that, as editor of the only science fiction magazine being produced, he commanded the rapt attention of everyone in the emerging science fiction community; in the 1950s, as the editor of one of many magazines, Gernsback understood that his own influence and importance were greatly diminished.[6]

Throughout the pages of *Science-Fiction Plus*—jointly edited by Gernsback as "Editor and Publisher" and Sam Moskowitz as "Managing Editor"—there are numerous signs that the minds of those editors were frequently focused on the past. The first issue's "Book Reviews" by Moskowitz referred to Gernsback's 1934 publication of Stanley G. Weinbaum's "A Martian Odyssey" as "a red-letter day in the annals of science fiction" (60), and the "Science Questions and Answers" in the same issue notes that "As far as is known, your editor was the first to point out this condition. He called it 'space sickness.' If you have a copy of his novel, RALPH 124C 41+, you will find out all about it on page 202 (Second Edition)" (66). Phrases in biographical notes about the authors often harkened back to the days of Gernsback's first successes: John Scott Campbell "has been writing science-fiction for diversion since 1929, when he sold his first story, *The Infinite Brain*, to Hugo Gernsback" (March, 1953 12); Philip José Farmer "has been hailed as the greatest science-fiction discovery since Stanley G. Weinbaum" (March, 1953 21); "Encouraged when Hugo Gernsback purchased his first science-fiction stories, Raymond Z. Gallun left the University of Wisconsin after one year to become a free-lance writer" (April, 1953 5); Harry Bates "was a pioneer science-fiction editor, following Hugo Gernsback by editing a magazine for Clayton Publications in 1930" (May, 1953 4); Frank L. Wallace "has taken strongly to writing science-fiction, which he has been reading since Gernsback's first publication" (May, 1953 40); "Jack Williamson sold his first science-fiction story to Gernsback's *Amazing Stories* in 1929" (October, 1953 24); and "Like so many other authors [Roger Dee] began reading Gernsback magazines at the age of twelve" (October, 1953 36).

A strong interest in the science fiction of Gernsback's years of prominence — the 1920s and 1930s — can also be discerned by looking at the contents page of each issue. True, the works of some new authors were included, including Philip José Farmer and Chad Oliver, but there was a clear emphasis on earlier authors: Gernsback himself was represented by two stories in each of the first two issues and by one story in the third issue and the fourth issue, and the magazine featured several other authors who had originally come to prominence in the 1920s and 1930s, including Harry Bates, Eando Binder, John Scott Campbell, Raymond Z. Gallun, Murray Leinster, Frank Belknap Long, Eric Frank Russell, Clifford D. Simak, and Jack Williamson. One might imagine that the editors were *deliberately* seeking out older authors and encouraging them to write some new stories for the magazine, and this suspicion is confirmed, first of all, by a comment about coming attractions in the last issue's "Chain Reaction" column: "we're hard at work on Nat Schachner" (40), Moskowitz reported, describing an effort to obtain a new story from another author very active during the 1930s who had recently stopped writing science fiction. And Mowskowitz later noted that, even before the magazine appeared, Gernsback "began to solicit manuscripts from authors he had published in his earlier magazine and whose work he liked and remembered" ("The Return of Hugo Gernsback" Part II 217), such as John Scott Campbell. And when Moskowitz himself began sending letters to authors requesting submissions, he also acknowledged making an "effort to reach competent authors who had not written science fiction for some years" ("The Return of Hugo Gernsback" Part III 117), contacting older authors such as Harry Bates, Eando Binder, Raymond Z. Gallun, Frank Belknap Long, Thomas Calvert McClary, and Richard Tooker.

This backward-looking inclination of the editors of *Science-Fiction Plus* did not go unnoticed by readers, as reported by Moskowitz in "The Return of Hugo Gernsback": some "brutally critical" readers, "disappointed in the quality of the stories," "placed the blame on me as a fellow-traveler with Hugo Gernsback and his old-fashioned ideas" ("The Return of Hugo Gernsback" Part IV 194, 195). Indeed, although Moskowitz states the magazine never had a letter column solely "Due to space limitations" ("The Return of Hugo Gersnback" Part IV 194), it may have been that he and Gernsback decided to limit themselves to reports of readers' reactions in the "Chain Reaction" column because they preferred paraphrase and summary to the presentation of the actual scathing prose of the letters.

Acknowledging these criticisms in the first "Chain Reaction" column, "the Editors"—officially Gernsback and Moskowitz, though the piece was probably written entirely by Moskowitz, who later signed these columns—tried to put a positive spin on matters: "Some readers state that our fiction may prove 'old-fashioned' or too heavily scientific.... We are not trying to turn back the clock, but we *are* attempting to restore the proper balance between science and fiction in stories" (25). Some modern stories, their argument went, were overly "literary," creating a need to return to an emphasis on science; as Gernsback himself said in his final editorial, "Status of Science Fiction: Snob Appeal or Mass Appeal?," "*Modern science-fiction today tends to gravitate more and more into the realm of the esoteric and sophisticated, to the exclusion of all other types*" (2). Thus, by this argument, the editors' efforts to recruit authors from the 1920s and 1930s, and their manifest nostalgia for that era, only reflected an appropriate preference for science fiction which had scientific value as well as literary value.

However, there seems to be something disingenuous in the manner that Moskowitz and Gernsback are framing their argument. After all, in 1953, science fiction which stressed literary merit at the expense of scientific content was a relatively recent phenomenon, best represented by the contents of *The Magazine of Fantasy and Science Fiction*, which began publishing in 1949. If a return to science was the editors' primary concern, they could have turned to any number of writers who became prominent in the 1940s, ranging from luminaries like Robert A. Heinlein and Isaac Asimov to reliable professionals like Hal Clement and George O. Smith, all writers with a proven ability to write science fiction with a heavy emphasis on accurate science. Yet none of these writers appeared in *Science-Fiction Plus*, which instead chose to go a bit further back, to the 1920s and 1930s, to recruit its authors. As if anticipating this criticism, Moskowitz states that this policy was purely because "The better authors did not need a new market, putting me as a distinct disadvantage" and thus requiring him to "contact the better old-time writers not contributing to the present field and determine whether they could meet modern standards" ("The Return of Hugo Gernsback" Part I 218, 169). But it should be noted that other emerging magazines of the era, presumably in a similar predicament, failed to resort to this strategy of seeking out authors from previous eras of science fiction, suggesting that it was a matter of preference as much as a matter of necessity.

What Gernsback and Moskowitz were primarily trying to avoid, then, was not the science fiction of the 1950s but the science fiction of the 1940s, as most significantly represented by John W. Campbell, Jr.'s *Astounding Science-Fiction*. Recall that the biographical blurb for Harry Bates had conspicuously declined to mention the name of the magazine he had edited, *Astounding Stories*, suggesting a strong aversion to the magazine that Campbell inherited and renamed *Astounding Science-Fiction*. For Campbell, I believe, had championed a form of science fiction that Gernsback could not really understand, and that Moskowitz disliked: science fiction in which the scientific contents were not merely paraded before readers but integrated into the background developed for the stories; science fiction which did not simply toss out ideas for inventors, but created plausible future worlds that could be employed to evaluate the possible effects of new inventions or the value of proposed new social initiatives.[7] This was a sort of science fiction that Gernsback simply could not write, and a sort of science fiction that, from Moskowitz's perspective, replaced the thrilling stories of the 1930s that appealed to one's "sense of wonder" with less imaginative and more subdued narratives.[8]

In a sense, Gernsback had unknowingly described his own plight in one of his editorials for *Science-Fiction Plus*, "Skepticism in Science Fiction: Who Are the Disbelievers in Science-Fiction...?":

> As he grows older, man loses much of his enthusiasm, his drive. He becomes more cautious, much more skeptical. New ideas are no longer such a compelling challenge. They simply mean more work, more effort. Hence, the mature and aging mind actually *resents* the new and the untried. He begins to dislike the mul-

titude of new technical ideas that pour out incessantly in ever-increasing amounts. They now bewilder him — in truth, he can no longer cope with them, *they overwhelm him.* He finally finds himself no longer able to absorb the new [2].

Here, of course, Gernsback is placing himself in the group of eternally young minds always open to new scientific ideas, in contrast to the older minds that resist new scientific ideas; still, one must recognize that, at the time he wrote this editorial, Gernsback was already sixty-eight years old, and hence fully susceptible to all of the failings he had just listed. True, as someone with a lifelong interest in science and in publishing scientific magazines, Gernsback may have made a special and extraordinary effort to keep up with the latest scientific theories and speculations. But he clearly had not made a similar effort to keep up with the latest approaches of science fiction, since he no longer spent much time reading science fiction stories and novels.[9]

Thus, in the editorials he contributed to *Science-Fiction Plus,* one consistently notes three things: signs of a visible interest in noticing and commenting on new developments in science fiction; a lack of detailed knowledge about recent stories and novels illustrating those developments; and an impulse to turn the discussion away from contemporary science fiction and toward the subjects that had occupied his mind in the past. For the first issue's editorial, he reprinted his Guest of Honor speech at the 1952 World Science Fiction Convention, in which he noted the tremendous growth in the field of science fiction during the past twenty-five years and argued that science fiction had greatly contributed to scientific progress; however, seemingly unable to think of any recent texts, the only examples he could cite all appeared before Gernsback launched *Amazing Stories* in 1926 and truly launched the genre: Jules Verne's *Twenty Thousand Leagues under the Sea* (1870), H. G. Wells's *When the Sleeper Wakes* (1899), and his own *Ralph 124C 41+* (1911–1912). He then drifted into a new version of one of his most ridiculed proposals from the 1920s — the idea that science fiction writers should be able to patent their ideas — with the modest new wrinkle that writers not yet able to realize their imagined new inventions might qualify only for a special new kind of patent, a "Provisional Patent" ("The Impact of Science-Fiction on World Progress" 67).

In the second issue's editorial — "Pseudo Science-Fiction: What Type of Science Fiction Do You Read?" — he began by complaining that "nowadays, an increasing number of authors write a vast array of pseudo Science-Fiction" (2), an observation one would expect to be followed with some examples of recent stories with egregious scientific errors (such as those lambasted by Damon Knight in reviews later collected in his *In Search of Wonder*). But Gernsback has no examples to offer; instead, he contrives to change the subject by claiming, implausibly, that the cause of all of these inaccurate stories is that authors are being misled by "a periodical crop of pseudo-scientists, charlatans, and out-and-out fakers, who try to cash in on the public's igno-rance of science. Often authors, who should know better, fall prey to these perverted science-peddlers and base their Science-Fiction stories on such non-sense" (2). This allows Gernsback to devote the rest of his editorial to a favorite preoccupation of his during the 1920s — namely, the denunciation of various scientific hoaxes, none of which — with one fascinating exception — ever seem to have had any influence on science fiction. The fascinating exception was the work of a noted science fiction writer turned religious leader:

> One of the recent perpetrators is L. Ron Hubbard, author of the ludicrous book *Dianetics*, a hodgepodge of pseudo-medical pseudo science, which, believe it or not, fooled many thousands of innocents.
> Recently he has branched out in "Scientology"—a term he invented—then promptly bestowed upon himself the title of "D.Scn."—Doctor of Scientology! [2].

Gernsback may have particularly enjoyed attacking Hubbard because, as he was surely aware, he first promoted his ideas in an article that appeared in *Astounding Science-Fiction* with the implicit blessing of John W. Campbell, Jr., the rival that Gersnback would now never mention by name.

In the third issue's editorial, "The Science-Fiction Industry: A New Industry in the Making," Gernsback becomes one of the first people to notice what he terms the new, *"third dimensional world of science-fiction"* —"toys, games, gadgets, scientific instruments of all kinds, wearing apparel for young-sters, and countless other constantly-evolving, ingenious devices" (2). How-ever, he mentions only one recent work inspiring this sort of merchandise, the television series *Space Patrol* (1950–1953), with one other example, the long-standing comic strip, serial, and television hero Buck Rogers, who of course originated in two novellas Gernsback had published in his *Amazing Stories*. Furthermore, instead of envisioning these objects as interesting com-mentaries, or possible influences on, other forms of science fiction,[10] Gerns-back concludes by implausibly and inaccurately predicting that the market will soon turn to an emphasis on more educational toys of the sort that would perfectly accord with Gernsback's vision of the educational role of science fiction: "We may therefore soon see a similar boom in all sorts of scientific instruction merchandise" (2).

The editorial in the fourth issue, "Skepticism in Science-Fiction," can-not be broken down to illustrate these three aspects of Gernsback's 1953 sci-ence fiction commentaries, but the pattern returns in the editorial in the fifth issue, "Science Fiction Semantics: New Words and Definitions for S-F." He begins by calling attention to an aspect of science fiction that has increasingly fascinated some commentators — namely, that the genre "has spoken a lan-guage all its own," with "new terminology, new words, new meanings being added constantly" (2). But he then reproduces a passage, purportedly filled with contemporary science fiction jargon, that he had recently contributed to a recent time-capsule, although the passage actually only employed terms dating from the 1920s, 1930s, and early 1940s, as can be verified by consulting the *Oxford English Dictionary*'s online list of earliest known uses of various science fiction words. The novel terms that are both in Gernsback's paragraph and in the database are "visi-screen" (earliest known use: 1938), "Contraterrene matter" (1941), "astrogator" (1935), "Force-field" (1931), "space-drive" (1932), "disintegrators" (1925), and "positronic" (1941). Even more significant is the revelation in Moskowitz's "The Return of Hugo Gernsback" that "I myself had written this sample for Gernsback" (Part IV 213), suggesting two conclusions: Gernsback had so little knowledge of science fiction that he was even unable to reproduce some of its characteristic language from the 1930s; and Moskowitz, as already postulated, remained mentally fixated on this era.[11] Unsurprisingly, then, Gernsback's editorial does not go on to discuss some more recent examples of science fiction neologisms; instead, he proposed some of his own, characteristically inept neologisms: "orbitemp" for the distance a planet takes to circle the Sun, "light unit" for the distance from the Sun to Alpha Centauri," and "solex," "ulvio," and "cosrar" for the times it would take for x-rays, ultra-violet rays, or cosmic rays to kill a person.[12]

As he was working on this editorial, Gernsback was also becoming aware, by means of sales figures, that his curiously antiquated vision of science fiction was not proving popular with magazine buyers, as anyone could have deduced by considering two noteworthy features of the fifth issue: the elimination of Gernsback's own stories, which manifestly were not appealing to science fiction readers of the 1950s, and the shift to a bimonthly publication schedule, historically a clear signal that a magazine is failing. Moskowitz's "The Return of Hugo Gernsback" confirms that the magazine was hardly doing well: "early circulation results were coming in daily for both the April and May issues. They were even worse than for the first, and Gernsback was beginning to wear a grim expression at our regular Thursday group lunches" ("The Return of Hugo Gernsback" Part IV 200). As he contemplated the dismal sales of *Science-Fiction Plus* and recalled the unenthusiastic response to the patent proposal at the 1952 World Science Fiction Convention and the highly critical letters he had (by Moskowitz's report) carefully read, Gernsback may have felt that the science fiction community he had effectively brought into being was now turning on him, rejecting its father figure. In an effort to explain why this was happening, Gernsback then devised one more argument about the changing nature of science fiction, which he unveiled in the editorial for the seventh issue of *Science-Fiction Plus*, "Status of Science-Fiction: Snob Appeal or Mass Appeal?"

Here, Gernsback first notes that science fiction is now popular in a variety of media — "newspaper strips, comics, motion pictures, radio and television programs, books, and science-fiction magazines"; oddly, however, the least popular venue for science fiction is now the science fiction magazine, which is "at the bottom of the heap as far as mass penetration is concerned" (2). To explain this phenomenon, Gernsback presents an indictment of science fiction fans — "the *central concrete core* of science fiction — the all-important, all penetrating Fan the amateur — that vociferous and voluble voice of all science-fictiondom" (2). Despite their relatively small numbers — Gernsback's estimate is 25,000, which he surely got from Moskowitz — these fans are the ones who write most of the letters to science fiction magazines. In these, "The fan praises the stories he likes with enthusiasm, but throws corrosive acid in driving stream on the stories which — to him — don't pass muster" (2). On the one hand, Gernsback goes on to say, "this is quite as it should be — because it helps to drive the art to higher accomplishments" (2), but it also has the unintended negative consequence of possibly "destroy[ing] the very edifice which they helped so laboriously to rear" (2). For, as a result of their criticism, "*Modern science-fiction today tends to gravitate more and more into the realm of the esoteric and sophisticated literature, to the exclusion of all other types*" (2). Thus, magazine stories do not attract readers because they are driven by a sort of "snob-appeal," while science fiction in other media thrives because it "is nearly always simple, understandable to the masses, young and old" (2). Thus, "At present, science-fiction literature is in its decline — deservedly so. The masses are revolting against the snob dictum 'Let 'em eat cake!' They're ravenous for vitalizing plain bread!" (2)

Previously, Gernsback had contrasted his brand of properly science-centered science fiction with "pseudo science-fiction" which ignored or distorted scientific facts; now, in this somewhat parallel but equally self-serving argument, he is presumably contrasting his brand of "simple, understandable" science fiction with the "*esoteric and sophisticated literature*" appearing in the other magazines which, while promoted by science fiction fans, fails to attract large numbers of readers. Now, there may well have been an element of truth in this distinction, for the stories in *Science-Fiction Plus*, largely written by authors who first became popular in the 1920s and 1930s, probably were generally less sophisticated than the stories then appearing in magazines like *Galaxy* and *The Magazine of Fantasy and Science Fiction*. Yet if Gernsback's argument was correct, then his magazine of "vitalizing plain bread" should have been thriving while those other, more sophisticated magazines should have been failing. In reality, of course, those other magazines were doing well enough while *Science-Fiction Plus*, despite modest improvements in the sales figures of later issues, never turned a profit. Furthermore, and not incidentally,

Gernsback was hardly increasing his magazine's chances for a comeback by launching an attack, however couched in introductory laudatory language, on the science fiction fans which he acknowledged to be "a power to reckon with" in the field.

In "The Return of Hugo Gernsback," Moskowitz offers some additional, and contradictory, explanations as to why the magazine failed. One implicit and recurring argument is that the magazine failed to attract readers because of its inferior contents, a problem Moskowitz was willing to attribute entirely to Gernsback's bad decisions and old-fashioned attitudes. If Moskowitz had been allowed to make all of the decisions himself, he implies, it would have been a much better, and more successful, magazine. Thus, the all-important first issue made a bad impression on readers because "the policy of secrecy [Hugo Gernsback and Harvey Gernsback] insisted on maintaining for four months of the magazine seriously lowered the quality of its first issue" (Part IV 228); he generally complains that "Hugo Gernsback's insistence on second-guessing and changing submissions, often seemingly just for the sake of change, was becoming my biggest problem," while also expressing sympathy for "the victims of his authoritative behavior" (Part III 125); because of the way that Gernsback would overrule Moskowitz to accept bad stories and reject good stories, "it was becoming obvious that, out of touch with science-fiction for sixteen years, he no longer was aware of what was novel and what was old hat" (Part III 118); and "during the entire life of the magazine not a single one of the stories on which Hugo and Harvey overruled me was worth publishing" (Part IV 228). The notion that Gernsback was devoting a tremendous amount of energy to editing the magazine is reinforced by the official reason he gave Moskowitz for ceasing publication of *Science-Fiction Plus:* "While he could continue, absorb losses, and possibly break even within a few issues, he felt that age was beginning to tell on him, and he needed a prolonged vacation for recuperation; he just didn't think the effort was worth the risk to his health" (Part IV 234).

However, Moskowitz concludes his account with another surprising theory: when he heard Harvey Gernsback say of the magazine's demise that "We took it in our stride and wrote it off on our income tax," Moskowitz surmises that that might have been the plan all along: "He emphatically denied that his father had started *Science Fiction* + as a tax loss — a reasonable question, considering how expensively it had been produced. Yet I always wondered whether the fact that the magazine appeared close to turning a profit had entered into Hugo Gernsback's decision to drop it" (Part IV 236). However, one must ask, if Gernsback had wanted his magazine to fail, why would he work so hard on the project? Wouldn't he, instead, be doing as little work as possible on the magazine? Indeed, Moskowitz's entire account seems to tell a different story: that while he may not have been reading much science fiction, Gernsback still cared a great deal about the genre, so much so that he had, in his own eyes, threatened his own health by devoting so much of his declining energies to producing a science fiction magazine. It also seems as if he had thoroughly enjoyed the experience of working on this new magazine, because Moskowitz at one point says that *Science-Fiction Plus* was clearly "a new and very attractive toy for Gernsback to play with" (Part IV 195). In sum, one can never be certain about such things, but if Gernsback in fact had been plotting all along to deliberately create a failing magazine, he concealed his intentions with extraordinary skill.

It would seem wiser to attribute the cancellation of *Science-Fiction Plus* to an attribute Gernsback had displayed throughout his career: an attachment to the bottom line which outweighed any sentimental value. No matter how much he loved editing a magazine, and even if he could afford the losses, Gernsback could never bring himself to maintain any enterprise which was not making money. He sold *Wonder Stories* in 1936 because it was no longer profitable, not because he had tired of science fiction; he stopped publishing *Superworld Comics* for the same reason, and that was undoubtedly the reason why he abandoned *Science-Fiction Plus*. If he subsequently contrived to take advantage of its failure on his tax returns, that was only an instance of Gernsback making lemonade out of a lemon, not the culmination of some insidious scheme.

While Gernsback would never again be the editor of a science fiction magazine, Gernsback would have the opportunity to write one more science fiction magazine editorial; for in 1961, the current editor of *Amazing Stories,* Cele Goldsmith, graciously invited him to contribute a "Guest Editorial" to the April, 1961 issue, which commemorated the thirty-fifth anniversary of the magazine by reprinting seven classic stories that had first appeared in its pages. Except for a few speeches later reprinted in Forecast, this represented Gernsback's final opportunity to address the science fiction community he had founded so long ago.[13]

It is a curious, but revelatory piece. First, Gernsback has not forgotten or abandoned his original definition of science fiction, as announced in his very first sentence: "As we look back over the vista of modern science fiction, we are struck by the fact that the outstanding stories in the field — the ones that endure — are those that almost invariably have as their wonder ingredient true or prophetic science" (5). Here, identified as clearly as they were in the first editorial of *Amazing Stories,* are the three essential elements of science fiction are announced: fiction ("stories"), science ("true ... science"), and prophecy ("prophetic science").

Second, Gernsback reveals yet again that, despite protestations to the contrary, he really did not know very much about science fiction, especially its more recent texts. In the discussions of Jules Verne and H. G. Wells that follow his introductory comments, Gernsback twice quotes from the *Encyclopedia Britannica*—indicating that even when talking about the two classic authors who appeared repeatedly in *Amazing Stories*, Gernsback felt obliged to consult a reference book in order to ensure that his comments were accurate. And the editorial mentions not a single science fiction author who first published in the 1930s or thereafter.

Third, Gernsback once more displays his fixation on the past. Other than his remarks on Verne and Wells, the only detailed information on the history of science fiction he provides is an extended account of the authors and works that appeared in his science magazines prior to the launching of *Amazing Stories*. He mentions his own novels *Ralph 124C 41+* and *Baron Münchhausen's New Scientific Adventures* as well as his early authors Charles M. Adams, Jacque Morgan, George Frederic Stratton, and Charles S. Wolfe; when he moves on to the 1920s, he lists Ray Cummings's *Tarrano the Conqueror*, A. Merritt's *The Metal Emperor*, and Victor MacClure's *The Ark of the Covenant*. Particularly incongruous is his extended celebration of Clement Fezandié, who is described as a "celebrated" "titan of science fiction" who wrote his "famous" stories about eccentric inventor Mr. Fosdick ("Guest Editorial" 7). It is as if Gernsback is entirely unaware that he is talking about a writer that, surely, the overwhelming majority of readers of *Amazing Stories* in 1961 had never heard of.

Fourth, there are indirect indications of Gernsback's concealed, or subliminal, awareness that he was now an aged, old-fashioned figure. After summaries of Verne's and Wells's careers, Gernsback identifies the problem that eventually afflicted their careers in science fiction:

> Both of these illustrious authors had succumbed to the phenomenon of science fiction fatigue — the creative science distillate of the mind had been exhausted. New prophetic visions could no longer be generated.
> Science fiction exhaustion is well known to every author in the genre; some succumb to it early, others late in their careers. It is a phenomenon only too well understood by all editors and publishers, who must cope with it. Nor is it any wonder that the science fiction output of nearly all authors who have ever tried it is so limited. Only those who have attempted it can know how difficult and exhausting the subject can become ["Guest Editorial" 6].

Now, if asked about the matter, Gernsback no doubt would have identified himself as a rare, exceptional case who remained capable of "New prophetic visions" well into his seventies — since he was seventy-six years old at the time of writing this editorial, and as if to demonstrate that, he would conspicuously conclude his editorial with a brand new prediction. But exhaustion of another sort may have been haunting his thoughts — exhaustion in the face of having to make yet another attempt to talk about the contemporary science fiction that he no longer understood, leading to the understandable strategy of limiting his discussion to authors who worked before 1930.

Finally, however, one observes Gernsback striving to keep up with the times and to stay focused on the future. The final section of the editorial begins with the question, "What is the future of science fiction in this country?" ("Guest Editorial" 7) He notes that "like the stock market, [science fiction] has its ups and downs, its peaks and its valleys" (7), and he may have been thinking about his own career in science fiction publishing as much as the genre as a whole. And while the elderly Gernsback elsewhere expressed concerns that science fiction was almost entirely abandoning its involvement with genuine science (most fervently in his 1963 Address to the M.I.T. Science Fiction Society, later published as "The Prophets of Doom"), he chooses to be optimistic in this forum, arguing that "Because of the present unusual interest in science by our young generation, it would seem certain that there will be far more science fiction authors in the future than there ever were in the past. Hence there should be more and better stories, too" ("Guest Editorial" 7). He then says his farewell to the science fiction community, characteristically, with a touch of humor and yet another clunky neologism: as a coming solution to the problem of "Science Fiction Fatigue," he predicts the invention of an "*electronic biocomputer-menograph*" which will, instead of humans, someday write all the materials published in *Amazing Stories* (88). Perhaps, though he does not mention it, he is also hoping that a mechanical brain would be more likely to maintain the strong focus on science in science fiction that Gernsback always cherished and celebrated.

Judging solely by this editorial, and the seven reprinted stories in this issue of *Amazing Stories* — only two of them from issues edited by Gernsback — one might well conclude that Hugo Gernsback had essentially become someone who was unimportant to science fiction, an antiquated, out-of-touch figure who was no longer relevant to the contemporary science fiction scene. Certainly, there were times when Gernsback felt the same way, as most vociferously expressed in "The Prophets of Doom." In that speech, he bitterly complained that "the genre of Jules Verne and H. G. Wells has now been prostituted to such an extent that it often is quite impossible to find any reference to science in what is popularly called science fiction today." Instead, one mostly finds only "mutations" of the genre such as "Pseudo Science Fiction, Fantasy Science Fiction, Sexy Science Fiction, Fairytale Science Fiction, and, lately — believe it or not — even Computer (i.e., *Analog*) Science Fiction, and then the so-called *psi* deviations, from psychic phenomena to spiritualism, including astrology" (176–177). Still, even as he observes little to celebrate about contemporary science fiction, Gernsback refuses to surrender to pessimism in that speech, as he goes on to condemn "the many prophets of doom" ready to "write off genuine science fiction as *passé*" (178). Then, evidently inspired by the example of Arthur C. Clarke, who he describes as "perhaps the most outstanding true science fiction personality" (179), he goes on to predict that "Given enough such outstanding authors, true prophetic science fiction could very well stage a massive comeback — it could become the renaissance of the Jules Verne-H. G. Wells type of technological science fiction so badly needed in our present idea-impoverished world" (181).

In light of the new prominence and energy of hard science fiction in recent decades, one might say that this was one Gernsback prediction that came true; however, one does not need to appeal to developments after his death in order to demonstrate his lasting impact. Instead, as I searched for evidence of Gernsback's influence at the time when he wrote his final editorial for *Amazing Stories*, I turned away from that special issue, which unusually consisted entirely of classic stories and lacked the magazine's regular features, and instead picked up another, more typical issue of *Amazing Stories* from that period which I happened to own, the May, 1963 issue. It contains four stories, all of them preceded by brief editorial introductions. It also features an "Editorial" by Editorial Director Norman M. Lobsenz in which he discusses a *New Yorker* review of Arthur C. Clarke's collection *Tales of Ten Worlds* which singles out for special praise a Clarke story first published in *Amazing Stories* in 1951. There are two other brief editorial commentaries: "Coming Next Month," discussing the stories scheduled to appear in the next issue, and "A Message to Readers," in which the editor explains and apologizes for a recent rise in the magazine's cover price. In a letter column, "Or So You Say," there are four letters, three responding to a recent letter, and the other praising a recent short story; one of the letters is accompanied by a brief editorial response. A book review column, S. E. Cotts's "The Spectroscope," offers long reviews of two recent science fiction novels and a collection of science fiction-inspired nursery rhymes. There is a science article, Ben Bova's "Where Is Everybody?," in which he discusses possible reasons why humans have so far been unable to detect extraterrestrial civilizations. Most interestingly, there is an article about science fiction — Alexander Kazantsev's "A Soviet View of American SF" — which is actually the translated and edited preface to a recently published Soviet anthology of American science fiction.[14]

In sum, one should not make the mistake of Alexei Panshin, in his 1971 essay "The Short History of Science Fiction," of measuring Gernsback's important solely by the scientific content of published science fiction stories — even if Gernsback himself at times seemed to make the same mistake. Rather, it is in these regular arrays of accompanying features, found in

Amazing Stories and other science fiction magazines, that one finds Gernsback's true legacy. Other editors before Gernsback had published science fiction stories of various sorts, but Gernsback surrounded his stories with editorials discussing science fiction, letter columns allowing readers to talk about science fiction, reviews of science fiction books, articles about the science found in science fiction stories, and articles about science fiction writers. As already discussed, Gernsback launched a great conversation about science fiction, which continues to this day in many forums, including the science fiction magazines. Like some other people who start very long conversations, Gernsback eventually found that the conversation was drifting into areas where he did not always feel comfortable and did not always enjoy, and so he tended to say less and less, and when he did say something, the other people in the conversation tended to pay less and less attention to him. And for this reason, people who entered the conversation at a later time might mistakenly conclude that Gernsback had nothing to do with the conversation. Yet those who have studied the entire history of this conversation will recognize that Hugo Gernsback has had an enduring impact on both the forms and the contents of that conversation; and his sporadic and diminishing contributions during the last decades of his life should not be allowed to obscure that basic truth.

PART II

HUGO GERNSBACK THE AUTHOR

5

Evolution of Modern Science Fiction

The Textual History of Hugo Gernsback's Ralph 124C 41+

Throughout the twentieth century, as science fiction developed into a recognized literary genre, Hugo Gernsback's novel *Ralph 124C 41+: A Romance of the Year 2660* has repeatedly emerged at crucial defining moments. It was first published as a serial of twelve installments in Gernsback's magazine *Modern Electrics* from April, 1911 to March, 1912, an era when other magazines were struggling with several short-lived terms to describe their science fiction stories,[1] and its popularity led to the policy of offering science fiction stories in all of Gernsback's science magazines, establishing the first markets exclusively for works of "scientific fiction." Its appearance as a book in 1925 immediately preceded the birth of Gernsback's first science fiction magazine, *Amazing Stories*, in 1926, and its success may have been one factor in the decision to publish that magazine; and Gernsback soon reprinted *Ralph* in *Amazing Stories Quarterly* in 1929, explicitly identifying it as an exemplary work of "scientifiction." In the late 1940s and early 1950s, when companies were first publishing lines of science fiction books on both sides of the Atlantic Ocean, a second hardcover edition of *Ralph* appeared in America as part of "Fell's Science Fiction Library," quickly followed by a British hardcover edition. Later in the 1950s, as paperbacks increasingly dominated the science fiction market, a paperback edition of *Ralph* was published in 1958. And when the twentieth century drew to a close, as more and more older texts were being posted online, and as more and more scholarly presses were publishing works of and about science fiction, it was only to be expected that portions of *Ralph* would become available on the Internet, and that a new edition of

Ralph would emerge from the University of Nebraska Press. If one also considers Gernsback's prominence and visibility as a magazine editor, it is hardly daring to hypothesize that *Ralph* is an important document in the history of science fiction and to justify a detailed study of an admittedly poor novel on those grounds.

The problem, however, is that the various editions of the novel often display significant differences, and the first one in particular is radically unlike all of its successors. To fully understand this novel, one must examine its complete textual history, exploring how and why each version differed from its predecessor. It is a story about a narrative built out of fundamentally incompatible elements, of massive efforts to resolve those incompatibilities, and of later attempts to ameliorate those incompatibilities by polishing its surface. It is a story, I will finally suggest, that is not unlike the story of science fiction itself.

The 1911–1912 Version

A serialized novel appearing in *Modern Electrics* was incongruous, since as already noted the magazine might have been better described as a kind of *Notes and Queries for Inventors*. Yet *Ralph 124C 41+* was dropped into this milieu virtually without comment. Aside from an introductory paragraph accompanying the first installment (quoted below), summaries of earlier episodes, and reminders in tiny print that back issues with previous installments could be ordered, Gernsback made absolutely no mention of his story anywhere in *Modern Electrics* while it was appearing, even when describing, in moments of editorial boosterism, how the contents of his magazine were constantly improving; nor did he publish any letters with reader responses to the story (though, admittedly, he published very few letters of that type anyway). Perhaps Gernsback was at the time not too sure about what he was doing and hence reluctant to discuss the work at length.

There are two stories about Gernsback's plans and reasons for writing *Ralph 124C 41+*. First, Sam Moskowitz's "Hugo Gernsback: 'Father of Science Fiction'" says that when Gernsback "found himself a few pages short of material to fill the April 1911 issue of *Modern Electrics*, he sat down and dashed off the first installment of *Ralph 124C 41+*, a work of science fiction" (232). Whether Moskowitz created this story or heard it from Gernsback, it is almost certainly false. There has always been reason to doubt that Gernsback decided to write *Ralph* at the last minute: a scene from the story appearing on that issue's cover (as was the case for the next eleven issues) implies that there was forethought involved, as does the fact that the story began in the first issue of a new volume; Gernsback also announced at the start that it would be a "serial story." (To fill space in one issue, an editor might well dash off a short story but would be unlikely to commit himself to a *continuing* story simply for that reason.) Examining the published text raises more questions. The preceding three issues of the magazine — January, February, and March, 1911 — were respectively 64, 64, and 60 pages long; the April, 1911 issue was 64 pages. The first installment of *Ralph* in April occupied little more than a page and a half. Perhaps publishing exigencies demanded an issue of either 60 or 64 pages, so Gernsback could not have solved his hypothesized space problem by printing an issue of 62 pages; but there was still no need to add a piece of fiction, as he could have easily left out a few things to bring the magazine in at 60 pages, or he could have used some of his standard filler material — excerpts from magazines, cartoons, jokes, book reviews, advertisements — to fill one and a half pages. In sum, all the evidence suggests that Gernsback carefully planned from the start to add a serialized story to his magazine.[2]

The second story is Gernsback's own, in his 1950 "Preface to the Second Edition" of *Ralph*:

> today I must confess I do not recall just *what* prompted me to write *Ralph*. I do recall that I had no plan whatsoever for the whole of the story. I had no idea how it would end nor what its contents would be.... As the story developed from month to month there was the age-old scramble to beat the deadline — but somehow or other I always made it — usually under duress, finishing the installment at 3 or 4 a.m. on the last day [8].

Moskowitz agrees that "He had no ideas beyond the first chapter, but each month at the approach of the deadline he would sit down and carry the story forward, with no concept of how it would develop or end" (232). These accounts ring truer, since ample evidence in the text suggests that *Ralph* was not carefully planned. As one major example, the key characters of Fernand and Llysanorh'[3] are not introduced until the eighth installment, intimating that the extended melodrama of the kidnappings and space flights was not anticipated. More generally, there is reason to believe that, in response to a specific influence, Gernsback decided halfway through his serial to radically alter the contents and style of the story.

To understand how *Ralph* changed, one must examine its twelve installments. Despite many changes, the 1911–1912 text corresponds to portions of the 1950 edition, the most accessible uncorrupted text. (The other editions published during Gernsback's lifetime — in 1925, 1929, 1952, and 1958 — differ in various ways, but they are generally similar in their contents, as will be discussed.) Reading the portions listed in the table below will provide a rough picture of the serial's contents.

Table. The 1911–1912 Text of *Ralph 124C 41+*

Original magazine installment	*Roughly corresponds to this portion of 1950 edition*
1. April, 1911	Chapter 1 (25–29), to "became apologetic"
2. May, 1911	rest of Chapter 1 (29–39)
3. June, 1911	Chapter 2 (40–51), without references to the faces of Fernand and Llysanorh'
4. July, 1911	Chapter 3 (52–65)
5. August, 1911	Chapter 4 (68–78), without the conversation about Fernand and Llysanorh,' and without the meeting with Fernand
6. September, 1911	Chapter 5 (79–88), to "this timely night"
7. October, 1911	rest of Chapter 5 (88–96)
8. November, 1911	Chapter 10 (141–146), from the start of Fernand's letter to end of chapter Chapter 11 (147–51), to "damn you"
9. December, 1911	rest of Chapter 11 (151–163)
10. January, 1912	Chapter 12 (164–171)
11. February, 1912	Chapter 14 (176–181)
12. March, 1912	Chapter 16 (195–207)

Looking at these texts, one sees that the original *Ralph* was, in essence, two significantly different stories. First consider installments one through seven: the first is a scene from a technological utopia, celebrating the wonders of picturephones and instantaneous language translation; the second introduces a bit of what might be termed scientific melodrama, a story of danger and rescue achieved by scientific wizardry, not derring-do; and the third through seventh installments settle comfortably into the familiar combination of the utopia and travel tale, as Ralph gives Alice a guided tour of his future world. Installments eight through twelve are quite different: they take place almost entirely in outer space, while the first seven occurred exclusively on Earth; and far from utopian, they seem drawn more from traditional melodrama with touches of Gothic horror, as Ralph must pursue and overcome two villains, observe three violent deaths, and finally rescue Alice from the grave itself. Quite evidently, Gernsback had dramatically changed his mind about the type of story he wished to tell; and I believe I can identify one reason for that change.

At times, as noted, *Modern Electrics* would include brief book reviews of scientific books as fillers; but at least once, a work of fiction was reviewed. The August, 1911 issue, which featured the fifth installment of *Ralph 124C*

41+, also had a "Book Review" section which discussed a recently published novel, Mark Wicks's *To Mars via the Moon*:

> This book is published at a timely epoch, when all the world at large has become interested in our neighboring planets, and the question of their inhabitation. The book is dedicated to that eminent astronomer, Professor Percival Lowell, and based on his theories and discoveries.
>
> While the book contains fiction that will hold the reader spell-bound until the last page is reached, nevertheless, from a scientific point of view, it is a very valuable book for advancing new theories and probabilities. Not only may it be read as a pastime, but it is recognizable as a text book. The description of the conditions on Mars, are unique, the people, cities, method of transportation, canals and other features, while based on the most conservative theory, make interesting reading. The very clear maps of the planet with its "canals" are especially worth mentioning.
>
> This book should appeal strongly to those interested in the researches in connection with the planet Mars, and almost as appealing for the average readers seeking an enjoyable scientific novel [371].

This is probably the first commentary on science fiction published in a Gernsback magazine and also contains the first Gernsback-magazine use of a term for science fiction: "scientific novel." Since the review was unsigned, one cannot establish beyond doubt the identity of its author. However, its publication does prove that someone in Gernsback's circle had read the book in 1911 and that Gernsback was aware of its contents; furthermore, given how much of the magazine was written by Gernsback himself, either under his own name, under a pseudonym, or with no attribution, it is highly probable that Gernsback himself read the book and wrote the review. In fact, the unfolding text of *Ralph* gives strong evidence that Gernsback had read, and had been impressed by, that book.

First, there are some similarities in contents between *To Mars via the Moon* and the later installments of *Ralph*. In Chapter XXVI of Wicks's book, the narrator and his friends witness "Wonderful Aerial Evolutions" staged by the Martians:

> We were gazing upwards at the vast assemblage of air-ships, which were lit up by the ordinary lamps used when travelling at night, when suddenly the whole sky became brilliant with the flow of countless thousands of coloured lights, and the air-ships began to move into their allotted positions.
>
> Every ship — and there was a very large number of them — was covered all over with electric lamps. Some of the ships had all red lights, others all blue, others yellow, and so on through the whole range of tints known to us, besides many tints which we had never seen before.

The Martian airships then form "simple geometrical designs," a rainbow, the spectra of several stars, interesting mixtures of light, and light displays corresponding to music (Wicks 184–188). The scene clearly anticipates

the "aerial carnival" that Ralph and Alice witness in the October, 1911 installment:

> The spectacle which unfolded itself below his guests was indescribable. As far as
> the eye could see a broad expanse studded with lights, like a carpet embroidered
> with diamonds, was laid out. Thousands of aerial craft with their powerful
> search lights moved silently about and once in a while an immense transatlantic
> aerial liner would swish over the horizon with tremendous speed, the flare of its
> flashlights long in evidence after the disappearance of the liner....
>
> Suddenly overhead at a great height the flag of the United States in immense
> proportions was seen. It was composed of about 6,000 aerial flyers all flying
> together in the same plane.... Each one of course had very powerful lights on
> the bottom; some had white lights, other red ones, other blue ones [7:420–21].[4]

Later displays show the Solar System and the Planet Governor.

More broadly, Gernsback's decision to take his story into space may have
been inspired by Wicks. The first seven installments contain no references to
Martians or space travel; Ralph's future society is evidently an earthbound
one. Only in the eighth installment (published in November, 1911 issue) are
readers abruptly informed that Earth has mastered space travel and enjoys regular contact with humanoid Martians. And particular devices suggest the
space travel motif stemmed from Wicks. *To Mars via the Moon* includes three
charts showing the orbits of Earth and Mars, including one which also shows
the flight path of his protagonists' spaceship, the *Aeronal* (Figure 1, facing
page 118); this may have inspired Gernsback's chart in the January, 1912 installment showing the orbits of the inner planets and paths of Ralph's and
Llysanorh's spaceships (Figure 2, 10: 691). Wicks includes a description of the
Martians:

> I could now see that they were very much taller than myself, being quite seven
> feet nine inches in height. They were, however, so splendidly proportioned that
> at first their stature had not impressed me as being much above our ordinary
> standard; whilst their features were most beautifully formed and regular, their
> complexions being very clear and fresh-looking.
>
> One great peculiarity I noticed in all around us, and that was a peculiar soft
> and liquid glow in their eyes, which seemed to light up the whole of their fea-
> tures, adding greatly to their beauty and nobility of appearance [165].

This has affinities with Gernsback's briefer descriptions of his Martian: Fernand calls him "this lanky seven foot Llysanorh" and refers to "his big black
horse eyes" (8:498). Finally, one subplot of Wicks's novel is a romance between
the narrator's companion and a beautiful Martian woman, which the narrator ends by telling his friend that a relationship with a seven-foot woman
would never work back on Earth; this vignette of thwarted romance between
human and Martian may have inspired Gernsback to feature a Martian man
helplessly in love with an Earth woman but forbidden to marry one.[5]

More important that these apparent borrowings of content, however, is the fact that Gernsback evidently adopted the *form* and *purpose* of Wicks's novel. Consider the paragraph that introduced *Ralph* in April, 1911 (here, I reproduce the actual text, not the slightly altered text Gernsback presented in the 1950 edition):

> [Note. This story, which plays in the year 2660, will run serially during the coming year in MODERN ELECTRICS. It is intended to give the reader as accurate a prophesy [*sic*] of the future as is consistent with the present marvelous growth of science, and the author wishes to call especial attention to the fact that while there may be extremely strange and improbable devices and scenes in this narrative, they are not at all impossible, or outside of the reach of science] [1:19].

To readers of Gernsback's later commentaries on science fiction, these remarks have a conspicuous omission: while Gernsback promises a "narrative" that will include prophecies, he does not stress that the narrative will provide "scientific fact" along with "prophetic vision" (as he did in "A New Sort of Magazine" 3), since stating that his predictions are "consistent with the present marvelous growth of science" and not "outside of the reach of science" does not exactly promise scientific information, and he nowhere indicates that his narrative will be in any way "educational." At this time, Gernsback has not fully formed the idea of science fiction that he would later proclaim in *Amazing Stories*.

Then, in the summer of 1911 (we are with some confidence assuming), Gernsback read *To Mars via the Moon*. Wicks's "Preface" to the novel explicitly asserts that it is designed to educate readers by providing current, accurate information about astronomy:

> In the course of my experience as an occasional lecturer during the past twelve years, I have been much impressed by the keen interest evinced, even by the most unlettered persons, when astronomical subjects are dealt with in plain untechnical language which they can really grasp and understand ... it occurred to me that it would be much more useful and appeal to a more numerous class if, instead of writing a book on the usual lines, I wrote a narrative of events which might be supposed to occur in the course of an actual voyage to Mars; and describing what might be seen on the planet during a short visit.
>
> This is the genesis of my story; and, in carrying out my programme, I have endeavoured to convey by means of natural incidents and conversations between the characters portrayed, the most recent and reliable scientific information respecting the moon and Mars; together with other astronomical information: stating it in an interesting form, and in concise, clear, and understandable language. Every endeavour has been made to ensure that this scientific information shall be thoroughly accurate, so that in this respect the book may be referred to with as much confidence as any ordinary textbook [ix–x].

And in writing a book with such goals, Wicks employed some devices usually associated with nonfiction: astronomical maps, charts, and photographs, with "Notes on the Maps and Charts" (xix–xxi) and a table of data on the Sun, moon and planets (xxiii), and, on three occasions, informative footnotes in the main text (52, 55, 126).

Reading *To Mars via the Moon*, then, may have showed Gernsback that a "scientific novel" could fruitfully include scientific data as well as predictions, and could thus be educational as well as inspirational. The author of the review picked up on the idea, saying that "Not only may it be read as a pastime, but it is recognizable as a text book." And, with this missing piece of the puzzle in place, as it were, Gernsback was able to go on, in later installments of *Ralph* and other works, to write exactly the sort of science fiction that he would later extol in *Amazing Stories*.

As evidence for this hypothesis, note the *formal* differences between the two parts of the original *Ralph*. The first seven installments have no footnotes and only two small visual aids: drawings of a Menograph tape (3:167) and the trans–Atlantic tube (4:231). The last five installments have seven footnotes (9:596 [two], 10:691; 11:788 [two], 790; 12:883) and five larger visual aids: the diagram of Gernsback's "radar" (9:593); a picture of the "Principle of the Anti-Gravitator" (9:595) omitted from later texts; the chart of planetary orbits (10:691); and two photographs of artificial comets (11:788). The first seven installments include only one sentence describing present-day science: "In 1909 Cove of Massachusetts invented a thero-electric sunpowergenerator which could deliver ten volts and six amperes, or one-sixtieth kilowatt in a space of twelve feet" (6:359). Yet the ninth installment includes a long description of conditions in space (9:596,616); the tenth describes the asteroids (10:690–91); and the eleventh offers extensive data about real comets and experimentally produced artificial comets (11:788). The fact that this information is astronomical further suggests the impact of Wicks's novel.

Acknowledging Wicks's influence, however, does not imply that *Ralph* simply became an imitation of *To Mars via the Moon*, since there remain significant differences between the works. First, while Wicks does discuss some marvelous Martian inventions and developments, he does so only in the most general terms; the policy of describing in detail the principles and workings of such devices, followed in all installments of *Ralph*, was uniquely Gernsback's. Second, the other dramatic change in the later installments of *Ralph*— the lunge into melodramatic action — cannot be attributed to Wicks. *To Mars via the Moon* is a conventional utopia and proceeds placidly: there are no villains, no violence, and no conflicts other than trivial ones. Ralph's daring pursuit of two kidnappers through space, and his efforts to restore a dead woman to life, are utterly unlike anything in Wicks.[6] Overall, then, what happened during the writing of *Ralph* might be imagined in this way: after proceeding for a while with his guided tour of a marvelous future city,

Gernsback came to realize that the story was unsatisfactory; seeking improvements, he borrowed from Wicks the ideas of space travel and scientific explanation in the manner of a textbook; he borrowed from somewhere else — other popular fiction of his day, no doubt — the colorful story lines of villainy, pursuit, and resurrection; and he retained his own emphasis on imagining and explaining at length new scientific achievements.

At times, it must also be noted, Gernsback's original *Ralph* also strayed into another, quite different generic territory: the love story. Consider, for example, the 1911–1912 description of the tennis game between Ralph and Alice:

> It was a delightful game and although 124C 41 was an expert, his companion beat him almost from start to finish. To be frank, he was not very attentive to the game, as it interested him far less than his fair opponent. He did not see the ball, nor did he notice the net. All he could do was to watch her in rapture and this alone kept him pretty busy. He had never imagined that a human being could be so swift and graceful all at the same time. She darted hither and thither, she swished from right to left, smiling and beaming all the time. It seemed to him that she never touched the ground; one moment she would be straight up in the air, straight as an arrow, trying to catch an impossible ball; the next second her lithe and wonderful, flexible body would fly almost horizontally over the field after a hopelessly "out" ball. And she always smiled and beamed upon him, no matter what her pose, her white and perfect teeth, glittering in the sunlight, trying to outdo the fluorescent sparkle of her wonderful, tantalizing, ever dancing eyes. 124C 41 under this bombardment of feminine charms became as awkward as never before in his life. He could play mechanically only and as the game proceeded he became more and more confused. It was hopeless. Instead of seeing balls, he saw nothing but waving hair, a set of wonderful teeth and a pair of almost impossible, wonderful eyes which kept him spellbound.
>
> He was almost ready to give up when the remarkable happened.
>
> Miss 212B 423, when she left the house, had of course not known that she was going to play tennis, and for this reason had come to the game without her usual hair-net protecting her heavy hair. It was, therefore, little wonder that suddenly, while jerking her head to catch an extremely low ball, her hair came down without warning. Nor was there any half way about it.
>
> It became unfastened neatly and thoroughly. Down it came, farther and farther; it passed her waist, then her knees and stopped short a foot from the ground. It completely enveloped her, and what hair it was! 124C 41, who was only ten feet away from her, had stopped short as if thunderstruck, completely flabbergasted, as it were. His racket had slipped from his hand and his mouth was far from being closed. He looked anything but intelligent. If he had ever given the subject thought, he would have come to the logical conclusion that a mass of hair, and such hair as he saw now before him, was an absolute impossibility. He would have told anyone that such hair was preposterous, a mad dream of a mad brain.
>
> Presently, however, before his astonished eyes, a pink nose disentangled itself out of the forest of blue-black, heavy hair. Next a dimpled, well rounded pink chin appeared, followed immediately by a blushing, annoyed face, and a plaintive, embarrassed voice complained:

"*How* dreadful, oh what will I ever do..." but catching sight of our hair-struck young friend, whose face was the very personification of amazement, she burst into a ringing laugh, which to his ears sounded much like church chimes. It furthermore had the beneficial effect of waking him up by bringing him gently back to earth. Unfortunately, or perhaps fortunately — who knows? — it did not stop there. No indeed. He did not turn his head for the very simple reason that his head had become turned. [This is not intended for a pun.] Consequently, he watched her. The very admiration shining out of his soul by way of his eyes embarrassed her at first, but it quickly wore off, while she began to put up her hair again.

It was not the easiest task either. 124C 41 for the life of him could not see how on earth she was ever going to get it back again in place. Besides he could not understand where all these masses of heavy hair could find shelter and he continued gazing at her, watching every move. Little by little, however, it found its way back and in a short while it once more crowned a queenly head — not in time, however, — for 124C 41+ had made a solemn oath that he would never consider himself happy if he could not call himself part owner of that wonderful hair.

For the next ten minutes, he rhapsodized in ardent terms over her hair, and she became so embarrassed that he had to put a stop to it.

"You know," he concluded, "some individuals, like Samson, are conquered by the loss of their hair; and on the other hand, some individuals, by the achievements of other's hair are conquered in turn!"

"Now," he said, having become a matter-of-fact scientist again, "I will show you where New York gets its light and power from." [6:358–359]

Here, Gernsback's prose is certainly exuberant and flowery, and he seizes upon a scenario that must have already been a cliché in 1911 — the prim, proper girl who lets down her hair and reveals herself to be a beauty — and exaggerates it to an absurd extent. (Surely, only undiscussed technological advances would enable a woman with hair extending to her feet to pin it all up.)

Significantly, this is one of the few passages that is greatly shortened in the 1925 edition (from 819 to 343 words), completely recast, and toned down:

In the game that followed, Ralph, an expert at tennis, was too engrossed in the girl to watch his game. Consequently, he was beaten from start to finish. He did not see the ball, and scarcely noticed the net. His eyes were constantly on Alice, who, indeed, made a remarkably pretty picture. She flung herself enthusiastically into her game, as she did with everything else that interested her. She was the true sport-lover, caring little whether she won or not, loving the game for the game itself.

Her lovely face was flushed with the exercise, and her hair curled into damp little rings, lying against her neck and cheeks in soft clusters. Her eyes, always bright, shone like stars. Now and again they met Ralph's in gay triumph as she encountered a difficult ball.

He had never imagined that any one could be so graceful. her lithe and flexible figure was seen to its best advantage in this game requiring great agility.

Ralph, under this bombardment of charms, was spellbound. He played mechanically, and, it must be admitted, wretchedly. And he was so thoroughly and abjectly in love that he did not care. To him, but one thing mattered. He knew that unless he could have this girl life itself would not matter to him.

He felt that he would gladly have lost a hundred games when she at last flung down her racket, crying happily: "Oh, I won, I won, didn't I?"

"You certainly did," he cried. "You were wonderful!"

"I'm a little bit afraid you let me win," she pouted. "It really wasn't fair of you."

"You were fine," he declared. "I was hopelessly outclassed from the beginning. You have no idea how beautiful you were," he went on, impulsively. "More beautiful than I ever dreamed anyone could be." Before his ardent eyes she drew back a little, half pleased, half frightened, and not a little confused.

Sensing her embarrassment he instantly became matter-of-fact.

"Now," he said, "I am going to show you the source of New York's light and power" [25:96–98].

While a few passionate phrases are retained, the falling of Alice's hair is eliminated (and, in fact, her hair is shortened along with the passage so that it only reaches her "neck and cheeks"), so the incident qualifies as one of two passages in the 1911–1912 edition that was completed removed from later versions of the story.[7]

Another passage of this sort that was considerably condensed and revised is the romantic moment Ralph and Alice enjoy right before Fernard's kidnapping. In the original version:

It was a beautiful night. The moon was full and the early autumn air was invigorating.

Ralph 124C 41 and Alice 212B 423 were enjoying a ride in a two-seated aerocab above the ocean, in the neighborhood of New York. This was one of Alice's favorite diversions and both enjoyed these rides immensely.

For some time already both had stopped talking. During the weeks of their acquaintanceship both had not lost time studying each other thoroughly. They had the same likes and dislikes for most things, and they usually agreed on the most vital subjects. They were moreover extremely sympathetic to each other, so much indeed that each one when blind-folded or in the dark could tell the presence of the other in a room full of people without difficulty.

The great scientist 124C 41, who two months ago was an avowed enemy of the fair sex, had at last been conquered. The great scientist had been turned into a meek lover, and he had, moreover, forgotten his own lectures ridiculing love as being nothing but a "Perfumed animal instinct." Ralph, the lover, had indeed changed his mind on the subject. Alice, who for sometime past had watched the moon with a dreamy expression in her eyes, was building aircastles — a favorite habit of hers. In fact she was so engrossed in a lovely pink dream with baby blue edges on it that it was some time before she became aware that Ralph had taken her hand in his. She had never held hands with anyone in such a shocking manner and consequently withdrew it violently — in her imagination. However, as the novel feeling of holding hands with a very sympathetic young man was surprisingly delicious, she actually did not, of course, withdraw her hand violently. Quite the contrary. She sat perfectly still and both for a time enjoyed the thrill of the sympathetic flux surging back and forth between them through the clasped hands.

Centuries back on a like occasion the young man would have said or perhaps whispered a lot of sweet as well as foolish things — and thereby most likely have spoiled the whole effect. He would of course asked her if she wanted to be his wife, if she would love him all her life, and other equally unnecessary questions.

Ralph and Alice, however, being highly advanced beings with the refinement and culture of past civilized centuries behind them, neither talked nor whispered. Sitting close together, the exchange of their thoughts was attended with no difficulty. Both felt in the same manner, both understood and thought through similar channels.

By and bye their two other hands met and clasped and still further by and bye their lips met, and neither of the two spoke. In fact speech had become impossible, obsolete. Both were electrified; every nerve in them tingled and pulled and vibrated. They were not sitting in an aerocab any longer, they floated in a rose-red sea of delicately scented emotions, in which time stood still. Their ears heard nothing but far-off sonorous chimes, ringing and singing in regular intervals — at least that is what it sounded like to them; what they did hear, or rather feel, however, was the rhythmical beating of their hearts. Just how long they floated on the sea of their emotions and just how long they heard the chimes in each other's hearts is difficult to ascertain, as no authentic report on these subjects is available. It is, however, well known that both were brought back to earth, or rather to their aerocab, by another aeroflyer, which hailed their driver, asking for assistance. The strange flyer seemed to be having trouble with its motor and asked permission to draw up to our friends' cab, which permission was of course granted. When the two cabs had been made fast, the driver of the aeroflyer asked the other driver for a few copper connectors which would enable him to repair the damage. Ralph, who had his head turned away, annoyed by the unpleasant interruption, was holding the left hand of Alice, as if he were loath to break away even for a second. He suddenly became aware of a sweet, pungent odor, which rapidly became sickening. He tried to turn his head to ascertain where the odor originated, and everything was blotted out...
[8:499–500; author's ellipses].

Again, a heavily romantic passage was shortened (from 722 to 393 words) and toned down:

It was the night of the full moon. There was a faint touch of crispness in the early autumn breeze that now and again gently ruffled the waters of the ocean. A thousand stars danced lightly in the sky and were reflected in the undulating waves below. And in the moonlit path over the waters hovered an aerocab gleaming silvery white in the radiance.

The cab was far from New York, away from the beaten traffic. Occasionally other aircraft came into view but always at a distance.

To Alice and Ralph this solitude was Paradise. Night after night they hired an aerocab and flew to this lonely airway, where seated side by side, with only the driver for a chaperon, they were absolutely happy.

The driver was a silent man who, as long as he was well paid for his time, was content to describe endless circles indefinitely.

On this particular evening Alice seemed, to Ralph, more lovely than he had ever before seen her. In the caressing light of the mellow moon her flowerlike face glowed with a new radiance, and her dark eyes, shadowed with long curling lashes, were mistily tender.

Between these two there was no need for words. So perfectly were their thoughts attuned that each knew what the other felt.

And so, presently, their hands stole out and met, and clasped. And it seemed to both that Heaven could hold no greater happiness than this, until, with one accord, they turned their faces to each other, and their lips met. To them nothing existed beyond themselves and their love.

The voice of another aerocab driver hailing them made them realize that there were still ties that bound them to earth, and they moved apart a little self-consciously, as a cab drew alongside their own.

"Having some trouble with my motor," called the newcomer. "Could you let me have a few copper connectors to repair the damage?"

"Sure," returned their driver, and the two cabs came together and were made fast.

Ralph, seeing that his man could attend to the matter, turned away from them towards Alice, and again drew her hand into his own, where it snuggled confidingly.

Quite suddenly he was aware of a sickish, sweet odor, which almost instantly became suffocating. He was conscious of the pressure of Alice's fingers and then blackness overwhelmed him [25:197–99].

While one passage of the 1911 version — the remark about "Perfumed animal instincts" — was moved to the new beginning of Chapter 10, much of the other material was simply deleted, shortened, or revised; and to further dampen the spirit of romance, the presence of the driver, ignored until the climactic moment in the 1911 version, is established at length at the beginning of the passage.

There are two reasons why Gernsback may have revised passages of this kind. First, Gernsback seemed to regard such writing as ridiculous, as shown by two ancillary texts in *Modern Electrics*. While lists of Gernsback's "firsts" can grow tiresome, he does qualify as the first person to parody *Ralph*. In two editions of "The Wireless Screech," the humor section of *Modern Electrics*, he parodied his own "serial story." The first (August, 1911) went as follows:

RALPH + − x :−! ?
By "Fips."

"HELLO, Ralph!!"

"Hello, Alf!!!"

Ralph put his proboscis into the *smell piece* of his *telephot* and took a long sniff.

"Punk," he said, "that cigar of yours smells terrible."

"That so?" chirped Alf; "next time give me a better one!"

"You don't mean to say that that is the cigar I gave you?" angrily demanded Ralph.

"Quite so," quietly responded Alf, "but I guess it smells queer because our telephot wire passes through your stable! Consequently, you smell my cigar plus the stable!"

"Darn it," muttered Ralph, "will you please...."

At this juncture, by one of the pranks of Central, the two friends were disconnected from each other. For four minutes Ralph fumed and swore trying to get his friend back, and he was just going to hang up his receiver when a soft light appeared on the face plate of his telephot and immediately after the face of a beautiful young French cow appeared.

Ralph was so surprised at the beautiful sight that for a few minutes he could do nothing but gasp. By the soft light, lit up by a beautiful stable lamp, Ralph could see that she wore evening dress, i.e., none at all.

He finally managed to stammer.

"Pardon my intrusion, I assure you it was not intentional."

"Moo-ooh, moo-ooh!" came the answer, in a voice that went down deep in Ralph's heart.

"Aha, she's French," thought Ralph, "I'll fix that in a hurry."

He quickly turned the knob of his *language rectifier* to French, but somehow or other, the cow continued to say "Mooh-mooh!" which is the French for the English "Mooh-moooh."

For a minute or two the great inventor was stunned. He looked about himself and then looked again at the cow. The cow was mooning plaintively and looking closer through the telephot, Ralph could see that the cow stood in three feet of water. Ralph turned white.

"Heavens!" he muttered, "a flood! What can I do to save that poor cow? and she's a French cow, too, 4,000 miles distant!" He tore his hair in despair. He had never met such a difficult problem in his life. The water was rising rapidly and the poor cow was frightened out of the little wits she had. It was frightful, awe inspiring.

Note: So far the story is O. K. I like it but I must confess I got both Ralph and the cow into a tight position. If Ralph saves the cow, it is customary that he must marry her and that wouldn't be the story. If he don't save her he isn't as smart as I thought he was. Besides, I don't think he can save her anyhow, because the cow don't know enough to assist him. I am puzzled. It started so nice and easy and I had hoped to make a nice big story of it. I think I'll chuck it up and let you guess the rest.... No — an idea! I got it! So here goes:

In despair Ralph looked on. Suddenly....

[To be continued] [5:308; author's ellipses]

The second [April, 1912] went as follows:

ALF 12B 40.
By Fips.
(Concluded.)
(Coffeeright by Fips. All rights preserved.)

He could see himself and his assistants working over the wretched canine with a fine-toothed comb and insect powder, and how suddenly the dog had shown signs of life and a violent desire to scratch himself, and how finally he had been brought back from the valley of the shadow.

He could see himself surrounded by the famous men congratulating him on his unheard of, wonderful success, and he could hear himself making the little speech in which he said:

"What I have achieved with this dog can be achieved with my poor "Valise." [punctuation *sic*]

All this passed through his brain with lightning rapidity — a light ray in the utter darkness.

But could it be done? For the first time in his life he began to doubt his ability. He was almost afraid. What if he failed? He knew he could not live without his betrothed; only the solemn vow he made then and there, to die if she could not be brought back from the Beyond, finally gave him sufficient courage to act.

In a second he was himself again, not the lover, but the cold scientist. He instinctively felt that if he were to be successful he must not let his feelings interfere with his work.

A most important task was now before him. He had to pump an antiseptic solution through the veins of "Valise," and after that the blood vessels had to be filled with a weak solution of Radium-K Bromide, which, taking the place of the blood, has the important property of restraining the body from undergoing physical and chemical changes.

After this task had been completed to his full satisfaction, Ralph returned to the laboratory to fetch down the insect powder.

When, however, he came to examine the steelonium bomb, labeled "Insect Powder," he found that for unknown reasons the powder had escaped.

He had all he could do to keep from collapsing. His head swam and he had to sit down to keep from falling to the floor. This last blow was almost enough to drive him out of his mind. After he had had a reasonable assurance that "Valise" could be brought back, everything had been snatched away from under his very hands.

He became so despondent that he broke down completely and wept like a child. Without the insect powder he knew he could never hope to save his dead sweetheart, as there was nothing to keep the dead body from disintegrating.

Can you imagine what the poor young man's feelings were, on his flight back to Earth? Imagine yourself enclosed in a metal flyer, all alone out in space, millions of miles from anywhere, with a **dead French cow** as sole company, with the chances ten to one that you will bury her on your arrival home. It is not very cheerful.

(Note. On account of lack of space we can't conclude this thrilling narrative in this issue. We will positively complete it in the next number. To our lady friends who have read this story with breathless interest we would say that the story finishes alright. Alf will positively fetch back to life the dead cow. It's going to be excitingly thrilling. Order your copy now) [44–45].[8]

It is not clear why Gernsback found it so hilarious to substitute a cow for the woman Alice; and given his later insistence on science fiction as wholesome entertainment, the implication of bestial sex seems incongruous. Still, these feeble parodies do offer some insight regarding Gernsback's attitude towards his work. Later parodists of *Ralph,* like Harlan Ellison and John Sladek,[9] would focus on the long passages where Ralph didactically describes the marvelous inventions of his future world; but Gernsback apparently did not see anything funny in those parts of his story. Rather, for him, the romantic passages chiefly invited ridicule.[10]

The latter parody suggests a second reason for Gernsback's shift away from this type of writing: the idea that the romantic element appealed only to "lady friends" in the audience. However, while scanning every 1911 and 1912 issue of *Modern Electrics*, I do not recall seeing a single female name; while it is possible that I missed a few, or that some female contributors or questioners concealed their gender with initials, the readership of *Modern Electrics* must have been almost entirely male. This was also true of its successor magazine, *Electrical Experimenter*, in which Gernsback responded to a rare letter from a female reader by noting, "We might as well admit it; we are not burdened with many letters from the gentler sex" ("Editor's Mail Bag," December, 1916 568). Thus, some time between 1912 and 1925, Gernsback had evidently concluded that the potential audience for science fiction was also overwhelmingly male, perhaps influencing his decision to shorten and dampen the romantic passages in *Ralph*.[11] A mild irony is that even as he downplayed the element of "romance" — in its modern sense — in his 1925 version, Gernsback also added a subtitle to the novel — *A Romance of the Year 2660* — using the term "romance" in its older sense — an adventurous narrative in an exotic locale.

Overall, Gernsback's willingness to make fun of his own novel suggests that he was dissatisfied with it — as does the fact that, after finishing *Ralph*, Gernsback temporarily stopped publishing fiction and waited thirteen years until he returned to Ralph's story to revise it for book publication.

1912–1925: The Interregnum

Early in 1912, *Modern Electrics* twice published a form with several questions about the magazine and invited readers to send in responses. While the survey covered all aspects of *Modern Electrics*, the timing of its appearance suggests that Gernsback was particularly anxious to receive some feedback about his novel. The results, published in April, 1912 as "What Our Readers Want" on page 46, listed these results for the five questions pertinent to fiction:

I like Mr. Gernsback's serial story	**3005**
I do not like Mr. Gernsback's serial story	1074
I would like another serial story by Mr. Gernsback	**2520**
I like short stories	**2155**
I do not like short stories	1387

Several things can be said about this survey. First, readers were evidently interested in responding to *Ralph*: while the survey had twelve pairs of "like/do not like" questions, the pair of questions on *Ralph* was one of four pairs that attracted more than 4000 total responses. Second, most respondents liked the story — almost 74%, to be exact. Third, the more general question about "short stories" generated a less enthusiastic response: far fewer responses overall, and a smaller percentage of positive responses — almost 61%. This suggests that Gernsback's story was appealing to some readers who did not otherwise like fiction, which presumably was one of Gernsback's goals in writing a heavily scientific story; but the question about "another serial story" did not attract as many positive responses as *Ralph* itself, indicating limited enthusiasm for fiction as a regular part of the magazine.

However, since this was still a generally positive reaction, why didn't Gernsback immediately begin another work of fiction? The heading to the survey weakly explained that "Owing to Mr. Gernsback being in rather poor health at present, we will not immediately publish another serial story by him, but hope to be able to do this later on." But the statement is suspicious, since Gernsback was during this time still managing to write his editorials and, with increasing frequency, the "Wireless Screech" feature. It is more likely that Gernsback simply did not feel ready to tackle the problematic task of writing another serial at that time; and when fiction did return to *Modern Electrics*, in October, 1912, it came in the form of Jacque Morgan's "The Scientific Adventures of Mr. Fosdick," the first of several Morgan stories, and not another serial by Gernsback.

Evidence of Gernsback's ambivalent feelings about such work surfaced when, later in 1912, *Modern Electrics* added a Table of Contents page to each issue, which meant that Gernsback had to classify the fiction he was publishing in one of his categories. In the October, 1912 and November, 1912 issues, the contents pages listed Jacque Morgan's first two Mr. Fosdick stories under the vague title "Miscellaneous Subjects" (pages 672, 785); but in the December, 1912 issue, the third Fosdick story was instead listed with other articles under "Electricity and Magnetism" (page 897). So — were scientific stories predominantly fiction, or predominantly science? Gernsback could not make up his mind.

Not until May, 1915, the first issue of the third volume of the successor to *Modern Electrics*, *The Electrical Experimenter*, did Gernsback return to writing a "serial story" with the first of thirteen installments of *Baron Münchhausen's New Scientific Adventures*. Gernsback evidently wanted to produce a quite different kind of story, a rollicking satire in the manner of the original Münchhausen stories; however, as will be discussed at length in the final chapter, the story did not work out well, and Gernsback abruptly abandoned the novel in 1917.

Gernsback's later ventures into science fiction before 1925 were brief: two short stories, "The Magnetic Storm" (*Electrical Experimenter*, August, 1918) and "The Electric Duel" (*Science and Invention*, August, 1923). and two speculative articles, "10,000 Years Hence" (*Science and Invention*, February, 1922) and "Evolution on Mars" (*Science and Invention*, August, 1924). But the form of writing he would call science fiction was increasingly on his mind: as the stories that he published in his science magazines grew increasingly popular, he made the August, 1923 issue of *Science and Invention* a special "Scientific Fiction Number" and in 1924 began planning the all-fiction magazine that would emerge as *Amazing Stories* in 1926. This might have seemed like the logical time for Gernsback to revise and republish his first story, perhaps as a sort of trial balloon for his magazine; but he would now strive, for the first time, to produce a genuine science fiction *novel*.

The 1925 Version

In his one comment on the changes made in the 1925 edition of *Ralph*, Gernsback stated that "It has been necessary, in view of scientific progress since the time the story was written, and in order to present the book to a much wider reading public, to rewrite much of the story and to make many changes. Yet, the ideas and conceptions embodied in the original manuscript have been little altered" ("Preface [to the First Edition]" 25:3). The implication of the phrase about "scientific progress"— that Gernsback extensively reworked and updated the novel's scientific passages — is false; except for usually replacing the word "wireless" with "radio," Gernsback retained virtually all of his original scientific language, even maintaining outdated references to the "ether" that could have been recast with little thought. Instead, all his energies were focused on "present[ing] the book to a much wider reading public"— improving the literary quality of *Ralph*, making it a better story.[12]

Comparing the 1911–1912 and 1925 texts, one sees that Gernsback had a few definite priorities in revising *Ralph*. First, he simply had to make the story longer, to achieve the typical length of a novel; second, he needed to better integrate the two parts of his story, particularly by incorporating materials in the early chapters that would foreshadow and lay the groundwork for the events in the later chapters; third, he sought to do what he could to make the conversational scientific lectures in *Ralph* a little more plausible; fourth, he tried adding a little more satire to the generic mixture of *Ralph*; fifth, he worked to better develop and sharpen the differing characters of the two villains, Fernand and Llysanorh'; and finally, he had an evident desire to generally make the novel more entertaining and to polish its prose style.

To lengthen his story, Gernsback realized that extending Ralph and

Alice's tour of the future would be the easiest course; thus, he inserted four new chapters (6 through 9) immediately after the end of what was the seventh installment in the original text, having the lovers visit an Accelerated Plant Growing Farm, discuss twenty-seventh-century economics, confront the menace of Fernand and an "invisible cloak," and learn about and witness the "Conquest of Gravitation." Unfortunately, in adding the new scientific ideas, Gernsback paid little attention to his old scientific ideas, creating obvious inconsistencies between the older text and the new text. At the start of Chapter 9, Ralph excitedly explains and demonstrates his wonderful new invention, a machine that turns spoken language into writing; yet in the original and preceding text, Ralph had been shown using a Menograph that turns human thoughts into language. Surely, with such a machine in place, a new machine that transcribed voices would not be considered a significant or helpful innovation. At the Accelerated Plant Farm, Ralph and Alice enjoy a meal of solid vegetables, with no mention of their previous preference for liquefied food at the "Scientific Restaurant." The new discussion of anti-gravity seems to conflict with much of the technology earlier introduced, as such a powerful tool would surely supplant such crude electrical devices as the Tele-motor-coasters, and also conflicts with the earlier, retained explanation of the "Anti-Gravitator" that powers Ralph's space flyer.

The other entirely new materials — Chapters 13 and 15 — describe what happened to Alice while Ralph pursued her kidnappers through space and provide more information about Fernand and Llysanorh,' as will be discussed; but these are crudely inserted into the story, as they respectively relate events that had already happened in Chapters 12 and 14. One might call them flashbacks, but it seems awkward to have flashbacks that only go back a few hours. However, instead of putting these scenes at more logical points, Gernsback took a lazy approach: the old tenth installment became Chapter 12, followed by a new chapter, and the old eleventh installment became Chapter 14, followed by a new chapter.

Overall, these clumsy additions suggest that Gernsback lacked great concern for truly creating a unified narrative; yet he paradoxically worked very hard to knit the two parts of his story together and made several additions to passages from the earlier installment to achieve that sort of unity. First, while the first installment abruptly began with the Telephot conversation — "Hello, Edward!" "Hello, Ralph!" (1:19) — the 1925 version has a new two-paragraph introduction, with this first paragraph:

> As the vibrations died down in the laboratory the big man arose from the glass chair and viewed the complicated apparatus on the table. It was complete to the last detail. He glanced at the calendar. It was September 1st in the year 2660. Tomorrow was to be a big and busy day for him, for it was to witness the final

phase of the three-year experiment. He yawned and stretched himself to his full height, revealing a physique much larger than that of the average man of his times and approaching that of the huge Martians [25:9].

Not only does this better establish the milieu of the novel, and quickly provide a physical description of his protagonist, but the casual reference to "huge Martians" immediately conveys to readers that this is a future world that has mastered space travel.

Further foreshadowing is cleverly provided in the second chapter, where the old, rather dull description of the Telephot ovation for Ralph's rescue is enlivened by having Ralph notice the faces of Fernand and Llysanorh' and feel vaguely uneasy about them, even without knowing anything about them. The new Chapter 4 has two significant additions: a conversation between Ralph and James where the latter provides all the necessary background information about Alice's two suitors, and a brief and unpleasant encounter between Fernand and the pair after they notice the monument to the last work horse in New York. And the four new chapters in the middle include the exciting adventure of Fernand's abduction of Alice with an invisibility machine and Ralph's frantic effort to devise countermeasures and locate her. Thus, when the space adventure commences, readers of the 1925 version, unlike readers of the 1911–1912 version, already know that this is a world with space travel, are familiar with the characters of Fernand and Llysanorh,' and are prepared by the kidnapping episode for further melodramatic adventures of chase and rescue. (These new materials also resolve a minor inconsistency in the original text: when after the kidnapping Ralph exclaims, "Only that devil 6OO 10 could perform such a dastardly, cowardly trick" [8:600], the statement seems inexplicable, since Ralph at that moment has not displayed and has not been given any knowledge of Fernand; in the 1925 revision, when Ralph immediately suspects Fernand, it is totally understandable.)

As a third concern in revision, Gernsback was aware that all of the scientific lectures worked into his conversations were not always plausible, and he changed the text to ameliorate, if not eliminate, these problems. Consider this passage in the second installment, right after Alice has explained what has happened with the striking weather engineers of her district:

> "What a remarkable case!" he ejaculated, ["]and what a fine scientific understanding you have!"
> "Oh that is nothing. I am somewhat of a scientist myself, and like nothing better than to dabble in papa's laboratory. That's why I was so interested when I saw yours," she added.
> She opened her mouth as if to say something. But at that moment... [2:84].

In the 1925 version, the passage from "ejaculated" to "She opened her mouth" has been removed. When Gernsback was first writing his story, it might have seemed only logical to make the future wife of the world's greatest scientist a scientist herself. But this makes many of the later conversations between Ralph and Alice absurd; any scientist would already know how the Tele-motor-coasters work, how solar power plants work, and so on. So to make Alice a plausible audience for these explanations, Gernsback cannot describe her as a scientist. Yet he cannot go to the other extreme and make her a dummy, as then she could not understand Ralph's explanations; so he retained with slight alteration the assertion in the 1911 version that "Although Miss 412B 423 had a good scientific training, some of the wonders of New York kept her guessing" (5:294), which became, "Although Alice had had a good scientific training, some of the wonders of New York amazed her" (25:81).

There was also a passage in his fourth installment that seemed to bother Gernsback even as he was writing it: James 212B 423's explanation of the Sub-atlantic Tube. Originally, Ralph provokes the lecture abruptly: "and now the scientist spoke out of him, 'tell me all about the new tube.'" James then begins a lecture with "As you of course know" and later starts another phase of his explanation with "You know, of course" (4:231). Gernsback thus signals that he fully realizes this entire discussion is ridiculous. After all, James is talking to only two people: his daughter, who has just come with him through the Tube and knows everything about it, and the world's greatest scientist, who would be surely familiar with such a major scientific achievement. So there is absolutely no reason for James to be explaining everything about the Tube to these two people — except, of course, that *readers* need this information.

Gernsback attempts to eliminate the problem with a key addition to the dialogue. In the 1925 version, Ralph now provokes James' explanation as fol-lows: "And then, the scientist in him to the front: 'Tell me all about this new tube. Busy with my own work I have not followed its progress closely enough to know all the details'" (25:62). And James' description proceeds basically as before, without the "As you of course know" and "You know, of course." This is of course not an ideal solution, since it remains highly unlikely that Ralph would not know "all the details" about the tube, especially since this "Busy" scientist has been previously seen reading the afternoon newspaper, paying special attention to its "technical page" (25:45), and an event like the immi-nent opening of a Subatlantic Tube surely would have been extensively dis-cussed in the newspapers. Yet the additional sentence shows at least that Gernsback was aware of the problem, even if he did not entirely solve it. Again, this is arguably a sign of laziness, since he might have with a little more work simply made the description of the Tube part of the narration, elimi-nating the need to justify a conversation about it.

Fourth, to add some humor to his story, Gernsback expands and recasts the scene when Alice and James first visit Ralph. In both versions, Ralph initially refuses visitors, as he is engaged in scientific work, and after finishing up he warmly welcomes them. But the 1911–1912 text treats these events matter-of-factly:

> The next day Ralph 124C 41, engrossed in deep research work, was interrupted by Peter.
> The great inventor, irritated by the intrusion of his old servant, said a few unkind things and quite lost his temper.
> "But," Peter interjected, "won't you let me explain that the lady whom you ____"
> "Never mind your lady," was the angry reply, "and now, please disappear, and quickly at that!"
> With that he pressed a button nearby, an electromagnet acted and the heavy plate glass door slid down from above, almost brushing Peter's displeased face.... [and Ralph returned to work. Later:]
> As this was all that could be done for the moment 124C 41 summoned Peter.
> "Sir," announced the servant, "Miss 212B 423, the young lady you saved yesterday, has just arrived with her father; both are in the reception room, anxious to see you."
> "Oh, Oh, really!" the great inventor exclaimed, beaming with pleasure. "I shall be down immediately!" [4:229,230].

Here, Ralph's initial refusal and later reversal are not treated in a particularly humorous fashion. But the 1925 text elaborates:

> An apologetic cough came through the entrance to the laboratory. It was nearing one o'clock of the following day.
> Several minutes later it was repeated, to the intense annoyance of the scientist, who had left orders that he was not to be interrupted in his work under any circumstances.
> At the third "ahem!" he raised his head and stared fixedly at the empty space between the door jambs. The most determined optimist in the world could not have spelled welcome in that look.
> Peter, advancing his neck around the corner until one eye met that of his master, withdrew it hastily.
> "Well, what is it?" came from the laboratory, in an irritated harsh voice.
> Peter, in the act of retreating on tiptoe, turned, and once more cocked a solitary eye around the door-jamb. This one feature had the beseeching look of a dog trying to convey by his expression that not for worlds would be have got in the way of your boot.
> "Beg pardon, sir, but there's a young —"
> "Won't see him!"
> "But, sir, it's a young lady —"
> "I'm busy, get out!"
> Peter gulped desperately. "The young lady from —"
> At this moment Ralph pressed a button nearby, an electromagnet acted, and a heavy plate glass door slid down from above, almost brushing Peter's melancholy countenance, terminating the conversation summarily ... [and Ralph returned to work. Later:]

This being all he could do for the present, he pressed the button that raised the glass barrier, and summoned Peter by means of another button.

That individual, looking a trifle more melancholy than usual, responded at once.

"Well, my boy," said Ralph good-humoredly, "the stage is all set for the experiment that will set the whole world by the ears.— But you don't look happy, Peter. What's troubling your dear old soul?"

Peter, whose feelings had evidently been lacerated when the door had been lowered in his face, replied with heavy dignity.

"Beg pardon, sir, but the young lady is still waiting."

"What young lady?" asked Ralph.

"The young lady from Switzerland, sir."

"The— which?"

"The young lady from Switzerland, sir, and her father, sir. They've been waiting a half an hour."

If a bomb had exploded that instant Ralph could not have been more astounded.

"She's here— and you didn't call me? Peter, there are times when I am tempted to throw you out—"

"Pardon sir," replied Peter firmly, "I made bold to assume that you might be interested in the young lady's arrival, and presumed to step into the laboratory to so inform—"

But his master had gone, shedding his laboratory smock as he went. Peter, gathering his dignity about him as a garment, reached the doorway in time to see the elevator slide downwards out of sight [25:51–52,57–58].

Now, not only is the butler Peter a more developed and sympathetic character, but Ralph is being made fun of— the absent-minded scientist who does not pay attention to what he is told and later forgets what had happened — and two previously routine exchanges are considerably enlivened. Further, the passage provides evidence of another shift in Gernsback's approach to science fiction.

In the pages of *Modern Electrics*, it should be recalled, Gernsback presented two different personalities: as Hugo Gernsback, he wrote serious scientific articles and earnest editorials, but in the transparent guise of "Fips," he provided a steady stream of jokes, banter, and parodies. *Ralph 124C 41+*, except for a feeble joke about the Tele-Theater retained in later versions, was manifestly a product of the humorless Gernsback. But in revising this passage, Gernsback was seemingly trying to integrate the two aspects of his public character, to occasionally bring, as it were, the spirit of his parodies of *Ralph* into the text of *Ralph* itself. In the added Chapter 8, his antic muse surfaced again in Ralph's conversations with the befuddled, "none-too-intelligent shopkeeper" (25:165). Thus, even as Gernsback was working to downplay his use of the conventions of love stories, he was sporadically incorporating elements of a new genre — satire.

Fifth, Gernsback wanted to better clarify and differentiate the key characters of Fernand and Llysanorh'. The letters from the two men in the eighth installment of the 1911–1912 text, similar in content to those in Chapter 10 of the 1925 text, announce the differing personalities of the two suitors: Fernand is cold and interested in Alice primarily because of his ego, whereas Llysanorh' is sincere and driven by a genuine love for Alice. But Llysanorh', as it turns out, never actually makes an appearance in the novel, save as a dead body when Ralph catches up with his ship; and the single letter from Fernand and his one meeting with Ralph do not fully convey with any impact Fernand's evil nature.

In the 1925 version, Fernand's despicable nature is fully established by James's warning to Ralph that he might kidnap Alice, by his actual kidnapping attempt using the invisible cloak, and by his unctuous dialogue and evil behavior towards Alice in the new Chapter 13, with passages like this one:

> Fernand entered alone, carefully closing the door behind him. He wore his customary, rather bland smile, and his voice was suave to the point of oiliness.
> "All over our little fit of temper?" he asked.
> Alice stared at him, disdainfully, unanswering. Then her eyes fell upon something in his hand — manacles of glistening steelonium!
> The horror she felt was depicted in her face, for he said, holding them out for her to see, "A pair of bracelets for you, sweetheart. Just as a precautionary measure. You are rather too quick with those hands of yours. But I am not unkind, my dear. You need not wear them if you will only give me your word not to repeat your recent performance" [25:240–41].

In addition, Gernsback rewrites the scene where Ralph boards his flyer and finds Alice absent. Originally, Ralph confronted a surprisingly mild and apologetic Fernand:

> In his right hand he held the Radioperforer and his eyes were lit with intense hate. Facing his enemy he bellowed:
> "You damnable, low-down cur, I want every question answered truthfully and as quickly as I ask them. If you try any tricks or if the full truth is not forthcoming, by God, I will blow you to eternity as sure as I live. Now then: Where is Alice?"
> "I don't know, but let me explain and you will sympathize with me when you hear the story." Fernand was breathing hard, and was leaning heavily against the wall of the flyer. Only now did Ralph observe the careworn, hard drawn face of his enemy and instinctively he felt that he would hear the entire truth from him. A most amazing story it was that followed:
> "Go ahead," Ralph said. "I am listening."
> "First I wish to apologize for having abducted your fiancee. Only you, who love her, perhaps no more than I did, can understand my actions. I felt as if I could not live without her and I risked everything to conquer her. My mind was love-crazed, my actions, as perhaps you can understand better than anyone else, were like those of a drowning man coming up for the third time, trying to

clutch a sun-ray with his hands. But I have come to my senses, I am happy to say, and you need not fear any interference from me, quite the contrary, I will try to make good on whatever I have spoiled so far" [10:689].

And after hearing his story, Ralph is somewhat conciliatory:

For a while he sat deeply engrossed in thought, then he jumped up and said: "While I should leave you to your fate, I feel charitably inclined. I will turn your machine around and direct you Earthward, so you will intercept the Earth in about thirty hours. Although you cannot steer, you can accelerate and retard the speed of your flyer and you will thus not run any risk of a collision with the Earth. Good-bye" [10:690].

In the 1925 version of their final encounter, there is no effort to portray Fernand sympathetically — no mention of his "careworn, hard drawn face"— Ralph is more angry and confrontational, and Fernand makes no apologies. This is how they meet in the 1925 version:

"Where is she?" asked Ralph hoarsely. "What have you done with her? Answer me, or by God, I'll blow you into Eternity!" and, aiming his Radioperforer at Fernand's head, he spoke with such ferocity that the other shrank involuntarily.
"I don't know," he muttered, weakly. "It's God's truth I don't know. The Martian got her. He took her away and left me drugged." His voice trailed off and he seemed about to collapse.
"You're a liar!" growled Ralph, but his tone lacked the conviction of his words. There was that in the other's voice that rang true. Mechanically, he cut the cords that bound Fernand, and the man rolled over helplessly. He was weak and dazed, and altogether too broken in spirit to make any further trouble. His nerve was gone [25:226].

While the original version incongruously made Fernand suddenly sympathetic and noble, he is now only portrayed as weak — an impression further heightened by their equally different parting:

He turned savagely on Fernand still crouched against the wall. "I'm tempted to leave you to the fate the Martian intended for you. God knows it wouldn't be half what you deserve."
"Don't do that, in Heaven's name," mumbled the other. "Don't leave me here like this."
The scientist looked at him contemptuously for a moment.
"Bah!" he said scornfully, "can't you even take your medicine like a man? But I'll turn your machine around and direct it Earthward. You will intercept the Earth in about thirty hours. You can't steer, but you can accelerate or retard the speed of your flyer, and need not collide with the Earth if you are careful.
"And remember this," he added grimly, "if you and I ever meet again I will pound your miserable cowardly body into jelly!" [25:232–233].

Fernand thus fully becomes a melodramatic villain — thoroughly evil in his scheming, abject and weak in the face of reversal — and Ralph appropriately treats him with greater anger and less respect.

Finally, Gernsback seeks to blacken Fernand's character by revising his letter. In the 1911 text, the letter reads as follows (omitting a passage that is virtually identical in both versions):

Well, everything is fine — for everyone else not for me. However — you know me — I am not downed so easily. Fact is, I might just as well run against a steelonium wall as against Alice. One is as hard to conquer as the other. That, however, is to my liking. I love obstacles, especially if they are pretty as Alice. I never wanted her more in my life than now, now that she has thrown me down. I suppose if she really had given me encouragement, I would not care a lot for her. Now it is different. I will have her. I will make her love me and I will use force to gain my end.

I have told you already of Llysanorh', the funny Martian. It is too funny to seek him look at Alice with his big black horse eyes. I do believe he really is in love with her, but these Martians certainly can control their emotions.

If Alice should ever take a liking to this lanky seven foot Llysanorh', she'd be lost to me, Ralph, and the rest of the world. That fellow certainly can be sugary if he wants to. However, I really think she loves that crazy Ralph scientist and, as I said before, between him and that Martian I have absolutely no chance. I know Alice could learn to love me if she really knew me well, but she never had an occasion. I am going to provide for that occasion. Yes, I will carry her off....

The purpose of this letter is to ask you kindly to attend for me to the several matters as per enclosed rolls. You will understand everything after you read the instructions. I do not think I will be away longer than three months at the latest and you will see from the gray document that I empower you to take charge of my affairs. I thank you in advance for your pains. Now I must close; I will send you a message from on board the machine if everything goes right.

Sincerely yours,
FERNAND [8:498–99]

For the purposes of the story, this version of the letter is functional and could have been retained without change for the 1925 version. Instead, Gernsback completely reworked the letter:

You have heard the gossip, but don't fear my having a broken heart. I am not easily downed, and I have a card or two yet to play in this game.

Fact is, Alice is as hard to conquer as a steelonium wall is to break through. That, however, is to my liking, my dear Paul. I love obstacles, particularly when the goal is as pretty as Alice. I have never wanted her more than now that she has thrown me down. Perhaps if she had ever encouraged me I would not have cared a rap for her. But — this opposition inflames me! Now I will have her. I *will* have her, and she shall love me, mark my words.

I have mentioned to you before the ridiculous Martian, Llysanorh,' I believe. It is very amusing to see him staring at Alice with adoration in those enormous eyes of his. I really believe he is in love with her, but these Martians are so self-controlled it is hard to tell anything about them.

If Alice had fallen in love with this lanky, seven-foot Llysanorh' she would have been lost to me, and to all the rest of the world. That fellow certainly can be sugary when he wants to. However, she really imagines that she's in love with this crazy scientist, and right now I'm decidedly *de trop*. That worries me very little, I assure you. She will soon learn to love me once I can get her away from him. And I am going to provide for that....

Before I close I must ask you to attend to several matters for me, as per enclosed rolls. You will understand everything better after you read the instructions. I do not expect to be away more than three months at the latest, and you will see from the gray document that I empower you to take charge of my affairs. I will send you a message from on board the machine if all goes well.

Until then,
Fernand. [25:195–97]

In this version, Gernsback first emphasizes that Fernand is motivated more by his ego than by love with the language of gamesmanship — "I have a card or two yet to play in this game" and "I love obstacles, particularly when *the goal* is as pretty as Alice." His lack of genuine affection is underlined by changing the line "I would not care a lot for her" to "I would not have cared a *rap* for her." Instead of saying "I really think she loves" Ralph, this Fernand, too egotistical to accept Alice's genuine feelings, says "she really *imagines* that she's in love with" him, and the name of one of his rivals has not fully registered in the brain of this self-centered person: it is "Llysanorh', *I believe*." Sarcastic phrases like "don't fear my having a broken heart" and "my dear Paul" make Fernand sound more villainous, and the new Fernand is even less polite: he does not "ask ... kindly" for his friend's help, does not "thank [him] in advance for [his] pains," and closes with "Until then," not "Sincerely yours."

While he makes Fernand more despicable, Gernsback also adds material to make Llysanorh' more sympathetic and likeable. First, the added Chapter 15 fully conveys Llysanorh's sincere, tormented feelings with an exchange between him and Alice:

It was then that the pent-up emotions of months burst the bonds of self-restraint that he had forced upon himself.

"Why!" he cried passionately, "you ask me why! Can't you see why? How can you look into my eyes and not know why? Because I am a man — because I am a fool — good God, because I love you!" He flung himself upon his knees, clasping her about the waist with his arms.

"I worship you, I adore you — I always shall. You must love me, you cannot help but love me. I love you so much, Alice, Alice, my dearest, my beloved."

He threw his head back and looked into her face imploringly, as if by the very force of his love she must respond.... For a time neither spoke. At last he said in quiet tones strangely in contrast with his late passion, "You can't hate me, Alice, I love you too much."

"No," she said, gently, "I don't hate you, Llysanorh,' but oh, can't you see how hopeless all this is? I love Ralph, and if you keep me here forever I will still love him."

She got a glimpse, then, of the terrible struggle this man of Mars had had with his conscience.

"I know, I know," he groaned, "I have gone over that ground many times — many times, but I can not — will not — give you up. I tell you," he went on with a return of his former frenzied emotion, "that rather than let him have you I will kill you with my own hands. At least, when you are dead I will be sure that no other man can possess you" [25:268–70].

Next, rather than placing the two men's letters side by side without comment, as in the original version, Gernsback adds a transitional passage in the 1925 text:

Long after [Llysanorh's] missive had gone, he sat rigid, motionless, by the window with unseeing eyes fixed on the city below him. At last he rose with a sigh and left the room. Was there no way out of such misery? Was there no straw he could grasp?

Of a very different caliber was an epistle sent by Fernand 60O 10 to his friend Paul 9B 1261 [25:194–95].

These words emphasize the differences between the two men.

Finally, Gernsback also revised Llysanorh's letter — not as dramatically as he did with Fernand's, but with some small changes to place the Martian in a better light. In the 1911–1912 text:

Although I am booked on the *Terrestral* which departs to-morrow, I have cancelled my reservation and consequently will not arrive on Mars November thirty-first as planned. I do not know if I will book on the next transport, in fact I don't know where I am at. My case seems hopeless. I should never have come to this earth. As you have guessed already — it's love at first sight. Never mind her name. You who have never visited this planet cannot understand, consequently it does not matter. Inasmuch as intermarriage of Martians and Terrestrials is forbidden by law, here as well as on Mars, this makes it all the more hopeless for me. I have tried everything to free myself— in vain. Chemicals and Radio-treatments seem only to accentuate my longing for the wonderful creature I love so madly, and I know by this time that I can never free myself. The good part is that she does not know how violently I love her, as I have always been careful not to betray myself. I know she likes me, but she very probably does not love me — in fact I can only hope that she does not; it would only heighten my agony to know that she should have to suffer on my account.

I will, I suppose, go the way of all Martians who fall in love with Terrestrials. There is no return. A little Listadinide injected under the skin will free me from all. Don't be shocked — you know my strong mind. If I could get out of it, I would, that is all there is to be said. I have lost and admit it.

Please hand enclosed documents to my Second and break the news gently to him. I have arranged everything of importance and there is nothing I can ask you to do for me. Please do not mourn me, but keep me in mind and think sometimes of

Your unhappy friend,
LLYSANORH' [8:498]

In the 1925 text:

> Although I am booked on the *Terrestral* which departs tomorrow, I have cancelled my reservation and consequently will not arrive on Mars November thirty-first as planned. I do not know whether I shall take passage on the next transport or not. In fact, I don't know what I shall do. I am mad with despair and anguish. A thousand times over have I wished that I had never come to this planet!
>
> I have not told you before, but as perhaps you have guessed from my previous letters, I am in love with a Terrestrial woman. Never mind her name. I loved her from the first moment I saw her. You, who have never visited the Earth, can hardly understand. It does not matter.
>
> I have tried in every way to free myself from this mad infatuation, but it is hopeless. Chemicals and Radio-treatments seem but to accentuate my longing for that which is forever beyond my reach. I thought at first that I could conquer myself, but I know now that I cannot, and the knowledge is driving me to madness.
>
> She has never known, and I think no one else here does. I have told none but you, my friend. Always I feared that in some way I might betray myself to her. There are times now when I wish that I had.
>
> And yet — to have her suffer as I am suffering — I could not have borne that.
>
> I will, I suppose, go the way of all Martians who have had the misfortune to care for a Terrestrial. A little *Listadinide* injected under the skin will free me from an existence which has become a daily torture unless I find a way to evade the harsh laws.
>
> Please hand the enclosed documents to my Second. If I do not see you again do not grieve for me, but remember our friendship, and think sometimes of your unhappy friend.
>
> Llysanorh' [25:193–94]

While some information is omitted because it has now already been conveyed in previous chapters, the heightened and polished rhetoric definitely makes Llysanorh' a more likable and understandable character. The clichés are removed: "love at first sight," "break the news gently." The mild "My case seems hopeless. I should never have come to this earth" is replaced by the more passionate "I am mad with despair and anguish. A thousand times over have I wished I had never come to this planet!" The prosaic "my longing for the wonderful creature I love so madly" becomes "my longing for that which is forever beyond my reach," and the suicide drug will not "free [him] from all" but will "free [him] from an existence that has become a daily torture." And repeated and emphatic use of the terms "mad" and "madness" — "mad with despair and anguish," "this mad infatuation," "driving me to madness" — also illustrate his tormented mental state. In all these ways, then, a character only briefly sketched in the original version becomes a better developed, even sympathetic figure, and this new Llysanorh' starkly contrasts with the manipulative, devious Fernand.

The differences between the two versions of Llysanorh's letter also illustrate Gernsback's final concern in revision: to improve the quality of his writing. There are many places in the text where small changes were made seemingly only for stylistic reasons. Consider, for example, the conclusion of the dead-alive dog experiment. In the 1911–1912 text:

> From that moment on the dog made rapid progress, and at half past five — one hour and ten minutes after the dog had been lifted out of the glass case — the animal was able to lie on its paws and to lick up some milk with surprising avidity.
>
> At that moment the audience, who for almost thirty minutes had stood up in their seats, burst out in wild applause, scaring the dog almost to death. Everyone wished to shake hands with Ralph 124C 41 and he was visibly moved. He was the first man to give life to a dead body, dead for years; he had conquered nature, achieved the impossible; he had opened a new era for suffering humanity, for what could be achieved with a dog could be achieved with a human being.
>
> It would now be possible for human bodies to have life suspended for centuries, perhaps, and live again after the world had moved on and new generations had appeared. Truly, it was wonderful.
>
> As he descended in a dazed condition to his room a few minutes later, he could not forget a certain young lady, who with tears in her exquisite big black eyes had taken his hand into hers and with a vibrating voice full of emotion had said, "Oh you wonderful, marvelous being!" [4:233]

As first written, the scene seems implausible — after watching a dog gradually become active for over an hour, why would people suddenly "burst out in wild applause" when it drank some milk? — and not quite an appropriate response to Ralph's achievement, better suited to his rescue of Alice from the avalanche than to a remarkable scientific achievement; nor are the adjectives "wonderful" and "marvelous" really fitting. In revision, Gernsback added some dialogue to the description and presented a more subdued, and more effective, response:

> In a few minutes more the dog was lying on its paws and licking up milk when Ralph turned to the group and said:
>
> "Gentlemen, the experiment is concluded and I believe the condition of the animal at this moment establishes sufficient proof of my theory."
>
> As the reporters eagerly dashed from the laboratory to get to the nearest Telephot in order to communicate the news to the waiting world the scientists gathered around Ralph and one of them, a white haired old man considered to be the dean of the "Plus" men, voiced the sentiments of the entire group.
>
> "Ralph, this is one of the greatest gifts that science has brought to humanity. For what you have done with a dog, you can do with a human being. I only regret for myself that you had not lived and conducted this experiment when I was a young man, that I might have, from time to time, lived in suspended animation from century to century, and from generation to generation as it will now be possible for human beings to do."

The vista opened up by the results of this experiment in the minds of the other scientists had dazed them and it was with the most perfunctory good-byes that they left the scene of the experiment, enveloped with their thoughts of the future.

Tired and exhausted by the nervous strain of the afternoon Ralph, a few minutes later, lay down on his bed for a few hours' rest. But as he closed his eyes there came to him a vivid picture of a pair of warm dark eyes, radiating admiration, trust and something more that aroused an emotion he had never before experienced [25:71–72].

Here, Ralph's statement, not the dog eating, serves to signal the successful end of the experiment; the rushing reporters add a touch of reality to the scene; and the old scientist's speech and the stunned silence of the others seem a more logical and evocative reaction than their original "wild applause."

In addition to dramatically changed scenes, there are scattered throughout the text short passages that Gernsback tried to polish up a bit. Two examples: when Alice sees the monument to "the last Horse in Harness" in New York, this is her 1911 reaction:

"The poor thing," murmured the young lady, "but I think the world is better off without torturing poor dumb beasts when electricity can well take care of all the work."

Her companion, touched by this feminine remark, smiled softly [5:296].

The moment is elaborated on in the 1925 text:

"The poor thing," she said, "it looks so pitiful, doesn't it? To think that once the poor dumb animals were made to labor! It is much better nowadays with electricity doing all the work."

Ralph smiled at this very feminine remark. It was like her, he thought tenderly, to feel sympathy for even this former beast of burden [25:89].

Instead of running Alice's reaction into one sentence, Gernsback separates her reactions — sympathy for the animal, regret at the former practice of animal labor, and gratitude for the improvements in her world — into three sentences; and Ralph spells out in his thoughts exactly how these remarks reflect favorably on Alice's character. Also, consider her first reaction to the Signalizers:

It was an inspiring sight to watch the hundreds of light shafts, especially the ones changing colors, the weird beauty of it all thrilling sensitive Miss 212B 423 into ecstasy:

"Oh, if I could only watch this beautiful spectacle forever!" she exclaimed, "it is so amazing, so superb. A fairyland could not demand more to satisfy its tenants" [7:421].

In the 1925 text:

It was a wonderful sight and the weird beauty of the colored shafts thrilled Alice immeasurably.

"Oh, it is like a Fairyland," she exclaimed. "I could watch it forever" [25:115].

Here, Alice's rather overheated response to the traffic lights of future air travel is shortened and toned down: the sight no longer excites Alice to "ecstasy," and the awkward-sounding "A fairyland could not demand more to satisfy its tenants" is effectively reduced to "Oh, it is like a Fairyland."

These passages also convey another noteworthy aspect of Gernsback's prose revisions: a tendency towards shorter sentences — a difference in style that can be quantified. In the tennis game passages above, the 1911–1912 version consisted of 819 words and 41 sentences, an average of 20 words per sentence; the 1925 version consisted of 343 words and 28 sentences, an average of 12.25 words per sentence. In the abduction scenes, the 1911–1912 version had 722 words and 34 sentences, an average of 21.25 words per sentence; the 1925 version had 393 words and 23 sentences, an average of 17 words per sentence. Perhaps Gernsback simply came to prefer the clarity and forcefulness of short sentences; but consideration of his audience could have been another factor. While *Modern Electrics* consistently addressed an adult audience, Gernsback may have gradually learned that many of his readers were much younger; and he may have reduced his average sentence length for the benefit of posited young readers. Thus, just as the diminution of the romantic element suggests a growing perception that science fiction had mostly male readers, Gernsback's shorter sentences suggest a growing perception that science fiction had many younger readers.

As a final illustration of several concerns operating at once, consider the two versions of the scene after James completes his lecture on the Subatlantic Tube. In the 1911 text:

> [Alice] went on to explain the details of the journey and 124C 41 watched her with increasing interest.
>
> Here at last was a girl who interested him. He, who had long since given up hope of making the acquaintance of a girl who would excite more than passing interest in him, began to think that he had found her at last.
>
> Alice 212B 423 was tall and lithe. She carried a wonderful head on queenly shoulders, and her Greek masterfully chiseled profile, crowned with a mass of black curly hair, would command attention everywhere.
>
> Her sparkling, black, vivacious eyes had an impenetrable depth, and when they did not dance mischievously, as was invariable when she laughed, a sorrowful expression would sometimes light up those deep-sea eyes — an expression that was quite in contrast with her general appearance. She was quite tall and carried herself with unusual grace; moreover she was quick in all her movements, and a trained eye would soon detect that she must be a great lover of out-door sport.
>
> The more 124C 41 watched her, the more he knew that his search was ended and that here at last was a young woman worth his while. The afternoon having progressed, he invited father and daughter to be his guests for a few days. His invitation after some hesitation was finally accepted. He then summoned Peter to show the guests their rooms on the seventeenth floor of the tower, and before

they ascended he invited them to be present in the laboratory at four that afternoon [4:232].

The improved 1925 version:

> As she spoke Ralph watched her with keen interest. Here was a girl who attracted him. Beneath the vivacity that so fascinated him he sensed the strength of her character, and the depth of her mind.
>
> "I am so glad to be in New York," she was saying. "Do you know, this is my first visit here for ages. Why, the last time I can just barely remember, I was such a little girl. Father has been promising me a trip for years," with a laughingly reproachful glance at him, "but it took an avalanche to get us started."
>
> "I'm afraid I've been a neglectful father of late years," said her father, "but my work has kept me tied pretty close to home. I, too, am pleased to be here once more, and my visit promises to be doubly interesting, for I understand that your great dog experiment will be completed today. I am looking forward to receiving the earliest reports of it at the hotel."
>
> "But I can't permit you to spend your days here in a hotel," protested Ralph. "Of course you must both be my guests. Yes, yes," as they seemed about to demur, "I won't take no for an answer. I am counting on showing you New York, and, as for my experiment, it will give me great pleasure to have you both present in my laboratory this afternoon at four."
>
> He pressed a button. "Peter will show you to your rooms, and I will send some one for your luggage" [25:66–67].

Gernsback again reduces the romance element by severely shortening Ralph's reverie and eliminating some pretty-sounding but essentially empty description of Alice. He ameliorates two minor inconsistencies in the story: first, since James has already provided much superfluous description of the Subatlantic Tube, it seems doubly incongruous that Alice would continue the farce with her own extended account of the Tube; thus, the reference to Alice "explain[ing] the details of the journey" is removed. Second, it always seemed implausible that the daughter of a wealthy engineer working on an underground tube to connect France and New York would have never been to New York before; the original text's lame explanation is a brief comment preceding Ralph's tour: "for some unknown reason she had never visited New York" (5:293). Now, Gernsback offers a somewhat reasonable explanation for her unfamiliarity with the city. He also enlivens the passage by casting much of it in dialogue form, and he uses that dialogue to better characterize Ralph's guests: James, the caring but distracted father, Alice the loving but playful daughter.

No one has ever called *Ralph 124C 41+* a masterpiece of literature, and it manifestly is not. But in revising the novel for book publication, Gernsback demonstrated that he could at times recognize bad writing and faulty story logic, and that he could occasionally do something to ameliorate such flaws. To be sure, innumerable problems remain in the awkward construction, disparate moods, and inept writing of the novel; but the 1925 *Ralph* is in every respect significantly better than the 1911–1912 *Ralph*, and Gernsback deserves some credit for his many improvements.

The 1929 Version

Because Gernsback in the late 1920s was involved in many publishing and business ventures, as described in Ashley's *The Gernsback Days*, he surely lacked the time and inclination to revise *Ralph 124C 41+* again when he reprinted the novel in the Spring 1929 issue of *Amazing Stories Quarterly*. Yet *someone* spent an appreciable amount of time working on the text, as the innumerable minor changes are far too pervasive and frequent to attribute to accident or a presumptuous typesetter.

Other evidence indicates that Gernsback did not make these changes. First, none of these emendations were retained in the 1950 edition that Gernsback supervised,[13] which basically followed the 1925 text. This would suggest that Gernsback either was unaware of, or disapproved of, the 1929 changes. Second, the 1929 editor clearly lacked Gernsback's experience: growing up near the Alps, Gernsback knew exactly what an "avalanche" was, and describing Alice's plight in Chapter 1, he used that term every time; the 1929 editor, seeking word variety, often substituted "landslide," a different phenomenon. Finally, the 1929 changes consistently reflect fussiness about grammar and punctuation, clarity of phrasing, and parallel structure, all concerns foreign to Gernsback, who employed a looser, and at times colloquial style. But those concerns that characterize the prose of T. O'Conor Sloane, Associate Editor of *Amazing Stories* and *Amazing Stories Quarterly*, and Gernsback's successor as their editor.

Sloane is most probably the editor of the 1929 text for two additional reasons. By all accounts, Sloane was most responsible for the daily business of producing Gernsback's science fiction magazines, so he certainly had the means and opportunity to alter the prose of *Ralph 124C 41+*. As for motive, when Sloane became editor of *Amazing Stories*, he became known for compulsive tinkering with his contributors' prose, much to their displeasure. For example, Alva Rogers reports that E. E. Smith sent a novel to *Astounding Stories* in the 1930s because "he was thoroughly sick of *Amazing*'s rewriting his material" (*A Requiem for Astounding* 14). Sloane himself alludes to this tendency and the conflicts it generated in a 1929 *Amazing Stories* editorial, "The Editor and the Reader": "Many authors are unduly sensitive. In pre–Victorian days authors were very willing to submit their writings to critics for emendation. But the author of today often objects to even minor changes.... Any printer who has had extensive experience with authors can tell strange stories about the way they act with regard to corrections of their copy. They are a very sensitive class of people" (485). Though there is no definitive proof, then, ample evidence indicates that Sloane edited the 1929 text, and that is what I assume here.

The changes that Sloane made in *Ralph 124C 41+* can be conveniently categorized as beneficial, pointless, and ruinous.

First, to give Sloane his due, he occasionally improves Gernsback's writing. He was vigilant in correcting minor errors and standardizing Gernsback's erratic capitalization. At times, he notices and removes redundant or superfluous language: from Gernsback's "His own body could not grow cold as its heat could not be given off to the atmosphere, nor could his body grow cold" (25:28) he removes the repetitive "nor could his body grow cold" (29:8); from "All at once there was seen an enormous colored circle which revolved with great rapidity, becoming smaller and smaller, as though it were shrinking" (25:117) he removes the unnecessary "as though it were shrinking" (29:23); and from "This cool abduction of herself" (25:238) he removes "of herself" (29:43). He replaces long, wordy phrases with tighter constructions: "Students who have failed in their studies" (25:[5]) becomes "Poor students" (29:4); "the certain destruction of himself" (25:29) becomes "his own certain destruction" (29:8); "It seemed that the heat of those flames was so intense" (25:31) becomes "The heat of those flames seemed so intense" (29:8); "The vista opened up by the results of this experiment in the minds of the other scientists had dazed them" (25:72) becomes "The vista opened up by the results of this experiment had dazed the scientists" (29:16); "tobacco planted and harvested that day" (25:135) becomes "freshly harvested tobacco" (29:27); "such as sugar, milk, and many others" (25:137) becomes "such as sugar and milk" (29:27); and "Confident of success, sure of victory" (25:256) becomes "Confident of victory" (29:47). Some of his tiny word changes are defensible: a phrase referring to the novel, "the conception therein," (25:[5]) becomes "the conceptions therein" (29:4), and "swung onto the Intercontinental Service" (25:11) becomes "swung into" (29:4). And at least one revised sentence is a clear improvement: "she could not deny the fact of his genuine, and fervent love for her" (25:271) becomes "She could not deny the fact that his love for her was genuine" (29:49).

Other changes in the 1929 text are harder to defend. Some of them are manifestly purposeless: "for a minute" (25:162) becomes "for a moment" (29:30), and "the New Yorker, loving his town" (25:82) becomes "the New Yorker who loves his town" (29:18). Next, Sloane displays a mania for scientifically exact and accurate language, even when the problems are trivial: Gernsback's "permit the heat to pass from one atom to another" (25:28) becomes "from one molecule to another" (29:8), since heat is a molecular phenomenon, and "the original supply taken from the earth is used over and over by altering the carbonic acid by means of automatic generators" (25:219–20) becomes "is used over and over by absorbing the carbonic acid and organic emanations by means of automatic apparatus" (29:40), apparently because it seemed incorrect to speak of "altering" carbonic acid and to omit "organic emanations." When Gernsback wrote, "a head of wheat grown in the year 2900 was about three inches long, while the present year's crop showed a length of more than six inches, or twice as much flour content per stalk" (25:132), Sloane found this scandalously imprecise; if the new heads were "more than six inches," it must be "or more than twice as much flour content" (29:25). Other examples of revisions along these lines include "flat tennis racquets" (25:187) becoming "parchment covered tennis racquets" (29:35), and seeing if a package "was franked correctly" (25:110) becoming seeing "if it had the proper postage stamps on it" (29:22).

Finally, Sloane's desire for proper sentence structure often produces revisions that are neither better nor worse than the originals, like corrections of a faulty modifier (James's statement "but being one of the consulting engineers of the new electromagnetic tube, my daughter and I" [25:61] becomes "but I, being one ..." [29:14]), irregular sentence order ("Autograph-hunting women he usually dismissed" [25:14] becomes "He usually dismissed autograph-hunting women" [29:6]), and sloppy parallelism ("exactly as handwriting by different persons may vary, but still you can read because the characteristics are the same" [25:172–73] becomes "may vary, yet be easily read because" [29:32]). To epitomize this sort of revision, Sloane's alteration of "The silver mouthpiece was then placed in the mouth and one pressed upon a red button" (25:86) to "and a button was pressed" (29:18) does provide two balanced passive constructions, but it is hardly a better sentence.

Most noticeable, however, are the ways that Sloane makes Gernsback's writing worse. Occasionally, the contents of the narrative are seriously harmed. In Gernsback's Chapter 1, it seems perfectly logical that a powerful energy beam would be able to melt or vaporize an "avalanche" of snow and ice; but this would obviously not work against Sloane's "landslide" of dirt and rocks. Belatedly, Sloane seemingly recognized the problem, because he changed Gernsback's description of the beam's results, "the entire avalanche was being reduced to hot water and steam" (25:31), to "the entire landslide was being reduced to hot water, steam and gravel" (29:8); but the potentially damaging "gravel" generated by Sloane's revision has vanished in the next sentence, where both versions speak only of "A torrent of hot water" rushing towards Alice's house (25:31; 29:8). In Chapter 8, to justify his invisibility device, Gernsback provides a footnote: "In 1925 John L. Reinartz, working with ultra-short radio waves, actually made it possible to look through solid metal plates with the naked eye" (25:157), which sounds impressive enough. Sloane gives a more detailed version that only emphasizes how unreliable and irrelevant this work actually was: "In RADIO NEWS of June, 1925, it told how John L. Reinartz, working with ultra-short radio waves, thought that he had made it possible to look through solid metal with the naked eye. The metal, gold, if thin enough, transmits green light, and if still thinner, transmits purple light" (29:30). If, as Sloane implies, all Reinartz did was to beam light through extremely thin sheets of metal, this has absolutely nothing to do with the sort of invisibility effect Gernsback is describing. (Surely, a wise editor would have simply omitted this note.) Finally, in Chapter 13, when Alice responds to her kidnapping by rushing to the door of Fernand's spacecraft and trying to open it — which would of course kill all the occupants — Gernsback specifies that such a murder-suicide was precisely her intent: "Fernand wrenched at her hands in real fear that she would succeed in her purpose, which was evidently their destruction" (25:239). But Sloane ends the sentence prematurely, "in real fear that she might succeed in her purpose" (29:44), which could suggest that Alice was simply trying to escape and stupidly did not understand that opening a spacecraft door would be fatal.

Sloane also lacks even Gernsback's rudimentary sense of style. Gernsback's term "Menograph" is a reasonably euphonious and logical portmanteau blend of "mental phonograph": Sloane uses "mentigraph," a more formal word construction, but with an unfortunately playful, even trivial sound: "minty graph." Gernsback's Alice asks: "I wonder if you know where I am?" (25:12); Sloane's Alice asks: "I wonder if you know what city I am talking from?" (29:4,6) Gernsback says the avalanche "was sweeping down the mountain-side" and that it "rushed down the mountain" (25:29,44); Sloane substitutes the terms "creeping down" and "crept down" (29:8,11), perhaps more accurate descriptions of an avalanche's pace, but words clearly lacking in drama, implying that Alice might have escaped harm by calmly walking away. According to Gernsback, the fleeing Fernand "had a handicap of 400,000 miles" (25:221); Sloane says that he "enjoyed" such a handicap, hardly an apt word for the occasion (29:40).

On a few occasions, Sloane's revisions damage Gernsback's efforts to bring out his characters' personality. When Alice gets flustered because she called the great scientist "Ralph," he graciously replies, "I hope you will always call me that" (25:92). Sloane misses the point in changing this to "I hope you will always talk like that to me" (29:19). When Llysanorh' has captured Alice, he tells her "nothing is wrong with the flyer. It is I — I with whom everything is wrong" (25:267) — a statement whose poetic metaphor (the Martian is like a damaged spacecraft) and awkwardly formal construction are both perfectly suited to Llysanorh's personality. Sloane reduces this to the considerably less poetic "nothing is wrong with the flyer. It is I — I who am wrong" (29:49), further adding the false sense that Llysanorh' is in some way admitting guilt. And when Alice tells the Martian that "I thought you were serious," Gernsback's Llysanorh' dramatically responds, "I was never more serious" (25:268); Sloane's Llysanorh' prosaically responds, "I am serious" (29:49). And Gernsback often would deliberately use unusual word order in order to end a sentence on a dramatic note; Sloane insists upon standard word order, whatever the consequences. One conspicuous example is the sentence where Ralph discovers Alice is dead: Gernsback's sentence "The sight that presented itself to him as he crawled into Llysanorh's machine drew from him an involuntary agonized cry" (25:262) ends effectively with the evocative "cry"; Sloane numbly revises this to "drew an involuntary agonized cry from him" (29:48). Other cases include Gernsback's "on which lay his beloved" (25:283), as compared to Sloane's "on which his beloved lay" (29:52), and Gernsback's "she became increasingly aware that her situation was desperate" (25:270), as compared to Sloane's "she became increasingly apprehensive of her situation" (29:49).

And any discussion of Sloane's revising technique must mention his absolute obsessiveness about adding commas, though he did not fully understand the rules. He apparently believed, for example, that all participle phrases must be enclosed in commas, which at times led to infelicities. Gernsback's sentence "She looked at the man smiling in the faceplate of the Telephot almost dumb with an emotion that came very near to being reverence" (25:32) is perfectly clear; Sloane's version, "She looked at the man, smiling in the faceplate of the Telephot, almost dumb ..." (29:8) introduces an ambiguity: is Ralph or Alice smiling? More broadly, Gernsback's tendency to omit commas sometimes helps to make his prose move more rapidly; and Sloane's added commas in these passages needlessly slow down the pace. Thus in Chapter 8, arguably the most exciting chapter, Sloane adds no fewer than 13 commas, and in the equally fast-paced first part of Chapter 10, he adds 10 commas. To understand the problem, consider two sentences describing Ralph's actions after Alice's kidnapping. Gernsback's text: "Leaving the driver where he was Ralph dashed into the building. Meeting Peter he did not stop, only motioned him to the cab while he himself sprang to the nearest telephot" (25:202). Sloane's text: "Leaving the driver where he was, Ralph dashed into the building. Meeting Peter, he did not stop; he only motioned him to the cab, while he himself sprang to the nearest telephot" (29:37). Gernsback's prose appropriately moves at breakneck speed; Sloane, by adding three commas, changing Gernsback's one comma to a semi-colon, and making a verb phrase into a clause, slows it down to a snail's pace. Twice, Sloane also dampens the energy level with end punctuation: Ralph's exclamation to Alice "You were

wonderful!" (25:98) becomes "You were wonderful." (29:20) Ralph's rumi-
nations "Thoughts of high frequency wireless waves — of X-rays — of Fernand —" (25:156) becomes "Thoughts of high energy wireless waves — of
X-rays — of Fernand." (29:30)

To be sure, Sloane was not consistently energetic in revising *Ralph*: whole
pages of text were left virtually unchanged — save for the inevitable new commas — then there is suddenly a phrase added or paragraph rewritten. Also,
except for one short explanatory paragraph following Lylette's death in the
vacuum of space (25:82), nothing was omitted from Gernsback's text, and
there were no substantive changes in its contents. Still, the overall effect is of
a novel that is clumsier, stodgier, and grayer than Gernsback's 1925 novel —
a situation that leads to two interesting conclusions.

First, while the 1911–1912 version has long been unavailable, and while
the 1925, 1950, 1958, and 2000 book editions were not widely distributed, the
1929 *Amazing Stories Quarterly* text, thanks to many private collections and a
microfilm series, is easily accessible to modern scholars; thus, it is logical to
assume that this is the most frequently consulted version. Yet this is also a
significantly corrupted text that does not truly reflect Gernsback's writing style.
Gernsback surely deserves to be described as a terrible writer, but his reputation may be slightly worse than it should be, because so many people have
only read the work of this bad writer as it was edited by an even worse writer.

Second, it has long been supposed that Sloane chafed under the control
of Gernsback and that, when bankruptcy forced Gernsback to relinquish control of *Amazing Stories* in 1929, Sloane was more than happy to stay on with
the new owners as their chief editor. Yet there is now reason to suppose that
Gernsback may have had a reason to dislike Sloane. At the very least, Sloane
displayed a certain amount of chutzpah in revising his boss's prose, however
minimally in his eyes, and Gernsback would not have needed to carry out a
detailed, line-by-line comparison to detect Sloane's handiwork; merely by
glancing through the first few pages, Gernsback would have spotted what
were arguably Sloane's two most egregious and objectionable revisions, "landslide" and "mentigraph." Therefore, Sloane may have failed to accompany
Gernsback because he had not been invited; and when Sloane wrote about
the "very sensitive" authors who "object[ ] to even minor changes," one of
the writers he had in mind may have been Hugo Gernsback himself.

The 1950 Version

After Gernsback sold his remaining science fiction magazine, *Wonder
Stories*, in 1936, he officially withdrew from the field, though he maintained

his interest in science fiction by launching his short-lived science fiction comic book, *Superworld Comics,* and by writing farcical articles for the annual magazines he sent as Christmas cards. And in the late 1940s, when hardcover publishers were suddenly anxious to publish science fiction novels, it must have seemed to Gernsback that this was the appropriate time to publish a new edition of *Ralph.* In theory, Gernsback might have used this opportunity to further revise and improve his novel, but he actually left it relatively unchanged; and, as some will not be surprised to hear, this was essentially a marketing decision.

That is, instead of attempting the hopeless task of making the outdated *Ralph* seem like a modern novel, Gernsback consciously decided to present it as a museum piece, a forty-year-old novel that had incredibly predicted a number of modern scientific advances.[14] With due modesty, Gernsback could only boast about his own prophetic abilities to a limited extent — his "Preface to the 1950 Edition" briefly noted that "quite a number of the scientific predictions made in *Ralph* have come to pass" (50:10) — but he recruited two old friends, Lee De Forest and Fletcher Pratt, to write two "Forewords" making the case more forcefully. De Forest wrote, "The most outstanding, most extraordinary prophecies which this young clairvoyant had at that time conceived — all based on his keen observations and appreciation of their real significance and trend — he chose to record in the guise of a fanciful romance bearing the strange, cabalistic title of this book.... [The passage describing radar] constitutes perhaps the most amazing paragraphs in this astonishing Book of Prophecy" (50:15,18). According to Pratt, "This is a book of historic importance ... a book of prophecy, one of the most remarkable ever written.... Mr. Gernsback has been rather astoundingly successful in predicting actual developments" (50:19,21). Today, when *Ralph* is inaccurately described as only a series of predictions tied together by a perfunctory story line, we should recall that this is partially a result of the success of Gernsback's own marketing campaign.

Officially, then, Gernsback could not tamper with the text of *Ralph,* since this would virtually amount to rewriting history; and he added three footnotes in the 1950 edition which further call attention to the antiquity of the text. At the end of the paragraph declaring that "all the great baseball, tennis, and football contests are held after sundown," the note points out that "At the time this was written, no illuminated, night time sports fields existed" (50:81); when the "aerial carnival" depicted a Solar System of eight planets, a note says, "In 1911 the outer planet Pluto had as yet not been discovered" (50:94); and when Ralph was explaining the concept of converting paper money to gold coins, a note adds, "When this was written gold coins were legal tender. Gold payments were outlawed by Congress in 1933" (50:112).

The subtext of these notes is unambiguous: you are reading the unaltered text of a very old novel.[15]

Unofficially, however, Gernsback did make a number of small changes in the 1950 text. Of course, having attributed the changes in the 1929 text to another editor, I must ponder the possibility that another person revised the 1950 edition; but I consider that highly unlikely. First, for what it is worth, there is Gernsback's own testimony that he was personally involved in preparing the 1950 text: "when I was reading proofs for the 1950 edition, after a lapse of 25 years" ("Preface to the Second Edition" 50:7).[16] Second, I can claim a degree of familiarity with Gernsback's prose, and while the 1929 text sounded inauthentic from the very beginning, all the changes in the 1950 text seem consonant with Gernsback's own prose style. Finally, since Gernsback was a wealthy and prominent publisher in 1950, it hard to imagine any employee of the Frederick Fell Company having the temerity to make unauthorized changes in his writing; but it is relatively easy to imagine Gernsback taking a little time to go through the manuscript with a blue pencil, making a few changes here and there.

First, there were two tiny but substantive changes in the novel's contents. In the 1925 version, the Planet Governor was described as "the ruler of 90 billion human beings" (25:36); having the second thoughts about the difficulties of supporting such a huge population, Gernsback changes it to "15 billion human beings" in the 1950 edition (50:42). Also, in all previous versions, both Alice's and her father James's surnames were given as 212B 423; in the 1950 edition, James's surname is consistently given as 212B 422, implying that the second number of the surname somehow represents a number of generations.[17]

Second, Gernsback was willing in a few ways to "update" the text, despite his commitment to historical accuracy. First, in the 1925 edition, Gernsback tried to change all uses of "wireless" to "radio," but a number of "wireless's" remained in the latter part of the novel. For the 1950 edition, Gernsback changes seven more of them to "radio," though there were still a few "wireless's" toward the end of the novel that forever escaped his scrutiny. Also, while justifying his new voice-writing machine, the 1925 Ralph explains the defects of phonograph records, including this comment: "under that method it was possible for one to speak a will, but it was a clumsy way and was rarely used; on account of its high cost, and because the voice was not reproduced faithfully" (25:169). Because the final clause was not true of the improved records of 1950, Gernsback deletes it, so the sentence ended "and was rarely used on account of its high cost" (50:128; also, for no clear reason, "a will" became "one's last will and testament"). Third, Ralph's 1925 explanation of anti-gravity included this long description of then-current research: "The first work along this line was conducted by Majorana, the Italian scientist in the year 1920. He floated metal balls on top of mercury and claimed to have discovered a diminution of the weight of the balls when thus floated. He thought he had discovered here a means that partially screened gravitation from the iron balls, thus making them lighter" (25:181). By 1950, it was clear that Majorana's work had no scientific value, so Gernsback deletes the entire passage. Also related to a desire for modernization were the change from "'etherized'" (25:27) to "energyzed" (50:36; though all other references to the ether were retained) and from "telephone thanks were not nearly so nice" (25:59) to "telephot thanks" (50:57).

Finally, in addition to various minor corrections, including updated spelling and punctuation, Gernsback made about forty changes in his language, usually involving a few words at most. He tried to avoid repeated use of the same word in quick succession: "He stepped to one side of his Telephot so that his friend could see the apparatus on the table about ten feet from the Telephot faceplate" (25:10) becomes "He stepped to one side of his instrument ..." (25:26); "he proceeded to point out the finer points of the tube construction" (25:62–3) becomes "he proceed to elaborate on the finer points ..." (50:59); "the scientist made a minute examination of the instrument. It was a complicated instrument" (25:162) becomes "... It was a complicated machine" (50:123); and "the Governor felt that the task of keeping Ralph content had been lifted from the Governor's already over-burdened shoulders" (25:191) becomes "... from the official's already over-burdened shoulders" (50:141). In a few cases, he adds more specific information: "Ralph applied a small electric device to the back of the insensible man" (25:225) becomes "Ralph applied a small electric shocking device to the spine...." (50:164); "when he had generated enough" (25:251) becomes "when he had generated enough of the gas" (50:180); "the blood will begin to flow" (25:282) becomes "blood will begin to flow from the mouth, nose and ears" (50:200); and "he was forced to sit down to keep from falling" becomes "he was forced to sit down to keep from slumping over in the gravitation-less flyer" (50:198). At times, Gernsback simply substitutes a more dramatic word: on two occasions in addition to the above, a form of "fall" is replaced by "slump" (25:226,273; 50:165,194); "the avalanche rushed down the mountain" (25:44) becomes "the avalanche thundered..." (50:47); and "said Ralph in exasperation" (25:161) becomes "shouted Ralph in exasperation" (50:122).

Rarely, an entire phrase is reworked: "all of a sudden, the sound stopped" (25:24) becomes "suddenly, all sound stopped abruptly" (50:34), and "in order that all might get a good look at him" (25:39) becomes "in order that all might see him perfectly" (50:44). And there are a number of unimportant word changes: "power" (25:19) to "energy" (50:31), "began" (25:23) to "started" (50:33), "aerial vessels" (25:114) to "the traffic" (50:92), "numerous" (25:123) to "many" (50:98), "steadiness" (25:129) to "continuance" (50:102), and "just" (25:276) to "now" (50:197). Certainly, Gernsback did not undertake any thorough polishing of the text, but if he happened to notice a little something that might be better, he went ahead and made the change; and the fact that he bothered to do so again demonstrates that, for all his concerns about science, Gernsback always retained some interest in the quality of his published writing.

The 1952 British Edition

A British edition of Gernsback's *Ralph 124C 41+* (with subtitle dropped) was published as a Cherry Tree Novel in 1952. This is generally a faithful and accurate rendering of the 1950 Second Edition from Frederick Fell, Inc.; for once, Gernsback's prose received the respect it did not deserve. True, the Lee De Forest and Fletcher Pratt "Forewords" were removed, as was the 1925 "Preface to the First Edition," leaving only the 1950 "Preface to the Second Edition" as "Preface"; yet the main text was not meaningfully altered; only on rare occasions does one note the removal or addition of one small word. Signs of inattentiveness are equally infrequent, such as "no dirt or germs" (50:70) given as "no dirt or gems" (52:57) and "eating salon" (52:73) given as "eating saloon" (52:60). In addition, one long but clear sentence with faulty parallelism —

> Ralph learned from him that the purchaser of the new machine, one of the very latest models, was Fernand, beyond any doubt, and when he was informed that the latter had plentifully supplied himself with spare parts as if for a long journey, and moreover, the most significant fact that the cabin had been fitted out as a lady's boudoir, then indeed were his worst suspicions confirmed [50: 150–541].

is in apparent haste recast as two confusing sentence fragments —

> Ralph learned from him that the purchaser of the new machine, one of the very latest models, was Fernand, beyond any doubt, and when he was informed that the latter had plentifully supplied himself with spare parts as if for a long journey.
> Moreover, the most significant fact that the cabin had been fitted out as a lady's boudoir, then indeed were his worst suspicions confirmed [52:135–36].

Other than such infelicities, there are three major sorts of changes in the 1952 text.

First, and demanding no comment, is the regular use of British instead of American spellings.

Second, like T. O'Conor Sloane editing the 1925 text in 1929, but with less energy, the 1952 editor attempted to expand and regularize Gernsback's use of the comma. A few principles were unfailingly followed: the phrase "of course" was always enclosed in commas, and adverbs or phrases modifying a verb of speech were always set off with commas: "she gasped faintly" (50:122) becomes "she gasped, faintly" (52:107). Otherwise there are no consistent patterns: commas are sometimes added where they are clearly needed, sometimes added where they are not needed, and sometimes not added where they are clearly needed. However, since the added commas are not as numerous or as intrusive as Sloane's, the flow of the prose is not significantly slowed down.

Finally, the 1952 editor is bothered by, and frequently breaks up, long paragraphs, and even some not-so-long paragraphs. Since Gernsback's detailed explanations often drone on at great length, one might defensibly break some long paragraphs in half, and that occurs; more strange is the habit of removing the first sentence, or the last sentence, of a paragraph while leaving it otherwise intact, which sometimes results in the separation of a topic sentence from its development. At times, this tendency to create short paragraphs arguably heightens the effect, as in one crucial moment of realization: the 1950 text proceeds

> Suddenly an electric thrill seemed to pass through his body and his clouded mental vision cleared. A picture flashed upon his mind. He saw himself in his laboratory on Earth, bending over a "dead" dog. And there came to him a memory of the words of that Dean of scientists:
> "*What you have done with a dog, you can do with a human being*" [50:195–96].

while the 1952 edition provides

> Suddenly an electric thrill seemed to pass through his body and his clouded mental vision cleared. A picture flashed upon his mind.
> He saw himself in the laboratory on Earth, bending over a "dead" dog.
> And there came to him a memory of the words of that Dean of scientists:
> "*What you have done with a dog, you can do with a human being*" [52:179].

In other cases, however, the splits into shorter paragraphs are pointless and serve only to make Gernsback's prose seem even more juvenile than it is, as in his description of the "vacation city." Gernsback's version:

> "There is one unique place, I am sure you will be interested in." Ralph led the way to the elevator and they quickly shot up to the roof, where they boarded one of Ralph's flyers and within a few minutes were heading north. The machine rose until they were up about 20,000 feet. The cold made it necessary to turn on the heat in the enclosed cab. In the distance, just ahead there shortly appeared a brilliant spot of light suspended in the dark sky, which quickly increased in size as they approached. From a distance it appeared like an enormous hemisphere with the flat side facing the earth below. As they drew close, they could see that it was a great city suspended in the air apparently covered with a transparent substance, just as if a toy city had been built on a dinner plate and covered with a bell-shaped globe.

They alighted on the rim, at a landing stage outside the transparent covering. They were soon walking along a warm, beautifully laid out street. Here was neither bustle nor noise. The deepest calm prevailed. There were small houses of an old-fashioned design. There were shops in great profusion. There were playgrounds, neatly-laid-out parks, but without looking at the humans that were walking around, the visitors felt as if they had gone back many centuries.

There were no power roller skates, no automatic vehicles. There were no aeroflyers beneath the glass ceiling. Instead a serene calm prevailed, while people with happy expressions on their faces were leisurely walking to and fro [50: 131–132].

The 1952 text:

"There is one unique place, I am sure you will be interested in."

Ralph led the way to the elevator and they quickly shot up to the roof, where they boarded one of Ralph's flyers and within a few minutes were heading north. The machine rose until they were up about 20,000 feet. The cold made it necessary to turn on the heat in the enclosed cab. In the distance, just ahead there shortly appeared a brilliant spot of light suspended in the dark sky, which quickly increased in size as they approached. From a distance it appeared like an enormous hemisphere with the flat side facing the earth below.

As they drew close, they could see that it was a great city suspended in the air apparently covered with a transparent substance, just as if a toy city had been built on a dinner plate and covered with a bell-shaped globe.

They alighted on the rim, at a landing stage outside the transparent covering. They were soon walking along a warm, beautifully laid out street. Here was neither bustle nor noise. The deepest calm prevailed.

There were small houses of an old-fashioned design. There were shops in great profusion. There were playgrounds, neatly-laid-out parks, but without looking at the humans that were walking around, the visitors felt as if they had gone back many centuries.

There were no power roller skates, no automatic vehicles. There were no aeroflyers beneath the glass ceiling.

Instead a serene calm prevailed, while people with happy expressions on their faces were leisurely walking to and fro [52: 116–117].

Still, if these are the only sorts of changes one can find to discuss, it is obvious that British readers of the Cherry Tree edition, unlike readers of the 1929 *Amazing Stories Quarterly* version or the 1958 Fawcett Crest version to be discussed next, may generally trust the book as a reasonably reliable transcription of what, for better or worse, Gernsback actually intended to write.

The 1958 Version

As the 1950s progressed, Gernsback's novel faded from view in America, but it seems that there was the brief possibility of its reemergence in a new and more prominent form. In "The Return of Hugo Gernsback," Sam

Moskowitz reports that, early in 1953, Gernsback had received an undated letter from famous science fiction fan and agent Forrest J Ackerman that included these comments:

> Tuesday, a Hollywood film producer on the Sunset Strip called me to his office and in effect said, "Mr. Ackerman, I know your reputation. I know you know more about science fiction than anyone else in the world, and represent more of the authors than anyone else. You can help me. I want a story. Right away. If you were a producer, what science fiction would *you* make?" [...].
>
> But, remembering our conversation a couple of years ago, I took a chance on you; and along with Van Vogt's *Slan*, Homer Eon Flint's "Nth Man" [I represent his widow], and two others, the next day I laid down on the producer's desk a copy of your novel *Ralph 124C 41+* [...] I have given him quite a pep talk about it.
>
> If you approve of the negotiations I have instituted on your behalf, and wish me to consummate the transaction if *Ralph* is the lucky winner, please wire me authorization to close the deal for you "if and when," stipulating that my fee is to be 15% ["The Return of Hugo Gernsback" Part IV 210].

Gernsback responded positively (although, characteristically, he insisted that Ackerman should only receive 10%), but Ackerman's next report said only, in Moskowitz's paraphrase, that "things were progressing very slowly" (Part IV 210), though he does mention that the producer he talked to was Ivan Tors; and Moskowitz's subsequent silence on the subject suggests that the topic of a film version of *Ralph* never came up again.

A look at Tors's filmography suggests that he eventually decided to go with two of his own original stories as the basis for his next two science fiction films, *Riders to the Stars* (1954) and *Gog* (1954), which was more economical both because it eliminated the need to purchase rights but also because Tors's stories, set in the near future, could be filmed for much less money than any of Ackerman's more expansive suggestions would have required. Still, if Ivan Tors's papers are still extant somewhere, it is just slightly possible that they include another odd item to include in the textual history of this novel — Tors's notes regarding a possible film version of *Ralph 124C 41+*.[18]

Even without the boost of a film, science fiction novels in the 1950s were regularly sought after by paperback publishers, so it is not surprising that a paperback edition of the novel came out in 1958. The Fawcett Crest paperback edition marketed *Ralph 124C 41+* as a venerable antique full of remarkable predictions: the front cover described it as "One of the most prophetic books of science-fiction ever written"; both front and back covers call *Ralph* Gernsback's "famous classic," further emphasizing its antiquity; and there is a new subtitle, *One to Foresee for One*, which both explains the meaning of the title to baffled browsers and again communicates its prophetic qualities. Though presented as a reprint of the 1950 Frederick Fell edition, this version was not exactly that, since there were a number of new changes in the text. Almost certainly, Gernsback was not personally involved in preparing this edition, as he most definitely would not have approved of the decision to omit both of his "Prefaces," leaving only a drastically shortened version of Pratt's "Foreword" and a brief quotation from De Forest's "Foreword" as introductory materials. So it is logical to attribute these changes to an editor, or copyeditor, working for the Fawcett company who, predictably enough in preparing a mass-market paperback, brought new priorities to the revision of *Ralph*: intermingled concerns for economy, brevity, and modernity.

First, undoubtedly to avoid the hassle and expense of reproducing illustrations, the 1958 editor removes all of the textual drawings and diagrams that had previously been part of the text — another change that Gernsback surely would have opposed. So this is the first version of *Ralph* that does not present the drawing of the Menograph tape, the diagrams of the Trans-atlantic Tube and of Ralph's journey through space, the photographs of the real and artificial comets, and even the well-known diagram illustrating the principle of radar. At times, this meant that some of the text has to be removed as well; so, the two short paragraphs in parenthesis surrounding the Menograph drawing (50:48) are taken out, as is a sentence in the footnote about comets describing the two photographs (50:179). To be sure, the diagrams were not essential, and removing them arguably made for a more conventional and readable novel; but without them, some of the unique flavor of Gernsback's story is undeniably lost. And for that reason alone, while the 1958 editor's changes were otherwise less frequent and less objectionable than Sloane's, this edition qualifies as the more corrupted of the two unauthorized revisions.

While removing the diagrams served to shorten the length of the novel, there are many other small reductions in the 1950 text. Since it states something that is repeated two sentences later, the sentence "Alice tasted it, however, and found that it tasted exactly like a good rich cow's milk" (50:108) is properly deemed superfluous and removed. While Gernsback fully describes why Ralph had "one great advantage over Llysanorh'—"The latter was wholly unprepared, believing he had to deal with a comet. This facilitated Ralph's movements" (50:185)— the 1958 editor feels this is already clear enough and simply states, "The latter was wholly unprepared" (58:125). Gernsback writes, "When the farms came into view, the entire country below, so far as the eye could see, appeared to be dotted with the glass-covered roofs ... she had never seen so many grouped together of such immensity" (50:98); in the 1958 version, "When the farms came into view, the entire country below appeared to be dotted with the glass-covered roofs ... she had never seen so many grouped together" (58:61). From "The girl, desiring to know what it represented, approached and read this inscription" (50:75), "desiring to know what it represented" is removed (58:45). Sometimes only a small phrase is taken out: "can then be accurately and quickly calculated" (50:152) becomes "can then be accurately calculated" (58:101); "to which humanity had been chained for ages" (50:155) becomes "to which humanity had been chained" (58:104); "she became increasingly aware that her situation was desperate" (50:193) becomes "she became increasingly desperate" (58:131); "which he was certain was that of the Martian, as he had reasoned, heading for Mars" (50:169–70) becomes "which he was certain was that of the Martian heading for Mars" (58:114); and references to "James 212B 422" (50:58,88,95) are shortened to "James" (58:32,54,58). Only twice is this type of trimming harmful: when Gernsback's "six to twelve large anti-gravitators ... which could be worked in unison, or operated independently in order to control the direction of the flyer" (50:157) is changed to "to control their direction" (58:105), the function of the devices is obscured; more significantly, when the 1958 editor omits two seemingly redundant lines of dialogue from the scene with Peter quoted above — "The young lady from Switzerland, sir." "The — which?" (50:56) — the humor is spoiled, as this eliminates the precise moment of Ralph's double-take.

Finally, the 1958 editor at times wishes to modernize, smooth out, or improve Gernsback's often creaky prose. "These thoughts obtruded themselves into his consciousness" (50:55) becomes "These thoughts were uppermost in his mind" (58:30); "That is a great relief to me, I assure you, for I speak French very indifferently" (50:58) becomes "That's a great relief, I assure you, since my French is terrible" (58:32); "Busy with my own work I have not followed its progress closely enough to know all the details" (50:59) becomes "I've been busy with my own work so I have not followed its progress" (58:33); "to ascertain at what hour they would be ready" (50:66) becomes "to find out what time they would be ready" (58:38); "it may be taken as an axiom that" (50:99) becomes "we know that" (58:61); and "Certainly, he would not hesitate to murder Ralph if the opportunity presented itself" (50:175) becomes "to murder Ralph if he could" (58:118). There are a number of minor word changes: "Ralph ejaculated" (50:31) becomes "Ralph said" (58:14; perhaps because the term seemed suggestive); "in readiness" (50:33,165) becomes "ready" (58:15,111); "desired to know presently" (50:79) becomes "wanted to know" (58:47); "think collectively" (50:119) becomes "think clearly" (58:76); and "his missive" (50:143) becomes "his letter" (58:95). Generally these revisions are either harmless or beneficial; so, while Sloane gave the world a slightly stuffier *Ralph*, the 1958 editor presented a slightly breezier, more accessible novel.

When editors produce a revision of a novel, they also provide a commentary on it, which is why the 1929 and 1958 versions merit discussion; and while Sloane and the 1958 editor had very different attitudes and concerns, their responses to *Ralph* are generally parallel. First, while they were surely aware of the larger problems in the novel's structure, pace, and consistency, they had no desire, and were not in a position, to deal with them. On the other hand, they both recognized Gernsback's consistently awkward prose as one problem they could unobtrusively attack, and they both took some time to try to improve the style of *Ralph*. However, neither Sloane nor the 1958 editor attempted the herculean and probably impossible task of bringing the entire text of *Ralph* up to the level of competence; they would occasionally spot and work on some clumsy sentence, but they would then look at several equally inadequate sentences without making any changes. Both editors were helpless, therefore, in confronting the fundamental weakness of *Ralph*: the fact that its author was consistently unable to write a fluent English sentence. If Gernsback had only had a smidgen of talent to go along with his scientific imagination and literary aspirations, *Ralph* might have actually become a "famous classic" in the eyes of the general public; instead, after the 1958 edition went out of print, everyday readers no longer enjoyed ready access to the novel, and they undoubtedly became less and less aware of its existence.

Improbably, however, some members of the science fiction retained a strong interest in Gernsback's inferior novel and worked to maintain its visibility in the science fiction community of the 1960s, 1970s, and 1980s in a number of ways, including homages like William Gibson's story "The Gernsback Continuum" (1981), the noted parodies of Ellison and Sladek, and the invariable, though usually disparaging, comments of science fiction historians, which occasionally generated responses defending the novel and its value. It is also true that, in one sense, *Ralph 124C 41+* remained in print during this era because of six anthologies which published excerpts from Gernsback's novel, suggesting a strong belief that the novel was in some way important or interesting; these anthologies were I. O. Evans's *Science Fiction Through the Ages 2* (1966), Richard Curtis's *Future Tense* (1968), Russell Hill's *Reflections of the Future* (1975), Ralph S. Clem, Martin H. Greenberg, and Joseph D. Olander's *The City: 2000 A.D.* (1978), Patricia S. Warrick, Greenberg, and Olander's *Science Fiction: Contemporary Mythology* (1978), and Eric S. Rabkin's *Science Fiction: A Historical Anthology* (1983). And there are other stray indications that Gernsback's science fiction has not been forgotten, such as the name of the science fiction author in the future world of Philip José Farmer's "Riders of the Purple Wage" (1967), "Huga Wells-Erb Heinsturbury" (129), which pays tribute to Gernsback along with H. G. Wells, Edgar Rice Burroughs, Robert A. Heinlein, Theodore Sturgeon, and Ray Bradbury as the major science fiction writers of the past which this future author wishes to pay tribute to and emulate.[19] Then, in the 1990s, a widespread reappraisal of Gernsback, and increased critical attention, led naturally to two other editions of the novel.

The 1998 Online Edition and 2000 Reprint Edition

The two recent editions of *Ralph 124C 41+* require little comment. In 1998, Gernsback's nephew Patrick Merchant was producing a monthly online edition of Gernsback's Forecast, and he began to include monthly installments of the 1950 edition. However, the installments, and the magazine itself, stopped after three chapters. As of 2006, however, the first three chapters remained online at the URLs given elsewhere. The website also reproduces two illustrations from the 1925 edition and the contents page for the final December, 1998 issue interestingly displays the cover of a Russian edition of *Ralph 124C 41+* — raising the possibility that other foreign editions, either in English or translated into other languages, await the attention of scholars.

In 2000, the University of Nebraska Press published a photographic reproduction of the 1925 edition, including Frank R. Paul illustrations. The book included a few other features: Gernsback's Preface to the 1950 edition, a new introduction by science fiction writer Jack Williamson, and a "List of Specially Named Inventions and Technological Devices" with 27 terms accompanied by brief explanations. Most interestingly, this edition includes three pages from an advertising brochure that accompanied the first edition. As one might expect, this brochures features a list of scientific wonders in the novel and laudatory quotations from reviews, but one might not expect the novel to be described in this fashion:

> Against a vivid and pulse-thrilling background of mechanical, electrical and chemical wonders is a fascinating story of romance and adventure — the love story of the greatest scientist of his day, and a beautiful stranger.
> The climax of the story, the thrilling battle in the realms of space, between supermen with incredible weapons, will hold you enthralled [3].

There is a lesson here, to be expanded upon in later chapters, about the centrality of melodrama in science fiction, both as a way to attract readers and as a way to sustain a narrative.

The book does not identify the editor of the volume, or the creator of its annotated list, but there is at least one indication of editorial inattentiveness: on the back cover, Gernsback's birth and death dates are incorrectly given as "(1887–1964)" instead of the correct 1884–1967.

Conclusion

With its full story revealed, *Ralph 124C 41+* emerges as a novel which interestingly straddles all of the boundary lines typically erected in the field of science fiction.

Some, building upon the apparent dichotomy in its name, would divide science fiction between those primarily interested in science and those primarily interested in literature; and Gernsback is presented as a leader of the science-first camp. Yet despite his obvious fascination with scientific ideas, Gernsback devoted an equal amount of energy to improving the literary qualities of his novel. True, he was reticent about these ambitions and displayed little writing ability; but lack of public commitment and lack of talent should not be mistaken for lack of desire.

There is also Brian W. Aldiss's division of science fiction into the "thinking pole," represented by the somber speculations of H. G. Wells, and the "dreaming pole," represented by the exotic adventures of Edgar Rice Burroughs. Again, Gernsback displays both tendencies. The first seven installments of the original *Ralph* stand solidly near the thinking pole, strongly emphasizing scientific gadgetry, to be sure, but also projecting a broader picture of a benevolent world government that has prospered by recognizing and supporting the work of its scientists. But in the last five installments, Gernsback veers near the dreaming pole with a melodramatic account of pursuing evil kidnappers through space.

Finally, some see science fiction as either basically utopian — stressing the positive effects of scientific progress — or dystopian — stressing its negative effects — and Gernsback is said to exemplify the utopian school. Yet Gernsback could recognize that there were dangers in advanced science: people in his future world are being driven crazy by their "labor-saving devices," an invisibility machine and modern chemicals are employed in kidnapping schemes, and Ralph reveals the power to create a comet and aim it at a vulnerable planet. Certainly, Gernsback was more inclined to celebrate the benefits of technology, but he was not completely blind to its possible drawbacks.

After examining its multifaceted nature, and seeing signs of its influence throughout modern science fiction, I have elsewhere argued that *Ralph 124C 41+,* and the ideas that Gernsback developed and promulgated after writing it, constitute the true origin and foundation of the genre of science fiction. To others, who find the roots of science fiction in other, more exemplary texts, *Ralph 124C 41+* is only an aberration, a brief, catastrophic interruption in the genre's otherwise distinguished history. Yet those who see *Ralph* as a wellspring, and those who see it as a backwater, might find common ground in considering the novel as a microcosm.

That is to say: when science fiction historians look back at the seventeenth and eighteenth centuries, the texts they find usually fall into the categories of utopia or travel tale, and their scientific marvels are presented as either pleasant accoutrements to life in exotic lands or the basis of an ideal society — as in the first seven installments of the original *Ralph*. But when those historians move into the nineteenth century, the mood abruptly changes: whether because of the general Romantic revolt against Newton's clockwork universe, as a specific reaction to the unpleasant effects of the Industrial Revolution, or simply due to a desire to generate more exciting stories, writers begin to present scientific progress in a negative light: scientists replace necromancers in Gothic horror tales, and amazing inventions once seen as instruments of a benign government are now placed in the hands of madmen and criminals — as in the last five installments of the first *Ralph*. Throughout this time, there is a disinclination to combine scientific predictions with tales of romantic love, save as a perfunctory subplot in melodramas, and there are occasional times when science is viewed in a humorous fashion or as an object of satire. At the beginning of the twentieth century, most notably in the works of H. G. Wells, one sees all of these elements coalescing — as in the 1925 version of *Ralph*— and they have remain blended in modern texts, sometimes effectively, sometimes uneasily, while their literary quality has gradually improved.

This is the story of the evolution of modern science fiction; and in miniature, it is also the story of the evolution of Hugo Gernsback's *Ralph 124C 41+*.

6

"Man Against Man, Brain Against Brain"

The Transformations of Melodrama in Science Fiction

As previously discussed, the first version of Hugo Gernsback's *Ralph 124C 41+* began as a combination of utopia and travel tale, providing a guided tour of a seemingly ideal future world, and then in its final chapters plunged into melodramatic adventure; one can also detect signs of Gothic horror and of satire, particularly in the 1925 revision. I have elsewhere discussed the problems Gernsback encountered in endeavoring to employ these genres to achieve his purposes, and the reflections of those problems observed in later science fiction[1]; however, along with its connections to utopia, the novel's peculiar relationship to melodrama, and the enduring impact of that relationship, demand more extensive attention.

For of all modern forms of fiction and film, none seems more closely linked to melodrama than science fiction: Garff Wilson's *Three Hundred Years of American Drama and Theatre* observes that "The western, cops-and-robbers, and science fiction serials are all as melodramatic as any play of the nineteenth century" (107); and in describing modern descendants of melodrama, Frank Rahill's *The World of Melodrama* mentions that "Science fiction, in its more lunatic manifestations, and the monster theme formed a fruitful alliance (*King Kong*, *The Thing from Outer Space*, etc.), the scientific binge of our generation contributing to the size of their public" (301).[2] However, these commentators have failed to note that in adopting this theatrical form, science fiction reconstructed the melodrama in a manner which often complicated and undermined its traditional clarity; and in examining these transformations, as first observed in Gernsback's *Ralph 124C 41+*, we

149

see both the inherent limitations, and the continuing power, of this dramatic genre.

The direct descent of modern science fiction from nineteenth-century American melodrama is unusually well documented. First, when melodrama became a major American form in the nineteenth century, there simultaneously arose the genre of dime novels, crude adventures which were, as Michael Denning's *Mechanic Accents* notes, "clearly connected to popular melodramas" (24). To support the idea that the two forms are related, Denning cites an 1879 reviewer describing some dime novels simply as melodramas "narrativized for the story paper" (24) and discusses authors like Albert Aiken and Bartley Campbell who wrote both melodramas and dime novels (215). In addition, David Gerould mentions that "stories [for melodramas] could be appropriated from dime novels" (9); and Rahill calls Wild West melodrama "Plays of the Beadle dime novel school" (237) and notes that "The dime novel discovered [the cowpuncher] (circa 1885), and his numerous stage representations in the proletarian theatre stemmed from this source" (238). In addition to these documented links, we repeatedly find in dime novels the sorts of virtuous heroes, imperiled heroines and dastardly villains featured in stage melodrama.

One prominent author of dime novels, Luis Senarens, virtually created the subgenre of the form known as the "invention story," where the plucky hero is typically a young inventor who, as the story opens, has just built a wonderful new device which then figures in the otherwise routine melodramatic action. One representative invention story is Senarens's *Jack Wright and His Electric Air Rocket, or, The Boy Exile of Siberia* (1884), where the eponymous hero jumps in his newly constructed airplane and goes to Russia to rescue a young lad who has been kidnapped by an evil uncle trying to steal his inheritance. This adventure is obviously related to melodrama, since it includes a scene where the friend is tied to the railroad tracks, and Jack must fly his airplane and untie him before the train comes!

The influence of Senarens can then be seen in the theories and writing of Hugo Gernsback: in the 1920s, he published an article calling Senarens the "American Jules Verne"[3]; he came to define science fiction stories as "thrilling adventure" ("Science Wonder Stories" 5); and his seminal novel *Ralph 124C 41+: A Romance of the Year 2660* is melodramatic both in its plot—a virtuous young scientist named Ralph must rescue his fiancée from a villain named Fernand who has kidnapped her—and in its dialogue:

> "You coward," [Alice] blazed, "how dare you keep me here!
> Turn around and take me back at once—at once, do you hear?"
> Fernand, in the act of opening her door and going back to his laboratory, paused smilingly.

"My dear girl," he said mockingly, "ask of me anything and I will grant it — except that. You have a temper that delights me. Your smiles will be all the sweeter, later" [172].

Gernsback had a powerful impact both on written science fiction, as even his critics acknowledge, and on filmed science fiction; for in 1928 and 1929, Gernsback published two stories by Philip Francis Nowlan, "Armageddon 2419 A.D." and "The Airships of Han" (later published together as the novel *Armageddon 2419 A.D.*) which became the basis for the popular *Buck Rogers* comic strip. Its success led to the similar *Flash Gordon* comic strip and the *Flash Gordon* and *Buck Rogers* film serials, which later served as the models for various television series of the 1950s — including *Buck Rogers*, *Flash Gordon*, and *Space Patrol*; and these in turn led to the superior, but equally melodramatic television series *Star Trek,* which later spawned four successor series and ten films. The *Flash Gordon* serials also helped to inspire George Lucas's 1977 *Star Wars*— a film which Lucas created only after he had first tried and failed to obtain the rights to *Flash Gordon*. Thus, the continuing prominence of melodrama in written and filmed science fiction can be traced through an unbroken chain directly back to Gernsback's influence.

However, while Gernsback took the form of melodrama from Senarens, he also embedded special purposes in his new genre which disturbed and distorted the melodramatic structure. First, Gernsback wanted science fiction to incorporate accurate scientific information, so that science fiction could be "a means of educating the public to the meaning of science" ("Science Fiction Week" 1061); and second, he believed that stories should describe proposed new inventions in detail, in order to offer useful and stimulating ideas to scientists: "The professional inventor or scientist ... gets the stimulus from the story and promptly responds with the material invention" ("$300.00 Prize Contest" 5). In these ways, science fiction could inspire support for, and improve, science and scientific progress. One problem is immediately clear: while melodrama, according to Peter Brooks's *The Melodramatic Imagination*, is dedicated to "Emotions ... given a full acting-out ... a full emotional indulgence" (41), science fiction mandates unemotional accounts of scientific data and ideas far exceeding the traditional amount of exposition needed to explain the plot, thus compromising the characteristic tone of melodrama. But the structure is altered as well: for to make melodrama serve the ideology of science fiction, Gernsback had to make Ralph, the hero of his novel, resemble both a conventional hero and a conventional villain, thus threatening the integrity of the melodramatic form.

To explore Ralph's strange character, I developed in *The Mechanics of Wonder* a model of melodramatic conflict derived from Robert Heilman's argument in *Tragedy and Melodrama* that melodrama is "a polemic form" in "the realm of social action" (97), that it works with "whole rather than divided" characters (81), and that particularly in its American form, characters are, in Wilson's words, "either completely good or completely bad" (101). In this framework, I noted three important and interrelated themes in the conflict between villain and hero.[4]

The first is *intellect versus emotion*: David Grimsted's *Melodrama Unveiled* notes that August von Kotzebue, one influence on American melodrama, preached that "impetuous feeling rather than reason or custom was the proper basis of conduct" (13) and that melodramas usually had villains with "intelligence" (177) and heroes who "seldom showed signs of great learning or rationality" (210). In addition, Rahill describes the archetypal melodramatic hero in Pixérécourt's *Coelina* in this way: "Somewhat stupid, he will often be outwitted by the clever villain in his long stage career, but not in a hundred years will he be worsted in a fair fight" (31); and Michael Booth's *English Melodrama* claims "The basic hero is really rather stupid" (15) and quotes one stage villain who proclaims, "Men of brains and cunning must rule the world" (152).[5]

In melodrama, then, the villain is usually older, more knowing, and better educated than the hero; he is described as cold and calculating; and he uses sophistry in making his case, perhaps with logic or the letter of the law on his side in foreclosing a mortgage.[6] In contrast, the hero is young, naive, and unschooled; he seems emotional, impulsive; and he opposes the villain based on simple morality, not complex reasoning — despite the law, people should not be thrown out of their homes.

A related theme is *indirect action versus direct action*. The villain, typically employing what Grimsted describes as "diabolic subterfuge" (178), has henchmen do the dirty work so he is elsewhere, with a perfect alibi, when the crime is committed, or sets events in motion and leaves, tying the heroine to the railroad tracks or the hero to a log in a sawmill, so that machines, not the villain, will do the actual killing. However, the hero acts on his own without relying on other people or devices; the villain may be absent at the climax, but the hero is always there to save the day. And though the hero may occasionally indulge in his own scheming, this is justified as a needed response to the villain's machinations.

A third theme is *the elite versus the common man*; Booth points out that "Melodrama clearly reflects class hatreds. Villains tend to be noblemen, factory owners, squires; heroes peasants, able seamen, and workmen" (62). Also, Heilman points out that "royalty and nobility were the first villains" in American melodrama (104), while, as Grimsted observes, melodrama "took the lives of common people seriously and paid much respect to their superior purity and wisdom" (248); William Paul Steele observes in *The Character of*

Melodrama that the villain "is often of high rank" (4); and Brooks says that in melodrama, "Villains are remarkably often tyrants and oppressors, those that have power and use it to hurt. Whereas the victims, the innocent and virtuous, most often belong to a democratic universe" (44).

Thus, the villain is typically a wealthy man, owning considerable property, and he may enjoy power over others, the open or covert support of law officers, or an official position; but the hero is poor, with no friends in high places, no official cooperation in opposing the villain, and no title or social status. Indeed, the hero may be seen as a rebel, an outcast, or even, as Booth says, a "criminal-hero" (64).

These villainous and heroic qualities illustrate Gernsback's dilemma in creating science fiction melodrama: celebrating the value of science, Gernsback was promoting intellect over emotion; depicting new inventions to replace manual labor, he was advocating indirect action over direct action; and supporting the scientific community, he was favoring the interests of an elite over those of the common man. Yet his chosen genre — melodrama — was antithetical to these concerns. His solution was to create a hero who alternately displayed the attributes of both hero and villain, so that Ralph could be a traditional hero while also advancing Gernsback's untraditional agenda.

Ralph's contradictory qualities emerge repeatedly. Ralph is "one of the greatest living scientists" (25) who once called love "nothing but a perfumed animal instinct" (140), but his love for Alice leads this intellect to scream at his servant, lose a tennis game because he cannot concentrate, and madly dash off to save Alice when she is in danger.

Second, he first rescues Alice with scientific indirect action: when Ralph learns an avalanche is about to destroy her faraway home, he tells her to set up an antenna, goes to his laboratory to create a storm of energy, and broadcasts heat to melt away the threatening snow. Yet when Fernand later kidnaps Alice and flies into space, Ralph eschews complicated scientific scheme and simply gets in a spaceship to go after her.

Finally, due to his vast intellect Ralph is "one of the ten men on the whole planet earth" with "the Plus sign after his name" (25); because of that title, he enjoys generous financial support and personal access to the Planet Governor who controls the entire world. Yet to keep Ralph hard at work in the laboratory, the government forbids dangerous activity and Ralph comes to believe that he is "nothing but a prisoner" (42). And when the Planet Governor expressly tells him not to pursue Fernand, Ralph defies the order and leaves anyway, effectively becoming an outcast and criminal.[7]

In displaying these conflicting impulses, Ralph might become a divided and, in Heilman's terms, tragic character, thus moving away from melodrama; however, this does not occur because Ralph, as Heilman says of Bosola in

Webster's *The Duchess of Malfi*, "is one thing at one moment and another thing at another moment; rarely ... a human totality in which rival urgencies are operative at the same time" (293). That is, in his alternating and contradictory modes, Ralph fails to become a character at all — a minor problem with a secondary figure like Bosola, but a crucial flaw in a melodramatic protagonist with whom audiences must identify.

Later creators of science fiction devised a solution to Gernsback's problem which I have called the *counterhero*: the hero, stripped of scientific knowledge and abilities, reverts to his traditional character, while a new hero with villainous traits is created to be his companion. While this figure first begins to emerge in the scientific Dr. Heur who becomes a key character in the *Buck Rogers* comic strip, the Flash Gordon serials (*Flash Gordon* [1936], *Flash Gordon's Trip to Mars* [1938], and *Flash Gordon Conquers the Universe* [1940]) set the pattern. Here, melodramatic conventions initially seem in place: Dale Arden is the lovely heroine, Ming the Merciless is the despicable villain, and Flash is the perfect hero — handsome, brave, and not too bright. But the troublesome figure of Dr. Zharkov, his mentor and companion, does not fit in so well. Zharkov's Russian name, in the political climate of the times, suggests villainy, and the stories at times cast doubt on his character, his loyalty, and even his sanity. Yet Zharkov is indispensable: his spaceship takes Flash to the planet Mongo, and when a situation arises that cannot be handled by Flash's physical strength, Zharkov's scientific knowledge provides the answer.

In these ways, Zharkov and Flash embody the antithetical elements in Ralph's character: Zharkov cold and intellectual, willing to employ devious scientific methods, and, by virtue of his title, rather patrician; Flash passionate, inclined to direct action, and lacking in social position. Creating two separate heroes with opposing attributes eliminates the need for an implausible two-sided character like Ralph, apparently strengthening the melodrama; however, the counterhero, who himself is necessarily a divided character — essentially a villain supporting heroic causes — can, if examined, move the melodrama into tragedy. This does not happen in the Flash Gordon serials, as Zharkov is never the center of attention.

That problem does emerge, though, in the original *Star Trek* series (1966–1969), where there is another pairing of two heroes with different attributes: Spock cool and logical, skilled in indirect science, and from an aristocratic family on Vulcan; and Kirk emotional, direct in his actions, and of undistinguished parentage. Like Zharkov, Spock is a counterhero whose competence and character are questioned: "The Galileo Seven" (1967) and "The Tholian Web" (1968) suggest that due to his logical nature, Spock is not suited to command, and "The Menagerie" (1966) and "The Enterprise Incident"

(1968) seem to catch him in the act of treason. Yet Spock's knowledge and abilities, also like Zharkov's, are essential in threatening situations.

As a divided character, half-human and half–Vulcan, driven to both heroism and villainy, Spock can become, as Daniel Cohen notes in *Strange and Amazing Facts about Star Trek*, "an almost tragic figure" (26), shifting the focus from external conflicts — melodrama — to internal conflicts — tragedy. Thus, for example, a sense of victory over the Romulans in "The Enterprise Incident" is weakened and complicated by Spock's sympathy for the Romulans and regret over the underhanded tactics he used against them.[8]

At this point, one might argue that the device of the counterhero is really nothing new, since many nineteenth-century melodramas have second heroes — typically comical, energetic, and perhaps a bit brighter than the hero. However, there are significant differences between these figures and the counterheroes of science fiction. The second hero is, in keeping with the name, a secondary figure, presented as the hero's sidekick or assistant, and often absent from the stage. In contrast, the counterhero observes no hierarchy: Spock's position as second in command of the *Enterprise* gives him a large degree of authority and autonomy, and he is sometimes obliged to take actions which Kirk does not endorse; and since Zharkov built and commands the spaceship that takes Flash to Mongo, he can in some ways be considered Flash's commander. In addition, the counterhero is almost always at the center of activity, fighting alongside the hero, and in some cases the counterhero may even usurp the hero at the story's most crucial point — the climax — and perform the final rescue. In *Star Trek* episodes, for example, it is striking how often Kirk, the ostensible hero, is reduced to a helpless position in crisis situations, sitting in his captain's chair and barking out pointless orders while Spock, or the similar Mr. Scott, is busy jury-rigging the device which will actually save the *Enterprise* from doom.

Space does not permit a full discussion of the many counterheroes found in science fiction. In film, the most familiar version is the older scientist who is also the heroine's father, and robots sometimes fill the role, like Robby the Robot in *Forbidden Planet* (1956). More unusual variations are found in Hal Clement's *Needle* (1950), where a friendly protoplasmic alien invades the young hero's body so that they can work together to track down an alien criminal; in the *Outer Limits* episode, "Demon with a Glass Hand" (1964), where the hero has a mechanical hand which knowledgeably guides him as he battles mysterious foes; and in Gregory Benford's *Great Sky River* (1984) and *Tides of Light* (1987), in which the hero has several "Aspects" — personalities of prominent dead people — implanted in his brain, with one of these, the Arthur Aspect, ready to regularly provide scientific information and explanations.

One particularly interesting example is the computer HAL in the film and novel *2001: A Space Odyssey* (1968), apparently a helpful companion to the astronauts but actually a tragically divided counterhero, driven insane by his conflicting instructions to cater to all the crew's needs — a heroic trait — and to withhold from them the true nature of their mission — a villainous trait. Despite his murderous acts in *2001*, he is explicitly rehabilitated, exonerated, and restored to heroic status in Arthur C. Clarke's sequel, *2010: Odyssey Two* (1982), filmed as *2010: The Year We Make Contact* (1984), and appears as a reborn companion to the deceased David Bowman and Heywood R. Floyd in Clarke's other *2001* books, *2061: Odyssey Three* (1987) and *3001: The Final Odyssey* (1997). (As a culminating indication that Bowman and HAL were the true, twin heroes of the *2001* saga, the final novel merges the spectral Bowman and HAL into a single being, Halman.)

The device of the counterhero need not damage the structure of melodrama because the undivided main hero may dominate the action, shifting attention away from the divided, potentially tragic double hero. But the double hero can generate another complexity with more ruinous effects: as hero splits into heroic hero and villainous hero, the villain may split into villainous villain and heroic villain.

This pattern of a *countervillain* does appear in Gernsback's novel, where Ralph has two rivals for Alice's affections: Fernand and a Martian, Llysanorh.' Fernand is a conventional villain: aloof and uncaring, he wants Alice simply for the satisfaction of conquest; devious and indirect, he seizes Alice with an invisibility device and uses confederates to seize her again; wealthy and well connected, his schemes suggest a high social status. Llysanorh' is completely different — "a very decent chap," who is "hopelessly infatuated" with her (68). Alice "could not deny the fact of his genuine ... fervent love" (193), even after he kidnaps her; his abduction is an impulsive, individual action; and as a Martian, he is by definition a social outcast, legally forbidden to marry an Earth woman despite his deep love — thus, he is a victim of society and to Alice seems "very pathetic" (190). Though ultimately driven to kidnap and murder Alice, he resembles a melodramatic hero, and one wonders why Gernsback chose to complicate his narrative with this character; the novel's final chapters are particularly clumsy, as Ralph, after flying to Alice's rescue and confronting Fernand, discovers that Llysanorh' has now kidnapped Alice from Fernand, which forces Ralph to effect a second rescue.

However, Llysanorh's presence is readily explained as a consequence of Gernsback's resort to melodrama in his science fiction story: since Ralph has the attributes of both hero and villain, a purely evil character like Fernand is not sufficient to serve as his foil; while Fernand can oppose Ralph when the scientist is emotional and daring, he cannot be his adversary when Ralph is intellectual and prudent. Thus, a second, more sympathetic villain is required as a counterpart to the sometimes unsympathetic hero.

We see the two villains functioning exactly this way in *Ralph 124C 41+*. In response to Fernand's deviousness, Ralph acts directly and personally: after Fernand invisibly abducts Alice, Ralph rushes after her, finds where she is hidden, and frees her. When Fernand kidnaps Alice in his spaceship, Ralph flies into space, locates and overtakes Fernand, and confronts him with startling passion and violence, exclaiming "If you and I ever meet again I will pound your miserable cowardly body into jelly!" (169)

Ralph acts differently in response to Llysanorh's direct actions: learning that Llysanorh' has taken Alice from Fernand and is heading to Mars, Ralph calculates he will not have enough time to overtake Llysanorh's ship before he reaches Mars and arranges to forcibly marry Alice. He then resorts to a trick: in his spaceship laboratory he creates an artificial comet and sends it towards Mars. He reasons that Llysanorh', for the sake of his fellow Martians, will change his course to intercept and destroy the comet, thus giving Ralph time to catch his ship. Though the stratagem works, it seems unheroic to play upon an opponent's altruism; the scheme resembles the moment in a melodrama when the trapped villain grabs an innocent bystander and puts a gun to his head: surrender, or I will kill him. The difference is that Ralph is pointing a gun at the entire planet of Mars. And there is something cold about his reaction when Ralph finds Llysanorh' has killed both himself and Alice: while returning to Earth, he methodically drains Alice's blood and tries to invent a way to bring her back to life. While understandable, these actions are an oddly unemotional way to respond to the death of a loved one.

The pattern thus emerges: cold and devious Fernand opposes Ralph's passions, while emotional and direct Llysanorh' opposes Ralph's intelligence; hero and counterhero have spawned villain and countervillain. Therefore, when Ralph proclaims his "fight is to be man against man, brain against brain" (153), Gernsback, perhaps inadvertently, suggests the complexity of his narrative, with one difference: the fight is Ralph the man against Fernand the brain, and Ralph the brain against Llysanorh' the man.

The countervillain also appears in the first major alien races of the *Star Trek* universe: the Romulans and the Klingons. Romulans are classic villains; like the Vulcans they resemble, Romulans are cold and unemotional; their characteristic weapon is a "cloaking device" making their ships invisible, allowing for sneak attacks; and their manner is haughty and aristocratic.[9] In contrast, Klingons are emotional and violent; they prefer direct attack and personal combat; and their unkempt appearance, crude language, and bad table manners mark them as proletarians. Therefore, the Romulans fit the model of villainy, while the Klingons, though repulsive and violent, fit the model of heroism.

These countervillains serve to further blur the division between good and evil, compromise the clarity of the melodramatic conflict, and create the possibility of inappropriate alliances — that is, the villainous counterhero may be drawn to the villainous villain while the heroic hero may be drawn to the heroic countervillain. Several episodes of the original *Star Trek* series suggest such linkages. In "Balance of Terror" (1966) Spock is suspected of secretly sympathizing with the Romulans; in "The Enterprise Incident," he apparently betrays his human friends and joins forces with the Romulans; and in an episode of *Star Trek: The Next Generation*, "Unification" (1991), an older Spock makes a return appearance, attempting to achieve a peace treaty between the Federation and the Romulan Empire.

Similarly, there are episodes which explicitly link Kirk and the Klingons: in "The Trouble with Tribbles" (1967), Kirk enjoys a kind of camaraderie with a Klingon captain; in "Errand of Mercy" (1967), Kirk and a Klingon become bizarre allies in arguing with aliens for their right to continue a war; and in "Day of the Dove" (1968) Kirk and a Klingon commander unite against an alien invader and defeat the being by joining in derisive laughter.[10]

The original series never carried these tendencies to their logical conclusions, and Spock has never joined the Romulans in villainy — some lines, it seems, cannot be crossed. Still, it should be noted that the traditionally evil Romulans continued to serve as villains in episodes like "The Enemy" (1989) and "The Defector" (1990) of *Star Trek: The Next Generation*; and Romulan characters in *Star Trek V: The Final Frontier* (1989) and *Star Trek VI: The Undiscovered Country* (1992) remained unsympathetic. However, the Klingons in fact became heroic: in the second series, the Klingons belong to the Federation, a Klingon serves on board the *Enterprise*, and Klingons are depicted as hot-headed but basically good characters. In *Star Trek V*, a Klingon general becomes Kirk's ally, and even a violent Klingon captain trying to destroy the Enterprise is finally recast as an impetuous youth. And in the final *Star Trek* film featuring characters from the original series, *Star Trek VI*, the peace process that brought the Klingons into the Federation is visibly initiated, with Michael Dorn, the actor who plays the Klingon crewman in the new series, on hand playing a sympathetic Klingon defense attorney.

This virtual transformation of countervillain into hero can create awkwardness and further distort the conventions of melodrama, as shown by one episode of *Star Trek: The Next Generation*, "A Matter of Honor" (1989). Here, the Klingons again function as enemies, as their warship approaches the *Enterprise* and threatens its destruction; but to maintain their new image, the conflict is laboriously framed as a misunderstanding — the Klingons believe the *Enterprise* is responsible for an infestation attacking their vessel — and when matters are explained, they become friendly again. In addition, the

Klingons are defeated not by space combat, but by an elaborate ruse, as Captain Picard's First Office Ryker contrives to assume command of the Klingon vessel. Thus, just as the device of the counterhero can lead melodrama into tragedy, the device of the countervillain can lead melodrama into comedy: that is, we move from a pattern of fundamental conflict leading to victory in violent battle — the structure of melodrama — and reach a pattern of confusion leading to clarification and reconciliation by means of gentle trickery — the structure of comedy.

This tendency toward comedy also emerged earlier in episodes of the original *Star Trek* series involving Klingons. "The Trouble with Tribbles" is frankly comic, and Kirk's only "victory" over the Klingons is that he infests their ship with the alien pests called tribbles; Klingons and Kirk's crew interact peaceably under truce conditions in both "The Trouble with Tribbles" and "Day of the Dove," suggesting the compromising spirit of comedy; and "Errand of Mercy" makes both Kirk and the Klingons seem ridiculous in their desire to carry on with a pointless war. Thus, even before the Klingons' official conversion to heroic status, we detect an urge to reconcile Klingons and humans, a resolution typical of comedy, but antithetical to melodrama.

While the later *Star Trek* series have for the sake of novelty introduced other alien races as adversaries, all of them have been variations on the sinister and remote Romulans — such as the Borg and the Cardassians — or variations on the more genial and accessible Klingons — such as the Ferengi. And while defectors from the Borg or the Cardassians have occasionally served as sympathetic characters — such as the ex–Borg Seven of Nine in *Star Trek: Voyager* and the gentle Cardassian tailor occasionally seen in *Star Trek: Deep Space Nine*— these races as a whole have remained implacable enemies of the Federation, while the adversarial Ferengi were quickly recast as lovable scoundrels in *Star Trek: Deep Space Nine*, their relentless greed now regarded only as a charming eccentricity.

Again, one might observe that there are many secondary villains in earlier melodramas, usually serving as comic, sympathetic, and stupid assistants to the main villain; and again, the science fiction countervillains do not fit this pattern. To be specific, the countervillain is not a subordinate of the other villain, but an independent agent, and he is often as menacing as, or more menacing than, the traditional villain. For example, Ralph can brush away the machinations of the villain Fernand, but his climactic struggle and triumph involve the countervillain Llysanorh'.

While not as common as the counterhero, countervillains can be found in other science fiction works. In the film *Forbidden Planet*, Dr. Morbius has unconsciously spawned the completely malevolent Monster of the Id, which emerges as the ultimate threat; and although he often functions as an opponent to the film's heroes, Morbius himself is finally cast as a sympathetic, though tragically divided, character. In Spider and Jeanne Robinson's *Stardance* (1979), the first villain in the final scenes is thoroughly callous, driven by his own desire for wealth and power, while the second, more sensitive villain is driven to act by a misguided concern for the future of the human race. And in the film *Superman II* (1980), the major menaces are the implacably diabolic super-villains from Krypton, while Superman's traditional foe, Lex Luthor, emerges as an oddly likable and not particularly evil character.

Science fiction melodrama does not always grow complex and generically mixed, since writers can always ignore the potential problems and proceed in a conventional way, as in most comic books and cartoons. However, when a work of science fiction is created with care and intelligence, complications of this kind frequently emerge, as seen, for example, in George Lucas's first three *Star Wars* films.

The opening of *Star Wars* (1977) presents a classic melodramatic trio: virtuous young hero Luke Skywalker, captured heroine Princess Leia, and heartless villain Darth Vader. Yet there must be another character, Ben Kenobi, to contribute the experience and knowledge Luke needs to fight the evil Empire. As a counterhero, Kenobi is prominent in the action: he obtains the needed spaceship, begins training Luke, and battles Darth Vader when he knows that Luke is not ready. Even after he dies, the story cannot do without him, for he returns as a ghost, helping Luke attack the Death Star. In the second film, *The Empire Strikes Back* (1980), the dead Kenobi makes another brief appearance, but since a living counterpart is manifestly necessary, a new character, Yoda, appears to replace him as the counterhero. However, the sedentary Yoda is fundamentally unsuited to the role, remains behind when Luke prematurely abandons his training program, and dies in the next film.

In *Return of the Jedi* (1983), the story line suddenly lurches in another effort to replace Kenobi. When Leia is revealed to be his sister, Luke can no longer romance her and so cannot serve as the main hero; Han Solo, previously serving as the secondary comic hero,[11] is structurally promoted to the protagonist's role, since he will now rescue and marry the Princess. Luke, assuming Kenobi's role of counterhero, dresses in black and becomes cold and withdrawn. As Luke takes on these unemotional, unsympathetic attributes, emerging as a divided and potentially tragic counterhero, the villain correspondingly becomes emotional and sympathetic; so the despicable Darth Vader, already revealed as Luke's father, now emerges as a divided countervillain, a good man corrupted by the Dark Side and thus another tragic figure. And because an heroic countervillain cannot stand alone, a new main villain must be created — the Emperor, as evil and heartless as Darth Vader once seemed to be.

These transformations are artful, but the contrast between the triumphant conclusion of *Star Wars* and the subdued ending of *Return of the Jedi* shows how much melodramatic clarity has been muddled to produce a hopelessly compromised happy ending. The final celebration in the third film is not a grand ceremony but a small gathering around a campfire, symbolizing a shift from attention to the public issue — defeating the Empire — to the private matter of Luke's personal tragedy. The audience's presumed joy over the coming marriage of Han and the Princess is alloyed by their disappointment that Luke has been denied that satisfaction, and he stands aloof from the merriment; the ghostly visits of Kenobi, Yoda, and Darth Vader — now depicted as a sort of tragic hero who found peace[12] — do not mitigate the isolation of the tragic hero who has found no peace. Having reached this problematic conclusion, Lucas abandoned *Star Wars* for twenty years to work in less troublesome genres like pure melodrama (the Indiana Jones films) and fantasy (*Howard the Duck* and *Willow*); then, when he finally resolved to make more *Star Wars* films, he elected to produce three "prequels" instead of trying to continue the story after the conclusion of *Return of the Jedi*. Despite previous suggestions that Lucas originally envisioned *Star Wars* as a nine-film epic, with three films to follow *Return of the Jedi,* Lucas has since confessed that he really has no ideas about how to extend his saga; and one reason for his ongoing uncertainty is that surely, the first priority in any sequel would be devising some sort of happy ending for Luke Skywalker, yet it is difficult to see how this might be attained.

In written science fiction, we find many authors apparently determined to ignore melodrama and write in a different style; but melodrama still rises to the surface, as for example in the aforementioned *Stardance*. The Robinsons's novel begins as a sensitive, lyrical depiction of six dancers' efforts to create and perfect the art of zero-gravity dance; and the descriptions of their practice and performance seem far away from a sense of melodrama. But later, when the dancers become "interpreters" on a diplomatic mission to aliens who communicate by movement, the climax is incongruous — and melodramatic — as not one but two of the diplomats pull out a gun, threaten to kill the dancers, and reveal a scheme to seize control of the ship. Now the dancers must use their skills to overpower the villains and thwart their schemes. Melodrama in science fiction, then, is like the beast-flesh in the creatures of H. G. Wells's Doctor Moreau: invisible at first, it inexorably and inevitably emerges.

Three other examples of this phenomenon come to mind. First, Frederik Pohl and C. M. Kornbluth's *The Space Merchants* (1953) begins as a satirical depiction of a world driven mad by advertising, with the ultimate joke being that the hero's unprincipled advertising agency is persuading people to migrate to Venus, a planet that is a living hell; yet it ends with the hero rescuing his girl friend from an evil rival and desperately attempting to escape to Venus — now recast as a desirable haven from a corrupt Earth. Interestingly, one contemporary reviewer, P. Schuyler Miller, thought that the novel was "suffering principally, it seems to me, from its concessions to melodrama" ("The Reference Library" 153). Second, John Brunner's *Stand on Zanzibar* (1968) is first structured like a futuristic version of John Dos Passos's *U.S.A.* trilogy, with a kaleidoscope of different scenes and characters, but ultimately comes to focus on the efforts of one reluctant hero to carry out a daring rescue of a defector from a totalitarian enemy nation. Finally, as will be later discussed in more detail, William Gibson's *Neuromancer* (1984) opens as a tribute to the hard-boiled detective story and the *film noir*, with a thoroughly amoral hero, but concludes with the protagonist's struggle to rescue his girlfriend from the clutches of evil villains — a classic melodramatic structure, though not immediately apparent due to Gibson's overlay of irony.

In all three cases, then, a science fiction novel which initially seems based on a radically different generic model concludes with a situation right out of melodrama; and these are hardly the only examples that could be cited. Speaking of another science fiction novel — Fritz Leiber's *A Specter Is Haunting Texas* (1968) — reviewer Alexei Panshin offers this summary judgment: that it "is not the first science fiction book crippled by melodrama.... Melodrama has been the main vehicle of science fiction expression" ("Books" 50).

The importance of melodrama in science fiction is also shown — paradoxically — by the notably anemic genre of science fiction theatre: although science fiction derives from stage melodrama, Maxim Jakubowski and Peter Nicholls have noted that "specifically stage-bound science fiction is rare ... a small number of unrelated plays" (600). The reason is that unlike written and filmed science fiction, shaped by Gernsback's insistence on melodrama, science fiction theatre, unaffected by Gernsback and lacking a strong contemporary tradition of melodrama, has attempted unsuccessfully to build upon other genres: the symposium play — Richard Ganthony's *Message from Mars* (1912); satire — Karel Capek's *R.U.R.* (1921); comedy — Ray Bradbury's *The Day It Rained Forever* (1966); and farce — Spike Mulligan and John Antrobus's *The Bed-Sitting Room* (1969). In the weakness of such plays, we observe the weakness of the genre of science fiction when it is separated from melodrama.[13]

In all these works the basic problem of melodrama in science fiction emerges: if science fiction writers begin with melodrama, their genre's concerns create complications and generic confusion; but if they try to escape from melodrama, they risk either being driven back to its structures or losing needed vitality. Simply put, science fiction cannot cope with melodrama, and it cannot avoid melodrama.

The relationship between melodrama and science fiction, as exploited and revealed by Hugo Gernsback's *Ralph 124C 41+*, leads to two conclusions about melodrama in other genres. First, there are limits in the form's adaptability. Heilman argues that melodrama can be employed both by "dissenters" and "the order that is attacked" (96–97)—that is, by either side in a given dispute—suggesting the genre lacks ideology; similarly, Brooks calls melodrama "a remarkably adaptable form" (89). However, the example of science fiction suggests that through the very act of simplifying reality, melodrama in fact generates a populist ideology of simplicity—favoring simple emotions, simple actions, and simple people—which ill accords, for example, with the ideology of science fiction.[14] Thus, certain cases and causes cannot be effectively advanced by means of melodrama.

Second, there is true power in melodrama. Even though I have shown that melodrama is an inappropriate vehicle for the argument of science fiction, its creators have not abandoned, and cannot abandon, the form. As one of its contradictions, the elitist genre of science fiction has always sought, as Gernsback said, to "influence the masses" ("Editorially Speaking" 483); and the best way to do so is apparently melodrama. If science fiction is truly a predictive literature, then, one of its implicit predictions is that melodrama will continue to be a major literary force.

7

Gadgetry, Government, Genetics, and God

The Forms of Science Fiction Utopia

When Hugo Gersnback's *Ralph 124C 41+* is briefly discussed in critical studies, it is, as will be noted, most frequently described as a scientific utopia, despite the strong dose of melodrama which, one can argue, actually comes to dominate the narrative. But matters are actually a bit more complex, in a manner that merits some extended exploration.

Introduction: Science Fiction and Utopia

More so than in the case of melodrama, science fiction critics will usually acknowledge that there is a strong relationship between utopia and science fiction; however, their views of that relationship are noticeably different. In *Metamorphoses of Science Fiction*, Darko Suvin declares that "utopias ... are the sociopolitical subgenre of [Science Fiction]" (95) and constructs an imagined history of science fiction which prominently includes a number of utopias, including Thomas More's *Utopia*— identified as the first modern work of science fiction. Employing another constructed history of science fiction, Brian Stableford sees utopia as Hugo Gernsback's unsuccessful imposition on the genre; he "intended to establish [genre science fiction] as a Utopian literature," but "despite Gernsback's inspiration and intention, [science fiction] was never strongly utopian" ("Utopia" 623). In *Science Fiction: History, Science, Vision*, Robert Scholes and Eric S. Rabkin take a mediating position: they note on the one hand that "science fiction has drawn upon the literary heritage of a third great narrative form, the utopia" (173); however, they see later utopias as "atavistic" and, since "Science and atavism are enemies" (174), there can be little common ground between utopia and science fiction.

In a sense, all of these views are correct: science fiction is both compatible and incompatible with utopia, and science fiction has both built upon and rejected the model of utopia. Nevertheless, two elements are lacking in current critical perceptions of the relationship of these genres.

First, while utopia has existed as a self-conscious and coherent literary tradition for the last 400 years, science fiction emerged as such only in the twentieth century, as a result of the critical work of Hugo Gernsback; thus, any account of the interactions of the two genres must begin with Gernsback's pioneering novel *Ralph 124C 41+: A Romance of the Year 2660*, their first point of true intersection.

Second, the differences in theories of utopia and theories of science fiction have created not only interesting individual works but a number of distinct and peculiar subgenres of science fiction utopia: first, the simple collision of the two theories produces an unsatisfactory hybrid which I call the *pointillistic utopia*, best exemplified by *Ralph*; second, modifications in the theory of science fiction lay the groundwork for a true *science fiction utopia*; third, modifications in the theory of utopia engender another hybrid form which I call the *evolutionary utopia*; and finally, there are examples of the science fiction utopia which falls back on religious mysticism, which I call the *mystical utopia*.

All these forms both solve and do not solve the problem of science fiction utopia, and one must therefore conclude that there is indeed some fundamental incompatibility between utopia and science fiction, rooted in the fundamental incompatibility of utopia and modern science itself.

As background for the argument that follows, I offer a brief summation of the basic characteristics of the form of utopia as I see them. First, as a matter of definition, a utopia presents a society where virtually all citizens are happy and virtually all problems are solved; or, at the very least, the utopia must be a society seriously attempting to become perfect — Chad Walsh's *From Utopia to Nightmare* notes that "Wells and many modern utopians conceive of utopia not as a final perfection but as a goal and movement towards a goal; it is a *process*. In their terms, to be utopian is simply to have a utopian sense of direction, and work at it" (56). Still, I would argue that any utopia must then either be perfect, or significantly better than existing society, in order to convincingly argue for its positions.

Second, the utopia is to some extent designed to function as a thoroughgoing model, blueprint, or plan for an entire society. Long ago, Lewis Mumford's *The Story of Utopias* describes "the utopia of reconstruction" as "a vision of a reconstituted environment which is better adapted to the nature and aims of the human beings who dwell within it than the actual one; and not merely better adapted to their actual nature, but better fitted to their possible developments." Mumford even uses the metaphor of an architect's blueprint: "It is absurd to dispose of utopia by saying that it exists only on paper. The answer to that is: precisely the same thing may be said of the architect's plans for a house, and houses are none the worse for it" (21, 25).

It follows, finally, that a utopia must imply that such radical improvements in human society are possible, and that the focus of the utopia must be on describing and defending its proposed "reconstruction" of the world, not on matters such as plot or characterization.

If these are the priorities of utopia, they have not always been the priorities of science fiction, and in that incompatibility lie the origins of the tensions I intend to explore.

Hugo Gernsback and Pointillistic Utopia

In discussions of science fiction and utopia, Hugo Gernsback traditionally functions as the token buffoon, the idiot who believed that marvelous inventions and new gadgets would in themselves create a perfect, utopian society. As Stableford has argued, "Scientifiction, of course, as Gernsback envisaged it, was an implicitly Utopian literature. Its most fundamental proposition was the notion that the advancement of science would remake the world, irrespective of any political and moral questions, for the benefit of all mankind" (*The Sociology of Science Fiction* 124). And Gernsback's novel, *Ralph 124C 41+: A Romance of the Twenty-Sixth Century*, described by Sam Lundwall as a "pitiable utopian novel" (*Science Fiction: An Illustrated History* 76), is routinely offered as one crude example of Gernsback's "implicitly Utopian literature."

There are only two problems with these analyses: Gernsback did not believe in a scientific utopia, and *Ralph 124C 41+* is not really a utopia.

First, as already indicated by Stableford's use of the term "implicitly," and by his consistent inability to produce supporting quotations, Gernsback never made any statement arguing or even suggesting that scientific progress would create a perfect world. Here are Gernsback's strongest words of support for science that I can locate, offered in the editorial "Science Fiction Week":

> Not only is science fiction an idea of tremendous import, but it is to be an important factor in making the world a better place to live in, through educating the public to the possibilities of science and the influence of science on life which, even today, are not appreciated by the man on the street.... If every man, woman, boy and girl, could be induced to read science fiction right along, there would certainly be a great resulting benefit to the community, in that the educational standards of its people would be raised tremendously. Science fiction would make people happier, give them a broader understanding of the world, make them more tolerant [1061].

Note Gernsback's use of comparative, not superlative, adjective forms: science fiction will make the world a "better place" and people will be "happier" and "more tolerant." Yes, Gernsback thought that scientific advances, aided by science fiction, would *improve* the world, but he never claimed that scientific advances would *perfect* the world.

As for his novel *Ralph*, a careful reading of the text clearly shows that it is not a utopia in any conventional sense of the term. As a matter of definition, a utopia presents a model society where virtually all citizens are happy and virtually all problems are solved; but in Gernsback's world of 2660, this is manifestly not the case.

First, Ralph is unhappy because of the restrictions placed on his life: to maintain Ralph's scientific productivity, the government does not allow him any harmful activities, and Ralph "grew restive under the restraint" (41), calling himself "nothing but a prisoner" (42). Alice is threatened by an avalanche in the first chapter because, as she tells Ralph without anyone expressing surprise, the weather-engineers in her district, on strike for more "luxuries," have sabotaged the equipment, indicating that many workers are deeply dissatisfied with their lives (31). As a further indication of widespread discontent, criminal activity of all kinds is still rather common: Ralph is supplied with criminals "under sentence of death" to use in his experiments (42), he tells Alice about a recent embezzlement scandal (131), and a large and effective police force springs into action whenever Alice is abducted. The Martian Llysanorh' is driven to despair because the law does not allow him to marry the Earth woman Alice, and though he later emerges as a major villain, the novel displays remarkable sympathy for his predicament.[1] There have been major famines as recently as a generation ago, and science is described as constantly struggling to increase food production for the world's growing population (97–100). This society cannot even, it seems, maintain an efficient picture-phone system, since Ralph initially contacts Alice because of a wrong connection. And when Ralph is about to marry, the Planet Governor expresses relief that at least one of his problems — keeping Ralph happy — has been taken off "his already over-burdened shoulders" (141). This is a perfect world?

Beyond these large, blatant indications of continuing social difficulties, there are casual asides in the novel which, when examined, reveal much about the world of 2660. When Ralph is approaching the spaceship of the villainous Fernand, he quickly produces a device called the radioperforer designed to disable the ship and render its occupants unconscious. This is not a machine that Ralph has just invented; instead, it seems to be a standard item in any spaceship's equipment. Thus, Ralph lives in a society which has found it necessary, as a matter of course, to create a device which attacks spaceships.

Further, there is even one indication, when Ralph explains the need for flying "vacation cities," that scientific progress is not only failing to improve human life, but is making it worse: "with all the labor-saving devices [people] have, their lives are speeded up to the breaking point. The businessman or executive must leave his work every month for a few days, if he is not to become a wreck" (132). Strangely enough, the "labor-saving devices" provided by science are not making work easier; they are driving people crazy.

With all of these unmistakable signs of imperfections in the world of 2660, one has to wonder why this novel is regularly described as a utopia. While in part this indicates that critics have rarely bothered to read it very carefully — as indicated by a few erroneous comments noted elsewhere[2]— the common misreading of *Ralph* also stems from the fact that Gernsback's novel does frequently incorporate what might be termed utopian tableaux: a new invention is introduced, its marvelous effects are described, and people express their extreme happiness about it. For example, in reference to the new trans-Atlantic tube, Ralph exclaims, "This new tube is going to revolutionize intercontinental travel. I suppose it won't be long now before we will regard our tedious twenty-four hour journeys as things of the past" (61). Contemplating a statue of the last work-horse in New York, Alice says, "It is so much better now with electricity doing all the work" (76). Sitting down to watch a play on the Tele-Theater, Alice comments, "Can you imagine how the people in former centuries must have been inconvenienced when they wished to enjoy a play...? They probably would have rejoiced at the ease of our Tele-Theaters, where we can switch from one play to another in five seconds, until we find the one that suits us best" (86–87). "Alice was much impressed with the automatic-electric packing machines" (88), the narrator notes, and while enjoying the "aerial carnival," she says "Oh, it is like Fairyland. I could watch it forever" (93). Because of such scenes, inattentive readers like Brian W. Aldiss or Lundwall might regard the entire novel as a utopia without noticing the many signs of pain and unhappiness permeating the world of 2660.

If *Ralph* is to be described as a kind of utopia, then, it must be called a *pointillistic utopia*: there are tiny points of brightness in the foreground, suggesting perfect bliss, but a few steps backwards reveal a broader and different picture of continuing unrest and imperfection. Specifically, one can define the subgenre of pointillistic utopia in these terms: a story involving a society which is manifestly far from perfect and not designed to serve as an ideal counterpart to modern society; a story with a melodramatic context of good and evil locked in constant struggle; and a story in which scientific progress and new inventions provide small moments of joy and incremental improvements in the human condition, while promising no final perfection.

If this is the kind of work that *Ralph* is, one must ask why Gernsback wrote such a work. An unflattering answer would be that he was simply an inept writer who failed to notice that he was undermining his carefully projected utopia with thoughtless references to continuing social problems. However, one might first respond that the later chapters of his second novel, *Baron Münchhausen's New Scientific Adventures,* do function (as will be discussed) as a reasonably cohesive utopia, indicating that Gernsback was capable of producing such a story if he chose to. Furthermore, there is evidence suggesting that the inconsistent *Ralph* was exactly the kind of novel that Gernsback chose to write — one cannot say "he planned to write" because, in fact, he began writing without any plans. Recall that Gernsback said in 1950 that "I had no plan whatsoever for the whole of the story. I had no idea how it would end nor what the contents would be" ("Preface to the Second Edition" 8). Thus, from the very start Gernsback deliberately neglected the careful thought and preparation that must go into crafting a blueprint for an ideal society. That Gernsback had no desire to write a utopia is further suggested by the novel's subtitle — *A Romance of the Twenty-Sixth Century*— linking the work to the unrelated genre of "romance," a term suggesting little more than adventures in an exotic locale.

In addition to his use of a writing process that could not produce a utopia, there are three other problems in considering *Ralph* a utopia: Gernsback focused on subject matter which would not logically yield a utopia, he chose as a secondary model a genre which could not fully combine with utopia, and these choices of writing process, subject, and genre were informed by purposes which were different from those of utopia.

First, although he made gestures toward recognizing fields like biology and psychology as true sciences,[3] Gernsback saw the main focus of science fiction as the hard sciences of physics and engineering; and not being an idiot, he fully realized that marvelous new inventions of this type — voice-writers, Tele-motor-coasters, Language Rectifiers, and the like — would not, despite their beneficial effects, in themselves produce a perfect world. Since he is therefore disinclined to speculate about sciences like psychology and sociology that might have a more direct salutary effect on human society, he must provide his future society both with helpful scientific advances and a host of unresolved problems.

Second, while the first seven installments of the first version of *Ralph*, as previously explained, roughly adhere to the utopian pattern, Gernsback grew dissatisfied with that approach and shifted the story into the realm of melodrama for its last five installments, and in revising the novel in 1925 he gave even more prominence to melodramatic elements. His public position on the proper genre for science fiction underwent a similar shift, from "charming romance" ("A New Kind of Magazine" 3) to "thrilling adventure" ("Science Fiction Week" 1061). As discussed in the last chapter, the world of melodramatic adventure is a Manichean universe, with forces of light and darkness engaged in a continual struggle which only at the end is, for the moment, resolved in favor of light. And it stands in stark contrast to the world of the utopia, where the static perfection of a society in some faraway time or place is implicitly contrasted with static imperfection of the writer's and reader's society, with no sense of active conflict or confrontation between the two. In foregrounding "romance" and "adventure," then, Gernsback was borrowing a narrative pattern quite unlike that of utopia.

Finally, Gernsback's purposes in choosing such content, and such a form, were quite different from the common purposes of writing a utopia. In presenting science primarily as a practical matter of invention and engineering, science fiction, Gernsback believed, could serve as a way to inspire new inventions. This might mean, as already discussed, an author suggesting a new device which a scientist then actually builds; however, works in the genre could also inspire new discoveries in a more indirect fashion, as Gernsback pointed out in one editorial:

> An author, in one of his fantastic scientifiction stories, may start some one thinking along the suggested lines which the author had in mind, whereas the inventor in the end will finish up with something totally different, and perhaps much more important. But the fact remains that the author *provided the stimulus* in the first place, which is the most important function to perform ["Imagination and Reality" 579].

Thus, science fiction is not always designed to tell inventors and scientists what to think; rather, it is supposed to make them think. A picture emerges of science fiction writers and readers engaged in a kind of brainstorming session — writers throwing out ideas and their scientist readers responding with their own, possibly similar but possibly different, ideas. So there is a reason why Gernsback wrote *Ralph* with "no plan whatsoever"; the kind of overall systematic design commonly seen and emphasized in a utopia would inhibit the spontaneous creative thought of both authors and readers.

In addition, the genre of melodrama provides a good context for exciting incidents and adventures and an effective mode of writing to attract younger readers — one of Gernsback's other main priorities in publishing science fiction. Gernsback clearly sought to interest his young readers in science and possibly encourage them to become scientists themselves[4]; and the format of melodrama was ideally suited to make one scientist — Ralph — seem like a glamorous and exciting figure. In contrast, while it is difficult to say what sorts of people would be heroes in a utopia, such an ideal society would surely not be especially fond of scientists — people who, by nature, continually upset the status quo, make new discoveries, and change patterns of life; hence, a pure utopia could not serve to celebrate scientists and their work, and to make his scientist Ralph a hero, Gernsback was obliged to create an imperfect, melodramatic world as a background — because a world with problems will need, and properly appreciate, a working scientist.

In a deeper sense, Gernsback's choice of melodrama may reflect his own perception of the state of scientific knowledge in his day. Commonly regarded as a confident believer in continuing scientific progress, Gernsback was nonetheless acutely aware of its limitations, as shown by repeated comments: "we have as yet not scratched the surface of the possibilities of nature, or come anywhere near the limit of our progress" ("Hidden Wonders" 293); "we do not know what electricity is; we do not know what light is, in their ultimate states, and there is practically nothing in the entire world that surrounds us, that we know anything about at all" ("The Amazing Unknown" 389); and "Why there should be stars and what their purpose is, we have not, as yet, the slightest conception; perhaps in a thousand years we shall know a great deal about all of it" ("Our Amazing Stars" 1063). Thus, not only is the current level of scientific knowledge woefully inadequate, but there is not even confidence that it will be ultimately complete — Gernsback says that "perhaps" we will know more about stars "in a thousand years." With so many unanswered problems confronting the scientists of Gernsback's era, one could not with assurance predict they would all be quickly resolved, and the world of science emerges as fundamentally melodramatic, with heroic scientists struggling against a host of mysteries. Thus, the genre of *Ralph*, so different from that of utopia, may be the most appropriate choice for a depiction of a scientist at work.

In sum, the man who created the first complete theory of science fiction endowed that genre with a characteristic content, a characteristic form, and characteristic purposes which were antagonistic to those of utopia, which led to only a strange and limited form of the genre, the pointillistic utopia. And I would argue that this remains the standard depiction of future human civilizations in science fiction: there are marvelous machines and scientific advances which have in some ways made life easier and have in some ways made life harder; but the basic problems of human nature and human society remain more or less as they always have been. This description would apply to works like Isaac Asimov's *The Caves of Steel* (1953), Philip José Farmer's "Riders of the Purple Wage" (1967), James Blish and Norman L. Knight's *A Torrent of Faces* (1967), John Brunner's *Stand on Zanzibar* (1968), and Bruce Sterling's *Islands in the Net* (1988).

Of course, the continuing imperfections of these societies may be a bit more conspicuous than those of Gernsback's world of 2660 — which may create the impression that these works are actually dystopias. But such a characterization simply cannot be supported. Just as Gernsback could not bring himself to argue that technological progress would in itself create a perfect world, these authors cannot bring themselves to argue that such progress in itself would create a nightmare world. Indeed, both Farmer and Brunner display delight in, as well as dissatisfaction with, their future societies, and neither work can be accurately read as a call to abandon scientific advances as a way to return to a simpler and happier existence.

It seems misleading, therefore, to interpret works like *Ralph* which lean toward optimism as utopias and works like *Stand on Zanzibar* which lean toward pessimism as dystopias, for this distinction is too fine, considering that both types of work essentially depict societies fundamentally unaffected by scientific progress, with problems that are identical to those of present-day society. Were I given to intolerable puns, I might describe all works of this form as the subgenre of *isotopia*—"same place"—because their scientific marvels finally cannot conceal the fact that nothing basic has really changed in their future worlds.

Since it seems, then, that Gernsback's theory of science fiction cannot yield a true utopia, writers and critics who wished to see a true science fiction utopia faced two choices: they could modify the theory of science fiction to suit the form of utopia, or they could modify the theory of utopia to suit the form of science fiction; and both strategies in fact can be observed.

Ursula K. Le Guin and Science Fiction Utopia

Although that was not his primary goal, John W. Campbell, Jr. effectively changed science fiction into a form suitable for utopia when he revised and expanded Gernsback's theories, which, among other consequences, resolved the all the conflicts between science fiction and conventional utopia which Gernsback had so conspicuously displayed.

First, to assist writers in creating science fiction stories that could serve as utopias, Campbell insisted that depictions of future societies in science fiction must be thoroughly planned and thoughtfully worked out before one begins writing: "Mapping out a civilization of the future is an essential background to a convincing story of the future ... you've got to have that carefully mapped outline in mind to get consistency of minor details" ("The Old Navy Game" 6).

Next, to eliminate problems with the limited subject matter of science fiction, Campbell explicitly included the social sciences in the realm of possible subjects for the genre: "Sociology, psychology, and parapsychology are, today, not true sciences; therefore, instead of forecasting future results of applications of sociological science of today, we must forecast the *development of a science* of sociology. From there, the story can take off" ("The Science of Science Fiction Writing" 91).

Third, to change the narrow generic focus of science fiction, Campbell abandoned Gernsback's insistence on "thrilling adventure" as the characteristic form of science fiction; instead, he claimed that "science-fiction is the freest, least formalized of any literary medium" ("Introduction," *Who Goes There?* 5) and, in 1946, described "Adventure science fiction" as only one of three types of science fiction, the others being "Prophecy stories" and "Philosophical stories" ("Concerning Science Fiction" vi).

Finally, to expand the characteristic purposes of writing science fiction, Campbell as noted once described science fiction as "a convenient analog system for thinking about new scientific, social, and economic ideas" ("Introduction," *Prologue to Analog* 10, 13); and with this larger purpose established, the genre now effectively incorporated utopia: "science fiction is ... a great way to study social concepts — to consider the logical human consequences of various cultural propositions, from absolute dictatorship to absolute anarchy. Which is, of course, why so many utopian, and negative-utopian novels, ranging from Plato's *Republic*, through *Utopia* itself, to Orwell's *1984*, have been science fiction" ("Introduction," *Analog 6* xv).

In sum, Campbell described a methodology for writing science fiction that was compatible with producing a utopia, expanded the subject matter of science fiction to include the sorts of social and political issues associated with utopia, announced an end to the fixation with melodramatic adventure in science fiction that had interfered with utopia, and defined a new purpose in science fiction which was identical to that of utopia.

Given this new critical climate, it is not surprising that science fiction writers from 1940 on have occasionally produced works that seem more or less like classic utopias, including Eric Frank Russell's "And Then There Were None" (1951), Theodore Sturgeon's *Venus Plus X* (1960), Ursula K. Le Guin's *The Dispossessed: An Ambiguous Utopia* (1974), and Mack Reynolds's *Looking Backward, From the Year 2000* (1973). And these are the sorts of novels that are normally discussed in the context of "science fiction utopia." However, there is still something not quite right about these works.

Of course, as befits its status as the first true work of science fiction, Gernsback's *Ralph* is not completely without some elements of this sort of science fiction utopia. There is, after all, a world government in 2660, ruled by a benevolent Planet Governor, and the feeling emerges that such a society is superior to previous divisions into nation-states. In addition, Gernsback includes a brief discussion of the improved economic system, which has little to do with scientific progress and much to do with social engineering.

However, to see the full dimensions of the true science fiction utopia, one might consider Le Guin's *The Dispossessed*, one of the few science fiction novels that explicitly labels itself as a utopia — albeit an "ambiguous" one. In all respects, it seems a fulfillment of Campbell's reforms: Le Guin offers a richly detailed and logically developed imaginary world to illustrate her ideas; her novel involves a posited "science of sociology" and is primarily concerned with politics and government; the novel is certainly more a "Philosophical story" than an "Adventure"; and it is definitely designed as "a great way to study social concepts — to consider the logical human consequences of various cultural propositions, from absolute dictatorship to absolute anarchy." In every way, then, a context has been prepared so that Le Guin can write a true utopia; and in her novel, to be sure, the influence of utopia and its relatives is perhaps stronger than that of science fiction. However, examined in the generic context of utopia, her novel reveals a number of paradoxes.

First, there is at least one aspect of *The Dispossessed* which is pure pointillistic utopia, a moment reflecting the influence of Gernsback in an otherwise dissimilar work. Preoccupied by her political and social concerns, critics sometimes fail to notice that this is also the story of the brilliant scientist who invented the ansible, the communication device which figures in and links several of Le Guin's novels; and a discussion of this machine and its marvelous effects recalls the spirit of *Ralph 124C 41+*:

> "But they can make the ansible, with my equations, if they want it.... It will be a device that will permit communication without any time interval between two points in space. The device will not transmit messages, of course; simultaneity is identity. But to our perceptions, that simultaneity will function as a transmission, a sending. So we will be able to use it to talk between worlds, without the long waiting for the message to go and the reply to return that electromagnetic impulses require...."
>
> "So I could pick up the — ansible? — and talk with my son in Delhi? ... And I could find out what's happening at home *now*, not eleven years ago. And decisions could be made, and agreements reached, and information shared.... Do you know, Shevek, I think your very simple matter might change the lives of all the billions of people in the nine Known worlds? ... It would make a league of worlds possible. A federation. We have been held apart by the years, the decades between leaving and arriving, between question and response. It's as if you had invented human speech! We can talk — at last we can talk together" [300].

As in Gernsback's novel, here is a new scientific invention that will significantly improve — but not perfect — a civilization, in this case that of all inhabited worlds.

In addition, Le Guin has not entirely escaped from Gernsback's old insistence on "thrilling adventure." The scenes on Anarres, to be sure, involve conflicts that are more muted and elemental — opposition from conservative superiors, a merciless drought, long periods of separation caused by continuing crisis, and the like. But on the other planet Urras, Le Guin indulges in a few scenes of violent action and derring-do involving a demonstration attacked by police, days of hiding out from the authorities while unrest continues, and a daring escape to the Terran Embassy. Since these incidents contribute little to her political and social messages, one might argue that Le Guin still feels some lingering urge to include a few moments of excitement in a novel that is generally written in a quite different manner.[5]

Despite the galactic importance of the ansible and Le Guin's adventures on Urras, the primary focus of *The Dispossessed* is, of course, on the world of Anarres, and in many ways it seems a traditional utopia. On the one hand, Anarres is clearly designed to show the kind of benevolent society that might have emerged from a true Communist revolution, one which produced anarchy instead of totalitarianism. Its egalitarian spirit, its freedom from possessions, its smooth functioning all testify that it is superior to the other world Urras, which represents our world. As the protagonist Shevek announces when talking to a group of Urrans,

> Here you see the jewels, there you see the eyes. And in the eyes you see the splendor, the splendor of the human spirit. Because our men and women are free — possessing nothing, they are free. And you the possessors are possessed. You are all in jail. Each alone, solitary, with a heap of what he owns. You live in prison, die in prison. It is all I can see in your eyes — the wall, the wall! [200].

However, Anarres is also a society with a host of unresolved and worsening problems; specifically, a growing sense of authoritarian control, of personal pettiness intervening in decisions, of resistance to new ideas. As one character says to the protagonist Shevek, "Change is freedom, change is life — is anything more basic to Odonian thought than that? But nothing changes any more! Our society is sick. You know it. You're suffering its sickness. Its suicidal sickness!" (146) And one early rumination by Shevek implies that a perfect society of any kind is in fact impossible:

> Suffering is the condition on which we live.... But no society can change the nature of existence. We can't prevent suffering. This pain and that pain, yes, but not Pain. A society can only relieve social suffering, unnecessary suffering. The rest remains. The root, the reality. All of us here are going to know grief; if we live fifty years, we'll have known pain for fifty years. And in the end we'll die. That's the condition we're born on [53].

Despite this insight, and his own personal difficulties, though, Shevek remains a firm supporter of his culture; and it becomes important to realize in exactly what sense of the term Le Guin's utopia is "ambiguous." The word does not imply that Le Guin harbors any doubts about the superiority of Anarres to Urras, for I see no evidence of that in the novel; the ambiguity is a matter of different contexts. Compared to the materialistic and unjust countries of Urras, Anarres is indeed a utopia; but compared to the ideals that created that new world, the reality of Anarres seems more like a dystopia. That is why Shevek vigorously defends his world when he is talking to residents of Urras, and why he vigorously criticizes his world when he is talking to his fellow Anarrens. Anarres both is and is not a utopia, depending on the contexts it is placed in.

It is also not without significance that Le Guin chose to make her protagonist a physicist, for no other field of modern science has been so obliged to live with ambiguity — photons that sometimes behave like a wave and sometimes behave like a particle, phenomena of gravity that are sometimes best explained by general relativity and sometimes best explained by a theory of quantum gravity. That is why Shevek spends so much time reading the works of Albert Einstein — this is a field where perceptions are necessarily relative. And in relation to time, as Shevek explains, "time has two aspects. There is the arrow, the running river, without which there is no change, no progress, or direction, or creation. And there is the circle or the cycle, without which there is chaos, meaningless succession of instants, a world without clocks or seasons or promises" (196). Similarly, any well-governed society has two aspects: perfection in relation to some societies and some ideals, imperfection in relation to other societies and other ideals; and linear progress is both possible — according to the "arrow" perspective on time — and ultimately impossible — according to the "cycle" perspective on time.

And the way that Shevek finally resolves his own mixed feelings about his society is significant, as indicated by a reflection late in the novel: "For her, as for him, there was no end. There was process: process was all. You could go in a promising direction or you could go wrong, but you did not set out with the expectation of ever stopping anywhere. All responsibilities, all commitments thus understood took on substance and duration" (291). Anarres is a utopia because it is moving in "a promising direction," unlike Urras, trapped in capitalism and tyranny; yet Anarres can never be a static, perfect society because that is impossible. Thus, Le Guin offers a utopia that is purely relative, a process of improvement, not an absolute ideal, not a perfection.

In other science fiction utopias, despite the apparent perfection of the societies they create, the authors also seem to lack the sense of confidence and moral certitude that traditionally governs this type of work. Thus, the humorous tone of Russell's "And Then There Were None" undermines its polemics; the hermaphroditic society of Sturgeon's *Venus Plus X* seems frail and threatened, more an anomaly than a model for future human society, and, as Stableford notes, it ultimately "fails the test" ("Utopia" 623); and *Looking Backward, From the Year 2000* pays tribute to Bellamy's classic work while at the same time suggesting that its optimism was a bit naive.

Seeing all of these misgivings emerging in a form of writing which traditionally embodies a clear and vehement polemic, one might simply argue that ours is not an age of moral certitude; and yet, outside the genre of science fiction, conventional and confident utopias have continued to appear, like Austin Tappan Wright's *Islandia* (1942), B. F. Skinner's *Walden Two* (1948), Aldous Huxley's *Island* (1962), and Ernest Callenbach's *Ecotopia: The Notebooks and Reports of William Weston* (1975). Thus, the failure to project complete perfection in science fiction, even though a theoretical groundwork for such projections was firmly established, must reflect some peculiar characteristic of the modern genre.

To understand the apparent failure of these science fiction utopias, one must look at another type of utopian science fiction: those works which reflect the second transformation, changing the theory of utopia to suit the form of science fiction.

Arthur C. Clarke and Evolutionary Utopia

Despite the reforms of Campbell and others, Gernsback's insistence on melodramatics and mechanics remained a powerful force in the genre, and many writers still sought to work within such frameworks. From them, we see an entirely different type of utopia emerging.

In these cases, there are four major changes in the form to deal with the four problems that *Ralph 124C 41+* revealed: first, to deal with the rather chaotic process of writing that Gernsback recommended, the utopia will involve not a complete social blueprint but a single major scientific innovation. Second, to accord with Gernsback's emphasis on invention and scientific ideas, the focus of the utopia will shift from improving human society through social engineering to improving human beings through biological and genetic engineering. To make the perfect world, one must now invent the perfect human. Third, to accord with Gernsback's insistence on melodramatic adventure, the appearance of this perfect human is moved from the center of the work to its very end — the one moment in melodrama where a vision of complete perfection is temporarily sanctioned — and the rest of the story can be freely adventurous in describing the exciting events that led to the creation of this perfect human. Finally, to achieve Gernsback's goals of interesting young readers and stimulating scientific thinking, the story can endow the new race with certain childlike qualities — as discussed below — and devote considerable attention to the scientific principles and methods used to change humanity. All in all, these transformations create another possible solution to the difficulty in writing a science fiction utopia.

One example of this form is Spider and Jeanne Robinson's *Stardance*. Here, after a series of adventures involving efforts to develop a new form of dancing in space, aliens previously regarded as unfriendly are revealed to be mankind's mentors, preparing the race for a new level of civilization. The dancers are then transformed into beings which can survive in the vacuum of space and which can function as a group intelligence — thus creating the possibility of a new and superior human race, as the changed protagonist Charlie Armstead triumphantly explains to one skeptic:

> We would never die, Silverman. We would never again hunger or thirst, never need a place to dispose of our wastes. We would never again fear heat or cold, never fear vacuum, Silverman; we would never fear anything again. We would acquire instant and complete control of our autonomic nervous systems, gain access to the sensorium keyboard of the hypothalamus itself. We would attain symphysis, telepathic communion, becoming a single mind in six immortal bodies, endlessly dreaming and never asleep. Individually and together we would become no more like a human than a human is like a chimpanzee [249].

And later, Armstead exclaims, "All the evil men and women on Earth will not stop us, and the days of evil are numbered" (268). Here is the true utopian spirit, though focused now on a new and ideal type of human being, not a new and ideal type of society; and while ordinary humans will continue to exist, more and more people in the future will want to undergo the transformation and become true space creatures, as Armstead urges them to do in the novel's last sentence: "my message to you is: the stars can even be yours" (278).

The type of novel, involving a new form of human being, might be called the *evolutionary utopia* and could be specifically defined as follows: a story which, like the pointillistic utopia, takes place in a manifestly imperfect world; a story where the solution to social problems involves the scientific evolution or creation of a new type of human or other intelligent being; and a story which describes how that new type of being came into existence and why it will enjoy a superior life.

Other novels which more or less fit this pattern include Clifford D. Simak's *City* (1950), wherein imperfect humans withdraw to live on Jupiter, leaving behind mentally advanced animals to create a superior civilization; Sturgeon's *More Than Human* (1953), where a few people with extraordinary powers come together to form "homo gestalt"; Clarke's *Childhood's End* (1953), where alien overlords help most humans come together as a group intelligence; John Wyndham's *Rebirth* (1955), where nuclear war creates a new race of people with advanced telepathic powers; Fritz Leiber's *A Specter Is Haunting Texas* (1968), depicting an ideal society in a space station orbiting the Moon; Brunner's *Stand on Zanzibar* (1968), which concludes with the suggestion that a remarkable gene present only in one African nation might lead to an end to all human conflict; George Zebrowski's *Macrolife* (1979), in which societies in space colonies gradually merge to become one massive being called Macrolife; Charles Sheffield's *Between the Strokes of Night* (1985), where people learn how to slow down their life span and live indefinitely in "S-space" or "T-space"; Frederik Pohl's *Heechee Rendezvous* (1984) and *The Annals of the Heechee* (1987), wherein Robinette Broadhead is transformed into a computer construct with nearly unlimited knowledge, abilities, and lifespan; and William Gibson's *Neuromancer* (1984), where Case and his comrades assist in the creation of a true Artificial Intelligence which can reach out to the stars and contact other beings of its kind.[6]

In addition, this pattern can be detected — faintly — in Gernsback's *Ralph*, with the description of how Ralph developed a method for bringing dead people back to life — tested on a dog in Chapter 3, and used to revive Alice at the end of the novel. And with Alice brought back to life, she in effect becomes, as previously noted, the first of a new type of human being, capable of living and continuing to improve indefinitely.[7]

I am by no means the first critic to seek a link between this kind of work and utopia; for example, in *Science Fiction: History, Science, Vision*, Robert Scholes and Eric S. Rabkin argue that these developments represent a "fourth phase" of utopia:

> Most twentieth-century writers have seen no way to get beyond the enslavement to technology, and thus we find a series of distinguished dystopias [like Huxley's *Brave New World*, 1932) that predict a dismal future for humanity. Some writers, however, have tried to get beyond this doom by postulating psychic growth or an evolutionary breakthrough to a race of superpeople. These tactics, of course, presume the possibility of a basic change in human nature; they do not so much see a way beyond technology as around it. In postulating such radical improvement in humanity, the utopians of this fourth phase are modernizing the dreams of the Christian humanists of the second [174].

Still, to defend these works as transformed utopias, I must first differentiate them from the two traditions to which they are apparently related. The first is the apocalyptic vision, alluded to in Scholes and Rabkin's reference to "Christian humanists"— stories where humans face a final judgment leading either to eternal bliss or eternal damnation. *Childhood's End* in particular is often discussed in apocalyptic terms; yet there are key differences to consider. Despite its air of discontinuity, the apocalypse is informed by people's previous behavior and affects all people; in contrast, the emergence of a new type of human being may seem unrelated to past human events and usually has no effect on those who are not transformed, leaving them behind to observe and despair, as in *Childhood's End*, or to continue their previous lives, as in

Stardance. The lack of a relationship between the old and new humans reflects the separation of the actual imperfect society and the imagined ideal society in the traditional utopia, rather than the transitional mood of the apocalypse.

Second, in some "scientific romances" which were written before and outside of Gernsback's tradition of modern science fiction, there are also depicted new future beings or transformed humans who appear in some ways to be improvements on present-day mankind; however, these works project a different attitude towards these new beings, as noted by Brian Stableford in *Scientific Romance in Britain, 1890–1950*:

> There is a strong vein of misanthropy in scientific romance.... A frequent corol-
> lary ... is the declaration that hope for the future [if there is any] must be tied to
> the transcendence of this brutishness, by education or evolution, or both.
> Utopian optimism was smashed by the realization that a New World would
> need New Men to live in it, and that we were neither mentally equipped nor
> spiritually equipped to be New Men. Writers of scientific romance disagreed
> about what manner of men those new beings might be, and were ambivalent in
> their attitudes to them, but their very ambivalence intensified their preoccupa-
> tion with the probable collapse of our civilization and its possible transcendent
> renewal [338].

This "ambivalence" towards these "New Men" can be seen in the two races of H. G. Wells's *The Time Machine* (1895), the helpless Eloi and the savage Morlocks; and these types of successors — mild-mannered midgets and malev-olent monsters — can also be seen in early science fiction: the pathetic and shriveled future men of G. Peyton Wertenbaker's "The Coming of the Ice" (1926) and John W. Campbell, Jr.'s "Twilight" (1934), and the evil creatures of the future depicted in Francis Flagg's "The Machine Man of Ardathia" (1927) and Edmond Hamilton's "The Man Who Evolved" (1931). However, modern science fiction grew beyond these stereotypical menaces and often began to see a new human race in a more positive light — indeed, to see such a race as the solution to the human race's intractable problems.

The successors to humanity typically have a number of posited charac-teristics which fall into three broad categories: new abilities, longer lifespans, and group intelligence. Authors are thus seeing three fundamental problems in the existence of present-day humanity — insufficient ability to accomplish one's goals, insufficient time in which to accomplish them, and inherent conflict between people — and, in response, are developing physiological and biological solutions to those problems.

There is little emphasis on new *physical* abilities, although these are occa-sionally found, as in the virtual invulnerability of the new beings of *Stardance.* A more common preoccupation is new *mental* abilities, such as increased intel-ligence, telepathy, and telekinesis — all seen in *More Than Human.* Immor-tality, or at least a greatly extended lifespan, is a common feature, achieved by living in zero gravity in *A Specter Is Haunting Texas*, by transformation into a computer construct in *The Annals of the Heechee*, and by slowing down humans' perception of time in *Between the Strokes of Night*. One specific form of immortality is achieved by becoming one element in a group intelligence, frequently seen as the next stage in human evolution. This idea is most grandly depicted in Olaf Stapledon's *Star Maker* (1937), of course, but also appears repeatedly in modern science fiction works, including *More Than Human*, *Childhood's End*, *Macrolife*, and *Stardance*.

While these increases in mental ability and lifespan, and surely with the formation of a group intelligence, society will clearly be more unified and less prone to conflicts; but writers also occasionally suggest the need for an improved sense of morality. Rather than an advance, however, this is usually depicted as a return and recommitment to the simple truths of earlier days. Thus, in *More Than Human*, the *homo gestalt* is perfected when a normal person is incorporated to provide the being with a conscience; and in *City*, the animals' moral code is ancient and fundamental, as suggested by the reference in the title of one later story to Aesop's Fables.

In fact, what all of these attributes suggest in some way is *a return to childhood.* that is, young people typically do not believe in their own mortality and seem to perceive time differently than adults, like the beings in *A Specter Is Haunting Texas*, *The Annals of the Heechee*, and *Between the Strokes of Night*; they may have an exaggerated belief in their own abilities, either physical or mental, like the beings in *More Than Human* and *Stardance*; the very young do not have a sense that they are separate from the rest of the universe, similar to the feeling of a group intelligence in *More Than Human*, *Childhood's End*, and *Stardance*; and children often have a strongly felt but simple sense of morality, like that seen in *More Than Human* and *City*.

In this way, we see one fundamental difference between traditional utopia and the evolutionary utopia: in traditional utopia, the dominant image is of a new maturity and the human race is essentially urged to grow up, to listen to the dictates of the old and wise philosopher-kings and to establish a mature, enlightened society. In contrast, the evolutionary utopias of science fiction have absorbed an important lesson from evolution, which reveals that new advances frequently occur by means of *neoteny*— the retention of juvenile features in adults. Thus, humans are very much like baby chimpanzees, and the successors to humanity, these stories suggest, will in some ways be very much like human babies in their attitudes and attributes. Thus, the new, improved people of these stories are not really older and wiser; they are better characterized as precocious children.

Scholes and Rabkin hint at this view of the evolutionary utopia when they speak of their "fourth phase" utopias as "clearly atavistic.... Atavism, though we see it here operating in a historical and intellectual way, is primarily a psychological phenomenon, a desire to return to what seems to have been a time in one's life when the world was better organized, when pressures were defended against by parents, when responsibility was easily borne" (174). Their error is to then argue that "science and atavism are enemies. Science allows no retreating in time" (174); but as I point out, atavism of a sort is in fact a common evolutionary strategy, and a return to childhood traits thus becomes both scientific and logical.

Of course, the title of one work I have mentioned — *Childhood's End*— apparently contradicts this picture, in describing the development of group intelligence as a sign of humanity at last growing up. However, it must be noted that the persons transformed in Clarke's novel are all children, while their parents and the distinctly parental Overlords remain powerless to transform themselves — indicating that age and maturity are enemies, not allies, of this change. And since Clarke is not incapable of subtlety, I suggest that another reading of his title would be "Childhood Is End"—that is, a reversion to a new and improved state of childhood represents the natural end, purpose, or goal of human evolution.

To understand both the nature of and the problems in this sort of narrative, Clarke's novel is a valuable and important work which describes how a race of aliens called the Overlords assume control of Earth, impose world peace, and thus prepare the human race for its transformation into elements of a vast group intelligence known as the Overmind. As in Le Guin's novel, there are first of all elements of the pointillistic utopia when Clarke identifies scientific progress as one factor in the improvement of the world:

> Production had become largely automatic: the robot factories poured forth consumer goods in such unending streams that all the ordinary necessities of life were virtually free. Men worked for the sake of the luxuries they desired: or they did not work at all....
> Thanks to the perfection of air transport, everyone was free to go anywhere at a moment's notice. There was more room in the skies than there had ever been on the roads, and the twenty-first century had repeated, on a larger scale, the great American achievement of putting a nation on wheels. It had given wings to the world ... the ubiquitous little aircars had washed away the last barriers between the different tribes of mankind [71–73].

In addition, Clarke is not above a little bit of "thrilling adventure"— some rebels seize the Secretary General of the United Nations who is cooperating with the Overlords — although he later refers to the incident apologetically as "This ridiculously melodramatic kidnapping, which in retrospect seemed like a third-rate TV drama" (49).[8] In this way also, Clarke pays tribute to the Gernsback tradition.

However, Clarke is also consciously drawing upon the genre of utopia, and he makes it clear that the main cause for the initial improvement in human existence was the Overlords' decision to impose a "World State" as the "first step" in solving humanity's problems (61). With the elimination of separate nations, and the Overlords' benevolent but forceful administration, an apparently ideal society is formed almost purely by political means:

> By the standards of all earlier ages, it was Utopia. Ignorance, disease, poverty, and fear had virtually ceased to exist. The memory of war was fading into the past as a nightmare vanishes with the dawn; soon it would lie outside the experience of living men.
>
> With the energies of mankind directed into constructive channels, the face of the world had been remade.... Crime had practically vanished [71–72].

And additional references to "Utopia" (75, 90) make it clear that Clarke is deliberately building upon this literary tradition.

However, Clarke also establishes that such political solutions are not sufficient, and several statements indicate that problems remain with Earth under the control of the Overlords. He speaks of "a decline in science" and "the virtual end of the creative arts," caused by "The end of strife and conflict of all kinds" (75)[9]; he refers to "boredom" as "The supreme enemy of all Utopias" (75); and he acknowledges that "No utopia can ever give satisfaction to everyone, all the time.... There still remain the searchings of the mind and the longings of the heart" (90). The full resolution of the human condition must involve the transformation of the human race, and that becomes the major theme of *Childhood's End*.

In depicting the change of all human children into a group intelligence, Clarke seems both celebratory and critical. The Overlord Karellan announces that "We are helping to bring something new and wonderful into being" (176), and Jan Rodricks speaks of the Overmind "bearing the same relation to man as man bore to the amoeba" (205). Thus, there is a sense of growth, of natural development to a higher plane. On the other hand, the blank faces of the transformed children are rather disconcerting, and viewing their activities in an early stage, Rodricks says "They might have been savages, engaged in some complex ritual dance. They were naked and filthy, with matted hair obscuring their eyes" (202). Perhaps this transformation is not so wonderful.

There are also indications that the Overmind itself is not happy, is not satisfied, in its present existence. Karellan says, "We believe — it is only a theory — that the Overmind is trying to grow, to extend its powers and its awareness of the universe" (183); and Rodricks asks of the Overmind, "Did it too have desires, did it have goals it sensed dimly yet might never attain?" (205) The analogy of amoeba is to man as man is to the Overmind carries the suggestion that the perfection of the Overmind is purely relative, just as a man might appear perfect from the perspective of an amoeba.

In other works of this type, there are also hints that the birth of a new human race may not be completely desirable, and that such new beings will continue to feel unfulfilled. First, the concept of group intelligence is often resisted: thus, in Robert A. Heinlein's *Methusaleh's Children* (1958), Lazarus Long flees in horror from a plantlike collective intelligence; the attitude of Michael Swanwick's *Vacuum Flowers* (1987) toward a group intelligence called the Comprise is at best ambivalent; and Richard A. Lupoff's *The Forever City* (1987) depicts a group intelligence as sinister, whispering voices — in a novel which also offers a briefly glimpsed genetic monster as another pessimistic view of humanity's future development. And the benefits of childhood traits are not always seen as unmixed: while one cannot be sure of Frederik Pohl's intentions, Robinette Broadhead in *The Annals of the Heechee*, for all his boasting about his superior abilities and lifestyle, begins to seem like an insufferable, pampered child, with every need tended to by two dutiful computer constructs that, respectively, perform all of the functions of father and friend, and mother, wife, and mistress. With such an exemplar of the new humanity, the fact that the mysterious Assassins are apparently reconstructing the universe for the benefit of beings like Broadhead sounds more ominous than promising.

In addition, when writers extend the story of the new improved humans beyond the moment of their creation, there emerge doubts about their perfection and their ultimate success in resolving fundamental problems that recall the pessimistic conclusions of *Star Maker* and other "scientific romances." Thus, at the end of *Macrolife*, the collective being falls apart and one of its constituent parts reemerges as an individual consciousness to observe the end of the universe. And *Between the Strokes of Night* offers a similar conclusion, as one person living in T-space remains to watch the universe die with some of his questions still unanswered.

Even humanity's successors, in the long run, cannot achieve perfection, it seems, so the development of the evolutionary utopia does not resolve the fundamental problem of how to achieve the ideal society. There remains, though, one more possible approach to this problem to explore.

Robert A. Heinlein and Mystical Utopia

To those who have trouble conceiving of a perfect society on Earth, there is still the refuge of religious belief, specifically, belief in an afterlife or Last Judgment which will provide — at least for the deserving — a perfect and eternal life by divine fiat. Such hopes, of course, predate the development of the genre of utopia, which is traditionally devoted to positing worldly solutions to worldly problems; nevertheless, divine intervention has sometimes figured in works related to utopia like Taylor Caldwell's *Your Sins and Mine* (1955), wherein a devastating drought ends when people discover that every place where they bow down and pray immediately becomes fecund again. A work presenting a religious or mystical solution to the problems of human existence might be termed a mystical utopia; but this is not a strategy that one would expect to find in the avowedly secular genre of science fiction.

Nevertheless, one very prominent science fiction writer, Robert A. Heinlein, has repeatedly presented heaven or an afterlife as the resolution and conclusion of his stories. In "The Man Who Traveled in Elephants" (1957), the story's likable vagabond is finally rewarded with an entrance into heaven; in *Stranger in a Strange Land* (1961), Valentine Michael Smith, having failed to establish an ideal society on Earth, dies and goes to heaven, where he will apparently have another chance to implement his ideas; and in *Job: A Comedy of Justice* (1984), Heinlein's hero escapes from his bewildering shifts through parallel universes by means of traditional Christian rapture, which leads to an afterlife where various deities are waiting to welcome and reward their followers.

To best understand how such visions are, and are not, compatible with utopia, one must turn to another work by Heinlein, *Beyond This Horizon* (1942), a novel which first seems to combine all three forms of science fiction utopia, then rejects all three approaches to move into the realm of mystical utopia.

Beyond This Horizon is first of all a pointillistic utopia, in that it presents many small inventions and improvements that have made life easier for the human race. Unlike Gernsback, to be sure, Heinlein, as has often been noted, tends to take these inventions for granted, rather than focusing on and celebrating them, but readers nonetheless get periodic glimpses of a society where doors dilate, where hot air cleans and mechanical fingers massage people who take showers, and where water beds provide complete sleeping comfort — and, by means a system for draining those beds, a uniquely effective alarm clock as well.

However, Heinlein also sets up his novel as a traditional utopia, in describing more fully than Gernsback a society governed by a humane world government, led by democratically elected Planners who are assisted by Moderators to monitor and assist individual citizens. An efficient and intelligent economic system insures continuing prosperity for all, and jobs are provided primarily because people feel the need to work, not because their work is really necessary. Politeness and social harmony are maintained by the practice of wearing arms and dueling when a dispute arises. And, like Clarke, Heinlein includes a specific reference to the genre when his hero Hamilton Felix says of a group of would-be revolutionaries that "I can't see them building a Utopia" (61).

Finally, *Beyond This Horizon* functions as an evolutionary utopia because it depicts a society obsessed with genetics, determined to improve the human race by encouraging marriages between well-matched partners and genetically engineering their offspring to be the best children possible. This program has not only eliminated congenital defects but promises to create "a stronger, sounder, more adaptable, more resistant race" (29); and a Moderator named Mordan is particularly anxious for Felix to have children, because genetic charts indicate that they will be excellent specimens. And the final section of the novel, focused on Felix's unusually intelligent and apparently telepathic son, reinforces the theme of a coming superior humanity.

These three simultaneous approaches to perfecting the human race — through gadgets, government, and genetics, as it were — do not exactly harmonize, however, which creates some tension involving the unsuccessful rebellion that occurs in the middle of the novel. Learning of a group of people planning to overthrow the government and establish totalitarianism, Felix is greatly alarmed, and he infiltrates the group while informing Mordan of what they are doing. Mordan, though, refuses to take the threat seriously, calling it a "pipsqueak conspiracy" (62). Even after the revolt leads to an unexpected attack on the valuable "plasm bank" which Felix and Mordan must fight off with guns and weapons, Mordan continues to insist that it was nothing of consequence: "the issue was never in doubt" (104). He even suggests fatalistically that it is a question involving not proper action but biological destiny: "If the rebellion is successful, notwithstanding an armed citizenry, then it has justified itself— biologically" (97). Thus, Heinlein seems torn between regarding the attempted revolution as a serious matter, a not-so-serious matter, and a matter of no consequence of all.

As reported in a 1941 letter to John W. Campbell, Jr. reprinted in *Grumbles from the Grave*, Heinlein, while writing *Beyond This Horizon*, found "the ideas it suggests really interest me — but I am finding it hard as hell to beat a *story* out of it" (24). Perhaps the plot to overthrow this ideal society was the best solution Heinlein could devise, and it might be attributed to the lingering influence of Gernsback's insistence on "thrilling adventure" as the normal pattern of science fiction; perhaps Heinlein himself regarded the story line as illogical and allowed the story to reflect his own ambivalence. But I would argue that there is a larger difficulty: the three forms of science fiction utopia that Heinlein draws upon — pointillistic utopia, standard utopia, and evolutionary utopia — all suggest different attitudes toward an event like an armed rebellion, and to maintain his balancing act, Heinlein must scramble to justify each one.

In a pointillistic utopia, evil and discontent are still rampant and one must be vigilant and energetic in fighting against it — which explains the many agents of law enforcement in *Ralph* and Felix's grave concern about the planned rebellion. However, this spirit of melodramatic struggle must fade in a true utopia, because in that context all fundamental social problems are presumed to be solved, and an attempted revolution must be regarded as a dim, atavistic echo of earlier, imperfect days — something to be opposed, to be sure, but not a real matter of concern.[10] Finally, in an evolutionary utopia, the new human race is by definition superior and sure to win out over its inferior predecessors; hence, there is absolutely no need to worry about a revolt by their opponents that will inevitably fail.

If these conflicting attitudes toward its central event somewhat muddle *Beyond This Horizon*, the more basic problem is that its protagonist firmly rejects all the approaches to perfecting humanity which its three models suggest, and the satisfying answers he finally reaches contradict the premises underlying all of these approaches.

The basic source of Hamilton Felix's angst is that he can see no purpose in human existence — "I know of no reason why the human race *should* survive.... There's no point to being alive at all" (25). His proposed resolution is to investigate the question of life after death: "The one thing that could give us some real basis for our living is to know *for sure* whether or not anything happens after we die" (100). And at his behest, the Planners then initiate the Great Research, which seems to be moving into fruitful directions; at the end of the novel, Felix is particular excited because his son Theobald, using his telepathic ability, deduces that his new sister is the reincarnation of a female Planner who recently died. And solid evidence of reincarnation, of course, would demonstrate beyond doubt the immortality of the soul. In this way, then, Heinlein moves away from other forms of science fiction utopia to suggest a mystical utopia.

In creating a story which validates such concerns, Heinlein effectively argues against all three quests for an ideal society. If human beings have an afterlife of some kind, then clearly any desire to improve civilization, either by gadgets or government, becomes less important. Heinlein seems to argue an opposite position in a completely specious argument offered by one Planner in support of the need to prove the existence of an afterlife: "It would seem obvious to me ... that the only rational personal philosophy based on a conviction that we die *dead*, never to rise again, is a philosophy of complete hedonism" (110–111). Yet earlier in the novel Mordan effectively refutes that argument when he tells Felix, "You don't want children. From a biological standpoint that is as contra-survival as a compulsion to suicide" (33). That is, the natural instinct and desire for species-preservation — not just self-preservation — provides ample justification for a "rational personal philosophy" based on altruism. Indeed, if that Planner's argument is accepted, then the society Heinlein depicts could never have evolved, since it does not offer its citizens any proof or demonstration of life after death. Everything else in the novel suggests that it is the very lack of proof regarding an afterlife that has motivated Heinlein's society to work so hard to provide its helpful machines, to devise an ideal government, and to improve the race by genetic manipulation.

Furthermore, proof of reincarnation in particular would render the desire to improve humanity through genetics pointless as well — a mere matter of creating better bodies for the same old souls. Indeed, in belatedly raising this possibility, Heinlein completely ignores the strong belief in genetics that informed the rest of his story. Earlier, Mordan had praised Felix because of his genes: "I know your chart. I know you better than you know yourself. You are a survivor type.... I counted not only on your motor reactions, but your intelligence. Felix, your intelligence rating entitles you to the term genius even in these days" (30–31). But now, it appears, Hamilton Felix's genes have nothing to do with his personality and characteristics, which would be, according to the doctrine of reincarnation, simply the personality and char-acteristics of the soul that happened to enter his body.

Heinlein's interest in spiritual matters may be idiosyncratic, but the way his story comes to a close, I believe, is ultimately similar to the resolutions of other forms of science fiction utopia. Felix is persuaded to have children not because any answers have been found, but because the process of finding them has begun; Felix finally becomes content with his life not because his doubts are quickly resolved, but because there are some promising hints in the Great Research; and in harkening back to the old concept of reincarnation, Hein-lein seems to support the old Hindu belief in the gradual improvement of humanity by step-by-step progress through lifetime after lifetime. In short, Felix — and Heinlein — do not need perfection to be happy; like Le Guin's Shevek, they merely need to observe progress towards perfection to be happy. In this way, Alexei Panshin seems to be correct when he describes *Beyond This Horizon* as "a story about process" (*Heinlein in Dimension* 38).

Looking at other Heinlein works, one sees a similar emphasis on the need for continuing improvement, even in the afterlife. Ignoring the idio-syncratic "The Man Who Traveled in Elephants," one sees in *Stranger in a Strange Land* a heaven which is in need of improvement, as Smith rolls up his sleeves to start making changes. The life after death in *Job: A Comedy of Justice* is also not exactly ideal, inasmuch as Heinlein's hero must struggle with the gods themselves in order to be reunited with his loved one. Thus, in looking beyond this horizon to a world after death, Heinlein finds a new world which, while better than our own, is still not perfect.

Through his peculiar use of the mystical utopia, then, Heinlein contrives to reach the same conclusion found in *Ralph 124C 41+*, *The Dispossessed*, and *Childhood's End*— that only the process of working towards utopia can be achieved, not utopia itself. Whether science fiction focuses on marvelous machinery, new forms of government, advances in evolution and genetics, or a divinely designed afterlife, the feeling of final perfection associated with the traditional utopia is never achieved. In asking why this is the case, one must notice the one factor that all of these works have in common — a focus on and knowledge of modern science — and seek answers there.

Conclusion: Science and Utopia

In all of these intersections of science fiction and utopia, then, we repeatedly find some incompatibility emerging: the gadgets of the pointillistic utopia, as even its authors freely admit, do not bring complete happiness; the political and social designs of the science fiction utopia do not seem presented with real confidence and conviction, as utopia emerges as at best a partial possibility; the improved human race of the evolutionary utopia does not appear to ultimately resolve any fundamental problems; and even the religious faith of Heinlein's mystical utopia does not offer full and final perfection. The question remains: why does science fiction resist utopia, in spite of these major efforts to combine those forms?

To account for the apparent incompatibility of utopia and science fiction, one might ask if there is a parallel incompatibility between science and utopia; and some of the major developments of twentieth-century science seem more than suggestive.

First, Albert Einstein's Theory of Relativity served to undermine traditional beliefs in a universe of certainty, since the theory posits that there is no such thing as a single fixed or privileged position; all perceptions will vary according to one's vantage point.

Next, there is Werner Heisenberg's Uncertainty Principle, stating that if one knows the momentum of an elementary particle she cannot know its position, and if one knows the position of an elementary particle she cannot know its momentum. Thus, by definition, a scientist can never obtain complete knowledge of the universe; one's understanding of it is forever destined to be, to borrow Le Guin's term, "ambiguous."

Finally, modern mathematics presents Kurt Gödel's incompleteness theorem, proving that if a given mathematical system is complete, it must be inconsistent; and that if a given mathematical system is consistent, then it must be incomplete. As a matter of mathematical proof, no single system can encompass all of mathematics. Again, one observes any claims for ultimate and complete knowledge, for complete perfectibility, utterly denied, this time in the cold symbols of a mathematical theorem. Indeed, since the failure to date of any mathematical system to explain and predict all aspects of individual and social human behavior suggests that people's thoughts and activities are more complicated than any mathematical system, and since it has been proven that no single system can absorb and reconcile all mathematical systems, one seems to obtain as a corollary the proposition that human behavior is beyond any single explanatory or regulatory system. In a sense, therefore, Gödel provides a mathematical proof that utopia cannot be achieved.

In the face of such fundamental and unsolvable barriers, then, what type of world does modern science presents us with? It is a world where ultimate and complete knowledge is impossible, but small victories in dispelling some areas of ignorance is possible; a world where ignorance can be struggled against and in some cases defeated, although its overwhelming, final, and complete defeat is impossible. This is not a utopian vision, since perfection can never be achieved; neither is it a tragic vision, since some feeling of partial triumph over external circumstances is always there to mitigate any sense of utter despair resulting from inner conflict. It is, rather, a vision of melodrama — an endless, Manichean battle of good against evil, knowledge against ignorance.

Thus, Gernsback's drift toward melodrama in writing *Ralph*, and his later insistence on "thrilling adventure" as the characteristic form of science fiction, were not simply cynical marketing ploys or unfortunate interruptions in the stately development of some imagined literary tradition of science fiction; instead, they represent an insightful realization that melodrama represents, in fact, the best possible narrative model for describing the universe that modern science reveals to us and obliges us to accept.[11] Science does not offer mankind utopia, final and complete perfection, and neither does it offer tragedy or dystopia, final and complete imperfection; rather, it presents a continuing struggle, where there are sometimes victories and sometimes defeats, where a final and complete resolution cannot occur. In another way, then, science fiction keeps returning to the spirit of childhood, not in celebrating the neotenic development of superchildren, but in seizing and holding on to a narrative model commonly associated with stories for children. Yet its attraction to melodrama does not represent, as is often implied, a sign of its immaturity; rather, it reveals a mature realization of the true limitations, and the true possibilities, which modern science offers.

And, as I have already suggested, this understanding of the message of modern science informs and accounts for the skepticism toward traditional utopia that all four forms of science fiction utopia ultimately display. Aware of how little modern scientists really knew, and of how difficult some of its mysteries were, Gernsback could not plausibly see a solution to all of humanity's problems through technological innovation. Operating from the perspective of twentieth-century physics and its necessary "ambiguity," Le Guin could not logically construct an absolute and a static utopia. Well known for taking the long view, for seeing events in human history as mere instants of time against a backdrop of a universe which is fated to finally expire, Clarke reflects an attitude of scientific atheism: just as individual creatures ultimately fail and die, and just as the universe itself will ultimately fail and die, so all human societies, regardless of their capacity for technological, political, or biological improvement, will ultimately fail and die. Finally, Heinlein, more so than most science fiction writers, both sees the inevitable failure of scientific progress and looks for a way out of it — typically in the manner of religious mysticism — but even these answers cannot be final, as supreme beings themselves surprisingly appear to be entities still groping toward a perfection that they have not yet achieved.

To be sure, as already discussed, science fiction can also develop problems when it adopts the approach of melodrama; but perhaps one of the genre's strengths and glories is that it emerges, from whatever perspective one chooses, as a product of conflicting generic models and conflicting priorities — giving science fiction a sort of inborn tension that helps to stimulate writers and make its works especially fascinating to readers. Science fiction tends to reject utopia, which seems incompatible with its objectives, only to display a natural attraction to melodrama, which seems a better match despite the fact that it brings its own set of incompatibilities.

In sum, there can be no true scientific utopia, whether created by gadgetry, government, genetics, or God; and any belief otherwise is pure and simple nostalgia for an outdated view of the universe. For that reason, therefore, in embodying the world view forced upon us by twentieth-century science, science fiction, despite its many problems and lapses, is more accurate — and more realistic — than any other form of modern literature.

"The Gernsback Continuum"

Cyberpunk in the Context of Science Fiction

A central paradox informs all discussions of cyberpunk fiction. On the one hand, its principal spokesman Bruce Sterling repeatedly emphasizes the relationship between cyberpunk and previous science fiction: cyberpunk is "a new movement *in* science fiction," "its roots are deeply sunk *in* the sixty-year tradition of modern popular SF," and "Cyberpunk has risen from *within* the SF genre; it is not an invasion but a modern reform" ("Preface" to *Mirrorshades* ix, x, xv; italics mine). On the other hand, Sterling proclaims the novelty of the form: cyberpunk is reinvigorating a genre that was "confused, self-involved, and stale," Gibson reflects "a growing new consensus in SF" in "the ease with which he collaborates with other writers," and he "is opening up the stale corridors of the genre to the fresh air of new data.... Eighties culture ... mainstream lit ... what J. G. Ballard has perceptively called 'invisible literature'" ("Preface" to *Burning Chrome* ix, xii, xii). Most fundamentally, cyberpunk embodies a new perspective towards science and technology:

> a new alliance is becoming evident: an integration of technology and the Eighties counterculture. An unholy alliance of the technical world and the world of organized dissent — the underground world of pop culture, visionary fluidity, and street-level anarchy.... The hacker and the rocker are this decade's pop-culture idols, and cyberpunk is very much a pop phenomenon.... Science fiction — at least according to its official dogma — has always been about the impact of technology. But times have changed since the comfortable era of Hugo Gernsback, where Science was safely enshrined — and confined — in an ivory tower. The careless technophilia of those days belongs to a vanished, sluggish era, when authority still had a comfortable margin of control ["Preface" to *Mirrorshades* xii–xiii].

Given both its alleged connections to science fiction and its alleged originality, the question is simply put: in which critical context is cyberpunk best examined — what Sterling calls "the sixty-year tradition of modern popular

SF" or the broader realms of "Eighties counterculture" and "mainstream lit"? I will contend here that the differences between cyberpunk and previous science fiction are at best superficial, and that claims to the contrary rest on a basal misunderstanding of the critical heritage of modern science fiction; and to demonstrate the strong connections and underlying structures which link cyberpunk to the science fiction tradition, I will discuss the similarities between Gibson's *Neuromancer* and *Ralph 124C 41+*, the major work by Sterling's favorite representative of older science fiction, Hugo Gernsback. In this way, I will also demonstrate the enduring impact of that seminal novel, even in a work which, at first glance, bears little relationship to it.

I first note that some of Sterling's effusive assertions can be immediately dismissed. Patrick Nielsen Hayden, for instance, has more than adequately shown in "Cyberpunk Forum/Symposium" that the science fiction of the 1970s cannot be accurately characterized as "confused, self-involved, and stale" (40–41). And Sterling's contention that Gibson's willingness to collaborate represents "a growing new consensus" is highly questionable, to say the least. Even in the 1930s, Gernsback was regularly arranging shotgun marriages between amateur and established writers through his "Interplanetary Plots" contests, which produced works like Everett C. Smith and R. F. Starzl's "The Metal Moon" (1932), and the early fanzines also brought about a number of collaborations, such as the twelve-author space epic, *Cosmos,* that appeared in the 1930s fanzine *Fantasy Magazine.* Later, a number of major science fiction writers regularly worked in tandem, including Earl and Otto Binder, Henry Kuttner and C. L. Moore, C. M. Kornbluth and Frederik Pohl, and Larry Niven and Jerry Pournelle; and almost every major writer in the field has collaborated at least once, including Robert A. Heinlein, Isaac Asimov, Clifford D. Simak, A. E. van Vogt, Jack WIlliamson, Gregory Benford, and Arthur C. Clarke. To call "the ease with which [Gibson] collaborates with other writers" something "new" in the field is simply absurd.

In addition, Sterling's determination to picture Gibson and other cyberpunk writers as rebellions against, and not continuations of, earlier science fiction leads him to what I regard as a willful misreading of Gibson's second published story, "The Gernsback Continuum." The story describes various artifacts from the recent past — buildings, objects, artworks — as remnants of a naive and outmoded view of the future that was never realized; later, the protagonist sees an alternate world based on those premises, with a woman in futuristic dress telling her companion, "John ... we've forgotten to take our food pills" (33). According to Sterling, Gibson is here defining what he is rebelling against, what he is trying to rise above: "'The Gernsback Continuum' shows [Gibson] consciously drawing a bead on the shambling figure of the SF tradition. It's a devastating refutation of 'scientifiction' in its guise as narrow technolatry" ("Preface" to *Burning Chrome* x).

However, this view ignores both the story's tone — the obvious knowledge Gibson has about this view of the future and the affection he displays for it — and its contents. The Gernsback Continuum of the story is not a dying or dead world; it remains as a force influencing present-day reality in its old artifacts and as a still-present alternate universe which continues to coexist next to reality — indeed, the hero is still haunted by his vision of it as the story closes. And Gibson is hardly "refuting" this world view; rather, he is consciously paying tribute to it. Given the strong identification of Gernsback with the genre of science fiction, it is furthermore easy to maintain that the Gernsback Continuum of the story is science fiction itself; that Gibson is arguing that the original vision of Gernsback continues to exist today as an force affecting that genre; and that Gibson is enthusiastically joining the tradition, not rejecting it.

To fully demonstrate that a work like *Neuromancer* in fact represents a relatively pure continuation of the science fiction tradition, I must briefly recall the critical theories of Hugo Gernsback, who, as even Sterling acknowledges, launched and deeply influenced the modern genre. Without going into detail, I note that Gernsback bequeathed to science fiction a number of fundamental tensions, reflected in his own stories and those of his successors. First, he maintained that science fiction "should not be classed just as literature" ("Imagination and Reality" 579) because it in fact represented a combination of fiction and scientific nonfiction, with "the ideal proportion" being "seventy-five per cent literature interwoven with twenty-five per cent science" ("Fiction Versus Facts" 291); thus, science fiction should consist of a narrative text which incorporated long passages of scientific explanation exactly equivalent to those found in scientific articles and textbooks. In order to incorporate this material, the author is obliged to create a protagonist who possesses scientific knowledge and the archetypal passivity often seen in such persons; and this leads to a second form of tension, since Gernsback is also committed to the idea that science fiction should provide "thrilling adventure" ("Science Wonder Stories" 5), mandating a less knowledgeable and more active protagonist. There is a third tension in that the scientifically adept hero is typically connected to a technological network which, while sustaining and supporting him, also becomes something he must ultimate reject and separate himself from in order to act. Finally, in pondering the overall effects of scientific progress on human society, the science fiction writer is driven simultaneously to pessimism about the future of the human race and optimism about the future of intelligent life in general. These peculiar combinations of qualities can readily be found in both Gernsback's *Ralph* and Gibson's *Neuromancer*.

As anyone familiar with Gernsback's work knows, his stories are filled with awkward interruptions where his hero or narrator provide lengthy and detailed explanations of scientific principles and proposed inventions. Gibson's concern with such expository material is less obvious but surfaces in a number of passages from *Neuromancer* rarely cited by critics; for example,

> "The matrix has its roots in primitive arcade games," said the voice-over, "in early graphics programs and military experimentation with cranial jacks." On the Sony, a two-dimensional space war faded behind a forest of mathematically generated ferns, demonstrating the spacial possibilities of logarithmic spirals; cold blue military footage burned through, lab animals wired into test systems, helmets feeding into fire control circuits of tanks and war planes. "Cyberspace. A consensual hallucination experienced daily with billions of legitimate operators, in every nation, by children being taught mathematical concepts.... A graphic representation of data abstracted from the banks of every computer in the human system. Unthinkable complexity. Lines of light ranged in the nonspace of the mind, clusters and constellations of data. Like city lights, receding...."
> "What's that?" Molly asked, as he flipped the channel selector.
> "Kid's show." A discontinuous flood of images as the selector cycled. "Off," he said to the Hosaka [51–52].[1]

Manifestly, we see here the clumsy interpolation into Gibson's text of scientific explanation which is significantly different in tone from the rest of the novel — exactly the sin for which Gernsback is routinely criticized. Consider another excerpt from an educational program about a terrorist group crudely inserted into Gibson's story:

> Cut to Virginia Rambali, Sociology, NYU, her name, faculty, and school pulsing across the screen in pink alphanumerics.
> "Given their penchant for these random acts of surreal violence," someone said, "it may be difficult for our viewers to understand why you continue to insist that this phenomenon isn't a form of terrorism."
> Dr. Rambali smiled. "There is always a point at which the terrorist ceases to manipulate the media gestalt. A point at which the violence may well escalate, but beyond which the terrorist has become symptomatic of the media gestalt itself. Terrorism as we ordinarily understand it is inately [sic] media-related. The Panther Moderns differ from other terrorists precisely in their degree of self-consciousness, in their awareness of the extent to which media divorce the act of terrorism from the original sociopolitical intent...."
> "Skip it," Case said [58].

Without a doubt, these jarring little lectures contrast sharply with the dazzling, pyrotechnic stylistics which is commonly regarded as Gibson's characteristic voice; and beyond these disruptive inserts, there are, even in the conversations between Case and various characters in the novel, moments which sound distinctly professorial, like these comments from Wintermute in the guise of Finn:

> "The holographic paradigm is the closest thing you've worked out to a representation of human memory, is all. But you've never done anything about it. People, I mean...."

"Can you read my mind, Finn?" He grimaced. "Wintermute, I mean."

"Minds aren't *read*. See, you've still got the paradigms print gave you, and you're barely print-literate. I can *access* your memory, but that's not the same as your mind.... You're always building models. Stone circles. Cathedrals. Pipe-organs. Adding machines.... But if the run goes off tonight, you'll have finally managed the real thing."

"I don't know what you're talking about" [170–171].

To be sure, Gernsback and Gibson handle explanatory passages in different ways: with a loquacious hero and his ever-curious girlfriend, Gernsback created an atmosphere unusually conducive to extended explanation, while with the taciturn Case and his supercool cohorts, Gibson is obliged to quickly force exposition into his story before Case impatiently cuts him off. However, in making the effort to include such material, Gibson repeatedly displays a desire to explain to readers the present state of scientific knowledge about computers, sociology, and human intelligence and to describe the real future possibilities of developing constructs like Cyberspace, new forms of terrorism, and a true Artificial Intelligence. While this motive may not be as dominant in Gibson as it is in Gernsback — certainly, Gibson has other things on his mind — it is nonetheless demonstrably present and fits *Neuromancer* comfortably into the explanatory tradition of science fiction as defined and demonstrated by Gernsback.

It is a quality, furthermore, which Gernsback and Gibson share with many noteworthy writers of modern science fiction. As is repeatedly noted, Heinlein regularly interrupts his stories to present lengthy lectures; the leisurely pace of Arthur C. Clarke's novels allows for a considerable amount of detailed explanation; and some works, like Isaac Asimov's original *Foundation* trilogy (1951, 1952, 1953) and Frank Herbert's *Dune* (1964), employ the device of extended quotations from imaginary reference books to present necessary background information. Thus, the nagging, intrusive voice of the compulsive explainer is one trait which unites Gibson with his predecessors.

A second characteristic of both *Ralph* and *Neuromancer* is a protagonist who is fully aware of the science and technology which infuse his future world and who at first seems inactive and emotionless as a result. To be sure, Ralph is primarily an inventor, one who creates new scientific marvels, while Case is more a manipulator, adept at maneuvering through Cyberspace and exploiting its opportunities[2]; however, what unites them is their thorough knowledge of and delight in the scientific advances of their time. That is, they are radically different from technological naifs like Winston Smith in George Orwell's *Nineteen Eighty-Four* (1949).

In our culture, the man who possesses intelligence and knowledge is often pictured as fundamentally passive and emotionless; and these are qualities which both Ralph and Case apparently display in the beginning of their stories. The scientist Ralph seems to prefer spending his life in his laboratory, constantly working on new inventions, and he once reacts angrily when his manservant ventures to interrupt him (52–53). In addition, when he first communicates with Alice while she is in Switzerland and learns she is threatened by an avalanche, he does not rush to her rescue, but rather contrives a method to beam energy to her house and melt the onrushing snow — thus saving her life without leaving his room. In keeping with his desire to avoid human contact, Ralph is also pictured as cold, almost inhuman: we are told he once pronounced love to be "nothing but a perfumed animal instinct" (140) and he likens himself to a "tool" (41). Similarly, Case desires nothing more than to be left alone to commune with Cyberspace; his efforts to appear callous and indifferent need hardly be documented; and his references to ordinary human experiences usually involve the word "meat": simstim is a "meat toy" and travel is a "meat thing" (55, 77). Thus, both men seem isolated from normal human contact and emotions and conceptualize themselves as objects — a "tool" or "meat."

However, as events in *Ralph* and *Neuromancer* unfold, both protagonists are obliged to abandon their passivity and lack of sentiment and play the role of the noble hero who rescues the fair maiden — a transformation mandated by the genre's commitment to "thrilling adventure," and one which in both cases is associated with a journey into outer space and a new romantic attachment. As they continue their tour through the world of 2660, Ralph gradually acknowledges his love for Alice and eventually announces marriage plans; and when Alice is kidnapped by the evil Fernand and taken into space, Ralph ignores a direct command from the Planet Governor forbidding any response, overcomes a guard sent to detain him, and leaves in his space flyer to rescue his beloved. As evidence of his sudden passion, Ralph at one point confronts Fernand and exclaims, "What have you done with her? Answer me, or by God, I'll blow you into Eternity!" (164) These impulsive actions, by the way, make nonsense of Sterling's repeated claims that Gernsback pictures the scientist as someone in his "ivory tower, who showers the blessings of superscience upon the hoi polloi" ("Preface" to *Burning Chrome* xi; a similar reference to an "ivory tower" is in "Preface" to *Mirrorshades* xiii); while this may be the way that Ralph is *initially* presented, at this later point in the novel, Ralph becomes as much a criminal as Case is, and his pursuit of Alice is a personal — and illegal — act of rebellion which perfectly accords with the spirit of cyberpunk as Sterling defines it: that is, Ralph now casts himself as part of "a pirate's crew of losers, hustlers, spin-offs, castoffs, and lunatics" ("Preface" to *Burning Chrome* xi).

In *Neuromancer*, Case and his cohorts travel to a space habitat to break into a computer complex; and once in space, Case seems to become a different person. First, he displays anger when Wintermute simply kills the agents who tried to arrest him — a highly unusual emotional response; then, when Molly physically ventures into their opponents' headquarters and is captured and threatened by members of the Tessier-Ashpool family, Case gives up his characteristically passive role: after announcing "I'm stayin' right here," he nevertheless immediately embarks on a daring rescue mission (192). At certain times, then, both Ralph and Case seem to undergo a complete character change, associated with a shift from Earth to space, and are newly presented as agents of action and emotion instead of men of inaction and intellect.

Although it is tempting to see these shifts as simple character transformations, the situation is actually more complex. After his initially passionate pursuit of Alice, Ralph becomes cold and analytical once again when he plots to divert her second kidnapper with an artificial comet aimed at the planet Mars; and after Molly's rescue and the successful completion of his mission, Case reverts to his unromantic self, as reflected in the novel's last line: "He never saw Molly again" (271). In fact, both sides of their characters are validated by the events of the novel, with neither emerging as completely dominant.

This combination of knowledgeable passivity and passionate activity is, I submit, also characteristic of many other science fiction works. One good example would be Robert A. Heinlein's *The Door into Summer* (1956). At the beginning of the novel, Daniel Boone Davis is content to sit in his workshop tinkering with new robots while others deal with the outside world; and though he expresses fatherly affection for his niece Ricky and a perfunctory love for his secretary, he hardly seems overly emotional or sentimental. However, when his secretary and partner swindle him and force him into suspended animation, he is galvanized into action; here, it is a trip through time, not through space, which provides the impetus, and Davis forcefully contrives to return to his original era and, awakening to his true love for Ricky, he arranges to meet and marry her when they are both adults. Another example would be Mitchell Courtenay in Frederik Pohl and C. M. Kornbluth's *The Space Merchants* (1953), initially content to work passively at his advertising agency but finally prodded to reject his society and seek escape, epitomized by his plans to go to Venus. In both cases, the passive and cold protagonist seems to metamorphose into a forceful, emotional hero.

This transformation in *Ralph* and *Neuromancer* is accompanied by another fundamental shift, a third common trait: although both protagonists are initially pictured as being connected to a large, technological network which benefits and sustains them, the network ultimately seems to confine and restrict them and in order to take action they must be separated from it.

In innumerable ways, Gernsback's Ralph is presented as part of a connected worldwide network, although it is jerry-built out of existing inventions and logical predictions of that time: Ralph meets Alice by means of a picture-phone conversation, facilitated by an instantaneous translation device called the Language Rectifier; when he beams energy to her house in Switzerland and saves her life, he is then applauded for his feat by thousands who broadcast their faces into a large auditorium where Ralph stands; he lives under a world government whose Planet Governor regularly consults with him; he reads his daily newspaper delivered on a tiny piece of microfilm; he is initially stopped from flying into space by a telegram from the Planet Governor; and he locates Alice's first kidnapper by inventing a form of radar. There is even the element of direct communication in and out of the human brain — the "powerful theme of mind invasion" which Sterling falsely describes as a cyberpunk innovation ("Preface" to *Mirrorshades* xiii): Ralph can record his thoughts in written form with a device called the Menograph; and while sleeping, he absorbs information conveyed directly into his brain by the Hypnobioscope. More generally, Ralph reveals himself as aware of and part of a larger scientific community; he calls other scientists in to witness his successful revival of a dead dog and, as noted, frequently acknowledges the work of previous scientists in his lengthy explanations.

As need not be elaborately stated, Gibson, of course, replaces all of these isolated connecting devices with the single medium of Cyberspace; and more generally, as Sterling says, "The tools of global integration — the satellite media net, the multinational corporation — fascinate the cyberpunks and figure constantly in their work" ("Preface" to *Mirrorshades* xiv). Despite his willful isolation from human society and contact, Case can always connect with others through his mind-link to Cyberspace, and he is further attached to a wider world through his network of underworld sources. For all their individual inventiveness, then, both Case and Ralph constantly have access to others who can provide help and information.

This sense of continuing connection is not without its drawbacks, though, which is another similarity between *Ralph* and *Neuromancer*: with their protagonists' connectedness come restrictions and harassment. Although the world government of 2660 gives Ralph the honorific title "+" and all the financial and scientific support he needs to produce his scientific marvels, Ralph also pays for these privileges with a significant loss of personal freedom:

> He was but a tool, a tool to advance science, to benefit humanity. He belonged, not to himself, but to the Government — the Government, who fed and clothed him, and whose doctors guarded his health with every precaution. He had to pay the penalty of his +. To be sure, he had everything. He had but to ask and

his wish was law — if it did not interfere with his work.

There were times he grew restive under the restraint, he longed to smoke the tobacco forbidden him by watchful doctors, and to indulge in those little vices which vary the monotony of existence for the ordinary individual....

"I can't stand it," he would protest. "This constraint which I am forced to endure maddens me, I feel that I am being hampered.... I am nothing but a prisoner," Ralph stormed once.

"You are a great inventor," smiled the Governor, "and a tremendous factor in the world's advancement. You are invaluable to humanity, and — you are irreplaceable. You belong to the world — not to yourself" [41–42].

Thus, when Ralph plans to rescue Alice, he receives this message from the Planet Governor: "under the law '+' scientists are not allowed to endanger their lives under any circumstances. I therefore command you not to leave the earth without my permission" (154).

Similarly, Case, because of past crimes, is initially deprived of his very ability to enter Cyberspace; and when that ability is restored, it comes with severe conditions: he can no longer metabolize and be affected by the drugs he loves to take — Molly tells him, "You're biochemically incapable of getting off on amphetamine or cocaine" (36) — and faces a renewed loss of his computer powers; as Armitage tells him,

> "You have fifteen toxin sacs bonded to the lining of various main arteries, Case. They're dissolving. Very slowly, but they definitely are dissolving. Each one contains a mycotoxin ... the one your former employees gave you in Memphis.... You have time to do what I'm hiring you for, Case, but that's all. Do the job and I can inject you with an enzyme that will dissolve the bond without opening the sacs. Then you'll need a blood change. Otherwise, the sacs melt and you're back where I found you" [45–46].

And to order to undertake the actions they feel are necessary, both Ralph and Case must severe their connections with their networks: Ralph flies off into space completely alone to rescue Alice, and, even though his presence in Cyberspace is absolutely necessary to the success of his mission, Case disconnects from that realm and ventures forth to rescue Molly from the Tessier-Ashpool family. And to again complicate any effort to see these actions as straightforward transformations, both characters finally revert to their previous state, with Ralph reinstated as a prominent scientist and Case returned to his old job of computer cowboy.

This ambivalence about the value of connectedness as opposed to the need for independent action surfaces in many other science fiction works. Pohl and Kornbluth's *The Space Merchants* can again serve as an example, in that it begins with its hero happily producing — and relating to — the clutter of advertising slogans that permeate his world and ends with the now-alienated protagonist fleeing to Venus to establish a new society. Also relevant in this context is Clifford D. Simak's *Way Station* (1963), with the human who maintains a teleportation station on Earth which connects alien worlds finally obliged to take personal action in a crisis. In the world of pervasive connecting media in John Brunner's *Stand on Zanzibar* (1968), Donald Hogan's job is literally to make connections by pouring through computer records and journals to find interesting correlations, although he is later pulled away from his synthesizing to be "eptified" into a skilled assassin on a dangerous solo mission. And innumerable *Star Trek* episodes illustrate the importance of communication, with Kirk receiving messages from Starfleet, talking to crewmen with his communicator, and reacting to any approaching starship with a command to "open hailing frequencies"— although the climax often finds Kirk, Spock, and McCoy cut off and isolated on some alien planet, left to their own devices. In all these cases, protagonists who are part of a technological network are later separated from it and forced to act as independent agents; and seeing all these examples of thoroughgoing communication and contact in science fiction, one can find nothing truly novel in the cyberpunk fascination with "The tools of global integration."

In the final actions of their now active, emotional, and separated protagonists, both *Ralph* and *Neuromancer* reveal a fourth similarity: both works present an attitude toward the future that is both pessimistic concerning the fate of the human race and optimistic concerning the fate of some transformed human race or new form of intelligent life. One might profoundly question the assertion that *Ralph* is an any way pessimistic, since the work is routinely presented as a naive scientific utopia; and granted, Gernsback devotes much time and attention to his world's diversions, providing a series of tableaux where characters express their delight about televised plays, the "aerial carnival," voice-writing, and other scientific marvels. As a result, readers can easily fail to note the pain and unhappiness that pervades Ralph's world of 2660, as has been previously discussed.

As for *Neuromancer*, no one would disagree, I suspect, that while the lives of Case and his contemporaries may be momentarily enlivened by simstim, exotic drugs, arcade games, and of course Cyberspace itself, none of these seriously affect the basic and drab unhappiness of their existence; here, the darkness of everyday life is strongly projected through the novel. Overall, although Gibson's vision is certainly more grim than Gernsback's, both works ultimately argue that there are certain fundamental difficulties in human existence that science may alleviate — or even intensify — but cannot solve. To employ Gregory Benford's apt phrase, both novels suggest that there is no "technological fix for the human condition."

However, there is also a note of hope in these novels: the possibility that human science might create or assist in the creation of new beings who can achieve what human beings cannot achieve. Thus, there is a possible techno-logical fix for the condition of *sentient beings who are other than or more than human*, but there is not a technological fix for the *human* condition.

In the case of *Ralph 124C 41+*, the final accomplishment involves a direct transformation of the human race: namely, the prospect of immortality. When Ralph finally catches up with Alice, only to find her dead, he frantically works to preserve her body with a special gas so that he can bring her back to life once they return to Earth; and the novel ends with her successful revival. In this case, a scientific process has been perfected which might bring immor-tality — and radical change — to human life and civilization. The magnitude of this achievement is foreshadowed and described in Chapter 3 of the novel, where other distinguished scientists witness Ralph's successful experiment involving the revival of a dead dog. With Alice brought back to life, as already noted, she in effect becomes the first of a new type of human being, capable of living and continuing to improve indefinitely. Still, there is a note of gloom in that not all humans will be able to undergo this transformation; those not especially prepared and older people are excluded, and the latter group may include Ralph himself, who, if his remarkable record of scientific achievements is any guide, must be at least middle-aged. Thus, some humans will advance through life extension, while others will be left behind.[3]

In the case of Gibson, this double message clearly emerges at the end of *Neuromancer*, where Case's ultimate triumph is to bring about the birth of a true Artificial Intelligence in the combination of Wintermute and Neuro-mancer; and this new being visits him one more time to explain that he has now become the matrix of Cyberspace itself, and that he has established con-tact with other similar beings from Alpha Centauri and elsewhere. Thus, a member of a new and entirely different species of intelligent life has been cre-ated, one who is obviously happy and excited to be alive, thrilled by the prospect of contact with other Artificial Intelligences and new possibilities for action and attainment. In contrast, Case's prospects are limited: the real world of technological progress that Case inhabits is obviously less than perfect, and despite the appeal of the scientifically created world of Cyberspace, that is not a realm that humans can permanently live in: such an option is effectively precluded in the unattractive depiction of the Dixie Flatline, the unhappy "construct" that has died in real life but lives on in Cyberspace while continually asking to be killed, and in the novel's final vision of a replica of Case still living in Cyberspace which evidently unnerves the living Case. Thus, there is no utopia for human beings in *Neuromancer*, either in reality or in Cyberspace.

This double message — despair for humanity, hope for its successors — is, I submit, found not only in these two authors, but in countless others as well, making it strongly characteristic of the genre of science fiction. As previously indicated, Brian Stableford finds this "ambivalent" attitude in many examples of the "scientific romance." But this same belief, usually expressed with a more hopeful outlook, is found repeatedly in American and British science fiction as well. The envisioned successors to humanity take several forms: superior robots and computers, like Wintermute/Neuromancer, Isaac Asimov's positronic robots, and the robotic pontiff of Clifford D. Simak's *Project Pope* (1981); animals given human intelligence and/or form, as in Simak's *City* (1950) and Cordwainer Smith's *Norstrilia* (1975); humans transformed by alien intervention, as in Arthur C. Clarke's *2001: A Space Odyssey* (1968) and in E. E. Smith's Lensman series; spontaneous human mutations with advanced intelligence and mental powers, like A. E. van Vogt's *Slan* (1940) and Stanley G. Weinbaum's *The New Adam* (1939); humans joining into a group mind, as in Clarke's *Childhood's End* (1953), Theodore Sturgeon's *More Than Human* (1953), and George Zebrowski's *Macrolife* (1979); and other scientific alterations in human characteristics, like hermaphroditism in Sturgeon's *Venus Plus X* (1960), immortality in *Ralph* and Robert A. Heinlein's *Time Enough for Love* (1973), aquatic adaptation in James Blish's "Surface Tension" (1952) and Hal Clement's *Ocean on Top* (1973), and genetic engineering to eliminate human conflict as envisioned in John Brunner's *Stand on Zanzibar*. And many other examples can be added to such lists.

Overall, then, we see that works like *Ralph* and *Neuromancer* share certain key characteristics which are also found in a wide range of science fiction texts: the simultaneous desire to offer entertainment and explanation in the context of narrative; a hero who is both cold and passive and emotional and active; one who is connected to a technological network and one who severs that connection; and a conclusive attitude which is pessimistic concerning the future of humanity but optimistic concerning the future of other forms of intelligent life.

To be sure, there are differences between the works, and one need not assert that Gernsback was the first cyberpunk writer or that *Neuromancer* is simply an updated version of *Ralph*. I would readily concede that Gernsback is more concerned with scientific explanation than Gibson, that Gibson is more suspicious of emotion and activity than Gernsback, that Gibson has more interest in networking than Gernsback, and that Gernsback is more optimistic than Gibson. However, these are differences of degree, not of kind; as suggested by the title of Gibson's story, the two works stand at two ends of a continuum, the continuum which is the modern tradition of science fiction launched by Gernsback and carried on most recently by the cyberpunk writers.

And the connections between cyberpunk and previous science fiction are, I assert, stronger and more significant than the posited relationship between cyberpunk and other modern genres—"punk music" ("Preface" to *Mirrorshades* x), for instance, or "mainstream lit" ("Preface" to *Burning Chrome* xii). In these realms, one first finds a fascination with the emotional and visceral and a suspicion of logic and rational explanation, which hardly describes the works of Gibson; thus, the injunction of the Talking Heads's David Byrne to "Stop Making Sense" cannot apply to Gibson, since he is manifestly committed to making sense out of his future world. Furthermore, while the archetype of the punk does involve a mixture of outward cool and inward passion, and while the computer hacker does function as a figure who is both connected to a wider world and isolated from it, the combination and integration of these images can be found only in previous science fiction—it is not a "new alliance," but a very old one. Finally, the prevalent attitude in these other fields is nihilism, energized perhaps by a giddy excitement concerning the coming apocalypse; nowhere except in science fiction does one see the careful blend of pessimism regarding humanity and optimism regarding its successors explicitly projected in the conclusion of *Neuromancer*. In short, Gibson and the cyberpunks can be logically explained primarily as an outgrowth and continuation of the modern science fiction tradition and cannot be logically explained primarily as a product of other genres and traditions.

If the clear links between *Neuromancer* and Gernsback's legacy have not been properly understood, that is simply because the modern genre of science fiction itself, and particularly its strange double message, have not been properly understood; and one consequence of this misunderstanding has been an incomplete and limited reading of Gibson's novel.

Comments by Brian W. Aldiss and other critics often suggest that science fiction writers can be neatly divided into two camps. On the one hand, there are the simpletons, the brainless technocrats who absurdly claim that science can solve all of humanity's problems; and Hugo Gernsback is most often called upon to represent this attitude. Thus, Aldiss complains in *Trillion Year Spree* of Gernsback's "simple-minded Victorian utilitarianism" (204), Lundwall calls *Ralph* a "pitiable Utopian novel" (76), H. Bruce Franklin describes Gernsback's tradition as "technocratic science fiction" (*Future Perfect* 394), and Sterling bemoans the "careless technophilia" of "a vanished, sluggish era" ("Preface" to *Mirrorshades* xiii). On the other hand, there are the mature writers, the ones worthy of literary analysis, who project a properly thoughtful view of unrelieved gloom concerning the future. This is the essence of Aldiss's implausible definition of science fiction as "characteristically cast in the Gothic or post–Gothic mode" (25), a genre which posits a world which is cramped, confined, and uncontrollable; and he celebrates as central works novels like Mary Shelley's *Frankenstein* (1818), H. G. Wells's *The Island of Dr. Moreau* (1896), and William Hope Hodgson's *The House on the*

Borderland (1908), which all maintain a rigorous pessimism regarding the future of both mankind and its possible successors.

As descriptions of the modern tradition which emerged under the label "science fiction," both views are plainly ridiculous.

That is, there are few if any writers in that tradition — including, as I have demonstrated, Gernsback himself— who have failed to point out that scientific progress will bring dilemmas as well as delights, and that science alone cannot be relied on to solve all of humanity's problems. Thoughtless optimism about the future is instead found only outside of that tradition, in tracts disguised as fiction like Gerard O'Neill's *2081: A Hopeful View of the Human Future* (1981) and in the exhibits of the 1939 World's Fair critiqued by Bruce Franklin in *Robert A. Heinlein: America as Science Fiction* (1980), a tradition seen today in the bland domesticity of space station Bravo Centauri in the Horizons ride at Walt Disney's Epcot Center. Conversely, few if any writers in the modern tradition have completely precluded the hope for some future transformation of humanity or a new species that will eliminate the pain of the human condition; instead, pure pessimism is more commonly located in works outside the genre like Orwell's *Nineteen Eighty-Four* (1949) and D. F. Jones's *Colossus* (1966). The characteristic attitude of modern science fiction, then, combines a degree of pessimism about mankind's future and a degree of hope about other possible beings; and this is the final message of *Ralph*, *Neuromancer*, and the innumerable other works between them in their continuum.

A determination to ignore part of this message, and put Gibson squarely in the envisioned camp of fashionable despair, leads directly to the misreading of *Neuromancer* as simply the story of Case and Molly; from that limited perspective, there might be some justice in seeing his relentless efforts to escape into inner worlds as an experience typical of the protagonists in Gothic novels.[4] However, if we see the novel as the story of Wintermute/Neuromancer, the human race and its concerns become a minor issue and the excitement of the new being's discovery of itself and others ends the story with an expansive, unlimited vision of continuing progress. And this second aspect of Gibson's novel cannot be ignored; Neuromancer is, after all, the title character, and his struggle to achieve a true identity is the motivating force for all that happens in the novel. I modestly suggest that excessive fascination with Gibson's human characters has shifted concern away from the Artificial Intelligence who is the real subject of the novel, precisely because this approach to the work makes it more difficult to fit *Neuromancer* into the questionable patterns proffered by Aldiss and other critics.

To state the point most broadly, the critical context of science fiction itself, with its message of future possibilities to relieve its logical extrapolations of disaster, poses one ultimate challenge to all other critical approaches to the genre. Certainly, the continuing fascination with intelligences beyond humanity in science fiction can be construed as an evasion of reality and responsibility: just as enthusiasts for space colonies sometimes seem to suggest that it is all right to continue polluting and destroying the environment of Earth because someday we will be living on other, pristine worlds, one could accuse science fiction authors of arguing that it is all right to tolerate human injustice and suffering because someday there will be other races who will live without such problems. However, science fiction repeatedly insists that humans are not the first, the last, or the most important intelligent beings in the cosmos; that in fact we are only one small part of a vast and alien universe; and that, perhaps, the only appropriate response to this environment is for humans to create, or transform themselves into, vast and alien beings. From this viewpoint, those who continue to focus only on human concerns and human limitations are the ones who are evading reality and responsibility.

Even if one accepts the logic of this position, there remain questions as to whether it is desirable, or even possible, for human beings to achieve an inhuman perspective. All that science fiction from Gernsback to Gibson asserts is that scientific progress is the one force that *might* be able to transcend the limitations of human nature and achieve something truly new, truly different.

One way in which Hugo Gernsback and Bruce Sterling emerge as spiritual brothers is that they repeatedly argue that the type of writing they are explaining and defending is something new and different, something that has never been seen in literature before. The strange thing, of course, is that, for all Sterling's rhetoric of revolution and novelty, they are both talking about the same type of literature — science fiction. The fact that this genre is routinely misrepresented and misunderstood is in a way not surprising: there are always those prepared to force any piece of writing into the same old categories, and science fiction has again and again been their victim. However, in the genre's ultimate double vision of simultaneous doom and transcendence, there is, I argue, evidence that science fiction is indeed distinguishable from other types of literature; and as we continue moving into a new century, this new perspective remains one of the most exciting aspects of science fiction. Thus, if a new name is necessary to make critics appreciate this unique genre, then the cyberpunk movement has indeed served a valuable purpose.

9

Scientific Adventures

Hugo Gernsback's Career as a Science Fiction Writer

Those who are relatively unfamiliar with Hugo Gernsback's *Ralph 124C 41+: A Romance of the Twenty-Sixth Century* will sometimes assert that it is simply a didactic tract thinly disguised as fiction, with a perfunctory plot deployed only to introduce and connect various scientific lectures. However, as the last four chapters have demonstrated, this simply is not the case. Gernsback's novel features four characters — Ralph, Alice, Fernand, and Llysanorh' — who are all, by the standards of the popular fiction of the times, reasonably well developed. There is a dramatic story line — Ralph must woo Alice while protecting her from two rivals and potential kidnappers who regularly imperil her — and while Gernsback never entirely forgets about science, there are several passages in his novel that are clearly focused more on advancing the plot than on presenting some scientific information or ideas. No one could say that *Ralph 124C 41+* is a good novel, but it most definitely is a genuine novel, and one that functioned as an influential model for later, better writers to fruitfully follow, and one that thus serves as an illuminating text for scholars seeking to better understand science fiction.

Rather, it is Gernsback's later works of fiction — most prominently, his second novel *Baron Münchhausen's New Scientific Adventures* and the self-published stories reprinted in *Science-Fiction Plus*—which offer virtually no story line and are devoted almost exclusively to explaining scientific principles and possible inventions based on those principles. And the question is: unlike other science fiction writers, why was Gernsback unable, or unwilling, to learn from and follow his own stimulating example in these later works of fiction?

Some possible answers come to mind when one looks through the pages of *The Electrical Experimenter*, Gernsback's magazine for do-it-yourself technicians and inventors in which *Baron Münchhausen's New Scientific Adventures* was originally serialized. While critical attention has quite naturally been focused almost exclusively on his fiction magazines, *The Electrical Experimenter* reminds us that, throughout his long career, Gernsback was primarily an editor and publisher of nonfictional scientific magazines. He spent the vast majority of his time reading scientific articles submitted to his magazines, preparing some of those scientific articles for publication, and writing scientific articles himself whenever there was a space that needed to be filled. Since Gernsback was thus constantly immersed in a world of expository prose, it may have been only natural that, when he set out to write a work of fiction, the results increasingly drifted toward the style and conventions of expository prose.

One must also recall that, until 1926, Gernsback was always publishing science fiction stories exclusively in, and occasionally writing science fiction stories exclusively for, various scientific magazines, and this placed a special burden on those stories: in order to justify their appearance in a scientific magazines, all of these stories, even if they were rather farcical, had to include and emphasize some sort of scientific principle or idea. In writing fiction for these magazines, then, Gernsback would inevitably feel inclined to foreground scientific matters and worry much less about the piece's qualities as fiction. Later, when he was publishing, and occasionally writing science fiction for, fiction magazines, Gernsback's inclination to maintain a focus on serious science remained strong, and as previously discussed, the results of this inclination became a cornerstone of his critical defense of science fiction — that the genre was more meritorious than other genres of popular fiction precisely because it so heavily emphasized the inclusion of valuable scientific data and stimulating scientific ideas.

Finally, Gernsback throughout his career always made his money as a publisher and editor, not as a writer. If he had been a struggling writer striving to sell science fiction stories to pulp magazines, he surely would have learned to pay more attention to developing his characters and keeping them involved in exciting situations and less attention to scientific discussions. However, as someone who wrote fiction purely as a hobby, Gernsback never had to worry about whether his stories would please editors and readers, so he could focus exclusively on talking about whatever he felt like talking about at the time — which was invariably some new scientific idea. Thus, driven by factors like these to stress didacticism over narrative, Gernsback after *Ralph 124C 41+* sporadically devoted his energies to producing generally unsatisfactory works of fiction that illuminate the genre of science fiction not because they were popular and influential, but because they were not.

The readers of *The Electrical Experimenter* first learned about Hugo Gernsback's second novel from an announcement in the April, 1915 issue of the magazine:

Mr. H. Gernsback has written a new serial story:

Baron Münchhausen's New Scientific Adventures.

The story will begin in the next issue. Each number will contain a complete story by itself; there will be a new adventure each month. You cannot possibly afford to miss this.

Watch for the next issue. As there will be an unusual demand for the May number, leave your order with your newsdealer now, otherwise don't feel disappointed if he will be "sold out" ["?" 220].

Thus, as was not the case with *Ralph 124C 41+*, there can be no controversies about whether or not Gernsback planned to write *Baron Münchhausen's New Scientific Adventures*; clearly, it was a carefully thought-out decision.[1] And while it can be difficult to distinguish promotional hype from genuine editorial expectations, one might reasonably conclude that Gernsback sincerely believed this novel would prove popular with his readers. As further evidence of this expectation, Gersnback placed paintings of Baron Münchhausen on the covers of the May, June, and July, 1915 issues, identifying the first three installments of the novel as the major attractions in those magazines.

It also seems clear that this "serial story" did not prove to be as popular as Gernsback had hoped. The next three installments — in the August, October, and November, 1915 issues — were not featured on the magazine covers, and after one more cover appearance — a painting illustrating the seventh installment in the December, 1915 issue — the serial was never featured on the cover again. In addition, despite that initial promise of "a new adventure each month," Gernsback offered no new installment in the September, 1915 issue, and in 1916, the skipped months became more frequent, as there were no Münchhausen chapters in the February, May, July, August, September, October, and December issues. And, after a thirteenth chapter in the February, 1917 issue, no further Münchhausen adventures appeared. While one might speculate that Gernsback was becoming too busy with other matters to continue writing his novel, these increasingly sporadic appearances manifestly suggest that there was little reader demand for more of Baron Münchhausen, and that his disappearance in 1917 inspired few complaints.[2]

In discussing the apparent failure of this novel in *The Mechanics of Wonder*, I characterized it as Gernsback's disastrous attempt to combine the three essential elements of science fiction — fiction, science, and prophecy — in a different way; here, instead of the constant intermingling of the three elements observed in *Ralph 124C 41+*, Gernsback began his novel with a section of fiction, describing Münchhausen's antics during World War I, then shifted to a section of scientific education, as the Baron visited the Moon and soberly described its features as they were known to scientists at the time, and finally moved into prophecy when the Baron went to Mars and was given an extended tour of its advanced utopian civilization. This is true as far as it goes, but it should not have been implied that it was perhaps Gernsback's intention to produce a three-part novel of this sort. Rather, the problem was that Gernsback made some terribly unwise decisions at the very beginning of his novel, which then required him to radically change his story as it went along.

A lengthy selection from the beginning of the novel's first chapter, which appeared in the May, 1915 issue of *The Electrical Experimenter*, will illustrate both what Gernsback was planning to do and why it was not going to work:

> My name is Ignaz Montmorency Alier. If that don't suit you, I suggest I. M. Alier for short. I am a Yankee by birth; no doubt you guessed that much. Both my father and mother came over on the Mayflower and settled in Yankton, Mass., where they are engaged at present in cactus and ostrich farming. Ever since I was a little boy my father, for reasons best known to himself, begged of me to be a worshipper of truth, no matter how painful it might prove. I am glad to say that my father's teachings fell on fertile territory. I have never knowingly uttered an untruth. The pursuit of truth since I have grown up has become a mania with me, so much so, in fact, that even an everyday exaggeration made by my best of friends will drive me frantic [...].
>
> I would not think of taking up your valuable time with the above statement were it not so vitally necessary for me to fully acquaint you with my character, for reasons which will be more apparent later. For this reason I also find it quite necessary to give you the following references; any of the below mentioned individuals and institutions will be only too glad to vouch for my integrity, honesty, as well as veracity.* I could give almost an indefinite list, but I prefer mentioning only the following:
> Hiram O'Rourke, lawyer, Yankton, Mass.
> [The above defended me in three breach of promise suits, as well as eight perjury charges of which I was accused.]
>   Patrick Flanagan, jailkeeper, Yankton, Mass.
>   Jeremiah Addlecock, jailkeeper, Coffeeville, Me.
>   Mike Whiffeltree, jailkeeper, Lyreville, Vt.
>   [The latter only knew me intimately for five months.]
>   The Ananias Club, Yankton, Mass.
>   Now that I have thoroughly established my standing I will proceed, and I sincerely hope and trust that no one will question any statements I may be called to make in these pages. They are the bare, unvarnished truth in each and every case. If called upon I will cheerfully swear to the truth of any of my statements before a notary. [I am a notary myself.]
>
> *On account of the numerous inquiries received concerning me, I suggest to enclose a 3-ct. stamp for your reply when writing. (1:2)³

The passage is striking for a number of reasons. First, it should be noted that Gernsback is establishing an unreliable narrator for his story, and that he is managing the trick of explicitly stating one message — I am a truthful narrator — while also contriving to convey a completely different statement to readers — the narrator is actually a habitual liar. One cannot say that it is marvelously clever or skillfully written, but it does definitely demonstrate an awareness of literary techniques and a desire to employ them — yet again decisively undermining Brian W. Aldiss's claim that Gernsback was "without literary understanding" (*Trillion Year Spree* 202).[4]

A completely unsophisticated writer, in other words, would never take the time to create an elaborately distinctive persona to serve as his story's narrator, and he would never begin his story with a long passage, unrelated to the plot, which was simply designed to present and to characterize that persona.

It is further evident that Gernsback is setting up what might become a highly complex text. As is already obvious from the title of the piece and its opening paragraphs, the story will have a notorious liar, I. M. Alier, reporting on what he has heard from the legendary Baron Münchhausen, one of literature's most notorious liars. This will naturally suggest a number of possible interpretations of Gernsback's narrative: Alier might be making up the entire story of radio messages from Münchhausen; or he may have actually heard from Münchhausen, but he is sometimes lying about what he heard; or he may be accurately reporting what Münchhausen told him, but Münchhausen himself might be lying. Thus, every "adventure" to be related in the novel might be the truth, might be Alier's lie, might be Münchhausen's lie, or might be some mixture of the above; and readers might therefore be forced to carefully examine subtle clues in the language to determine what is going on in each case. In the hands of a writer like William Faulkner, such a scenario might yield a brilliantly fascinating novel.

Needless to say, Gernsback is no Faulkner, and he will quickly be forced to steer his story away from any possibility of intriguing ambiguity. The reason might have become clear to Gernsback if, by chance, while composing this satirical introduction, he had glanced at a magazine cover lying on his desk and had remembered that he was writing this story for a magazine entitled *The Electrical Experimenter*. To justify its presence in such a magazine, *Baron Münchhausen's New Scientific Adventures* could not simply be a light-hearted satirical romp; rather, it would have to include accurate scientific information and imaginative but plausible scientific ideas — but how could any of these passages seem trustworthy to readers if they came from the mouths of proven liars?

Thus, instead of having fun with his cheerfully duplicitous characters, Gernsback is obliged to immediately turn around and demonstrate that they are really sober-minded truthtellers. In the first chapter, then, the major action

involves Münchhausen proving to Alier that he is telling the truth by means
of red lights on the Moon that Münchhausen generates for Alier's inspection:

> "My son," [the Baron's voice] came back in sepulchral tones, "I am not at all
> surprised at your astonishment. Rest assured I expected you would doubt my
> identity. However, I have proofs. It is now 12:50 A.M. terrestrial time. Kindly
> mount to the top of your roof. You will find it to be a clear night, the moon
> being half full. Take your watch along and observe the moon carefully. Precisely
> at 1 A.M. I will illuminate the dark half portion of the moon with a red phos-
> phorescence, three times beginning 1 a.m., each illumination to last five seconds
> with a 10 second interval between each illumination." [...].
>
> I recollect that I grabbed my cap and run up the stairs, knocking somebody
> down as I flew by, pushed the trap open and sank down on the roof almost
> exhausted [...]. A clock near by started to strike 1 o'clock. The sound was still
> vibrating in the air when I witnessed a most remarkable phenomenon. The dark
> portion of the moon was suddenly faintly illuminated with the same scarlet
> phosphoresence which I had seen but a few seconds before around my receivers
> [...] [1:3].

This edited passage, which was followed by another long paragraph describing the lights on the Moon, clearly is not providing the sort of playful humor
one might expect in a story about Baron Münchhausen, although there is a
somewhat lighter spirit in the Baron's subsequent account about how he was
accidentally injected with embalming fluid in 1797 and thus kept alive in a
form of suspended animation until his revival in 1907.

Then, in the second chapter, when the veracity of Alier's account is
understandably challenged by family members, a similarly dull passage is
required in order to in turn establish Alier's veracity:

> I hastened to reply that I was doing nicely, but that I found it difficult to per-
> suade my doubting Thomases that his Excellency had really come back to life.
> At this Münchhausen laughed heartily and said he had expected that much. He
> added that if further proofs were wanted, he would be happy to give another
> lunar exhibition [...].
>
> I will not go into lengthy details; suffice it to say that, true to his word, at
> exactly 11:30 P.M. Münchhausen swept the dark part of the moon's surface with
> an immense shaft of green phosphorescence, similar to the exhibition he had
> given to me the night before. If anything, the light shaft was more powerful;
> this, however, might have been due to the earth's atmosphere being clearer than
> on the previous night.
>
> I need not go to the trouble of explaining that every one of my family was
> thoroughly convinced. All were silent and awe struck, and all were as ready as
> myself to believe anything that Münchhausen might say, and I assure you I was
> convinced throughout [2:40].

By means of these passages, Gernsback is able to establish that the Baron
is a trustworthy reporter, and that I. M. Alier is a trustworthy narrator, so
that their forthcoming accounts of scientific facts and futuristic inventions

can be taken seriously. Still, before getting into such matters, Gernsback decides that he can safely indulge in a brief bit of the fun he originally envisioned when he decided to write about Baron Münchhausen. In the rest of the second chapter, then, Gernsback provides a satirical account of how the Baron assisted the Allies during World War I. First, he suggested that they use chloroform, or laughing gas, to disable enemies, a strategy foiled when the German soldiers began to wear diving helmets. Next, he creates "Salties," bullets made out of salt, which can be fired at German soldiers to give them an uncontrollable urge to stop whatever they are doing and start scratching themselves; but the soldiers begin wearing two layers of clothing to prevent this effect. Münchhausen's next idea is to ingeniously employ two cannons to propel a *"Human Self-binder"* (2: 42) which can quickly arrange to have over 500 enemy soldiers "baled together tighter than a bale of compressed cotton, and as helpless as the latter" (2: 43); and it was to avoid this damaging invention, Münchhausen claims, that the Germans then resorted to trench warfare. Finally, Münchhausen develops the audacious plan of digging tunnels to Berlin and secretly replacing the German high command with French and British soldiers in German uniforms. The plan proves remarkably successful — except that the Germans had hit upon the same plan and, while the Allies were at work, they had dug tunnels to Paris and secretly replaced the French high command with German soldiers in French uniforms. This then required a hastily arranged truce, during which time both combatants returned to their original commands. And, if someone were assembling a collection of modern stories in the tradition of Baron Münchhausen, this lively and mildly amusing passage would be the only portion of Gernsback's novel that could be included without seeming incongruous.

This is because the Baron, now "in disgrace with the Allies" because his plan had failed (2:73), decides to travel to America, and like Gernsback himself, once he arrives in the United States he abandons his youthful follies and begins to get down to some serious inventing. Specifically, in a passage clearly inspired by H. G. Wells's *The First Men in the Moon* (1901) — suggesting that Gernsback may have known more about earlier science fiction that some commentators have supposed — Münchhausen manages to invent a "gravity insulator" (2:76) which blocks the force of gravity and, like Wells's Cavor, he then builds an enclosed sphere coated with this substance that he can use to fly into space, and he decides to travel to the Moon. Again like Cavor, he brings along a friend, Professor Hezekiah Flitternix, and his own pet dog and the Professor's pet canary.

At this point, Gernsback begins a policy of providing long scientific lectures, usually consisting of information that the characters and readers already know. As in *Ralph 124C 41+*, Gernsback is sometimes forced to provide strained justifications for these expository passages. In the second chapter, Münchhausen apologetically explains a long discussion of gravity in the second chapter by saying "But of course this is all well known to you. I simply recite it so that the following may become plain to you" (2:76); in the fourth chapter, he introduces another lengthy discussion by stating, "Without desiring to deliver a dry astronomical lecture, I think it best to state a few fundamental facts in order that I can make myself better understood" (4:170). And in the fifth chapter, he concludes that "My little astronomical lecture," consisting entirely of information that Alier surely already knew, "was given solely for the purpose of refreshing your mind as to Mars in order that future reports which I shall make to you from the planet will be better understood by you and your friends" (5:298–299).

In the third and fourth chapters, Gernsback attempts to recapture a spirit of fun with introductory passages from I. M. Alier, but he may already be sensing that his story is becoming dull. Thus, in the third chapter, he begins with what reads like a stunning departure from the tone and content of the story so far:

> BANG!!!
> Bang! Bang! Bang!!!
> Four terrible shots rang out.
> A heartrending moan — a piercing cry.
> Then a long, ominous silence.
> BANG! BANG!!!
> Two more shots more terrible than the first ones.
> "Dick!! Dick!!!"
> No answer.
> "Oh, Dick!!! ..."
> Less answer.
> The pine trees on the cliff moaned plaintively in the oppressive silence. Suddenly a lone owl hoo-hooed sharply, and simultaneously a flash of lightning illuminated a scene of overpowering dread. I looked on aghast — my hair stood on end. I trembled violently, for what I had seen there was so terrible, so dreadful, so awful, that it is impossible for a human being to describe it. For that reason I must refrain [28:1151].[5]

Now, what does this violent and even horrific scene have to do with Alier's account of the Baron's adventures? Absolutely nothing; as is subsequently explained, it is purely an Alier invention designed to lure readers into the story: "advertising pays. Put something really exciting at the beginning, even if it has absolutely no bearing on the rest of the story. Almost anything goes; the more mysterious the better [...] Hence I beg your pardon for having taken an unfair advantage of you; in these times of fierce competition, however, 'us poor authors' must resort to unusual means" (28:1151). All of this makes for an unusual opening for the chapter; yet it also amounts to an admission from

Alier that, had he simply begun by continuing his actual story, that would not have been able to lure readers into the story. Gernsback, then, effectively admits that his story is no longer particularly involving. The introductory passages goes on to explain how Alier's proposal to have a statue of him erected in Yankton is violently rejected by the mayor, who complains that Alier's stories about Münchhausen had made Yankton "a permanent feature in all the comic supplements of the country" (28:1152).

The fourth chapter begins by quoting an error-ridden letter from "a uneducatet cowboy" (4:136) raising some objections to the Baron's story about the salt bullets, which he then responds to in his next radio conversation with Alier. But there is little else that is amusing in the rest of the third and fourth chapters, in which Münchhausen and his companion reach the Moon, begin exploring, and carefully describe its features in a manner that accorded with the best scientific information of the time. Some passages — particularly descriptions of lunar plants and fish, and accounts of how the Earth appears to people on the Moon — seem to recall Johannes Kepler's *Somnium* (1634), but there is no indication that Gernsback was familiar with this text.

By the time of the fifth chapter, one begins to suspect that Gersnback is getting complaints about this frivolous story taking up space in his scientific magazine, so that he begins with an extended discussion of how fiction may in fact become truth, citing as an example the submarine of Jules Verne's *Thousand Leagues under the Sea*, once regarded as fanciful, but now a reality. Presumably, readers are being invited to similarly regard the Baron's adventures as accurate predictions of future predictions. This discussion ends abruptly after the Verne example with Alier stating, "Hundreds of similar instances could be cited, but lack of space prohibits. Besides, I mustn't ramble!" (5:246) But one could say that Gernsback is beginning to work out in greater detail the arguments in favor of science fiction as prophecy that he will later present in the editorials of *Amazing Stories*.

As another indication of a new desire to emphasize the scientific value of his story, a footnote in fourth chapter announces that "The balance of this installment is based upon actual facts, according to the latest lunar researches" (4:137). The fifth chapter introduces an even more conspicuous device to let readers know about true information in the story: at the end of Alier's introduction in the fifth chapter, a footnote announces a new policy: "In order to distinguish facts from fiction in this installment, all statements containing actual scientific facts will be enclosed between two † marks" (5:246).[6] Later in his career, Gernsback would seek other ways to single out and call attention to the facts in his fictions: in *Amazing Stories*, by means of a regular science quiz based on information in that issue's stories; and in *Science-Fiction Plus*, to designate stories deemed to be "of a *serious scientific-technical* trend" containing "new ideas which are certain to be realized in the future," Gernsback devised the special accompanying symbol of a five-pointed star above a circle which featured the letters "SF" (*Science-Fiction Plus*, Table of Contents in each issue).

The fifth chapter of the novel is also noteworthy in that it is the last time that anything even remotely exciting happens. First, the fourth chapter had concluded with Alier's concern that Münchhausen had been struck by a meteor, though upon beginning his next message he explains that the impact of a meteor did in fact dislodge him from his position but did not otherwise harm him. Münchhausen then explains that he had subsequently fallen into a hole on the Moon's surface, had plummeted steadily downward, and had finally emerged on the other side of the Moon, having passed through the entire globe. Fortunately capable of "reaching for a projecting rock as soon as my plunge had come to a dead stop," Münchhausen then "fell down exhausted" (5:248). He soon recognized the full dimensions of his plight:

> My troubles were far from being terminated. No sooner had I regained my breath than I became conscious of the terrible cold; for I was now but a few feet from the surface of the moon, but on that side which was turned away from the sun, where nothing but icy cold, darkness and desolation reign. Aside from this, I was some 2,160 miles from Flitternix, my companion, and our "Interstellar." Walking around half of the moon was out of the question; neither could I stay where I was without freezing to death [5:248].

He then decided that "it was far better to attempt the flying journey through the moon once more than to perish with the cold on the dark side of the moon," and emerging from another perilous descent, he was lassoed and brought safely to the ground by Flitternix, who had figured out his problem, deduced what he would do, and prepared for his return (5:248).

Having learned all they could on the Moon, and still fearful of meteors, Münchhausen and Flitternix then decide to depart for the planet Mars, which leads to long discussions about scientific reasons for supposing Mars to be inhabited by intelligent beings and a system for relaying radio messages which Münchhausen sets up so that his transmissions from Mars can still be picked up by Alier's receiver. What is interesting is this new device soon becomes a recurring excuse for Münchhausen to abruptly terminate his messages; for example, at the end of the eighth chapter, , Münchhausen concludes, "But I note by my chronometer that the time is up and in a few seconds the telegraphone wire on my radiotomatic on the moon will be full to capacity. So I must cut off short" (8:526). This is one early indication that Gernsback is tiring of his monthly chore of writing this novel and thus eager to employ a device that will enable him to write no more than a minimal amount each time.

In the sixth chapter they approach the planet and are guided to a landing by three mysterious craft beaming bright yellow lights, confirming their belief that Mars has intelligent life. Their arrival on the surface brings a moment of slapstick humor:

> We lost no time in unbolting our steel door, and in our anxiety to get out in the open, all three of us, Flitternix, myself and Buster, our fox terrier, almost tumbled over each other. I admit that on a historical occasion like this the first time a human being sat foot on another planet, we should have appeared more dignified as, for instance, Christopher Columbus did when he first landed on San Salvador. Sad to relate, however, there was nothing dignified nor solemn to the occasion of our landing, and this was partly due to Buster. That infernal dog insisted on running between our feet and succeeded in tripping Flitternix just as he placed his foot on the ground; if it had not been for me he would have sprawled all over the grass [6:313].

The rest of the chapter, however, consists almost entirely of a long flashback providing Flitternix's prior suspicions about the likely appearance of the Martians, suspicions which were confirmed upon their arrival.

In the seventh chapter, a "metallic cap" placed on Münchhausen's head enables him to receive telepathic communications from his Martian hosts, and he learns how the planet had gradually evolved into a utopia:

> Our host launched into the "Evolution of Mars." We were first shown how the planet, millions of years ago, was but a nebulae floating in space and how the nebulae slowly became a solid sphere. The early life of Mars was then pictured, which must have been exactly like the evolution of our own Earth. We saw the prehistoric Martians with their clubs and stones, then we saw for a long period the slow evolution of Mars down through the ages till a civilization similar to that of present terrestrial conditions was reached. There were the wars, the barbarism and the thousand other evils exactly as those experienced by man on Earth. Evolution, after all, is the same throughout the Universe, given like conditions.
>
> As the story of the evolution went on we could see how the Martian's small head and his small chest both kept on increasing with each subsequent generation. We were shown how big oceans and inland seas, as well as vast rivers, dried by gradually, and how the whole population turned into mechanics, electricians and chemists. No true happiness and contentment, however, seemed to exist on Mars until thought transference was established, till gravity was conquered and money was abolished. There had been wars and disorders up to that period, but it seems that these three things, apparently invented and originated at about the same time, finally emancipated the race completely [7:387].

Münchhausen goes on to explain how telepathy led to adoption of a "one universal language" which eliminated the "evils" and "race hatreds" produced by multiple languages (7:387), and further explains how the conquest of gravity, together with other scientific advances, provided technological solutions to the problems of drought and a thinning atmosphere. Oddly, however,

Münchhausen does not elaborate on how the abolition of money significantly improved Martian society — perhaps reflecting the already noted aversion to economic speculations in science fiction, perhaps reflecting Gernsback's own lack of enthusiasm for any posited system which would abolish his beloved money.

As Münchhausen's account continues, readers learn more about Martian telepathy and how it works; the canals of Mars and how water is transported through them; the design of Martian cities, all placed on platforms 500 feet above the surface to avoid dust storms; what the Martians have learned about other planets by means of their advanced telescopes; and how Martians employ advanced science to create various sorts of delightful entertainments. Only one aspect of their civilization, mentioned only in passing, might raise the eyebrows of a contemporary reader: "While the Martians are enlightened enough to have no religion whatsoever, they know what we have known for some time, namely, that life on all planets is absolutely dependent on the sun" (9:625) Gernsback was evidently confident that his readers would not be unduly offended by this offhand dismissal of religion as a characteristic of the "unenlightened."

In depicting the Martians as beings far more advanced than humans, Gernsback was adhering to the common belief that Mars was an older planet than Earth, and hence one which would be home to beings that were older and more mature than humans and would therefore seem like wise parents to human visitors.[7] Yet in portraying Mars as a long-established utopia, Gernsback was also removing any possibility of involving narrative developments from his novel. Thus, although the purported utopia of *Ralph 124C 41+* was actually still afflicted by conspicuous and regularly mentioned problems, Gernsback's account of Martian civilization includes only one brief suggestion of a lingering imperfection when Münchhausen notes that "As the most vital question on Mars is invariably the supply of water, nine-tenths of the Planet Ruler's 'correspondence' is on this subject. So strenuous is the battle for existence on Mars that the inhabitants of the planet themselves are always considered after the water supply, never before it" (8:523). If Gernsback was truly intent upon making this into an interesting story, he might have seized upon this issue to confront the Martians with a water crisis — perhaps, a mechanical breakdown leading to a severe drought — which would have introduced some genuine conflict and suspense into the narrative. But the rest of the final chapters contain no other hints that the Martians' lives are anything but ideal, and the only activity in the novel becomes Münchhausen's leisurely exposures to various facets of Martian society, calmly explained at length by his accommodating hosts. And that, in essence, describes all of the remaining chapters of *Baron Münchhausen's New Scientific Adventures*.

In placing two humans in the midst of this ideal civilization, Gernsback effectively reduces his previously active and effective characters to the status of children, as several references suggest. Upon first meeting with the Planet Ruler, Münchhausen observes that "We were but uncomprehending children, and our eyes and senses were absolutely inadequate to do justice at once to the higher plane of civilization on which we had been thrown so suddenly" (15:386). Then, after hearing the Planet Ruler's account of Martian history, Münchhausen notes that "our host [...] watched our utter amazement with the benevolent smile a fond mother will bestow on her four-year-old child after she has finished telling him a particularly interesting fairy story" (7:388). Because the Martians are taller than humans, Münchhausen and Flitternix find that "The only trouble with the chairs was that they were too big for us," so they must sit "in the chairs just as children sit in big armchairs, that is with our backs resting against the inside back of the chair and our legs projecting straight out on the seat" (7:387). A subsequent illustration shows the men looking foolish as they sit in these oversized chairs in precisely that fashion (8:474). In the tenth chapter, when Münchhausen (as will be discussed) temporarily begins to talk like a Martian, humans are described as "still very young children" (10:697). And in the final chapter, Münchhausen says that "We are still very VERY young puppies, blinking uncomprehendingly about us in a wonderful and ancient world" (13:724).

Such diminished characters, unfortunately, cannot be expected to initiate adventures or accomplish anything significant; rather, in this milieu, all they can do, like children, is to do as they are told and listen to their lessons, and this further reduces any possibility for dramatic action. For example, if Gernsback had indeed decided to manufacture a Martian water crisis to enliven the narrative, one might like to see the Martians consulting Münchhausen about what they should do, as the French high command consulted with Münchhausen during World War I, and having Münchhausen then come up with some ingenious scheme to deal with the problem. But the Martians are so much more advanced than humans as to render such a scenario impossible. Instead, if a crisis had occurred, Münchhausen again would have found himself in a passive position, observing the vastly superior Martians handle the situation. With his characters reduced in this fashion, then it is not surprising that Gernsback himself was losing interest in his own story, as would become increasingly apparent as the novel progressed.

Now that Münchhausen's adventures are locked into a pattern which could yield no lively adventures, the only aspect of the story that might provide some conflict and humor is the frame story of narrator I. M. Alier — which would explain why Gernsback returns to a greater focus on Alier in the later chapters. Thus, in the sixth and seventh chapters, Alier was represented only by brief introductory passages before Münchhausen launched into a discussion of his latest experiences, suggesting that he was settling into a diminished role. But the eighth chapter has a more extended opening in which Alier describes the pleasure of smoking a "*Nargileh*— the Turkish water pipe" and says that he "would like nothing better than telling you how to make one." But he is unable to do so:

> Alas — I am supposed to report Münchhausen's doings; am supposed to be writing fiction, scientifiction, to be correct, and not "how-to-make-it" "dope!" The editor says he can get all the contributions he wants for that department, so he doesn't need mine. Between you and I, I like the "how-to-make-it-stuff" better myself. Mars, to be sure, is all right, but we're simply not educated enough to understand all this advanced Martian business. If I could only get a message to Münchhausen and ask him what kind of "dope" is published in the Martian Electrical Experimenter in their "How-to-make-it" department! [8:474].

This passage constitutes a startling admission: the narrator says that he would prefer to be producing the sorts of practical scientific articles that were typically featured in *The Electrical Experimenter*, instead of telling a story, and if that is not possible, he at least wishes that Münchhausen's reports could shift to a discussion of the sorts of practical scientific articles produced by the Martians. One is driven to suspect that Alier's comments reflect Gernsback's own increasing lack of interest in writing his novel, and his own desire to return to focusing on writing scientific articles.

In the ninth and twelfth chapters, Gernsback returns to the theme of the introductory passage to the second chapter: Alier's Münchhausen's stories are greeted skeptically, and Alier must struggle to convince others of their veracity. On these occasions, however, he is surprisingly unsuccessful. In the ninth chapter, a reporter visits Alier's home to listen to one of Münchhausen's broadcasts — but on this one occasion, Münchhausen mysteriously fails to contact him. This then inspires farcically skeptical stories in the local newspaper with these headlines:

I. M. ALIER
MAKES STUPEFYING INVENTION

———————

RECEIVES SOUNDLESS, VOICELESS,
MESSAGES FROM MARS

———————

ALLEGED HERO, MÜNCHHAUSEN,
SPEECHLESS WITH SURPRISE

———————

MÜNCHHAUSEN SAYS HE
AIN'T SAYIN' NOTHING'!!
——————— [9:624]

Later, Alier discovers that he had accidentally left his lightning switch in the wrong position, preventing him from receiving any messages. In the twelfth chapter, Alier discovers that, because Mars is moving farther and farther away from the Earth, he can no longer receive Münchhausen's messages, so he must hope that Münchhausen will be able to construct a more powerful broadcasting on Mars. Again, however, the local reporters respond with sarcastically skeptical reports:

PSEUDO SCIENTIST LOSES
ETHERICAL WAVE-CONNECTION
_____

Claims Earth and Mars Estranged, Are Suing
for Separation!
_____ [12:487]

Presumably, readers are still expected to believe that Alier is trustworthy, and that the reporters are being foolish in refusing to believe him because of these unfortunate problems. Still, the knowledge that residents of Yankton no longer think that Alier is telling the truth does serve to undermine Münchhausen's reports, and it is a further suggestion that Gernsback no longer finds this narrative either valuable or interesting.[8]

The tenth and eleventh chapters endeavor to enliven Alier's introductory passages in different ways. The ninth chapter had included an interesting comment about the Martians' lack of concern for personal privacy:

> The Martian loves nothing better than transparency and for that reason he builds nearly every object of Tos; from a table down to the floor, which, of course, is transparent, too. You might think that such a house, open to everybody's curiosity would bring with it many delicate as well as embarrassing situations, but this is not the case, at least not for the Martians. These people have long sense learned that anything worth doing cannot possibly be open to criticism from fellow inhabitants; while closeted, non-transparent rooms make for nothing but laziness and vice. When all of your actions are open to the entire world you are more apt to lead an upright life than otherwise. For that reason no false, make-believe civilization exists on Mars as is the case on earth. For that reason, too, the Martian is an upright, healthy, truth-loving individual, not a hypocrite as is the case on earth [9:660].

While the consequences of this lack of privacy are here described only in general and philosophical terms, Alier explains in the tenth chapter that he had gotten into trouble when he had decided to implement Martian policies in a crude and simple manner:

> As will be remembered, Münchhausen told us a little while ago that the Martian live in transparent houses, for reasons best known to themselves. As will also be remembered, he told us that anything that is worth doing — on Mars — is worth doing with everyone looking on [...].

I tried the Martian recipe the other day, and I must confess here that it was a dismal failure. Now everyone knows, of course, that everyone else is apt to take a bath once in a while for strictly personal reasons, the only difference being that the frequency varies with some individuals according to taste and according to the available water as well as soap supply. I know that *you* take a bath and you know that *I* take a bath; certainly there is no secret about that. Nobody should find fault with such universal custom. But when I tried it the other day, leaving my bathroom window wide open, it somehow didn't work out according to the Martian recipe, at least Officer Mulligan, on the beat, who I believe had not read about the Martians' habits, didn't approve of my custom and very promptly arrested me when a big crowd gathered in front of my bathroom, which happens to be on the ground floor. I have since given up trying to convert antiquated humans living on an uncivilized globe, to Martian standards of civilization [10:696].

And the eleventh chapter reintroduces the theme of Alier's desire to write scientific articles and the resulting conflicts with the editor: after Alier launches into a parenthetical discussion of how to construct his new invention, an "*Audi-Amplifone*," the editor interrupts the instructions:

> [NOTE.— *We contracted with Mr. I. M. Alier to furnish us one Münchhausen story a month. So far he has broken his contract twice. We, therefore, cannot allow him, in fairness to other contributors, to run "How-to-Make-It" articles in this department; furthermore our space is limited.*— EDITOR.]
> [Didn't I tell you that Editor of yours is an unappreciative, soulless old "crab"?— I. M. ALIER] [11:92].

This, however, represents the final effort to inject some humor into either portion of the novel, as the introduction to the thirteenth chapter only includes Alier's serious musings about the reasons why smaller worlds like the Moon lose their atmosphere, which prepares readers for the topic of Münchhausen's report, the "Martian Atmosphere Plants" which maintain the planet's breathable atmosphere despite its low gravity.

The later chapters also display signs of inattentiveness, as inconsistencies and some repetitiveness begin creeping into the narrative, further suggesting Gernsback's increasing lack of interest in a deteriorating narrative. In the first two chapters there are only two minor errors: a reference to the time being "11:59" when 12:59 was the intended time (1:3) and Münchhausen's reference to a "lapse of 100 years" between his embalming and revival when it was actually 110 years (2:41). But more significant problems later become evident. In the second chapter, Alier asserts that his brother was present during all of Münchhausen's transmissions that that "all conversations between Baron Münchhausen and myself, which I shall publish hereafter, are exactly as stated, taken from my brother's stenographic reports" (2:40). Yet in later accounts of visitors to Alier's home at the time of Münchhausen's broadcasts, the brother is never mentioned. In the first chapter, Alier says that he "had just lit a fresh pipe" (1:3), by all indications a conventional pipe, but the eighth chapter, as noted, depicts him as a regular user of a Turkish water pipe. When they first left the planet, Münchhausen and Flitternix were accompanied by Münchhausen's dog Buster and Flitternix's pet canary Pee-Pix; yet after another reference in the third chapter the canary is never mentioned again, and while there are continuing references to Buster up until the moment of their arrival on Mars, the dog then vanishes from the narrative as well. After their pratfall upon first arriving on Mars, Münchhausen reports that "It is a good thing that the Martians have a keen sense of humor, for the crowd that had collected around our flyer began to laugh uproariously in a queer, characteristically Martian falsetto voice" (6:312). Yet he later comments that "I had never before seen a Martian laugh" (11:133). A passage from the eighth chapter, cited above, notes that "life on all planets is absolutely dependent upon the sun," strongly suggesting that there is in fact life on all planets; yet in the very next chapter, Martian astronomy demonstrates, in fact, that "none of the planets except the earth bore life" (9:741) — a statement that is also surprising because of the various life forms that Münchhausen and Flitternix found on the Moon. In an editorial aside in the June, 1916 chapter, it is said that Alier, who promised to provide monthly installments about Münchhausen, "has broken his contract twice" (11:92); in fact, by this time there had been three months without a Münchhausen chapter. At one point in the tenth chapter, Gernsback evidently forgets that he is writing what Münchhausen is saying, not what the Martians are saying to Münchhausen, so that Münchhausen suddenly begins to speak to Alier as if he were a Martian: "When you consider how crudely you humans use your energy it must dawn upon you that you are still very young children" (10: 697). The narrative repeatedly identifies the leader of Mars as the "Planet Ruler"; yet in the final chapter, the figure is called the "Planet Governor" (13:751), which was of course the title used in *Ralph 124C 41+*.

As for repetitiveness, the eleventh chapter, "Martian Amusements," describes a spectacular show in which the sun and planets are depicted — but this is extremely similar to the "Aerial Carnival" described in *Ralph*. And, as already indicated, the humorous passage involving skeptical newspaper headlines in the twelfth chapter was extremely reminiscent of a similar passage in the ninth chapter.

At this point, was there any way that Gernsback could have revived his increasingly dull novel, and thus revived his own interest in the project? Apparently there were no viable options.

Münchhausen and Flitternix could remain on Mars, but that could only lead to more staid and stultifying presentations of the wonders of the advanced Martian civilization. They might leave to visit other planets, but since Münchhausen had previously established that none of the other planets had life, that could only lead to more descriptions of conditions on lifeless worlds like the Moon, hardly an improvement over the Martian utopia.[9] Finally, they could return to Earth, but that would provide no further pretext for introducing scientific information and prophetic ideas and would offer the further challenge of plausibly integrating the legendary Baron Münchhausen into ongoing current events.

Unable to resolve the problem of the novel, Gernsback abruptly terminated the novel with its thirteenth chapter. We know that this was not his original intent, since the February, 1917 issue includes an announcement about the March issue which promises that, in that issue, "Baron Münchhausen will hold forth again on Martian wonders. By Hugo Gernsback" ("In the March 'E.E.'" 725), and the chapter ends with the familiar "(*To be continued*)" (13:751). But as the months went by, and Gernsback found himself unable to come up with anything more that was worthwhile to say about Alier or Münchhausen, he must have gradually realized that the best thing to do about the novel was to silently abandon it.

In offering an overall assessment of *Baron Münchhausen's New Scientific Adventures*, one cannot say that the novel has been unjustifiably neglected. True, it is arguably better than one might expect, inasmuch as it does include some lively and clever moments which may represent Gernsback at the very peak of his limited writing skills. But the novel as a whole must be regarded as a complete failure, and its value for modern readers may be primarily to serve as additional evidence in support of lessons about the characteristic genres of science fiction which can also be extracted from *Ralph 124C 41+*.

First, science fiction with educational and prophetic goals will be highly resistant to satire. Here, even though Gernsback chose as his protagonist a famous satirical figure and creates his own satirical figure as his narrator, he found himself unable to write a satire and instead was obliged to incongruously employ these characters as conveyors of scientific facts and plausible ideas for future inventions. Second, such science fiction can blend more naturally with the genres of the travel tale and utopia, although the result may be a story with little narrative interest. Finally, the true genre that both may more accurately reflect scientific attitudes and typically drives successful science fiction, and the genre that is entirely absent in *Baron Münchhausen's New Scientific Adventures*, is melodrama. Ralph has a *reason* to go on a tour of an advanced future world: he is trying to entertain and to woo an attractive woman. He has a *reason* to go into outer space: to rescue that girl from a kidnapper. And despite Gernsback's poor writing skills, readers can develop an interest in Ralph's adventures and wonder as they read how his adventures will turn out. In contrast, once he gives up his efforts to win World War I,

Münchhausen has no *reason* for doing anything that he does; he does things purely for the sake of doing them, and there is nothing about his adventures to develop an interest in or to wonder about. Perhaps Gernsback had become embarrassed about the villains and derring-do that figured in *Ralph 124C 41+* and had consciously decided to produce a novel that had a bit more dignity; but the result was simply a story that nobody could care about, and a story that eventually even bored its own author, who could never be bothered to finish it.

As another sign that Gernsback was not fond of or impressed by this novel, one notes that, in the 1920s, Gernsback arranged for the republication in book form of *Ralph 124C 41+* and devoted a considerable amount of energy to revising and expanding the novel; however, he apparently never considered doing the same with *Baron Münchhausen's New Scientific Adventures.* Still, once he began to publish *Amazing Stories,* he repeatedly endeavored to save money by reprinting (presumably at no cost to him) stories that had previously appeared in *Modern Electrics, The Electrical Experimenter,* and *Science and Invention,* and it was inevitable that he would eventually decide to republish his second novel. So it was that, in the February, 1928 issue of *Amazing Stories,* there appeared the first of six installments of the retitled *Baron Münchhausen's Scientific Adventures,* following a schedule of two chapters per issue until the June, 1928 issue, which included the final three chapters. And, as was the case with the republication of *Ralph 124C 41+* in *Amazing Stories Quarterly,* one finds that the text has been altered in innumerable minor ways, undoubtedly by Associate Editor T. O'Conor Sloane.

However, while I have previously discussed how Sloane did significant damage to the text of *Ralph 124C 41+,* his work on *Baron Münchhausen's New Scientific Adventures,* overall, is much less objectionable — for two reasons. First, *Ralph 124C 41+* sometimes featured relatively exciting and fast-moving sequences, so that Sloane's relentless concerns for grammatical correctness, precise parallel structure, and proper punctuation at all times could have the effect of slowing down the pace of the narrative; but there is very little excitement in the goings-on of *Baron Münchhausen's New Scientific Adventures,* so this problem does not emerge. Second, and more important, Gernsback wrote *Ralph 124C 41+* in a consistently clear, and even colloquial style, so that Sloane's copyediting tended to make the text seem more stodgy and old-fashioned. In contrast, Gernsback created two artificial styles of writing for *Baron Münchhausen's New Scientific Adventures:* the naturally antiquated voice of the eighteenth-century Münchhausen, and the grandiloquent, posturing voice of I. M. Alier. The result was a text that often seemed wordy and over-written, so that Sloane's copyediting generally had the effect of making the prose more clear and concise. Indeed, and surprisingly, if one were planning to republish this novel, a case could be made that Sloane's text should be preferred over Gernsback's original version.

As always, Sloane was fastidious in correcting Gernsback's grammar. Thus, while the original second sentence began "If that don't suit you" (1:2), Sloane corrects the subject-verb agreement error by replacing "don't" with "doesn't" (28:1061). Reading "It seemed to me as if there was a gigantic searchlight" (1:3), the appalled Sloane imposes correct use of the past subjunctive: "as if there were" (28:1063), and when Gernsback casually writes, "Just as sudden the sweeping light shaft appeared anew" (1:3), "no one took him serious" (5:92), "hear the slightest 'rustling' in the ether perfectly plain" (5:92), or "Everything seemed to work entirely automatic" (13:751), Sloane inserts the correct adverbial forms: "Just as suddenly" (28:1063), "no one took him seriously" (28:38), "perfectly plainly" (28:346), and "entirely automatically" (28:357). When Münchhausen begins his explanation of how Flitternix had figured out how to rescue him after his fall, Gernsback's "This is what happened" (5:248) is revised by Sloane to correctly employ the past perfect tense: "This is what had happened" (28:41). Sloane knows that, with only two instances, one must use the comparative form of the adjective, not the superlative, so Gernsback's description of Phobos as "the largest moon" of Mars (6:313) becomes "the larger moon" (28:45); and of course it does not revolve "quicker" (6:313), but "more quickly" (28:45). Gernsback's Münchhausen rhetorically asks, "And who moves the waters on Earth? Who condenses the waters from the oceans and lifts up myriads of tons of water year in and year out, to form clouds, which latter produce the rains, without which your rivers would run dry within four weeks? The Sun, of course!" (7:443–444). But Sloane knows that he is not using the proper pronoun for an inanimate object and replaces "who" with "what" (28:153 — and yes, he further corrects "latter" to "later"). And at the end of the tenth chapter, when Gernsback momentarily gives the game away by twice referring to his narrator as "Aliar," Sloane corrects the spelling to "Alier."

Sloane is also vigilant in correcting or updating the scientific information in Gernsback's novel. Realizing that it was not proper to say that one was "falling through the whole length of the moon!" (5:246), a spherical body, Sloane replaces "length" with "diameter" (28:40). Gernsback's Münchhausen notes that the "moon revolves about [the Earth] in 27 1/4 days, always turning one side to the earth. For this reason, the inhabitants of the earth can never see more than one of the moon's hemispheres" (4:137). Sloane knew that, for a variety of reasons, people on Earth can actually see up to 55% of the Moon's surface, and so he adds an explanatory passage: "It is the same hemisphere always with the addition of a very small marginal area which periodically is obscured and illuminated. This periodical change is termed the libration of the moon" (28:1158). When Gernsback's Münchhausen raves about how the incredibly advanced Martians can make music which "can be heard plainly over a distance of 10 miles" (8:475), Sloane recognizes that this might not seem impressive to readers in 1928, and so he adds a footnote to acknowledge recent developments on Earth: "When this was written, radio loud speakers were not known. Recently radio loud speakers have been invented which can throw music and the human voice over a distance of several miles" (28:154); a similar footnote is added to a mention of Alier's "Audio-Amplifone" in the eleventh chapter (11:92; 28:346). Apparently drawing upon more recent information about Mars's moons, Sloane changes Gernsback's comment that Deimos is "12,300 miles from Mars" (9:658) to "12,480 miles from Mars" (28:245). Gernsback's Münchhausen states that if you emptied a pail of water in an area of zero gravity, "It would, therefore, hang freely in space like a cake of ice without falling apart" (11:134). Sloane knows this is not entirely accurate and says, "Instead the water would slowly begin to shape itself into a sphere, due to the phenomenon called 'surface tension.' It is this property that shapes small drops of water into almost perfect spheres when dropped upon a piece of cloth or velvet" (28:349).

Sloane updates Gernsback's text in other ways as well. Gernsback speaks of a posited "two cents a word" (1:3) as an attractive rate for working writers, but that would not necessarily be the case in 1928, so Sloane changes it to "ten cents a word" (28:1062). Gernsback cites "Prof. Percival Lowell, the greatest living authority on Martian research work" (5:297); since he had died in 1916, Sloane instead speaks of "the late Prof. Percival Lowell, the great authority on Martian research work" (28:42). Writing in 1915, Gernsback says that if Julius Caesar had been "transplanted" to present-day New York, that would be "a jump of but 1,965 years" (7:386); copyediting in 1928, Sloane alertly changes this to "a jump of only 1,978 years" (28:148).

None of these changes really affect the quality of the novel, either positively or negatively, but Sloane does improve Gernsback's prose by sporadically revising some passages. In the first chapter, "Now, as anyone can readily convince himself by trial" (1:2) becomes "Now, as anyone knows" (28:1061), and "But this brings me away from my story" (1:3) becomes "But I digress from my story" (28:1062). In the fourth chapter, "only the vast, rolling quantities of black smoke were easily discernible" (4:172) becomes "I could only see the vast, rolling quantities of black smoke" (28:1159). In the fifth chapter, "let's return to the original starting point" (5:246) is revised to "let's return to the place we started from" (28:38).

Furthermore, unnecessary or repetitive passages in Gernsback's originally are sometimes removed: in the fifth chapter, when Gernsback's Alier notices that Münchhausen's voice sounds different, he says, "in a short time, however, the mystery was cleared, and this is what poured in my astonished ears" (5:246); Sloane leaves out the "and this is what ... ears" (28:38). In chapter six, having already noted that a Martian "was dressed like them, the only difference being that his metallic cap appeared yellow in color," there was no need to add that "Otherwise there seemed to be no difference in his attire" (15:371), so Sloane removes the sentence. In the tenth chapter, after Alier comments, "Perhaps the above may have a certain bearing on this story and on the other hand it might not," the subsequent "probably that is quite true also" (10:696) seems redundant, and Sloane leaves it out (28:248). There are also several instances of superfluous transitional words like "however" and "now" being removed.

There are two cuts of considerably larger dimensions, although these are justifiable. As previously noted, the eighth and eleventh chapters include some extended introductory bantering involving Alier's desire to write practical science articles for *The Electrical Experimenter* and the exasperated editor's refusal to allow it. Since this conflict would seem incongruous in a novel being republished in a science fiction magazine, Sloane removes both passages. This does have the unfortunate effect, however, of eliminating the lingering sense of fun that Alier's opening flourishes were providing in this increasingly dull novel.

However, the most significant change Sloane made to the novel comes at the very end. Gernsback's thirteenth chapter ends abruptly, without even including Münchhausen's farewell and Alier's closing remarks; instead, the final sentence is a rhetorical question from Münchhausen: "How long will it be with your coal burning machinery till the earth's atmosphere will need cleaning plants?" (13:751). But the 1928 version continues as follows:

> For several more minutes the record ran on, but the voice grew so indistinct and so weak that it was impossible for me to hear the balance of Baron Münchhausen's message. All I heard distinctly was the final low click, when the recording mechanism on the moon had switched itself off.
> I suddenly began to realize that Mars was rapidly going further and further from the Earth. That evening, Mars had been some 80 million miles distant. This distance would now rapidly increase, and unless the Baron realized this and installed a more powerful transmitter, it will be impossible for me to hear his messages hereafter.
>
> * * *
>
> For several nights now, I have listened to Münchhausen's messages, but I have not been able to understand any of them. The recording apparatus on the moon was working in its usual manner, because I got the starting click sharply at 11 o'clock every night, and I got the sign off click as well. But in between the voice of Münchhausen was so low, that it sounded much like static and it was impos-

sible to make out a word except now and then, and as time went by, it got worse.

Every day, Mars retreats further into the heavens, until finally, it will be at its maximum distance from the earth, nearly 240,000,000 miles. Moreover, Mars will be directly behind the sun, and it would seem impossible that even a Martian radio transmitter could shoot radio signals around the sun at this tremendous distance and have them register on the recording apparatus on the moon.

I am, of course, desolate and heartbroken, but what can I do? Every night I strain my ears to the utmost, but I hear nothing. I know the world is waiting for further messages, and for more about the high culture of Mars, but it seems that for some time to come I will not be able to get in touch with the glorious old Baron.

Whenever I hear from him again, you will find me ready to give the news to the world [28:357].

Now, since Gernsback was after all working with Sloane in editing *Amazing Stories* at this time, it would seem possible that Sloane arranged for Gernsback himself to add some sort of ending to his incomplete novel, and that in this instance at least one might attribute a textual change to Gernsback instead of Sloane. However, this strikes me as extraordinarily unlikely, for two reasons.

In the first place, this purported explanation for Münchhausen's sudden silence directly contradicts what Münchhausen had just told Alier in the previous chapter about his new method of transmitting messages: "But you can rest assured that I will maintain communication with you even when Mars is in conjunction, that is, when the earth and Mars will be at their furthest separation, which is 230 million miles [...] Professor Flitternix figured it all out, and he thinks too that we will be able to maintain communication when the sun comes between Mars and the earth" (12:487). I have noted that Gernsback, while writing the original novel, began to become inattentive and some minor inconsistencies in the story, but I doubt that he would make a crucial element in his story's new conclusion dependent upon a development which completely contradicted what the text had so recently established. Rather, in this case, it seems that Sloane was the inattentive one, because he might have at least addressed the problem by removing or revising the passage in which Münchhausen assured Alier that his communications would continue no matter how far Mars moved away from the Earth; instead, he reproduces the above passage almost word for word.

The second, and more convincing, factor is that the new passage is thuddingly dull, both in its contents and its tone, and it seems entirely alien to the jocular spirit which Gernsback had consistently sought to maintain whenever he was speaking in the voice of Alier. Surely, if Gernsback had addressed the task of coming up with a way to end the novel, he would devised something a bit more clever. Perhaps, for example, he might have had an exasperated Alier report that, due to a ridiculously unfair legal decision imposed because of some purported act of chicanery, all of his radio equipment was suddenly impounded and sold at auction to pay for a judgment against him, rendering it impossible for him to hear any more of Münchhausen's transmissions.

While one can criticize Sloane's method of ending *Baron Münchhausen's New Scientific Adventures*, it must be acknowledged that he did face a real problem — a serialized novel that ended abruptly without a conclusion — and he did resolve that problem, however unsatisfactorily. And one might further defend Sloane by stating that, in the case of this increasingly boring novel, it was only appropriate to bring it to a close with the most boring conclusion imaginable.

After its republication in *Amazing Stories, Baron Münchhausen's New Scientific Adventures* essentially vanished from view: when the December, 1929 issue of *Amazing Stories* published a letter from a reader inquiring "By the way, what has become of the estimable Baron Münchhausen and the inventive Mr. Hicks, or who has sat by the side of Alier as he received the messages of the Baron?," the magazine's new editor, T. O'Conor Sloane, blandly responded, "We doubt if we shall get any more items concerning the travels of Baron Münchhausen" ("Discussions," December, 1929 362). It has never appeared in book form, and in contrast to the various anthologies that presented excerpts from *Ralph 124C 41+*, only one anthology — Peter Haining's *The Fantastic Pulps* (1976) — has ever included an excerpt from Gernsback's second novel (for the record, Haining chose Chapter 12, "How the Martian Canals Are Built"). And today, to say the least, any revival of interest in this seriously flawed novel seems extraordinarily unlikely.

Even while he was still working on *Baron Münchhausen's New Scientific Adventures* with a modicum of enthusiasm, Gernsback may have already been planning to retire from writing fiction — because, right in the middle of the text of the second chapter of the novel, *The Electrical Experimenter* printed this announcement:

Can you
write a snappy, short story having
some scientific fact as its theme? If
you can

Write
such fiction we would like to print it.
The story which is appearing in the
ELECTRICAL EXPERIMENTER at
present has aroused so much enthusiasm
among our readers that we have decided
to publish more

Stories
from time to time. If you have the
knack, try your hand at it. It is worth
while. However, please bear in mind
that only scientific literature is
acceptable, although not necessarily dealing with
electrical subjects. "Baron Münchhausen"
is a good example. Suppose
you try. We pay well for such original
stories [2:42].

Gernsback's apparent resolve to rely upon other authors to provide him with science fiction is evidenced by the fact that for the next thirty-eight years, until several works appeared in *Science-Fiction Plus,* Gernsback published precisely four stories, and three of them were extremely brief.

The first of these, "The Magnetic Storm" (1918), was expressly written in order to convey Gernsback's idea for winning World War I — unleashing a tremendous torrent of magnetic energy that would instantly disable all German equipment; he even obtained an accompanying endorsement from the great Nicolas Tesla to the effect that the scheme was possible. The story is briefly dramatic when, after a brief introduction, readers encounter the sinister Baron von Unterrichter, who establishes his unspeakable villainy by ordering a bombing raid on Allied hospitals. Inexplicably, his airplane and all other airplanes making the raid suddenly lose power; after making an emergency landing, von Unterrichter further discovers that cars and radio equipment are also dysfunctional. It is soon revealed that this is happening "all over Germany as well! Every train, every trolley car, every electric motor or dynamo, every telephone, every telegraph had been put out of commission. With one stroke Germany had been flung back into the days of Napoleon" (354).[10] Needless to say, the Allies quickly mark to victory. Then, the story halts, as Gernsback backtracks to allow his hero, the young inventor "Why" Sparks, to explain his brilliant idea to Nicolas Tesla in great detail, concluding that by means of his plans, "*Every closed coil of wire throughout Germany and Austria, be it a dynamo armature, or a telephone receiver coil, will be burnt out, due to the terrific electromotive force set up inductively to our primary current* [...] In other words, we will create a titanic artificial *Magnetic Storm* such as the world has never seen" (355). Tesla sees the merit in his proposal and takes the idea to the American government; soon, Sparks is in Europe installing the necessary equipment; and after its success he receives a medal from the President of France. Given Gernsback's evidently sincere belief in the plausibility of the scheme, it is surprisingly that he chose to present it in the inherently less persuasive form of a story, instead of writing an article; in any event, the work certainly commands little attention as fiction.

Gernsback's next work of fiction, his contribution to the special "Scientific Fiction" issue of *Science and Invention,* took a form that was to become characteristic of Gernsback: the mock news article. Indeed, the tone of "The Electric Duel" is so straightforwardly expository, and its prophetic content so unremarkable, that the piece at times is misidentified as an article; only the final sentence — "The frightfulness of the situation was so great that I myself woke up and promised myself never again to eat Welsh rarebits before going to bed" (333) — identifies the whole scenario as the author's fanciful dream. In the brief story, two young Italians, competing for the affections of the same young woman, agree to an unusual duel: while wearing helmets connected to a power line, each man will stand on an insulated platform and try to employ a large pole to push the other man off the platform and thus doom him to death by electrocution; when the men simultaneously knock each other off the platform, they both die instantly.

This sort of vignette, which is more an extended joke than a true narrative, soon came to fascinate Gernsback: as Moskowitz notes,

> from the early days of *Amazing Stories,* Hugo Gernsback had been obsessed with promoting interest in science-fiction short-shorts — stories of no more than 1,000 words that had novel endings. They are very difficult to write because so little wordage can be devoted to background and characterization. Yet their very brevity makes them seem easy. Gernsback had published a number of them, and had even written a few himself ["The Return of Hugo Gernsback" Part IV 197].

So it was that twice during his editorship of *Science Wonder Stories* and *Wonder Stories,* and once during his editorship of *Science-Fiction Plus,* Gernsback announced a contest of cash prizes for outstanding short-short stories. For the first of these, announced in the November, 1929 issue of *Science Wonder Stories,* he wrote his own sample story, "The Killing Flash."

It is difficult to interpret "The Killing Flash" upon first reading, but if a few omitted explanations are inferred, this seems to be its essence: John Bernard has been bested by rival Henry Lindenfeld throughout his college career, and he has further driven him out of business and stolen his fiancée. Enraged, he plots his revenge: he will rent a small loft, install some electrical equipment, call Lindenfeld on the phone, and kill him by sending a powerful electric current through the telephone line. He writes down a narrative of his plans — presented as the first part of the story — and, evidently experiencing a moment of doubt about its potential effectiveness, decides to send the manuscript to the telephone company to inquire about its practicality. The phone company writes a response — presented as the second part of the story — which explains that the scheme would not work because the electricity would largely be discharged before it reached its victim; however, before he reads the letter, he apparently overcomes his doubts and carries out the plan, although it actually causes his own death. As described in the newspaper story which is presented as the third part of the story, the loft he rented actually belonged to Lindenfeld, and when Bernard pulled the switch and sent the current racing through the telephone line, he also triggered "200 lbs. of high explosives stored on the floor above" (497), causing Bernard's death. One must guess that Lindenfeld found out about Bernard's plan, either by observing his new tenant or by receiving word from the telephone company, and decided to eliminate Bernard by placing explosives in the vicinity of his equipment. The fourth part of the story is a letter from "O. Utis, Ass. Editor" of *Science Wonder Stories,* which recasts all of the preceding material as a story that was submitted to the magazine; the editor rejects the story because of two implausibilities: Bernard would never have been foolish enough to write down his criminal plans, and he certainly would not have been foolish enough to send them to the phone company. The editor fails to mention another implausibility: Lindenfeld certainly would not have been foolish enough to devise a way to foil the plan which would inevitably cause considerable damage to his own property.

As in his other two stories following *Baron Münchhausen's New Scientific Adventures,* Gernsback again sticks to unadventurous predictions involving electrical devices, and he further betrays that he has insufficient writing skill to convey his story both clearly and succinctly. Still, the story unquestionably merits some attention as an early example of recursive science fiction, science fiction which is also about science fiction, and it is perhaps the first story to be built around the scenario of an author submitting a story to a science fiction magazine, including a letter from the editor — a pattern that would later be followed by many other stories, most prominently Jack Lewis's "Who's Cribbing?" (1953).

Gernsback continued to write science fiction stories in the 1940s, though only one of them, the soon-to-be-discussed "The Infinite Brain," appeared in a science fiction magazine. The others were only featured in his self-published "Christmas cards" of the 1940s, although several of these resurfaced in *Science-Fiction Plus.* For example, "The Exploration of Mars," which first appeared in the 1949 booklet Quip, later served as the lead story in the first issue of *Science-Fiction Plus.* In the fashion of a news story, the piece first discloses that intrepid scientist "Grego Banshuck" (one of several anagrams of "Hugo Gernsback" found in this and other Gernsback contributions to the magazine) had employed his amazing invention, the "atom-negative gravitator" (5), to fly a crew to Mars; Banshuck himself then takes over to describe the utopian civilization that he learned about during his visit. Needless to say, much of the account recalls the experiences of Baron Münchhausen on

Mars; in fact, when he offers an account of building the Martian canals that recalls a description in the novel, a footnote freely announces the borrowing in noting that "This atomic method of constructing the Martian canals was first suggested by Hugo Gernsback in his novel *Baron Münchhausen's New Scientific Adventures*, published in the *Electrical Experimenter*, November, 1916, page 513 — 26 years *before* the advent of atomic energy" (10). As in the novel, the humans, considered by Martian standards, are repeatedly described as "children" (9, 61), "puppies" (7, 8) and even "kittens" (9). And Gernsback gives these Martians similar physiologies, telepathic powers, great longevity, and vehicles that employ anti-gravity.

Still, these Martians are also different from Münchhausen's Martians in some mildly interesting ways. As he did not do in the novel, Gernsback expands upon the benefits of the Martian abolition of money in language that uncharacteristically sounds more like Lasser's socialism than Gernsback's passionate capitalism:

> There is, of course, no money and no such vicious, cancerous outgrowth as interest on money, no taxes. Consequently there is no such thing as business, as we know the term, because on Mars no one can make a profit.
> For over a billion years Martians have been conditioned to work for the good of the race and for each other. Whatever is produced belongs to the race [65].

Gernsback also gives this Martian utopia a proto-feminist twist in noting that "the females on Mars are the REAL rulers. They hold all the important positions of the entire planet, and the highest council, the *Planet Conclave* is composed of five *Universal Judges*, all females" (62). Females also choose the men that they marry. But female power never becomes too excessive because, "when their dominance becomes too great, the males go on strike *en masse*— millions of them refuse to make love to their wives. The last 'sex-strike' 14 years ago, involving over 2 ½ million males, lasted 5 ½ years. The males won!" (62) Finally, while these Martians also seem to lack religious beliefs — one Martian contemptuously refers to the humans' "fierce, childish belief in heaven and hell after death. What ludicrous, abysmal gibberish! As if they did not have an overabundance of continuous hell on earth!" (64) — they at least value the teachings of one of Earth's religious leaders: "The human race has produced one *and only one* individual who merits our complete admiration: the Hebraic Jesus Christ. Alas, his teachings continue to fall on deaf human ears" (64).

There is one other key respect in which "The Exploration of Mars" resembles *Baron Münchhausen's New Scientific Adventures*: it does not have any conclusion, but simply ends with a discussion of Martian economics without ever bothering to explain how Banshuck (one must assume) eventually left Mars and returned to Earth. Given that Gernsback indeed had a lifelong fascination with Mars, it is nevertheless striking that he could never be bothered to complete his two major works of fiction on the subject.

Along with three vignettes, *Science-Fiction Plus* published two other Gernsback stories of significant length — with one significant difference. In the first issue, the mock-article "The Exploration of Mars" had been identified on the contents page as a "Novelette." But similar mock-articles in the second and fourth issues, "World War III — In Retrospect" and "The World in 2046: The Next Hundred Years of Atomics," were instead identified as "Feature Articles." Someone working on the magazine — probably Managing Editor Sam Moskowitz — clearly felt uncomfortable about labeling such pieces as works of fiction, even though articles purportedly written in the future about events that have not yet happened can hardly be regarded as factual — even though the first piece had two footnotes that characerically related posited inventions to actual developments that had previously been described in Gernsback's science magazines, and even though the introduction to the second piece states, "You may think that much of the material is far-fetched, but it has been checked carefully by several noted scientists and no objections offered" (blurb to "The World in 2046" 34).

In the first of these stories, "World War III — In Retrospect" (previously published in Gernsback's 1950 Christmas booklet), Gernsback first envisions a near future of ominous Communist advances throughout the world: China conquers all the countries of Southeast Asia, South Korea, and Japan, while Russia takes Berlin and begins advancing through western Europe. Having previously reached an agreement with its enemies to avoid the use of atomic bombs, the United States turns the tide and achieves victory by means of other technological innovations which Gernsback names and describes: *Rasura* waves which unfailingly detected enemy submarines; *stratoradar* to locate enemy aircraft; new submarines termed *submarauders* equipped with tracks so they could also travel on land; *enclouders* to conceal the location of submarauders; *electronic autoguns* or *brainguns* which automatically strike their targets; *telehypnos* which disable enemy troops with inaudible ultrasound waves; atom-planes, run by a new form of atomic power, which could drop carefully guided *television bombs* to devastate enemy targets; and *magnetapalm* bombs which combined magnesium and napalm to produce destructive fires. Unable to resist all of these amazing weapons, Russia and China are driven back from conquered territories and soon forced to surrender.

While all of these imagined inventions are typical products of Gernsback's imagination, there is one passage near the beginning of "World War III — In Retrospect" which, less typically, again displays a new openness to radical economic reform. After commenting that the purchasing power of the dollar and other currencies has been disastrously declining up until 1967, the author discusses what may be the best solution:

> On the other hand, the atom-energy dollar — the AED — as a uniform world currency seems to gain strength as the months pass. Such a currency based upon the atomic-energy kilowatt — instead of gold — would have the same intrinsic value always — just as the meter or the yard. As atomic energy becomes cheaper the purchasing power of the AED increases. The only fly in the soup: how and on what basis could the world's nations convert their present state debts into atom-energy dollars? [27].

But this is nothing more than the "energy-credit" of technocracy under a new name; thus, to stabilize the economy of his future world, Gernsback surprisingly reaches back to a proposed system he once opposed to develop a possible answer.

While these two stories had at least some sort of narrative, "The World in 2046: The Next Hundred Years of Atomics" completely lacks such a structure. Its first section is a disorganized discussion of various aspects of the scientifically advanced world of 2046, filled with repeated references to new application of atomic power: Alaska is transformed into a temperate population center by means of weather control; the United States is upset because foreign countries are luring away its top scientists and are flooding American markets with cheap imitations of its products; workers stagnating because of a 20-hours-a-week schedule demand longer hours; Congress is divided between the Demorepub Party and the new Scientic Party; New York City's transportation problems are addressed by new networks of tunnels; atomic-powered machines are building sea walls to transform coastal waters into new lands for Earth's people to inhabit; a new art form combines dance with the release of pleasant odors; and new methods to permanently remove hair with atomic power have inspired most people to become bald. The second part of the article, "100 Years of Atomics," is simply a series of dates from 1958 to 2044 accompanied by lengthy descriptions of the atomic wonders that were first achieved on each date.

Gernsback's three other contributions to *Science-Fiction Plus* were vignettes, all attributed to pseudonyms that are anagrams of Gernsback's name. Two took the form of mock-articles: "The Cosmatomic Flyer," as by "Greno Gashbuck," describes the development of a rocket backpack enabling a man to fly through the air, while "The Electronic Baby," as by "Grego Banshuck," describes a secret new method of giving birth to a baby by employing an electronic fetus. "The Radio Brain," as by "Gus N. Habergock," takes the form of a story but is similarly uninteresting: a man with a metal plate in his head discovers that, by means of an electronic connection, he can hear radio broadcasts.

After the demise of *Science-Fiction Plus,* Gernsback continued to publish similar works of fiction in his Christmas booklets, now entitled Forecast,
but only one of these has ever been published. In the 1960s, Sam Moskowitz
set out to edit an anthology, *Masterpieces of Science Fiction,* that would include
stories by all of the famous figures profiled in his book *Explorers of the Infinite,*
and to represent Gernsback he chose a piece from the 1956 Forecast, "Extra
Sensory Perfection." The story takes the form of a letter written by a father
to his daughter, Maddy, who by means of her extra-sensory perception has
detected that her father is having health problems and contacted him for that
reason. Experiencing strange head pains and mental images, the man undergoes a series of tests employing advanced scientific equipment until the problem is finally diagnosed and solved: he has been experiencing mental pressures
because of an idea that was struggling to emerge from his brain; after the doctor administers an electric shock, the idea finally comes to the surface — and
it is, the man concludes, the idea for this very story! In a way, the story's mixture of scientific jargon and a trick ending is very typical of Gernsback, and
one might wonder why Moskowitz chose this particular story as Gernsback's
contribution. However, in taking on the voice of a father speaking to a beloved
daughter, Gernsback did manage to convey a certain amount of warmth and
personality that is largely absent from his other fiction; indeed, since Gernsback's oldest daughter was named Madelon, which could be naturally shortened to "Maddy," it seems highly probable that he had his beloved daughter
in mind as he wrote this story. Furthermore as a way to represent the man so
frequently termed "the Father of Science Fiction," Moskowitz might have
thought it appropriate to choose the only story he ever wrote in which Gernsback addressed the reader as a father.

Based upon all of the fiction discussed to date, one could readily dismiss
Gernsback — as he is often dismissed — as a writer obsessed with gadgetry,
only generating stories or mock-articles focused on present-day scientists
involved with modestly innovative inventions, future scientists involved with
more extravagantly imaginative inventions, and visitors to advanced civilizations listening as the inhabitants explain their amazing inventions. However,
there are two Gernsback stories yet to discuss which defy these standard expectations.

The first of these is "The Infinite Brain," the short-short story that Gernsback contributed to the June, 1942 issue of Charles D. Hornig's *Future Combined with Science Fiction.* It dramatically begins, "In its huge
vacuum-insulated globe, the Infinite Dimensional Brain had become restive"
(40), and it proceeds to offer further description of this "Ruler of his Universe," governing "myriads of worlds," who is "suspended high above the
northpole of the world 101^{20}" (40). The reason for his restiveness is that "a

Super-Sun from another Universe was heading for his own realm at terrific speed," and he recognized that it "was destined to cut a wide swath through his own Universe, destroying hundreds if not thousands of worlds in its path" (40). To counter this threat, he concentrates a beam of powerful energy "into a certain direction of the sky" to make his Universe "rotate at 12° upon its axis. 59,000 space-years hence, the foreign Sun, still pursuing its original course, would arrive where the Infinite Brain's Universe would have been, but thanks to his foresight, would then be in another, distant part of the Heavens. Safe" (41).

Even the generally supportive Moskowitz was compelled to describe this vignette as "a weak short-short story" ("The Return of Hugo Gernsback" Part I 161), and it is hard to argue with his judgment; one particularly wonders why this brain bothered to move its entire universe out of the way when it presumably would have required far less energy to simply repel the invading object. Still, "The Infinite Brain," the only Gernsback story published by an editor other than himself, does command some attention. In its cosmic vision of a far-future universe governed by a limitlessly powerful intelligence, it is completely unlike any other of Gernsback's fictions, which generally seemed tied to present-day people and possibilities even when they were set in the future or on alien worlds. Indeed, instead of representing the sort of science fiction Gernsback wrote and promoted, it seems an example of the "thought-variant story" championed by rival editor F. Orlon Tremaine, as it endeavors to convey breathtaking new possibilities transcending conventional notions of space and time. And the language of its opening passages is genuinely evocative, which serves to make its limp conclusion all the more disappointing.

The other distinctive Gernsback story is his final novel, *Ultimate World*, which was written in the late 1950s although not published until after his death. As reported in editor Sam Moskowitz's introduction to the novel, *Ultimate World* was originally unpublishable because "it was interposed with non-fiction essays" that Gernsback could never bring himself to entirely remove (17); when he died, Moskowitz removed all of the nonfiction material, reducing the original manuscript to half its original length, and finally found a willing publisher. The first few paragraphs suggest that we are in familiar Gernsback territory:

> They were sitting on their sumptuous *tempreg* [temperature regulated] foam-plastic couch opposite the fireplace. Above it the normally beautiful crystal mirror had, by the flick of a switch, become an illuminated chessboard with its thirty-two chessmen. The two players, each holding a miniature chessgame in his hands, watched the large board over the fireplace intently. As each player moved pawn or other piece on his hand-board, the corresponding move on the

large illuminated board followed electronically. Had there been company, everyone could have watched the progress of the game from all over the room.

But that memorable night they were alone — Duke Dubois, famed professor
of physics at Columbia University, and his wife, Donny, beautiful and sensuous
ex-haute couture model and daughter of Auguste Hawthorne, dean of the
School of Engineering at Columbia.

Professor Dubois, an inventor of note, was at home in practically any branch
of science, including sexology. A Nobel Prizewinner for his recent discovery, the
Cosmitronic Field Theory, he had won worldwide fame at the age of thirty-six.
The couple lived in a large two-story stone and marble villa in a secluded spot
on the Palisades overlooking the Hudson, in New Jersey. The house was
crammed with Dubois' own devices and inventions — from the tempreg couch
to the *electronichess* over the mantelpiece.

Dubois, who had patented a one-man *cosmiflyer* [a six-inch cosmic power
generator which is strapped to the back and operates like a rocket without a hot
exhaust], was accustomed to fly directly from his home over the Hudson to the
University, returning in the same manner evenings [19–20].

However, unlike the greatest scientist of the year 2660, this leading scientist
of the year 1996 is about to have his sense of complacency shattered, as unfolding events will leave all human inventions of this sort "relegated to the status
of children's toys" (80).

For within a few minutes, Dubois and his wife find themselves enveloped
in a mysterious force field that reduces gravity, and they feel mysteriously compelled to remove all of their clothing and to repeatedly have sex. When things
return to normal, it is revealed that unseen aliens have come to Earth in
strange vehicles consisting of spheres, and they have employed their advanced
technology to subject many couples to this sort of treatment. These people
have also, without their knowledge, been spirited away to the alien craft to
have eggs and sperm removed from their body. All of this logically suggests
that the aliens are intensely curious about human sexuality and have consequently embarked upon intensive research into the sexual practices of human
beings. Here, one might conclude, the editor of *Amazing Stories* and the editor of *Sexology* has finally felt free, for the first time, to combine his disparate
interests by writing a science fiction story that includes sex scenes and frank
discussions of sexual matters.

However, prurient interests are soon thrust into the background by the
unseen aliens' other activities. They begin to abduct large numbers of human
children, implant new organs into their brains, and return them as super-
intelligent and telepathic beings who uniformly express a visceral opposition
to all forms of warfare; the aliens also use the eggs and sperm they seized to
create new children with similarly advanced abilities who are eventually
dispatched to their human parents. The Xenos (as the humans come to call
them) then move the asteroid Eros into a near–Earth orbit and begin

hollowing it out and constructing buildings in its interior, apparently in order to use it as a spark ark to travel through space. Whatever further plans they might have had for humanity are left unrevealed when, at the end of the novel, they are visited by another alien race, seemingly their bitter opponents, and the two adversaries meet and completely destroy each other.

Whatever its other virtues and flaws, *Ultimate World* lays to rest another of Brian W. Aldiss's mischaracterizations of Gernsback, the charge that he was imprisoned in a mindset of "simple-minded Victorian utilitarianism" and championed science fiction that "neither thinks nor dreams" (*Trillion Year Spree* 202). In fact, the novel reflects the Gernsback who wrote "The Amazing Unknown" and "The Mighty Mite," a man capable of gazing up at the nighttime sky and regarding all human accomplishments, including scientific advances, as essentially trivial when one contemplates vast cosmic mysteries. Here, it is as if Gernsback deliberately took Ralph 124C 41+ and transplanted him into a new context that suddenly rendered his inventions and accomplishments completely insignificant and powerless, forcing him into the role of passive observer. In the face of *these* alien invaders, Duke Dubois cannot hop in a spaceship and rush off to heroically save the day; rather, all he can do is to observe the actions of these awesome and enigmatic beings, strive to interpret their behavior as best he can, and advise the people of Earth that it would be fruitless to attempt any countermeasures. Compared to the aliens, he argues, human are merely "silly, helpless ants, studied by the entomologist" (28). Needless to say, the situation Gernsback sets up does not allow for any possibility of melodramatic adventure, as his ineffectual hero can only watch and report on the mysterious activities of the aliens; the novel then becomes, as Stableford notes, a typically "quasi-journalistic" effort by Gernsback ("Creators of Science Fiction, 10" 50), but for different reasons this time.

As to why Gernsback might have chosen to write this sort of novel in the late 1950s, there is one tantalizing possibility. It will be recalled that Arthur C. Clarke was one of the few science fiction writers of the postwar period that Gernsback seemed aware of, since he referred to him in 1963 as "perhaps the most outstanding true science fiction personality" (179). And in 1953, Clarke had published a novel, *Childhood's End,* with a plot that in some ways seems similar to that of *Ultimate World*: in both novels, advanced aliens effortlessly conquer a future Earth and initiate a program to advance the evolution of humanity by altering children to possess new abilities. To be sure, there are also significant differences between the two novels: Gernsback's aliens remain unseen and mysterious, and their final destruction leaves many questions unanswered while Earth remains largely unchanged, except for a coming period of adjustment to a new breed of super-intelligent, telepathic humanity. Clarke's aliens reveal themselves, and readers learn that their plan is to transform humanity into a group mind so that the race can advance to the next level of evolution; and the novel ends with Earth abandoned, as the altered children employed their mental powers to collectively leave in order to find their destiny somewhere in the cosmos. Still, it remains possible, and even likely, that Gernsback read *Childhood's End* sometime during the 1950s and began thinking about writing his own story about superior aliens coming to Earth on a mission to scientifically improve the human race.

This possible connection inspires another thought about Arthur C. Clarke: while he is sometimes labeled an heir to Olaf Stapledon, it would provide a fuller and more accurate assessment of his career to describe him as a true successor to Hugo Gernsback. Both men energetically maintained active writing careers from their twenties until their eighties; Clarke shared Gernsback's fascinations with machinery, and they both produced stories that were focused on plausible scientific developments in the near future; like Gernsback, Clarke wrote several stories that read more like retrospective historical or journalistic accounts of future events than fictional narratives, and like Gernsback he sometimes displayed a sharp sense of humor in sometimes writing vignettes that amounted to little more than extended jokes; both men wrote considerable amounts of nonfiction along with their science fiction; while unquestionably a better writer than Gernsback, Clarke is also regularly criticized for a wooden prose style and unconvincing characterization; and both writers would occasionally abandon any concern for careful and practical extrapolation to indulge in mystical visions of extravagant future possibilities. And this last similarity is rarely noted because Gernsback revealed this side of his personality only in two stories — "The Infinite Brain" and *Ultimate World*—that are rarely if ever discussed.

None of this is intended to suggest that the two writers are comparable in terms of their skills, for the vastly superior Clarke consistently wrote capably, and sometimes brilliantly, while Gernsback struggled unsuccessfully to write adequately. "The Infinite Brain" and *Ultimate World* may represent distinctive additions to the Gernsback canon, but they are also, like all of his works, badly written and manifestly flawed. From the beginning of his career to its end, Gernsback may have brought sporadic enthusiasm to the task of writing, but he never revealed a talent that was sufficient to make him a science fiction author of genuine significance.

What makes Gernsback valuable is that, in both his nonfiction and his fiction, he suggests many stimulating possibilities for science fiction. In his most noteworthy work, *Ralph 124C 41+,* he provides a model for a combination of unlikely ingredients that, in the hands of others, could lead to successful work. In the less noteworthy works surveyed in this chapter, Gernsback at least identifies mistakes for other writers to avoid, and in *Ultimate World,* he joins a small group of writers, including Stapledon and Clarke, who have offered doses of cosmic pessimism to balance the spirit of undying optimism that Gernsback otherwise struggled to inculcate in the genre he named and created. In this way, as in many other ways, Gernsback perpetually retains the capacity to surprise his readers; and in this way, if in this way alone, he remains a writer who is indeed worth reading.

Notes

Chapter 2

1. Since I have extensively discussed Hugo Gernsback's theories — and those of John W. Campbell, Jr. — at length elsewhere, most extensively in *The Mechanics of Wonder*, the discussions of Gernsback and Campbell here will be relatively brief, to focus more attention on other figures who have elsewhere been dealt with either hastily or not at all.

2. I thank Richard Bleiler for providing me with information about this event and its possible significance.

3. Ashley's second statement actually is that "Merwin challenged..." but the context of the passages makes it clear that he is referring to Mines. No doubt because of the similarity of their names and occupations, Merwin and Mines are often confused: in "Beauty, Stupidity, Injustice, and Science Fiction," for example, Knight claims that Merwin published *The Lovers*, when it actually appeared after he had stopped editing *Startling Stories*.

4. As discussed in my *Cosmic Engineers: A Study of Hard Science Fiction*.

Chapter 3

1. This survey of science fiction symbols is necessarily not complete or comprehensive, and I remain interested in hearing about other symbols for science fiction, especially since the original publication of this chapter did yield two responses with valuable examples that are now included in this discussion.

2. The implicit meaning of the scene — that Verne's reputation and stories, presumably like those of other science fiction writers, would live forever — was later, ironically, repudiated by Gernsback in a 1933 editorial explaining why he no longer included reprints of older stories:

> I have, as yet, to see one old time science fiction novel which, in the light of today's advance in science fiction, is readable.
>
> Take, for instance, the majority of Jules Verne's books. Quite a number of them read so tamely today that the average reader would yawn. The incredible wonders of Jules Verne's day are commonplace today. The same is the case with a number of older science fiction books. Time has caught up with them, and progress has been such that the authors' predictions have mostly been fulfilled, leaving the present-day reader with a very ordinary story on his hands ["On Reprints" 99].

Regarding the enduring popularity of Verne's novels, Gernsback's picture proved more accurate than Gernsback's statement.

3. It would be interesting to learn if "Clarence Beck" of West Bend, Wisconsin, is actually the Charles Clarence Beck who later, under the name C. C. Beck, became the most prominent illustrator of the comic book hero Captain Marvel. In the biographical sketch in Rick Steranko's *History of Comic Books, Volume 2*, Beck is described as a Minneapolis native who lived in various cities in Minnesota and was once educated at the Chicago Academy; so it is at least possible that he was living in West Bend, Wisconsin, in 1928. Certainly, Beck's design is the only one Gernsback published that seems to be the work of a trained artist, and the style of drawing is not unlike Beck's later work.

4. Whether this actually represents the intent of the cover designer remains conjectural;

the editor of *Extrapolation* during that time, Donald M. Hassler, confessed in a letter that he himself was not sure exactly what the cover was supposed to mean.

5. Anthony Frewin's interpretation of the drawing: "Presided over by a cosmic muse, the magazine's stories encompass man's scientific knowledge and can be discussed, either with one's sweetheart, as on the left, or with one's contemporaries, as on the right" (*One Hundred Years of Science Fiction Illustration, 1840–1940* 101).

6. And, to briefly mention fantasy for comparative purposes, I should point out that fabulous or mythological creatures are the standard symbols for fantasy: for example, Ballantine/Del Rey Books's symbol for fantasy is a gryphon; the City Library of Ontario, California, identifies fantasy books with a mark showing the head of a unicorn; and the recent Baen Books symbol for fantasy books is the silhouette of a dragon. Also, one symbol employed by Gnome Press — a picture of a gnome sitting under a mushroom reading a book — should probably be taken more as a symbol of fantasy than as one of science fiction.

7. Consider, for example, the 1986 Atheneum cover of Brian W. Aldiss and David Wingrove's *Trillion Year Spree: The History of Science Fiction*— an Apollo astronaut standing on the moon with another astronaut reflected in his helmet — which seems to assert a close relationship between science fiction and space travel that would surely be anathema to the books' authors (though one might also read some statement about science fiction as a form of perception into that illustration).

8. I thank David Ketterer for pointing out this symbol in "Tesseracts," a 1995 letter to *Science-Fiction Studies*.

Chapter 4

1. Gernsback was evidently aware that most members of the science fiction community knew little about his early science magazines and the science fiction they contained, because in the later years, whenever he was called upon to discuss the history of science fiction, he always felt a need to pay special attention to his publications before 1926 — as in his 1953 pamphlet Evolution of Modern Science Fiction and in his 1961 "Guest Editorial" for *Amazing Stories*, to be discussed below.

2. Indeed, in heavily emphasizing the educational value of "The Man from the Atom," this introduction was far more enthusiastic than the entirely different introduction presented when the story was reprinted in the April, 1926 issue of *Amazing Stories:*

> In "Alice in the Looking Glass" the beautiful play of fancy which gave immortal fame to a logician and mathematician we read of the mysterious change in size of the heroine, the charming little Alice. It tells how she grew large and small according to what she ate. But here we have increase in size and pushed to its utmost limit. Here we have treated the growth of a man to cosmic dimensions. And we are told of his strange sensation and are led up to a sudden startling and impressive conclusion, and are taken through the picture of his emotions and despair [Introduction to "The Man from the Atom" 63].

Between 1923 and 1926, someone might have recognized that the story, in fact, had little to do with the Theory of Relativity and thus resolved to provide a more defensible blurb that foregrounded its imaginative and literary qualities.

As discussed in *The Mechanics of Wonder*, one can generally assume that the blurbs in *Amazing Stories* were written by either Gernsback or his Associate Editor T. O'Conor Sloane, and the same is undoubtedly true of the blurbs in *Science and Invention*. In this case, my own theory would be that the 1923 blurb was written by Gernsback, overselling the story's scientific aspect for the readers of his science magazine, and that Sloane objected to its contents and, in 1926, provided the second, more accurate blurb.

3. All page numbers for the first issue of *Superworld Comics* are based on my own count, since neither the comic itself nor any of its stories and features were paginated.

4. Ironically, one of those people would be Gernsback's successor as the editor of *Wonder Stories*—Mort Weisinger, first editor of the retitled *Thrilling Wonder Stories*, who later took control of the Superman franchise and brought many ideas and conventions from science fiction into his comic books.

5. In an extended discussion of science fiction fans in his editorial for the December, 1953 issue of *Science-Fiction Plus,* Gernsback talks about the fans' conventions and their letters to magazines, but does not mention

their fanzines, suggesting little awareness of these publications. It is harder to prove that his publications were never known to the science fiction community, but it is at least worth noting that the J. Lloyd Eaton Collection of Science Fiction and Fantasy, which now incorporates the extensive fanzine collections of three major fans — Terry Carr, Bruce Pelz, and Rick Sneary — contains no issues of Gernsback's Forecast.

6. Gernsback's colleague Sam Moskowitz — whose four-part series "The Return of Hugo Gernsback" provides a wealth of background information about the birth, production, and death of *Science-Fiction Plus* — also found the editorial striking, and offered somewhat parallel speculations about why it was so "atypically pessimistic": "Perhaps it was his advancing age. Gernsback would be 69 on August 16th [1953], and may have felt that despite his achievements he had fallen short of his goals, and had little time left to see his visions realized" ("The Return of Hugo Gernsback" Part IV 224).

7. As evidence that Gernsback's view of science fiction had never really changed, consider what Moskowitz reports were "the criteria on which we were supposed to judge each story. They were: Is it entertaining? Is the science sound? Is the writing good? Is it educational? Is it thought-provoking? Does it contain a new idea?" ("The Return of Hugo Gernsback" Part II 291). The order is irregular, but Gernsback had essentially established two questions involving the story's value as narrative ("Is it entertaining?" "Is the writing good?"), two questions involving the story's value as scientific education ("Is the science sound?" "Is it educational?"), and two questions involving the story's value as stimulating prophecy ("Is it thought-provoking?" "Does it contain a new idea?")

8. It is true that in his *Seekers of Tomorrow: Masters of Modern Science Fiction* (1966), Moskowitz had spoken with apparent enthusiasm about a number of writers who had become prominent in the 1940s, including Heinlein, Asimov, Theodore Sturgeon, and A. E. van Vogt, and it is also the case that Moskowitz did attempt to get some more recent authors to write for *Science-Fiction Plus*, such Philip José Farmer, who receives a great deal of enthusiastic praise in "The Return of Hugo Gernsback." However, Moskowitz's attachment to science fiction of the 1930s and declining enthusiasm for science fiction of the

1940s and 1950s might be discerned, for example, by examining the contents of two anthologies he assembled for Collier Books in 1963: *The Coming of the Robots* included five stories published in the 1930s, three stories published in the 1940s, and two stories published in the 1950s; *Exploring Other Worlds* including four stories published in the 1930s, two stories published in the 1940s, and two stories published in the 1950s. In both cases, then, 50% of the stories he chose came from the "Golden Age" of the 1930s.

9. In Part 1 of "The Return of Hugo Gernsback," Moskowitz reports Gernsback saying, in a talk on March 5, 1950, "that he now read very little science-fiction, and that the few tales he did seemed more like fairy stories than the type he had formerly presented" (162). Then, he summarized a recent story that appeared in *The Saturday Evening Post*, suggesting that he was not reading any science fiction magazines.

10. The argument I make in "Where No Market Has Gone Before: 'The Science-Fiction Industry' and the *Star Trek* Industry."

11. As further evidence that Gernsback's was not keeping up to date with his science fiction semantics, if such evidence is necessary, his 1952 speech included a discussion of a 1925 article he had written, "The Radio Teledactyl," envisioning mechanical hands that could be operated by distant doctors by remote control. He then notes that such devices are being used today in a different context — physicists using mechanical hands to manipulate radioactive materials from a safe distance — and he calls them "*telehands*" (67). Astonishingly, Gernsback seems unaware of the actual term for these devices, which had first appeared in a 1942 science fiction story and later entered the dictionary: "waldoes," from Robert A. Heinlein's 1942 story "Waldo."

12. Gernsback apparently was especially anxious to promote the use of "orbitemp," since Moskowitz notes that his editing of Albert de Pina and Henry Hasse's story "Ultimate Life" "chiefly involved changing the word 'year' to 'orbitemp' every time it appeared in the manuscript" ("The Return of Hugo Gersnback" Part IV 212).

13. After Gernsback's death, this editorial was republished under the new title "Science Fiction That Endures" in the December, 1967 issue of *Amazing Stories*; the text is identical except for the removal of the next-to-last paragraph, in which Gernsback made specific

reference to the occasion of the magazine's thirty-fifth anniversary.

14. As an aside, one might note that this article might offer some evidence of the special impact of Gernsback's original theories about science fiction; for Kazantsev seems utterly unaware that science fiction might be defended as a literature which provides scientific education and stimulating prophetic ideas. Instead, he can only see science fiction as a form of "fantasy," and he explains its purpose solely in conventional literary terms as either intentional commentaries on contemporary society — "It is characteristic of fantasy to reflect reality, emphasizing one or another of its aspects; invaluably for literature it is called to protest against the existing order, angrily to expose the gloomy side of contemporary society" (60) — or as unintentional but revelatory reflections of their authors' societies — "It is worth delving deeply into these jungles [of American science fiction] in order to understand better what is worrying Americans today" (56). Yet of course, any sort of literature might be defended in these fashions. And, lacking any unique way to defend or explain science fiction, the Soviet Union was yet another nation which did not develop its own strong tradition of science fiction until it was able, in the 1950s and 1960s, to begin emulating the globally influential American tradition which Gernsback had initiated and strengthened with his scientific arguments.

Chapter 5

1. As discussed in Sam Moskowitz's "How Science Fiction Got Its Name."

2. When this chapter was first published, Sam Moskowitz wrote a letter vigorously defending the accuracy of his story, noting among other things that the covers for *Modern Electrics* were in fact prepared quickly and at the last minute, so the appearance of Ralph on the cover did not necessarily suggest lengthy preparation ("On the Origins of *Ralph 124C 41+*"). Still, for the other reasons given, I continue to regard the story as improbable. This is also the opinion of Mike Ashley — surely the man who has researched this era most thoroughly — who argues that "it is unlikely that he wrote the first episode on the spur of the moment" for reasons similar to mine (*The Gernsback Days* 17).

3. Reflecting no doubt some novelty in

Martian pronunciation, as I note elsewhere, Gernsback spells the name with a final apostrophe; lacking a model in English for making such a name possessive, I have simply added an s: hence, Llysanorh', Llysanorh's.

4. In this chapter, future page references in the text to the 1911–1912 version will begin with the installment number (see Table), followed by colon and page number. Future page references in the text to the 1925, 1929, 1950, 1952, or 1958 texts will begin with 25, 29, 50, 52, or 58, followed by colon and page number. Later chapters will present quotations from *Ralph 124C 41+* exclusively from the 1950 edition and will simply provide page numbers from that edition.

5. There is another possible borrowing from Wicks that precedes the appearance of the review: Wicks's spacecraft is built out of "martalium," a metal "composed of aluminum and other rarer metals which, when combined together, produced a substance almost as light as aluminum, yet many times harder and tougher than case-hardened steel; whilst its surface shone like burnished silver and could never in any circumstances become tarnished or affected by rust" (27–28). The May, 1911 installment briefly mentions a similar substance, "steelonium (the new substitute for steel)" (2:85) and the August installment elaborates: "Steelonium, as you of course know, is unrustable and ten times as strong as steel" (5:294). Yet marvelous metals were common enough in the scientific fiction of the time, so that this may only be a coincidence.

6. Two other minor changes in later installments, that cannot be attributed to Wicks, reflect developments in Gernsback's writing style. In the first seven installments, Gernsback consistently referred to characters only by their last, numerical names: Ralph is "124C 41" and Alice is "Miss 212B 423." This must have sounded cold to Gernsback, for in the eighth and ninth installments, he alternated use of full names, last names only, and first names only: Fernand is variously "Fernand 60O 10," "60O 10," and "Fernand." In the last installments, only first names are used alone; and in the 1925 text, Gernsback substituted first names for numbers throughout the novel. Also, there are Gernsback's strange dates, introduced in the eighth installment: a letter to Alice is dated "August 35th, 2660" (8:497), Llysanorh's letter refers to "November thirty-first" (8:498), and the telegram from the Planet Governor to Ralph is dated

"Sept. 34th, 2660" (9:594). Since it is hard to imagine how or why future scientists would expand Earth's orbit — to lengthen the year — or speed up Earth's rotation — to shorten its days — there are two possible explanations: either the rational denizens of the future have adopted some calendar reform — perhaps ten months of 36 days each, with two months omitted and five or six holidays at the end of the year — or, because of the different lengths of "years" on the inhabited Venus, Earth, and Mars, they have adopted a uniform "year" that does not correspond to Earth's year. But since the text is silent on this issue, one must regard these dates primarily as a *literary* device, a novel way to convey the strangeness of Ralph's future world.

7. The other is the letter to Alice from her friend Vilonette 88B 90, beginning the eighth installment, that was eliminated in the 1925 because its background information about Fernand and Llysanorh' now had already appeared earlier in the text.

8. "Fips" was the pseudonym Gernsback regularly used for his humorous pieces. The surname in the second passage presumably should be read, "One to be for nothing" or "for naught."

9. Harlan Ellison's parody of *Ralph* came in his 1967 speech "A Time for Daring," when he needed a quick way to characterize — and criticize — the preferences of certain science fiction fans:

> Now Al Lewis believes that stories of science fiction [should be like this:] the man of the future is standing on this slidewalk going through future time and he looks around and says, "look at this fantastic world that we live in, isn't it incredible, I say to you, Alice of the future 20432209, isn't this a grand world in which the buildings rise up a full screaming two hundred feet into the air, isn't this a marvelous slidewalk that's going at 25 miles an hour, and we have one over there that goes to 35 miles an hour, and another one right next to it at 45 miles an hour, to which we can leap, if we want to" ["A Time for Daring" 106–107].

Sladek's parody, "Ralph 4F," appeared in *The Steam-Driven Boy, and Other Strangers* (1973).

10. Still, Gernsback was willing to have a little bit of fun with his science, imagining the telephot as a smell-transmitting device and replacing his *Permagatol* with "Insect Powder." One should also note that in the concluding remarks following these parodies, Gernsback presents himself as, first, an author who is not planning ahead, and second, an author who wishes to cynically exploit his story as a circulation-building device. One is naturally tempted to view these characterizations as autobiographical.

11. As evidence for this theory, there is a passage in an early *Amazing Stories* editorial where Gernsback noted the "unforeseen result ... that a great many women are already reading the magazine" ("Editorially Speaking" 483). It is also possible that Gernsback downplayed the romantic angle because he was increasingly aware that science fiction was attracting *young* male readers (as discussed below), presumably even less likely than adult males to appreciate passionate prose.

12. One unanswered question: did Gernsback make these changes entirely on his own, or were editors of the Stratford Company involved in the process? Given Gernsback's lifelong interest in writing fiction, and the many flaws remaining the 1925 version, it seems reasonable to assume that Gernsback did all the work on his own; but he may have received some outside prodding or advice.

13. The exceptions are a few identical corrections of minor errors, like changing "aeroflier" to "aeroflyer" at the beginning of Chapter 8, that could easily have been made by the preparer of the 1950 edition without reference to the 1929 version.

14. After writing this sentence, I found this statement in Gernsback's "Preface to the 1950 Edition": "In the meanwhile the book became a sort of museum piece" (50:7).

15. Oddly enough, the 1950 edition omitted all of Paul's illustrations, which would have served to emphasize the novel's antiquity, both because of Paul's old-fashioned technique and because most modern novels featured no illustrations; but a reproduction of the equally old-fashioned cover of the April, 1911 issue of *Modern Electrics*, showing Ralph at the Telephot, was included as part of Gernsback's "Preface to the Second Edition."

16. Also, the statement that he was rereading *Ralph* "after a lapse of 25 years" provides additional support for the theory that he was not involved in preparing the 1929 edition.

17. It is all but impossible, though, to make this seem reasonable. Assuming twenty years to a generation, Ralph's number 41 shows that

he can trace his ancestors back to 1840 or so, reasonably enough for an American; the evil Fernand's low number 10 might indicate that he is a social upstart of sorts; and Llysanorh's large number 1618 suggests that in the presumably older Martian civilization people can trace their ancestors back for thirty thousand years. But it is hard to see how Europeans could claim to trace their ancestors back 8000 years, as the numbers 422 and 423 imply; and other final numbers, like the Martian Rrananolh's 42 or Fernand's friend Paul's 1261, seem equally inexplicable. Like Gernsback's odd dates, these numerical names must be viewed primarily as literary devices, not scientific predictions.

18. Of course, it is also possible that Ackerman never mentioned *Ralph* in his conversations with Tors and was merely trying to curry favor with a man who, at the time, was providing a potential market for Ackerman's clients and for Ackerman's own pieces on science fiction films. Indeed, one finds it hard to believe that even a producer like Tors, noted for undramatic, "documentary"-style science fiction films that included large dollops of expository dialogue, would have been attracted to a stodgy property like Gernsback's novel.

19. Farmer may have been particularly inclined to remember Gernsback because, as previously noted, he was one of the few newer authors to appear regularly in his last science fiction magazine, *Science-Fiction Plus*.

Chapter 6

1. See Chapter 4 of *The Mechanics of Wonder*.

2. Rahill is no doubt inadvertently combining the names of two films, *The Thing (from Another World)* (1951) and *It Came from Outer Space* (1953).

3. This was high praise indeed, by the way, since Gernsback had called Verne his "favorite author" (Introduction to "Dr. Ox's Experiment" 421). The article, entitled either "The American Jules Verne" or "An American Jules Verne," was unsigned but probably written by Gernsback himself, as noted by Mike Ashley in *The Gernsback Days* (59).

4. I will use the terms "villain" and "hero" throughout this discussion strictly for convenience, for properly speaking, the structure of melodrama requires three characters — an heroic figure, a villainous figure, and a figure

whom the heroic figure must rescue from the villainous figure — and only tradition dictates that the heroic and villainous figures be male and the rescued figure be female. To note two variants, the invention stories of Senarens and other dime novels for young male readers often substitute a male friend for the heroine, and the film *Supergirl* involves a heroine's effort to rescue a handsome but helpless male from a villainess. If I pay little attention to the rescued figure — usually, the heroine — in this discussion, it is because she seems unaffected by the transformations of melodrama in science fiction; thus, throughout the complications involving the heroes and villains of the *Star Wars* films (discussed below), Princess Leia remains the same type of spunky heroine found in numerous nineteenth-century melodramas.

5. Of course, Grimsted also cites a play which describes a villain's "dauntless passion" (215) and I do not wish to imply in this model that villains are completely without emotions while heroes are completely without reasoning ability. The distinction is more in the realm of *how one publicly justifies one's actions*: for example, the villain may provide logical reasons why an evil act should be done, but the hero will offer a visceral and emotional rejection of evil.

6. This exact attitude appears in an exchange from T. P. Taylor's *The Village Outcast* (1846), cited by Booth:

> MUZZLE: What's the law to do with age? That's Nature's business. What's the law to do with infirmities? ... the law says this here wery [sic] building is to come down for improvements, consequently removal's the word.
>
> ALICE: And tomorrow I'm to be driven from the roof which has so long sheltered me — helpless and almost sinking into the grave — to die, perhaps in the fields.
>
> MUZZLE: That is the law, of which I am the executive [63].

7. One might protest that Ralph simply undergoes a character transformation and is related to other melodramatic characters who initially seem cold and uncaring but are converted to heroism by the love of a beautiful woman; but no such coherent pattern of change can be imposed on Gernsback's narrative. After every passionate outburst Ralph reverts to his cold, impersonal self; after taking direct action to rescue Alice from Fernand,

he returns, as described below, to indirect action in rescuing her a second time; and after he returns from his forbidden mission to space, all is forgiven and he is restored to his elite position.

8. Since Heilman discusses numerous instances of melodrama moving into the realm of tragedy, one might ask why this tendency is so noteworthy in science fiction. The answer is that in other genres, writers *have the option* of complicating and deepening the melodrama by introducing an element of tragedy, sometimes as a way to appeal to a more sophisticated audience; however, due to the unique critical tradition of science fiction, writers *are driven* into such complications, even while continuing to appeal to an unsophisticated audience.

9. Interestingly enough, Mark Lenard, the dignified actor who portrayed the first Romulan commander, was later recast as Spock's father, a high-ranking Vulcan official, appearing as such in episodes of *Star Trek* and *Star Trek: The Next Generation* as well as three *Star Trek* films. This further suggests the relatedness of the Vulcans and Romulans.

10. Incongruously, the sixth Star Trek film, *Star Trek VI: The Undiscovered Country* (1992), abruptly projects upon Kirk a lifelong hatred for Klingons which he had never before manifested — a feeling which, in any event, Kirk manages to overcome in the course of the film as he finally works to achieve the peace with the Klingons that had already been depicted in the series *Star Trek: The Next Generation*.

11. As described by Booth, "the comic man ... is a friend or manservant of the hero, and sometimes carries on the battle against villainy (though by comic means) in the absence of incapacity of his superior" (33). In the first two *Star Wars* films, Solo's constant wisecracks and blunders mark him as a comic hero, despite his occasional earnestness; but when transformed into the main hero in *Return of the Jedi*, he significantly begins to act in a more serious manner.

12. Interestingly, when Lucas later revisited the first three *Star Wars* films to produce "special editions," he was evidently troubled by the quiet, conflicted conclusion to *Return of the Jedi* and endeavored to make it all seem more cheerful, including awkwardly interpolated scenes of wild celebrations on an alien planet.

13. In his introduction to *Six Science Fiction Plays*, Roger Elwood maintains that the sheer scope of science fiction makes it incompatible with the stage: "The two forms do not meld easily. It is difficult to translate the imaginative leaps characteristic of science fiction writing into the hard reality of dialogue between articulate characters. Writing a science fiction play is a bit like trying to picture infinity in a cigar box" (vii). But it is difficult to argue that science fiction is so uniquely and incredibly "imaginative" that dramatization becomes impossible; certainly, any critic can cite scores of examples of plays that effectively present bold and vast ideas. I suggest instead that the problem is poor choice of genre: without the energizing framework of melodrama, science fiction tends either to become a stagnant airing of an author's ideas about man and society — as in Ganthony's, Capek's, and Mulligan and Antrobus's plays — or to dissolve into inconsequential pleasantries, as in Ray Bradbury's plays. And if further proof is requested for the notion that the genre of science fiction theatre is indeed "anemic," I note that in assembling his anthology, Elwood found only three actual *plays* and had to complete his collection with three *scripts* written for television or film.

14. Since Heilman sees melodrama and tragedy as complementary, all-encompassing dramatic forms, an interesting question emerges about science fiction: if the genre is not melodramatic, is it then tragic? A possible answer would go as follows: science fiction begins by accepting the melodramatic convention of simplified characters but rejects the convention of simplified events; reality is too complex, particularly in the light of scientific knowledge and progress. Since simple characters cannot be expected to cope with complex events, it becomes necessary for writers to create complex, divided characters — counterheroes and countervillains — although they tend to avoid focusing on them. Thus, for all his potential fascination, Zharkov is largely ignored in the Flash Gordon serials; and as Cohen observes, Spock is most tragic in "the early *Star Trek* episodes.... Later he is able to relax and become more comfortable with his dual nature" (24) — which is another way of saying that later episodes move away from confronting his dilemma. The cycle is repeated in the first six *Star Trek* films: the first two films reexamine Spock's tragic plight but the other four films essentially forget about it. While shying away from tragic characters, sci-

ence fiction does achieve a tragic sense in contemplating the situation of the entire human race: typically, writers conclude that the problems of humanity are fundamentally unsolvable but accept the possibility that a scientifically transformed human race, or some successor to humanity, might achieve satisfying solutions to human problems and a utopian existence. While this position might be seen as an evasion of tragedy — in asserting that only more advanced beings, not people themselves, might reach this heightened state — it can also be seen as a true expression of the ultimate meaning of tragedy, that humanity might gain from its experience insights to be fruitfully passed on to its successors. Shorn of dramatic terminology, this argument is developed in Chapter 8.

Chapter 7

1. Gernsback includes a letter from Llysanorh' in which he explains his plight and even discusses plans to commit suicide — clearly designed to contrast him favorably with the other villain, Fernand, whose motives are less noble (141–142); and even when Alice is kidnapped by Llysanorh,' she thinks that "He looked very lonely and remote, and somehow, to her, very pathetic" (190) and "She could not deny the fact of his genuine, and fervent love for her" (193).

2. See *The Mechanics of Wonder* 92–93.

3. For instance, the "Associate Science Editors" listed on the title page of every issue of *Wonder Stories* who "pass upon the scientific principles of all stories" included college professors in the fields of botany, entomology, medicine, psychology, and zoology.

4. It was first suggested that science fiction stories may be a necessary element in a scientist's development in a response to a reader's letter written by either Gernsback or his associate T. O'Conor Sloane: "It is not too much to say that a person who never reads fiction and who may be most morbidly self-conscious in that regard, is not on the road to become a good scientist" ("Discussions," *Amazing Stories* [June, 1927] 308). Gernsback also alludes to the goal of encouraging young people to become scientists when he says that science fiction "widen[s] the young man's horizon, as nothing else can" and "keeps [children] abreast of the times" ("Science Wonder Stories" 5); and after noting how many

young readers obtain "food for thought and a great stimulus" from *Amazing Stories*, he adds, "if we can make the youngsters think, we feel that we are accomplishing our mission, and that the future of the magazine, and, to a degree, the future of progress through the younger generation, is in excellent hands" ("Amazing Youth" 625).

5. As I hope is already clear, I am not attempting to demonstrate that Gernsback or *Ralph* constituted a major influence on Le Guin's novel; however, as I have argued elsewhere, Gernsback's theories and priorities have permeated modern science fiction to the extent that writers may reflect his ideas without even being aware of him; and in this way, Gernsback's theories have functioned as the major force binding the genre together. Thus, that fact that certain elements of Gernsback, however faint, are present in *The Dispossessed* indeed shows their continuing importance in maintaining science fiction as a distinct genre.

6. Of course, these are in some ways quite different works, and at least one of them —*A Specter Is Haunting Texas*— significantly departs from the pattern in that its ideal society in space is established before the novel opens, and the melodramatic action involves one resident's visit to Earth and his adventures there. In addition, the forms of humanity's successors — from transformed humans to intelligent animals and computer constructs — vary tremendously. Nevertheless, there are enough similarities in these works, and a sufficient number of similar works, to justly regard them as a subgenre.

7. This aspect of Gernsback's novel is discussed more fully in the next chapter

8. In Chapter 5 of my *Islands in the Sky*, I discuss this typical strategy of Clarke — to first exploit, then ironically distance himself from, episodes of melodramatic adventure — particularly as it is seen in his *Islands in the Sky*.

9. In noting that this apparently ideal society has little interest in or aptitude for scientific progress, Clarke seems to reinforce the point I made earlier — that a utopia is no place for a working scientist. However, Clarke does add that the presence of the Overlords, and their manifestly superior technology, apparently was also a factor in this tendency towards stagnation (75).

10. One example would be the insurrection that briefly disturbs the tranquility of the

utopian society in H. G. Wells's *Men Like Gods* (1923).

11. Of course, it is not only science fiction that has found the patterns of melodrama the most appropriate context for a discussion of modern science. I think of works like Berton Roueché's *Eleven Blue Men, and Other Narratives of Medical Detection* (1953) and the film *The Race for the Double Helix* (1993), which unabashedly present scientific research as a detective story or competitive sport; and I fondly recall a Bell television special called "The Strange Case of the Cosmic Rays" (1957), in which scientists offered the story of the discovery of cosmic rays as an entry in a mystery story contest.

Chapter 8

1. Unless otherwise noted, all Gibson page references are to *Neuromancer*, and all subsequent Gernsback page references are to *Ralph 124C 41+*.

2. One can argue that the difference between Ralph the creator and Case the manipulator is not as great as it might seem; for it is a carryover from medieval images of alchemists and wizards to envision the scientist as a sort of magician who goes into his laboratory and emerges with a fantastic new device, since an actual scientist consults and carefully builds upon the work of his myriad predecessors to produce assemblages and refinements of existing devices. Without a doubt, this is a good description of Ralph's methodology: consider his explanation of how he "invented" an anti-gravity device:

It took hundreds of years, however, before the correct solution was found. It was known that certain high frequency currents would set up an interference with the gravitational waves, for it had been found in the first part of our century that gravitation was indeed a wave form, the same as light waves, or radio waves. When this interference between the two waves, namely, the gravitational waves and the electrical waves was discovered, it was found that a metallic screen charged by electric high frequency waves would indeed nullify gravitation to a certain extent....

Thus things stood until about two years ago, when I began to occupy myself with the problem. I reasoned that while we had

achieved much, still much more remained to be done. Our anti-gravitational screen still let through some of the gravitational waves, or fifty percent of the energy, which we could not seem to counteract. I felt that it was not so much the effect of the current as the material of the screen which seemed to be at fault. Experimental work along this line convinced me that I was on the right track and that if ever gravitation was to be annulled in its entirety a screen of a special material would have to be evolved in order to obtain the desired results.

I finally found that only the densest material known, namely thoro-iridium, would completely stop the gravitational waves, providing that the metal screen was uninterruptedly bombarded with alpha rays which are continually emitted by radium [135–136].

What did Ralph do? He looked at the current state of progress in counteracting gravity, analyzed the one remaining problem, and located the existing material that would solve that problem. In short, he functioned not as a sorcerer but as a trouble-shooter — much as Case troubleshoots his way through Cyberspace. In this way, then, the division between scientist and technician is not that large.

3. The sense of human science achieving something beyond the human offers, by the way, one explanation for a puzzle in Gernsback's novel; while the meaning of "124C 41" is obvious enough, Ralph's full last name includes that "+" which does not seem to fit into the pun. Accepting that science fiction sees humanity's role as creating successors to humanity, one could then read Ralph's name as "one to foresee for one-plus"—*one* meaning man, and *one-plus* meaning a superior type of man (as in the title of Frederik Pohl's 1976 novel about one such being, *Man Plus*).

4. Case's efforts to achieve inwardness are described in another context in my book *Islands in the Sky*.

Chapter 9

1. A note on this novel's title: when Gernsback's second novel was republished in several issues of *Amazing Stories* in 1928 — the only text of the novel that today is readily accessible to scholars — it was consistently called simply *Baron Münchhausen's Scientific Adven-*

tures, and hence one finds that that title is sometimes employed. However, in all installments of its original publication in *The Electrical Experimenter*, it is called *Baron Münchhausen's New Scientific Adventures*, which would establish that, I believe, as the preferred title. As to why the "New" was dropped for its republication, perhaps Gernsback or his associate editor T. O'Conor Sloane thought that it might seem incongruous in 1928 to describe as "New" a story which began with an account of the Baron's adventures during the long-concluded World War I.

2. The only direct evidence of readers' reactions to *Baron Münchhausen's New Scientific Adventures* takes the form of two letters published in "Editor's Mail Bag," an occasionally published page of readers' letter. One of the magazine's rare female readers was unequivocally enthusiastic: "I have greatly enjoyed Baron Münchhausen's Adventures and have read them with as much interest as one of the weaker sex is supposed to have in the latest love story" ("Editor's Mail Bag," December, 1916 568). And a male reader seemed to move from initial displeasure to cautious approval: "I could not see, for the life of me, why it was that the editor continued the story of the 'Baron Münchhausen's Scientific Adventures,' but after reading a few installments I began to look at improbabilities with the far distant view of probability" ("Editor's Mail Bag," September, 1916 331). Perhaps this reader was won over by the novel's increasingly serious and scientific tone, as will be discussed below.

3. Following the pattern previously employed for *Ralph 124C 41+*, page references to the 1915–1917 edition of *Baron Münchhausen's New Scientific Adventures* will provide the chapter number, colon, and page number; references to the slightly different 1928 text will begin with "28" followed by a colon and page number.

4. As further evidence of Gernsback's "literary understanding," one might note that there is also a passage in the first installment which makes fun of common storytelling practices and conventions:

This story starts on a bitter cold December night. I could go to some length by writing two or three columns at two cents a word, stating how the wind sang weirdly through my aerial wires on the roof; how the flames of my log fire cast fantastic shadows about the room; how my cat was softly purring on a chair near by dreaming of some long departed appetizing canary; how the windows rattled uncannily in the storm; how the trees moaned plaintively outside, and so forth. Thus I could set the scene and prepare you for the story — getting you under tension, as the editor calls it technically.

As a plain matter of fact, however, the aerial wires were full of sleet and therefore could not "sing," furthermore I was glad that they didn't come down, which would have made some music, although not very pleasant music. Then the log fire, too, could not very well have cast fantastic shadows either, nor any other shadows for that matter, because the log fire happened to be a radiator. Instead of casting fantastic shadows, however, it cast a lot of rank noise about and every now and then made me jump clean out of my chair. Then, also, the cat could not have purred very readily on the chair because it wasn't a cat at all, but a dog to begin with, and he could not have purred even if he had taken lessons at $5 an hour. There were, however, good reason [*sic*] for this, too. Firstly, it was not a he; it was a she. Secondly, she had been dead for two years and only because she was stuffed so nicely did I keep her. Thirdly, she could positively not sat on a chair near by, simply because there was only one chair in the place and I was on it. Fourthly, dogs, especially dead dogs, are not known to dream about appetizing canary birds. Then, too, the windows could not have rattled in the storm where I was, for my wireless station is in the cellar and that cellar has no windows whatsoever. As for the trees moaning or not moaning I explained above that my people were engaged in cactus farming. There are no trees on the farm, and cactus does positively not moan in a storm. It squeaks [1: 3].

5. For quotations from the third installment, I am obliged to consult its republication in the March, 1928 issue of *Amazing Stories* (presumably a corrupted text, as discussed below), because the bound volumes of *The Electrical Experimenter* which I employed in my research unaccountably did not include the July, 1915 issue.

6. The same policy was followed in the sixth installment, as announced by an identical footnote, but the policy was abandoned for all later chapters.

7. As discussed in my "Reading Mars: Changing Images of Mars in Twentieth-Century Science Fiction."

8. There is another passage in the eighth chapter which was seemingly designed to subtly undermine Alier's credibility: after the cited introductory remarks about enjoying a Turkish water pipe, the chapter concludes with Alier saying, "A snap, a whirring click and the last ether wave from the moon had reached the earth for that night. I lighted my faithful Nargileh once more and gave myself up to a new series of pipe dreams" (8:526). The language thus invites readers to consider Münchhausen's preceding description of Mars as Alier's old series of pipe dreams.

9. Since this statement about the lifelessness of other planets had the obvious consequence of severely limiting the possibility of further Münchhausen adventures, one might wonder why Gernsback included it. The probable answer is that, for Gernsback, science fiction always had to adhere to and convey the latest and best scientific information. At the time, there were still solid scientific reasons for suspecting that Mars might be the home to intelligent life; but data from the other planets indicated that they were probably incapable of supporting life, and Gernsback was therefore compelled to report that

to his readers. It is interesting to note that, although little was made of the point, Gernsback's *Ralph 124C 41+* also contains no references to aliens other than Martians, implicitly suggesting that the other planets are also uninhabited and uninhabitable in its future world.

10. Because the March, 1918 issue of *The Electrical Experimenter* was also unavailable to me, I am again relying upon the presumably corrupted text of the republished version of the story in the July, 1928 issue of *Amazing Stories*.

11. One irony is this analysis is that, in Arthur C. Clarke's retrospective look at his youthful experiences with science fiction, *Astounding Days: A Science Fictional Autobiography,* Clarke emphasizes the influential role not of Hugo Gernsback's magazines, but of the rival magazine *Astounding Stories*, edited by Harry Bates, F. Orlon Tremaine, and John W. Campbell, Jr. Still, Clarke did pay tribute to Gernsback in that book by means of one footnote describing him as "the father of magazine sf, despite some claims to the contrary" (5), and he partially dedicated his non-fiction book *Profiles of the Future* to Gernsback: "and especially to the memory of Hugo Gernsback — who thought of everything" ([vii]).

Bibliography

Aldiss, Brian W., Brian Stableford, and Edward James. "On 'On the True History of Science Fiction.'" *Foundation: The Review of Science Fiction*, No. 47 (Winter 1989-1990), 28–33.

____, with David Wingrove. *Trillion Year Spree: The History of Science Fiction*. New York: Atheneum, 1986. A previous version, as by Aldiss alone, was *Billion Year Spree: The True History of Science Fiction*. New York: Schocken, 1973.

"An American Jules Verne." [no author given] *Amazing Stories*, 3 (June, 1928), 270–272. Presumably a republication of "The American Jules Verne," *Science and Invention*, 8 (October, 1920).

Ashley, Mike. "Introduction: From Bomb to Boom." In *The History of the Science Fiction Magazines, Volume III: 1946–1955*, edited by Mike Ashley. 1976. Chicago: Contemporary, 1977, 13–109.

____. Letter. *Interzone*, No. 128 (February, 1998), 3, 30.

____. *The Time Machines: The Story of the Science-Fiction Pulp Magazines from the Beginning to 1950*. Liverpool: Liverpool University Press, 2000.

____, and Robert A. W. Lowndes. *The Gernsback Days: A Study of the Evolution of Modern Science Fiction from 1911 to 1936*. Holicong, PA: Wildside, 2004.

"The Back Cover." *Science-Fiction Plus*, 1 (April, 1953), 47 [unsigned, written either by Hugo Gernsback or Sam Moskowitz].

"The Back Cover." *Science-Fiction Plus*, 1 (October, 1953), 19 [unsigned, written either by Hugo Gernsback or Sam Moskowitz].

Bates, Harry. "Editorial Number One: To Begin." In *A Requiem for Astounding*, by Alva Rogers. Chicago: Advent, 1964. viii–xvi.

Beck, Clyde F. *Hammer and Tongs*. Lakeport, CA: Futile, 1937.

Benford, Gregory. "Plane in Fancy: Alien Lands for Human Drama." Review of *The Science in Science Fiction* by Peter Nicholls. *Los Angeles Times*, February 20, 1983, Book Review, 2, 7.

Biographical Note about Harry Bates accompanying "Death of a Sensitive." *Science-Fiction Plus*, 1 (May, 1953), 4 [unsigned, almost certainly by Sam Moskowitz].

Biographical Note about John Scott Campbell accompanying "Utopia" (letters upside down in magazine). *Science-Fiction Plus*, 1 (March, 1953), 12 [unsigned, almost certainly by Sam Moskowitz].

Biographical Note about Roger Dee accompanying "Worlds Within Worlds." *Science-Fiction Plus*, 1 (October, 1953), 36 [unsigned, almost certainly by Sam Moskowitz].

Biographical Note about Philip José Farmer accompanying "The Biological Revolt." *Science-Fiction Plus*, 1 (March, 1953), 12 [unsigned, almost certainly by Sam Moskowitz].

Biographical Note about Raymond Z. Gallun accompanying "Captive Asteroid." *Science-Fiction Plus*, 1 (April, 1953), 5 [unsigned, almost certainly by Sam Moskowitz].

Biographical Note about Hugo Gernsback accompanying "Technocracy vs. Science." *Technocracy Review*, 1 (March, 1933), 83 [unsigned, probably written by editor David Lasser].

Biographical Note about David Lasser accompanying "Technocracy — Hero or Villain?" *Technocracy Review,* 1 (February, 1933), 5 [unsigned, probably written by editor David Lasser].

Biographical Note about F. L. Wallace accompanying "Worlds in Balance." *Science-Fiction Plus,* 1 (May, 1953), 40 [unsigned, almost certainly by Sam Moskowitz].

Biographical Note about Jack Williamson accompanying "Operation: Gravity." *Science-Fiction Plus,* 1 (October, 1953), 24 [unsigned, almost certainly by Sam Moskowitz].

Bleiler, Everett F., with Richard Bleiler. *Science-Fiction: The Gernsback Years.* Kent, OH: Kent State University Press, 1998.

Bleiler, Everett F., and T. E. Dikty, editors. "Preface." *The Best Science Fiction Stories: 1949.* New York: Frederick Fell, 1949, 19–27.

_____, and _____, editors. "Preface." *The Best Science Fiction Stories: 1950.* New York: Frederick Fell, 1950, 17–27.

Blish, James [as William Atheling, Jr.]. *The Issue at Hand* Chicago: Advent, 1964.

_____. [as William Atheling, Jr.]. *More Issues at Hand.* Chicago: Advent, 1970.

"Book Review" (of *To Mars via the Moon* by Mark Wicks). *Modern Electrics,* 4 (August, 1911), 371. [Unsigned, but almost certainly by Hugo Gernsback.]

Booth, Michael R. *English Melodrama.* London: Herbert Jenkins, 1965.

Brooks, Peter. *The Melodramatic Imagination: Balzac, Henry James, Melodrama, and the Mode of Excess.* New Haven: Yale University Press, 1976.

Budrys, Algis. *Benchmarks: Galaxy Bookshelf.* Carbondale: Southern Illinois University Press, 1985.

"Buzz Allen The Invisible Avenger!" *Superworld Comics,* No. 1 (April, 1940), 12–19. Comic book story. Author, Charles D. Hornig (as "Derwin Lesser"); artist Raymond Burley.

Campbell, John W., Jr. "Concerning Science Fiction." In *The Best of Science Fiction,* edited by Groff Conklin. New York: Crown, 1946, v–xi.

_____. "Future Tense." *Astounding Science-Fiction,* 23 (June, 1939), 6.

_____. "Introduction." In *Analog 1,* edited by John W. Campbell, Jr. Garden City, NY: Doubleday, 1963, xv–xviii.

_____. "Introduction." In *Analog 6,* edited by John W. Campbell, Jr. 1968. New York: Pocket, 1969, xi–xvi.

_____. "Introduction." In *Cloak of Aesir,* by John W. Campbell, Jr. 1952. New York: Lancer, 1972, 11–14.

_____. "Introduction." In *The Man Who Sold the Moon,* by Robert A. Heinlein. Chicago: Shasta, 1950, 11–15.

_____. "Introduction." In *Prologue to Analog,* edited by John W. Campbell, Jr. Garden City, NY: Doubleday, 1962, 9–16.

_____. "Introduction." In *Venus Equilateral,* by George O. Smith. New York: Prime, 1947, 8–12.

_____. "Introduction." In *Who Goes There?* by John W. Campbell, Jr. Chicago: Shasta, 1948, 3–6.

_____. "The Old Navy Game." *Astounding Science-Fiction,* 25 (June, 1940), 6.

_____. "The Perfect Machine." *Astounding Science-Fiction,* 25 (May, 1940), p. 5.

_____. "The Science of Science Fiction Writing." In *Of Worlds Beyond: The Science of Science Fiction Writing,* edited by Lloyd Arthur Eshbach. 1947. Chicago: Advent, 1964, 91–101.

"Chain Reaction." *Science-Fiction Plus,* 1 (May, 1953), 25 [unsigned, almost certainly written by Sam Moskowitz, possibly with some input by Hugo Gernsback].

Clarke, Arthur C. *Astounding Days: A Science Fictional Autobiography.* 1989. New York: Bantam, 1990.

_____. *Childhood's End.* 1953. New York: Ballantine, 1967.

_____. *Profiles of the Future: An Inquiry into the Limits of the Possible.* 1962. New York: Warner, 1985.

Clement, Hal. "Whirligig World." *Astounding Science-Fiction,* 51 (June, 1953), 102–114.

Clute, John. "Been Bondage." [Book reviews.] *Interzone,* No. 128 (December, 1997), 52–55.

Cohen, Daniel. *Strange and Amazing Facts about Star Trek.* New York: Pocket, 1986.

Conklin, Groff, editor. "Introduction." *The Best of Science Fiction.* New York: Crown, 1946, xv–xxviii.

Davenport, Basil. *Inquiry into Science Fiction.* New York: Longman, Green, 1955.

Davin, Eric Leif. *Pioneers of Wonder: Conversations with the Founders of Science Fiction.* Foreword by Jack Williamson. Amherst, NY: Prometheus, 1999.

de Camp, L. Sprague, and Catherine Crook

de Camp. *Science Fiction Handbook — Revised: A Guide to Writing Imaginative Literature.* New York: McGraw-Hill, 1975. A previous version, as by L. Sprague de Camp alone, was *Science Fiction Handbook: The Writing of Imaginative Fiction.* New York: Hermitage House, 1953.

Denning, Michael. *Mechanic Accents: Dime Novels and Working-Class Culture in America.* New York: Verso, 1987.

"Detective Crane: The Case of Super-Speed." *Superworld Comics,* No. 1 (April, 1940), 38–43, 45. Comic book story. Attributed solely to "Homer Porter," evidently a pseudonym for an author and/or artist; author probably Charles D. Hornig and/or Hugo Gernsback.

"Discussions." [Response to reader's letter.] *Amazing Stories,* 2 (June, 1927), 308. [Unsigned, either T. O'Conor Sloane or Hugo Gernsback.]

Donawerth, Jane. "Lillith Lorraine: Feminist Socialist Writer in the Pulps." *Science Fiction Studies,* 17 (July, 1990), 252–258.

Edwards, Malcolm J. "Schuyler Miller." In *The Encyclopedia of Science Fiction,* edited by John Clute and Peter Nicholls. New York: St. Martin's, 1993, 808–809.

Ellison, Harlan. "Cheap Thrills on the Road to Hell." In *Sleepless Nights in the Procrustean Bed: Essays by Harlan Ellison,* edited by Marty Clark. San Bernardino, CA: Borgo, 1984, 158–161. Essay originally published in *The Los Angeles Times,* January 1, 1982.

_____. "Introduction — Lurching Down Memory Lane with It, Them, the Thing, Godzilla, HAL 9000 ... That Whole Crowd: An Overview of the Science Fiction Cinema." In *Omni's Screen Flights/ Screen Fantasies: The Future according to Science Fiction Cinema,* edited by Danny Peary. Garden City, NY: Doubleday, 1984.

_____. "Introduction: Thirty-Two Soothsayers." In *Dangerous Visions #1,* edited by Harlan Ellison. 1967. New York: Berkley, 1968, 19–31.

_____. "Introduction: The Waves in Rio." In *The Beast That Shouted Love at the Heart of the World,* by Harlan Ellison. New York: Avon, 1969, 9–14.

_____. *The Other Glass Teat: Further Essays of Opinion on Television.* New York: Pyramid, 1975.

_____. "A Time for Daring." In *The Book of Ellison,* edited by Andrew Porter. New York: ALGOL Press, 1978, 101–115. Speech originally published in *ALGOL* (March, 1967).

_____. "A Voice from the Styx." In *The Book of Ellison* [see above], 117–140.

Elwood, Roger, editor. *Six Science Fiction Plays.* New York: Pocket, 1976.

England, George Allan. "Facts about Fantasy." 1923. In *Darkness and Dawn* by George Allan England. Westport, CT: Hyperion, 1974, i–vii.

Evans, Arthur B. "The Origins of Science Fiction Criticism: From Kepler to Wells." *Science Fiction Studies,* 26 (July, 1999), 163–186.

Farmer, Philip José. "Riders of the Purple Wage." 1967. *Dangerous Visions #1,* edited by Harlan Ellison. 1967. New York: Bantam, 1969, 70–144.

Franklin, H. Bruce. *Future Perfect: American Science Fiction of the Nineteenth Century.* Revised edition. 1968. New York: Oxford University Press, 1978.

_____. *Robert A. Heinlein: America as Science Fiction.* New York: Oxford University Press, 1980.

Frewin, Anthony. *One Hundred Years of Science Fiction Illustration, 1840–1940.* New York: Pyramid, 1975.

Gernsback, Hugo. "The Amazing Unknown." *Amazing Stories,* 3 (August, 1928), 389.

_____. "Amazing Youth." *Amazing Stories,* 2 (October, 1927), 625.

_____. *Baron Münchhausen's New Scientific Adventures. The Electrical Experimenter,* 3 (May, 1915), 2–3, 10; (June, 1915), 40–43, 72–77; (July, 1915), page numbers unknown; (August, 1915), 136–137, 170–172; (October, 1915), 246–248, 297–300; (November, 1915), 312–314, 371–372; (December, 1915), 386–388, 442–444; (January, 1916), 474–475, 523, 526; (March, 1916), 624–625, 658–661); (April, 1916), 696–697, 741–742; *The Electrical Experimenter,* 4 (June, 1916), 92–93, 132–134; (November, 1916), 486–487, 513, 539–540; (February, 1917), 724–725, 751.

_____. *Baron Münchhausen's Scientific Adventures. Amazing Stories,* 2 (February, 1928), 1060–1071; (March, 1928), 1150–1160; *Amazing Stories,* 3 (April, 1928), 38–47, 84; (May, 1928), 148–156; (June, 1928),

242–251; (July, 1928), 346–357. The 1915–1917 text, edited in numerous but minor ways by T. O'Conor Sloane.

_____. "The Cosmatomic Flyer." [As by "Greno Gashbuck."] *Science-Fiction Plus,* 1 (March, 1953), 53, 59.

_____. "Editorially Speaking." *Amazing Stories,* 1 (September, 1926), 483.

_____. "The Electric Duel." *Science and Invention,* 11 (August, 1923), 333.

_____. "The Electronic Baby." [As by "Grego Banshuck."] *Science-Fiction Plus,* 1 (May, 1953), 59–61.

_____. "The Exploration of Mars." *Science-Fiction Plus,* 1 (March, 1953), 4–11, 61–65. Originally published in the privately published *Quip,* December, 1949.

_____. "Extra Sensory Perfection." In *Masterpieces of Science Fiction,* edited by Sam Moskowitz. Cleveland: World, 1966, 428–434. Originally published in the privately published *Forecast,* December, 1956.

_____. "Fiction Versus Facts." *Amazing Stories,* 1 (July, 1926), 291.

_____. "The $500 Cover Prize Contest." *Amazing Stories,* 2 (June, 1927), 213.

_____. "Guest Editorial." *Amazing Stories,* 35 (April, 1961), 5–7, 88. Republished (with one paragraph removed) as "Science Fiction That Endures." *Amazing Stories,* 41 (December, 1967), 126–128, 144.

_____. "Hidden Wonders." *Science Wonder Stories,* 1 (September, 1929), 293.

_____. "How to Write 'Science' Stories." *Writer's Digest,* 10 (February, 1930), 27–29.

_____. "Humans and Martians." *Superworld Comics,* No. 1 (April, 1940), 32–33.

_____. "Imagination and Reality." *Amazing Stories,* 1 (October, 1926), 579.

_____. "The Impact of Science Fiction on World Progress." *Science-Fiction Plus,* 1 (March, 1953), 2, 67.

_____. "The Infinite Brain." *Future Combined with Science Fiction,* 2 (June, 1942), 40–41.

_____. "The Machine and the Depression." Technocracy Review, 1 (February, 1933), 20–25, 43–44.

_____. "The Mighty Mite: *Homo Sapiens*: A Study in Futility." *Science-Fiction Plus,* 1 (October, 1953), 2.

_____. "A New Sort of Magazine." *Amazing Stories,* 1 (April, 1926), 5.

_____. "On Reprints." *Wonder Stories Quarterly,* 4 (Winter, 1933), 99.

_____. "Our Amazing Stars." *Amazing Stories,* 3 (March, 1929), 1063.

_____. "The Prophets of Doom." In *The Science Fiction Roll of Honor: An Anthology of Fiction and Nonfiction by Guests of Honor at World Science Fiction Conventions,* edited by Frederik Pohl. New York: Random House, 1975, 175–182. Speech originally presented to the M.I.T. Science Fiction Society on October 25, 1963.

_____. "Pseudo Science Fiction: What Type of Science-Fiction Do You Read?" *Science-Fiction Plus,* 1 (April, 1953), 2.

_____. "The Radio Brain." [As by "Gus N. Habergock."] *Science-Fiction Plus,* 1 (April, 1953), 61.

_____. *Ralph 124C 41+. Modern Electrics,* 4 (April, 1911), 19–20; (May, 1911), 83–87; (June, 1911), 165–68; (July, 1911), 229–33; (August, 1911), 293–96; (September, 1911), 357–61; (October, 1911), 419–22; (November, 1911), 497–500, 516; (December, 1911), 593–96, 616; (January, 1912), 689–92; (February, 1912), 787–90, 796; (March, 1912), 881–86.

_____. *Ralph 124C 41+: A Romance of the Year 2660.* Boston: Stratford Company, 1925. 293 pp. Heavily revised and expanded version of the 1911-1912 text, with a "Preface" by Hugo Gernsback and several illustrations by Frank R. Paul.

_____. *Ralph 124C 41+: A Romance of the Year 2660.* In *Amazing Stories Quarterly,* 2 (Winter, 1929), 4–53. The 1925 text, edited in numerous but minor ways by T. O'Conor Sloane, with the 1925 "Preface" as untitled blurb and most of Paul's illustrations.

_____. *Ralph 124C 41: A Romance of the Year 2660.* Second Edition. New York: Frederick Fell, Inc., 1950. 207 pp. The 1925 text, lightly edited by Gernsback, with the 1925 "Preface" (as "Preface to the First Edition"), a new "Preface to the Second Edition" by Gernsback, two "Forewords" by Lee De Forest and Fletcher Pratt, and Paul's illustrations omitted.

_____. *Ralph 124C 41+.* Fantasy Books. A Cherry Tree Novel. Manchester, England: Kemsley Newspapers Ltd., 1952. 190 pp. Basically an accurate version of the 1950 edition, with very minor changes and including only the "Preface to the Second Edition," here entitled "Preface." The cover has a subtitle, "Thrilling Adventures in the Year 2660," not on the title page.

_____. *Ralph 124C 41+: One to Foresee for One.* New York: Fawcett Crest, 1958. 142 pp. Anonymously, lightly edited version of the 1950 text with a short version of Pratt's "Foreword" (as "A Preview of Tomorrow") and with all illustrations and diagrams omitted.

_____. *Ralph 124C 41+: A Romance of the Year 2660.* First three chapters of 1950 edition published online at the following addresses: Chapter 1, *http://www.twd.net/ird/forecast/1998chapter1-ralph.html*; Chapter 2: *http://www.twd.net/ird/forecast/1998chapter2-ralph.html*; Chapter 3: *http://www.twd.net/ird/forecast/1998chapter3-ralph.html.*

_____. *Ralph 124C 41+: A Romance of the Year 2660.* Lincoln: University of Nebraska Press, 2000. 300 pp. Photographic reproduction of 1925 edition, with Gernsback's preface to the 1950 edition and a new introduction by Jack Williamson.

_____. "Results of $300.00 Scientifiction Prize Contest," *Amazing Stories,* 3 (September, 19280), 519–521 [unsigned].

_____. "Science Fiction." *Science Fiction,* 1 (March, 1939), 3.

_____. "The Science-Fiction Industry: A New Industry in the Making." *Science-Fiction Plus,* 1 (May, 1953), 2.

_____. "The Science Fiction League." *Wonder Stories,* 5 (May, 1934), 1061–1065.

_____. "The Science Fiction League: An Announcement," *Wonder Stories,* 5 (April, 1934), 933.

_____. "Science-Fiction Semantics: New Words and Definitions in S-F." *Science-Fiction Plus,* 1 (August, 1953), 2.

_____. "Science Fiction Week." *Science Wonder Stories,* 1 (May, 1930), 1061.

_____. "Science Wonder Stories." *Science Wonder Stories,* 1 (June, 1929), 5.

_____. "Skepticism in Science Fiction: Who Are the Disbelievers in Science-Fiction?" *Science-Fiction Plus,* 1 (June, 1953), 2.

_____. "Status of Science-Fiction: Snob Appeal or Mass Appeal?" *Science-Fiction Plus,* 1 (December, 1953), 2.

_____. "Technocracy vs. Science." *Technocracy Review,* 1 (March, 1933), 82–85, 92.

_____. "Thank You!" *Amazing Stories,* 1(May, 1926), 99.

_____. "$300.00 Prize Contest — Wanted: A Symbol for Scientifiction." *Amazing Stories,* 3 (April, 1928), 5.

_____. *Ultimate World.* Edited with an introduction by Sam Moskowitz. New York: Walker, 1971.

_____. "We All Live in the Past." ["Stranger Than Science Fiction" feature.] *Science-Fiction Plus,* 1 (April, 1953), 38.

_____. "Whither Technocracy?" *Technocracy Review,* 1 (March, 1933), 53.

_____. "The World in 2046: The Next Hundred Years of Atomics." *Science-Fiction Plus,* 1 (June, 1953), 34–42.

_____. "World War III — In Retrospect." *Science-Fiction Plus,* 1 (April, 1953), 26–38.

"Gernsback, the Amazing." *Time,* 43 (January 3, 1994), 40, 42.

"Greetings, Electronitwits!" *Newsweek,* 23 (January 3, 1994), 54, 56.

Gibson, William. "The Gernsback Continuum." In *Burning Chrome,* by Gibson. 1986. New York: Ace Books, 1987, 23–35. Story originally published in 1981.

_____. *Neuromancer.* New York: Ace Books, 1984.

Gold, H. L. [Horace] "Ask a Foolish Question." *Galaxy,* 2 (August, 1951), 1–2, 159.

_____. "For Adults Only." *Galaxy,* 1 (October, 1950), 2–3.

_____. "In This Corner." In *The Fourth Galaxy Reader,* edited by H.L. Gold. 1959. New York: Pocket Books, 1960, ix–xii.

_____. "Introduction." In *The World That Couldn't Be and Eight Other Novelets from Galaxy,* edited by H.L. Gold. 1959. New York: Pocket Books, 1961, vii–xi.

_____. "It's All Yours." *Galaxy,* 1 (November, 1950), 2–3.

_____. "Program Notes." In *The Third Galaxy Reader,* edited by H.L. Gold. 1958. New York: Pocket Books, 1960, ix–xv.

_____. "Step Outside." *Galaxy,* 3 (November, 1951), 2–3.

_____. "Yardstick for Science Fiction." *Galaxy,* 1 (February, 1951), 2–3.

Grimsted, David. *Melodrama Unveiled: American Theater and Culture 1800–1850.* Chicago: University of Chicago Press, 1968.

Hardy, Phil. *The Encyclopedia of Science Fiction Movies.* 1984. Minneapolis, Minnesota: Woodbury, 1986.

Harrison, Harry. "Continuity." *Amazing Stories,* 41 (December, 1967), 2.

Hartwell, David. *Age of Wonders: Exploring the World of Science Fiction*. New York: Walker and Company, 1984.

Hayden, Patrick Nielsen. "Cyberpunk Forum/Symposium." *Mississippi Review*, Nos. 47–48 (1988), 16, 39–43.

Heilman, Robert Bechtold. *Tragedy and Melodrama: Versions of Experience*. Seattle: University of Washington Press, 1968.

Heinlein, Robert A. *Beyond This Horizon*. 1948. New York: Signet, 1960. Novel originally published in *Astounding Science-Fiction* in 1942.

____."Delilah and the Space Rigger." In *The Green Hills of Earth*, by Robert A. Heinlein. 1951. New York: Signet, 1952, 13–23. Story originally published in *Blue Book* (December, 1949).

____. *Expanded Universe*. New York: Ace, 1980.

____. *Grumbles from the Grave*, edited by Virginia Heinlein. New York: Del Rey/Ballantine, 1990.

"Hip Knox the Super-Hypnotist." *Superworld Comics*, No. 1 (April, 1940), 20–26. Comic book story. Author unidentified, though probably Charles D. Hornig and/or Hugo Gernsback; artist unidentified, though possibly Frank R. Paul.

Hornig, Charles D. "Station X." *Future Combined with Science Fiction*, 2 (June, 1942), 100–101.

Introduction to "How Technocracy Works." *Technocracy Review*, 1 (March, 1933), 68 [unsigned, probably written by editor David Lasser].

Introduction to "The Infinite Brain." *Future Combined with Science Fiction*, 2 (June, 1942), 40 [unsigned, presumably written by editor Charles D. Hornig].

Introduction to *The Island of Dr. Moreau*. *Amazing Stories*, 1 (October, 1926), 637 [unsigned, probably by either Gernsback or Sloane].

Introduction to "The Man from the Atom." *Science and Invention*, 11 (August, 1923), 329.

Introduction to "The Man from the Atom." *Amazing Stories*, 1 (April, 1926), 63.

Jakubowski, Maxim, and Peter Nicholls. "Theatre." In *The Science Fiction Encyclopedia*, edited by Peter Nicholls. Garden City, NY: Doubleday, 1979, 600.

Javna, John. *The Best of Science Fiction TV*. New York: Harmony, 1987.

Kazantsev, Alaxander. "A Soviet View of American SF." Translated by John R. Isaac. *Amazing Stories*, 37 (May, 1963), 56–63.

Ketterer, David. "Tesseracts." (Letter.) *Science-Fiction Studies*, 22 (July, 1995), 299–301.

Knight, Damon. "Beauty, Stupidity, Injustice, and Science Fiction." *Monad: Essays on Science Fiction*, No. 1 (September, 1990), 67–88.

____. *In Search of Wonder*. 1956. Revised and enlarged. Introduction by Anthony Boucher. Chicago: Advent, 1967.

____. Letter to Gary Westfahl, March 6, 1992.

Lasser, David. "How Technocracy Works." *Technocracy Review*, 1 (March, 1933), 68–73, 88–89.

Le Guin, Ursula K. *The Dispossessed: An Ambiguous Utopia*. New York: Harper & Row, 1974.

Le Guin, Ursula K., and Brian Attebery, editors. *The Norton Book of Science Fiction: North American Science Fiction, 1960–1990*. New York: W. W. Norton, 1993.

Lundwall, Sam J. *Science Fiction: An Illustrated History*. 1977. New York: Grosset & Dunlap, 1978.

"Mantra, Tantra, and Specklebang." *Ansible* No. 118, May, 1994. At *http://news.ansible.co.uk/a118.html*.

McCaffery, Larry, editor. *Storming the Reality Studio: A Casebook of Cyberpunk and Postmodern Fiction*. Durham, NC: Duke University Press, 1991.

"The Menagerie." *Star Trek*. New York: NBC, January 17 and January 24, 1966 [two-part episode]. The episode incorporates footage from the original *Star Trek* pilot, later renamed "The Cage" and released on videocassette.

Merril, Judith. "Introduction." In *SF: The Best of the Best*, edited by Judith Merril. New York: Dell, 1967, 1–7.

____. "What Do You Mean: Science? Fiction?" In *SF—The Other Side of Realism: Essays on Modern Fantasy and Science Fiction*, edited by Thomas D. Clareson. Bowling Green, OH: Bowling Green Popular Press, 1971, 53–95.

Miller, Donald L. *Lewis Mumford: A Life*. New York: Weidenfeld & Nicolson, 1989.

Miller, P. Schuyler. "The Reference Library." *Astounding Science-Fiction*, 52 (November, 1953), pp. 143–152.

"Mitey Powers Battles the Martians on the Moon." *Superworld Comics*, No. 1 (April, 1940), 1–11. Comic book story. Author unidentified, probably Charles D. Hornig and/or Hugo Gernsback; artist unidentified, but almost certainly Frank R. Paul.

Moorcock, Michael. "Why So Conservative?" *New Worlds SF*, 50, No. 166 (September, 1966), 2–3, 156.

Moskowitz, Sam. "Book Reviews." *Science-Fiction Plus*, 1 (March, 1953), 60.

_____. "Chain Reaction." *Science-Fiction Plus*, 1 (October, 1953), 40.

_____. "How Science Fiction Got Its Name." Moskowitz, *Explorers of the Infinite: Shapers of Science Fiction*. Cleveland: World, 1963, 313–333.

_____. "Hugo Gernsback: 'Father of Science Fiction.'" In *Explorers of the Infinite* by Sam Moskowitz, 225–242.

_____. "On the Origins of *Ralph 124C 41+*." (Letter.) *Science-Fiction Studies*, 23 (July, 1996), 315–316.

_____. "The Return of Hugo Gernsback." Part I, *Fantasy Commentator*, 9 (Fall, 1998), 160–172, 214–221, 229–230; Part II, *Fantasy Commentator*, 9 (Spring, 2000), 291–300; Part III, *Fantasy Commentator*, 10 (Winter 2001-2002), 101–129; Part IV, *Fantasy Commentator* (Spring, 2003), 193–236.

_____. *Seekers of Tomorrow: Masters of Modern Science Fiction*. Cleveland: World, 1966.

Mumford, Lewis. *My Works and Days: A Personal Chronicle*. New York: Harcourt Brace Jovanovich, 1979.

_____. *The Story of Utopias*. 1922. Gloucester, Massachusetts: Peter Smith, 1959.

Nicholls, Peter. "Futurology." In *The Science Fiction Encyclopedia*, edited by Peter Nicholls. Garden City, NY: Doubleday, 1979, 237–238.

_____. "Prediction." In *The Science Fiction Encyclopedia* [see above], 473–474.

Nowlan, Philip Francis. *Armageddon 2419 A.D.* New York: Ace, 1962. Originally published in two parts in *Amazing Stories* in 1928 and 1929.

Palmer, Ray. "The Observatory by the Editor." *Amazing Stories*, 12 (June, 1938), 8.

Panshin, Alexei. "Books." *The Magazine of Fantasy and Science Fiction*, 37 (November, 1969), pp. 46–51.

_____. *Heinlein in Dimension*. Chicago: Advent, 1968.

_____. "The Short History of Science Fiction." In *SF in Dimension: A Book of Explorations*, by Alexei Panshin and Cory Panshin. Second Edition. Chicago: Advent, 1980. Originally published as by Alexei Panshin alone in 1971.

Parkin-Speer, Diane. "Almost a Feminist: Robert A. Heinlein." *Extrapolation*, 36 (Summer, 1995), 113–125.

Pohl, Frederik. *The Way the Future Was: A Memoir*. 1978. New York: Ballantine, 1979.

Project Moonbase. Galaxy Pictures, 1953.

Rahill, Frank. *The World of Melodrama*. University Park: Pennsylvania State University Press, 1967.

"The Reader Speaks." [Readers' letters and responses.] *Wonder Stories*, 3 (June, 1931), 132.

Robinson, Spider, and Jeanne Robinson. *Stardance*. 1979. New York: Dell, 1980. An expansion of the novella of the same name originally published in *Analog Science Fact/Science Fiction* in 1977.

Rogers, Alva. *A Requiem for Astounding*. Chicago: Advent, 1964.

Scholes, Robert, and Eric S. Rabkin. *Science Fiction: History, Science, Vision*. New York: Oxford University Press, 1977.

"Science Questions and Answers." *Science-Fiction Plus*, 1 (March, 1953), 66 [author unidentified, though almost certainly Sam Moskowitz].

Scott, Barbara. "The Girls in Their Cosmic Dresses, or, The Thing of Shapes to Come." *Rhodomagnetic Digest*, 3 (July-August, 1951), 13–20.

Scott, Howard. "Technocracy Speaks." *Technocracy Review*, 1 (February, 1933), 10–13, 43.

Siringer, Norman. "Literature and Science Fiction." *Rhodomagnetic Digest*, 2 (August, 1950), 19–22.

Sladek, John. "Ralph 4F." In *The Steam-Driven Boy, and Other Strangers*, by John Sladek. London: Panther, 1973, 147–51.

Sloane, T. O'Conor. "Amazing Stories." *Amazing Stories*, 4 (May, 1929), 103.

_____. "The Editor and the Reader." *Amazing Stories*, 4 (September, 1929), 485.

Smith, E. E. [Edward Elmer]. *Children of the Lens*. 1954. New York: Pyramid, 1962. Originally published in *Astounding Science-Fiction* in 1947 and 1948.

_____. *Second Stage Lensman*. 1953. New York: Pyramid, 1962. Originally published in *Astounding Science-Fiction* in 1941 and 1942.

_____. *Skylark Three*. 1948. New York: Pyramid, 1962. Originally published in *Amazing Stories*, 5 (August, September, and October, 1930).

Stableford, Brian. "Creators of Science Fiction, 10: Hugo Gernsback." *Interzone*, No. 126 (December, 1997), 47–50.

_____. *Scientific Romance in Britain 1890–1950*. London: Fourth Estate, 1985.

_____. "Utopia." In *The Science Fiction Encyclopedia*, edited by Peter Nicholls. Garden City, NY: Doubleday, 1979, 622–623.

Star Trek: The Motion Picture. Paramount, 1979.

Star Trek II: The Wrath of Khan. Paramount, 1982.

Star Trek III: The Search for Spock. Paramount, 1985.

Star Trek IV: The Voyage Home. Paramount, 1988.

Star Trek VI: The Undiscovered Country. Paramount, 1992.

"Station X." *Future Combined with Science Fiction*, 2 (June, 1942), 100–101 [unsigned, but almost certainly written by editor Charles D. Hornig].

Steele, William Paul. *The Character of Melodrama: An Examination through Dion Boucicault's The Poor of New York*. With a Foreword by James B. Bost. Orono: University of Maine Studies, Second Series, No. 87, 1968.

Steranko, James. *The Steranko History of Comics 2*. Reading, Pennsylvania: Supergraphics, 1972.

Sterling, Bruce. "Preface." *Burning Chrome*, by William Gibson. 1986. New York: Ace, 1987, ix–xii.

_____. "Preface." *Mirrorshades: The Cyberpunk Anthology*, edited by Bruce Sterling. 1986. New York: Ace, 1988, ix–xvi.

Supergirl. Warner Brothers, 1984.

Suvin, Darko. *Metamorphoses of Science Fiction: On the Poetics and History of a Literary Genre*. New Haven: Yale University Press, 1979.

Table of Contents. *Future Combined with Science Fiction*, 2 (June, 1942), 4.

Table of Contents. *Science Fiction*, 1 (March, 1939), 4.

"Taxi Kills a Child Retrieving Pennies." *The New York Times*, November 19, 1928, 21.

"To Parents and School Teachers." *Superworld Comics*, No. 1 (April, 1940), inside front cover [attributed only to "The Publishers," but almost certainly written by Hugo Gernsback].

Tremaine, F. Orlon. "Ad Astra." *Astounding Stories*, 18 (September, 1936), 7.

_____. "Blazing New Trails." *Astounding Stories*, 17 (August, 1936), 153.

_____. "Looking Ahead." *Astounding Stories*, 17 (July, 1936), 155.

_____. "Star Dust." *Astounding Stories*, 17 (March, 1936), 65.

Walsh, Chad. *From Utopia to Nightmare*. London: Geoffrey Bles, 1962.

Warner, Harry, Jr. *All Our Yesterdays: An Informal History of Science Fiction Fandom in the Forties*. Chicago: Advent, 1969.

Weisinger, Mort. "The New Thrilling Wonder Stories." *Thrilling Wonder Stories*, 8 (August, 1936), 10.

Westfahl, Gary. *Cosmic Engineers: A Study of Hard Science Fiction*. Westport, CT: Greenwood, 1996.

_____. "Cremators of Science Fiction, 1 and 2: Brian Stableford and John Clute." *Interzone*, No. 130 (April 1998), 51–53.

_____. "The Dance with Darkness: The Limits of Human Interest in Science Fiction." In *Biopoetics: Evolutionary Explorations in the Arts*. Edited by Brett Cooke and Frederick Turner. Lexington, KY: Paragon House/International Conference on the Unity of the Sciences, 1999, 219–249.

_____. "The Dark Side of the Moon: Robert A. Heinlein's *Project Moonbase*." *Extrapolation*, 36 (Summer, 1995), 126–135.

_____. "Evolution of Modern Science Fiction: The Textual History of Hugo Gernsback's *Ralph 124C 41+*." *Science-Fiction Studies*, 23 (March 1996), 37–92.

_____. "Gadgetry, Government, Genetics, and God: The Forms of Science Fiction Utopia." In *Transformations of Utopia: Changing Views of the Perfect Society*, edited by George Slusser, Paul Alkon, Roger Gaillard, and Danièle Chatelain. New York: AMS, 1999, 229–241.

_____. "'The Gernsback Continuum': William Gibson in the Context of Science Fiction." In *Fiction Two Thousand: Cyberpunk and the Future of Narrative*. Edited by

George Slusser and Tom Shippey. Athens: University of Georgia Press, 1992, 88–108.

_____. "In Search of Dismal Science Fiction." *Interzone*, No. 189 (May/June 2003), 55–56.

_____. "'Man against Man, Brain against Brain': The Transformation of Melodrama in Science Fiction." In *Themes in Drama, Volume XIV: Melodrama*, edited by James Redmond. Cambridge: Cambridge University Press, 1992, 193–211.

_____. *The Mechanics of Wonder: The Creation of the Idea of Science Fiction.* Liverpool, England: Liverpool University Press, 1998.

_____. "The Popular Tradition of Science Fiction Criticism, 1926–1980." *Science Fiction Studies*, 26 (July 1999), 187–212.

_____. "Reading Mars: Changing Images of Mars in Twentieth-Century Science Fiction." *The New York Review of Science Fiction*, 13 (December 2000), 1, 8–13.

_____. "'Scientific Fact and Prophetic Vision': Marxism, Science Fiction, and 'The Fantastic Other.'" In *The Fantastic Other: An Interface of Perspectives*, edited by Brett Cooke, George Slusser, and Jaume-Marti Olivella. Amsterdam, Holland: Editions Rodopi, 1998, 187–208.

_____. "Superladies in Waiting: How the Female Hero Almost Emerges in Science Fiction." *Foundation: The Review of Science Fiction*, No. 58 (Summer 1993), 42–62.

_____. "The Textual History of Hugo Gernsback's *Ralph 124C 41+*: Addendum." *Science-Fiction Studies*, 25 (July 1998), 394–397.

_____. "Wanted: A Symbol for Science Fiction." *Science-Fiction Studies*, 22 (March 1995), 1–21, 1995.

_____. "Where No Market Has Gone Before: 'The Science-Fiction Industry' and the *Star Trek* Industry." *Extrapolation*, 37 (Winter 1996), 291–301.

"What Our Readers Want." *Modern Electrics*, 5 (April, 1912), 46.

Wicks, Mark. *To Mars via the Moon: An Astronomical Story.* New York: Arno, 1975. Reprint of 1911 edition published in London by Seeley and Co.

Wilson, Garff B. *Three Hundred Years of American Drama and Theatre: From Ye Bare and Ye Cubb to Hair.* Englewood Cliffs, NJ: Prentice-Hall, 1973.

Yep, Laurence. *The Lost Garden.* Englewood Cliffs, NJ: Messner, 1991.

Index